ISBN 978-0-483-11450-0
PIBN 10035796

AUSTRALIA'S AWAKENING

THIRTY YEARS IN THE LIFE OF AN AUSTRALIAN AGITATOR

BY

WILLIAM GUTHRIE SPENCE

AUSTRALIA:
THE WORKER TRUSTEES,
Sydney and Melbourne.

1909.

ILLUSTRATIONS.

W. G. SPENCE, M.H.R.,
President Australian Workers' Union.

CONTENTS.

PREFACE

THE hidden seed does not spring forth until it is surrounded by the necessary conditions to start its fermentation. When first its little bud reaches the light of day only the keen observer can tell to what family it belongs; by most it is unnoticed. In years it may become a very giant amongst trees. The Labor Movement in Australia has now become an almost dominant factor in the political life of the community; hence its history, its character and aims should be studied by every citizen of our great Commonwealth. The need of some work setting forth the causes leading up to the present position has been felt for some time. I have in this book attempted to meet that much-felt want from the Labor point of view. In what I feel to be an incomplete form I endeavor to furnish a mirror of the past, and to present from the inside what I conceive to be the future outlook. If the Socialist Movement of the world is helped, encouraged, and stimulated by this record of our success in Australia, I shall have ample reward.

W. G. SPENCE.

Parliament House, Melbourne,
June, 1909.

AUSTRALIA'S AWAKENING

CHAPTER I.

BEDROCK.

SETTLEMENT in Australia took place under conditions which differed vastly from those obtaining in other countries. At first it was merely a convict settlement under English rule. The Aboriginal race was a comparatively weak one, and gave but little trouble to the pioneers, and there were no dangerous wild animals. In America the pioneers were forced to settle on small areas of land, so that they could mutually help each other in defence and development. When the white man came to Australia he found in possession the aboriginal squatter, whose runs were tribal and whose stock were kangaroos and opossums. The white man gave no consideration to the black man's rights, but drove him off, took up enormous areas, and stocked them with cattle and sheep. The early white squatter secured Crown grants, others have since purchased; and thus we had the evil of private ownership of

11

land before we had population. Naturally the best
land was secured by the first landgrabbers. One of
these, in the Western district of Victoria, took up
blocks in his own name, then in the names of each of
his family and of the servants, and finally, when
these ran out, it is said he dummied blocks in the
names of his working bullocks. The story may not
be true, but it is a fact that Australia starts its
national life with its best lands monopolised by a
few families.

In Sutherland's " History of Australia " the
following appears, under the heading of " Edward
Gibbon Wakefield " :—

" In 1829 a small book was published in
London which attracted a great deal of attention, not only by reason of its manner, but also
on account of the complete originality of the
ideas it contained. It purported to be a letter
written from Sydney, and described the annoy-
ances to be endured by a man of taste and
fortune, if he emigrated to Australia. He could
have no intellectual society; he could not enjoy
the pleasures of his library, or of his picture
gallery; he could hope for none of the delights
of easy retirement, seeing that he had to go
forth on his land, and with his own hands labor
for his daily food. For, said Mr. Wakefield, the
author of this little book, you cannot long have
free servants in this country; if a free man
arrives in the colony, though he may for a short
time work for you as a servant, yet he is sure
to save a little money, and as land is here so
excessively cheap he soon becomes a landed

proprietor. He settles down on his farm, and though he may have a year or two of heavy toil, yet he is almost certain to become both happy and prosperous. Thus, the colony is an excellent place for a poor man, but it is a wretched abode for a man of means and culture.

"Wakefield, therefore, proposed to found in Australia another colony, which should be better adapted to those who had fortunes sufficient to maintain them, and yet desired to emigrate to a new country. His scheme for effecting this purpose was to charge a high price for the land, and so to prevent the poorer people from purchasing it; the money received from the sale of land he proposed to employ in bringing out young men and women as servants and farm laborers, for the service of the wealthier colonists. Now, said Wakefield, on account of the immense natural resources of these colonies, their splendid soil, their magnificent pasture lands, their vast wealth in minerals, and their widespread forests of valuable timber, which stands ready for the axe, a gentleman possessed of only £20,000 will obtain as large an income from it as could be procured from £100,000 in England; yet he will be able to enjoy his learned and cultured leisure, just as he does at home, because all the work will be done for him by the servants he employs."

As a matter of fact, South Australia was first settled upon the conditions advocated by Mr. Wakefield as far back as 1829. The South Australian Association acted upon his suggestion, and at the outset sold land at not less than 12s. per acre, and subsequently at £1 per acre. The system adopted by all the States of selling at £1 per acre land worth, in some cases, £3 or £4 an acre, and in others only 15s. per acre, had its origin in Mr. Wakefield's suggestion.

The foregoing gives us the bedrock of the Labor Movement. Place the essentials of wealth production in the hands of the few, and the rest of the community are little better than serfs. Those who control natural opportunities control the conditions of life for all. The worker depends on the will of another for the right to live. The other will only employ him if he pays tribute. In commercial life and in manufacturing, where employers compete with each other, they cut down the cost of production by lowering wages and by the displacement of labor by machines. Displaced labor increases the number of the unemployed, and decreases the purchasing power of the wage-earning class. Lessened demand affects output, and increases competition and the war of trade. The weakest are crushed out; the strong, the heartless, the least scrupulous, survive. Rapid invention forces the controllers of industries into combines, trusts, and monopolies, still further decreasing employment.

The few required to attend to the machines are but a part of the machinery of the factory, and are counted, not as human beings, but as "hands." They are unknown by name or person to the shareholders of the syndicate, company or combine whose riches they help to produce. The manager whose brains are hired to organize and supervise the work knows but a few of the workers, and to maintain what he thus terms discipline holds himself aloof as if made of superior clay. Employers all aim at securing a monopoly, and though they speak in favor of non-interference with a competitive system, in action they soon destroy competition and abolish the alleged law of supply and demand.

When workers, by forming trades unions, attempt to secure at least a living wage, the employers are against them. They argue against any restriction, and want the iron law of wages to operate. That law is that wages fall to the lowest rate that will maintain a sufficient supply of labor—in other words, such rate as the most needy individual workman will accept. In unrestricted competition there is no standard, and wages are fixed by the most greedy and unscrupulous employer and the meanest and poorest of the workers. The standard is set by the need of workers and the greed of employers.

With the lands and machinery in the hands of the few, the mass are forced into wage slavery, and hence the trade union is a necessity, and is always the first step taken by the intelligent worker towards securing better conditions of life. Every industrial gain secured to the workers is the result of the efforts of unionists and of no others. In the old world and in the new the history of Labor is the same in that respect. A few individuals outside of the workers have done good by writing and speaking, but practically the masses have had to fight for all they have now in the shape of improved conditions, and have had all the powers of law and law makers, of pulpit, press, and platform against them.

The history of the movement in Australia, as in the United Kingdom, is one of self-sacrifice, heroism, and suffering far greater that has ever been shown on any battlefield; and there are no rewards, no Victoria Crosses, no decorations or titles. On the contrary, there is misrepresentation, contumely, imprisonment, starvation. The unemblazoned courage of the wives of trades unionists locked out or on strike can never become known or appreciated until the world becomes humanitarian instead of commercial. The grit which enables men, women, and children to go hungry to bed every night, rather than that the husband and father should take the place of a fellowman with whom he is voluntarily united in fighting against injustice and tyranny, is evidence of a quality which inspires confidence as to the character of our race and gives us hope of our future. We read of the hardships of the long-enforced marches of soldiers on half rations. They are all men, and have the stimulus which comes of comradeship and emulation. There is the help of sympathy, in the keeping step of the march, and the music of the band. In the other case there is the appeal of innocent children who do not understand why food is short—an appeal which is heartbreaking to loving parents. It is the mentally strong and intelligent who are unionists and fight the battles which lead to lasting good. The soldier, with all his laudation, has never been noted as a class for intelligence. He is but a machine in the hands of others to do as he is told. Most wars are unjust, and in any case the soldier has no say in it. The unionist is ever on the side of the welfare of his fellows. His fights are against injustice and wrong. He sees good to be done for those who come after him by persistent resistance of evil. The trades unionist workers—men and women—are the true heroes and heroines of the world. Their names are unrecorded in history, but their work lives after them and has given color and force to a movement which cannot die, but is becoming more powerful and better understood as time goes on. After all names matter not; it is deeds that count.

B

CHAPTER II.

GOLD DIGGING DAYS.

THE discovery of gold in Australia not only brought a rush of very fine immigrants, but put Labor in a position not contemplated by Edward Gibbon Wakefield. There was no life more free and independent than that of the gold digger. He was no wage slave, but a free man, with all those high qualities only developed under free conditions. His influence counted for much in our early history. He was a democrat. He believed in law and order of the true kind—that which considers the interests of the mass as of first consideration—not that of the kind we hear so much of in late years, in which the mass and their wishes are to be suppressed for the gratification of the ignorant and selfish ideas of a few. No force was required in those days, as the digger recognised that he was a citizen interested in putting down anything calculated to work against the common good of all. Thieves were promptly dealt with by the diggers, and made to feel that honesty would pay best. No injustice was done. Freedom begets justice. If a dispute arose over a claim, as a mining property was called, the Commissioner rode on to the ground, heard both sides as he sat on his horse, and settled the matter at once. There was no delay, no lawyers nor other humbug, as is the case to-day.

Other and more important matters were not handled satisfactorily, however. The Government was 'autocratic. A Legislative Council and a Lieutenant Governor did as they liked. The Council was all the Parliament they had, and was practically nominated and appointed by the Crown. It imposed a license fee of thirty shillings per month for the right to dig for gold. This covered each calendar month only, no matter what date it was taken out on. If a digger had just arrived on the field on the morning of the last day, and had not started work at all, he was haled up and fined if he failed to show a license. If he took one out he would have to take out a new one next day. The police force of the time were a pretty bad lot. Many of them were ticket-of-leave men from Tasmania, who played the petty tyrant when they got a chance. These were paid—footmen 2s. 9d. per day, mounted men 3s. In addition the force was made up of black-fellows, who were paid 1½d. per day. In December, 1851, the license fee was doubled ; £3 per month was demanded, or 30s. if the license was taken out after the 15th of the month. Diggers were only allowed to take up a claim of eight feet square for one man, or eight by sixteen for a party. They were not permitted to dig for gold within half-a-mile of any homestead. Big squads of mounted men would ride around arresting all who had no license, and doing so in the most offensive and brutal way. Commissioners' boundaries were ill defined, and hence the ground was often gone over more than once in the same day under different Commissioners. Digger hunting became a pastime for Commissioners and police. The taxation was unreasonable, the manner of collection unendurable, and those who had to pay had no say in government. No body of intelligent men would justifiably stand such treatment.

The only injustice came from the Crown—from authority—and it was so great as to lead to our first great strike, known as the Eureka Stockade, or Ballarat Riot. I well remember the excitement of that period, as, though not present on the spot, I heard the firing and saw the digger hunting, etc., that led up to it. I saw diggers under arrest made to follow on foot the mounted police for the greater part of the day, and then saw them tied up to a tree at night in the open cold air. The law was unjust, its enforcement was cruel, and the democracy refused to stand it. The stand made led to lasting changes. Several circumstances combined to bring about the final attack by the soldiers on the diggers on Sunday morning, December 3, 1854. Fortunately there were but a small number within the enclosure wrongly termed a stockade. These resisted bravely enough, and 20 lost their lives. Of the military, Captain Wise and five soldiers were killed during the brief combat. The subsequent trial of the men arrested and the exposure of tyrannical government led to government by the people, so that though the diggers were beaten in the fight at Eureka they won politically.

Digging days could not last. The shallow leads ran under the basalt and into deep wet ground, and soon led to the days of big mining companies, and the free, independent digger became a worker for wages. In the opening up of the deep quartz mines it was the same. Towns and cities grew up, and so we soon had the civilization of the old land.

set up in the new, with all its evils and disadvan-
tages, modified as to degree, but there all the same.

The idea of Wakefield was put into force, and
land sold at £1 per acre quite irrespective of its real
value.   The object sought was gained; we had a
land-owning class; rent and interest added to profits
for the moneyed class, who also took over the law
making. Gradually manufacturing was introduced,
more especially in the cities, and sweating—long
hours and low wages—came to the workers.   In a
broad, general way the history of Labor and Capital
in England during the past century would describe
their history in Australia. Details vary, but the
fight is the same. Hundreds of artisans came to
Australia who were trades unionists before they left
the motherland, and they were naturally the first to
apply union methods to industrial conditions in
Australia so soon as circumstances gave rise to the
need for them. That strikes should eventuate was
inevitable. Commercialism should not complain of
strikes, as all buying and selling is built on such a
system. One man offers another an article at a
price; the article is refused at that price, even
though the person wishes to buy. That is a strike.
Any one man has the right to refuse to work under
conditions offered to him. A thousand have the
same right, and when they agree and do so it is
denounced as a wicked thing by the very class who
uphold the existing competitive system of trading.
Strikes are never sought by the worker. Almost
invariably every effort is made to avoid the
extreme step, but when employers absolutely refuse
even to meet the representatives of Labor, no course

is open but to strike, as that is the workers' only
weapon. It is common for the pretended friends of
Labor, as many of the clergy · are, , to tell the
workers in a patronising sort of way, that they
sympathise with them and believe in unionism ·so
long as it does not go too far—so long as they do
not strike. Practically this means that Labor shall
give way to the employers every time. But few of
the leaders of high moral and religious teaching and
thought denounce· the social system and conditions
which are responsible for all strikes and all forms
of injustice, industrial war, and misery.

Australia is a country of rapid development. In
a very few years we have the extremes of great
riches and dire poverty. Fortunes have been made
in a quarter of a century or less, and a rich and
idle class dwell in the suburbs of our cities who
assume airs of superiority characteristic of the small
mind and ignorant worshippers of gold. They have
been aptly termed the "wealthy lower orders."
For admission to their caste possession of riches is
all that is needed; moral character does not count.
They rule the social life to a large extent, and until
recently dominated political life. As they sneer at
the poor as persons dependent upon the capitalist,
and because poor, consequently inferior, so they
decline in any way to recognise the right of a worker
to have 'a voice as to the conditions he should be
permitted to· work under. The capitalist provided
the employment, and knew best how ·to manage his
business; therefore he ought to fix the terms. He
believed in freedom of·contract. The worker could
leave if he did not like it; but he, as ·the employer

and the benefactor of the whole community, must not be dictated to as to how he should manage his business. This tone amongst employers, together with the rapid change from individual to company, inevitably led to friction. Though forced to earn his living by working for another man, the Australian worker never lost his independence of spirit. He would not cringe to anyone. The employer was to him nothing more than a man—certainly no better than himself. Strong objection was early taken to the terms " master " and " servant," and in our later Acts of Parliament the terms " employer " and " employee " are adopted to express the industrial relationship; while in our electoral franchise for the Commonwealth Parliament, as also for the Assembly in the States, there is no recognition of property, but merely of manhood and womanhood in adult suffrage.

CHAPTER III.

THE A.M.A.

THE Australian Labor Movement naturally divides itself into two separate periods. One is that running from the days of early settlement, and more particularly from the period following the gold discovery to the year 1890; the other, the period since that year. The year 1890 is, by unanimous assent, the turning point in Australian Labor history, and marks the beginning of the abolition of class dominance and the introduction of truly democratic government. It was the period of a conscious awakening amongst the workers to the fact that social salvation could not be secured by the old methods of confining trade unions and their efforts each to its own industry, but that union principles must be applied politically, and reform and better conditions sought through political machinery. To understand the position it will be well for us to get a grip of the conditions leading up to the change, and then briefly review the results so far accruing from the departure. When we do so it will be seen that the value of industrial organization cannot be over-estimated. Prior to the gold discovery in 1851 wages were low and more on the basis of those paid in the United Kingdom. Wool-growing was the main industry, and squatters, as the owners of sheep and cattle were termed, were little kings on their large holdings. There was practically no Labor Movement in those days. Squatters and others in

New South Wales could get " free " laborers then ,
by having convicts assigned to them. The goldfields
period was from 1851 on to the sixties. When the
goldfields broke out in New South Wales there was
naturally a rush of men from other occupations. The
squatters actually·sent a petition to the Government
of the.,day, asking that martial law should· be
proclaimed, and digging for gold peremptorily
forbidden. Though such unions as the Stonemasons
existed in the fifties, it was not until the decade
following the falling-off in gold finding that
organized Labor began its fight.

The evils existing in connection with gold
mining, ·which·led to the formation of the Miners'
Association in 1872, were mainly a ten hours' day or
shift as it is termed; attempts to reduce wages; to
introduce Chinese workmen; and neglect of precau-
tions to safeguard the life·or health of the miner.
The miners ·of Bendigo, in Victoria, were the first to
move. They organized and made a demand for an
eight-hour shift. Opposition was shown to the
request, when the miners offered to stake their claim
on the result of one month's trial. If they failed to
do as much work in eight hours as had previously
been done in ten they agreed to forego their demand.
The mining companies accepted the· challenge, and
the trial took place, the result being that the miners
won, and established the eight hours. In October
following, in the same year, a big strike took place
at Stawell, in Victoria, for the eight hours, the men
winning the day. Unions were established in a number of other mining centres, and in 1874 a Conference
was held in Bendigo, when it was resolved all should

unite under the title of the Amalgamated Miners'
Association of Victoria. They adopted rules based
on those of the National Miners' Association of
Great Britain. Later, the association drafted a Bill
providing for eight hours, for proper ventilation of
mines, and inspection of machinery, etc. This was
laid before the Government, and owing to pressure
by the Association was taken as the basis of the
Regulation and Inspection of Mines and Machinery
Act of 1877, which repealed and took the place of
the Act of 1873. During the few years following,
the A.M.A. fell back, until in 1878 there were only
three branches, with a total of 250 members.

The revival came from the alluvial gold mining
field of Creswick, Victoria. The immediate cause
was an attempt to reduce wages from 7s. to 6s. 6d.
per shift. The conditions in that and the Ballarat
districts as to wages and ventilation were especially
bad. The system was what employers called contract
work. The manager fixed a price or piece work
rate of so much per foot of driving. The rate was
that by which a picked party of men working in the
best places in the mine could make equal to the
standard wage of 42s. per week. It naturally followed that the average made by other parties was
under the standard in spite of straining every nerve
in hard effort. Further, a practice grew up of the
manager deducting whatever sum might be earned
over wages and holding it in reserve to make up a
pay which might be under wages. Very soon, however, they improved upon this by paying the party
whatever they earned at the price fixed when they
earned less than wages, but when their true earnings

exceeded wages the excess was deducted and never paid. It was "heads I win tails you lose" all the time. Not only were miners' earnings very small; but much time was lost owing to foul air and lack of ventilation. The number of fatal accidents was very large, whilst more or less serious accidents ran up to over fifty per cent. each half year. A form of phthisis called "miner's lung" overtook men after a few years, and led to a more or less lingering death. We are told that a man cannot live where a candle will not burn, but the writer has worked many an eight hours' shift where no candle would burn, and where light was dimly secured by placing two candles one on the other horizontally in the mouth of the air pipe. The two candle flames would unite, and what air came through the pipe kept them supplied with oxygen, but left little for the miner working six feet away.

The lack of legislation to enforce sanitation and care for miners' lives and limbs applied to all forms of mining—gold, silver, coal, and copper. In the coal mines of New South Wales, where several thousand miners were employed, organization was forced upon the men as early as 1869. In order to secure trade in competition with each other, employers would cut the selling price of coal and then try to make a profit by cutting the men's wages. In such a field as Newcastle the employers require to have a sufficiency of labor always on hand to supply a full market, and as a consequence the average earnings of the men are very considerably under the rate shown by the mineowners' books on the working days. The

employers were united in a union of their own, and
were supposed to fix a selling price, but some of
them would every now and then blackleg on the rest
and thus bring trouble.   Many strikes have taken
place, and it has only been by loyalty to each other
and persistent resistance to reductions that the
miners have maintained a subsistence wage.

The attempt to reduce the wages of the miners
at Creswick, Victoria, was cleverly planned.   One
mine was almost worked out, a second nearly in the
same position, whilst a third was just opening up
and had only one man on wages.   It was expected
that the miners would not trouble to resist in the
mines which were so nearly worked out, and that
the temptation to get work would prevent refusal in
the new mine.   The directors in the mine in which
I was employed did not join in the movement at all,
and most of the workmen spoke pretty strongly
against the others accepting a reduction.   The first
step taken was a suggestion contained in an anonymous letter published in the press, that the miners
should organize and resist the reduction.   This was
written by the manager of the mine in which the
first move was made by the board to reduce wages,
a mine called Cameron's Freehold.   The letter was
followed by an advertisement calling a meeting at
Dibden's Hotel for Thursday, July 11; 1878.   No
name was attached, but the advertisement was put
in by one of the men in Cameron's Freehold.   The
afternoon shift in that mine wanted to attend the
meeting, but the manager, with apparent indignation, refused; and on the night of the meeting sent
them underground.   He called one of their number

into his office, however, and told him to go to the
meeting and speak on behalf of the others. This
man was named Jack McHenry, and it was his wife
and daughter who a few days later stoned a boss
Chinaman who was on his way to take the mine on
tribute. The attack on the Asiatic was so vigorous
that he retired, the two women chasing him over
the hill back towards where he had come from. The
meeting was largely attended, every man bar two
from my own shift being present, though our wages
were not affected. I was appointed chairman of the
meeting, some suggestions made by myself were
adopted, and a branch of the A.M.A. was formed.
I was elected secretary, and held the position for
nearly sixteen years. McHenry, who attended from
Cameron's Freehold, was paid his shift for that
night; so we had the unique experience of the mining
company which started the reduction paying the
men who fought against it.

One of the directors in an adjoining mine was
a farmer, and somebody told him that if he went for
reduction of wages he would find a firestick put into
his crop. This frightened the little wits he had out
of him, and he mounted his old grey horse and rode
down to the mine to assure the men that he was no
party to the reduction. One or two others were
also frightened, as there was considerable excitement. In troubles of this kind it is always wise to
help your opponent out rather than force him to
back down. Finding out privately that the directors
of the mine (Dyke's Freehold) were prepared to
give way, I drafted a letter which I got one of the
workmen in the mine to copy and send to the board

in the name of the rest of the workers, asking the directors to reconsider their decision regarding the reduction of wages. It also gave some reasons for the request. Immediately after the board meeting the men were informed that, owing to the absence of the chairman, the consideration of the letter had been postponed, but that in the meantime the old rate of wages would be paid. I had arranged with the chairman that he should be absent. Of course the matter never was reconsidered, though I had to use strong influence with the men in the mine to induce them to refrain from demanding a reply. Some men are great on dignity and formality, and too often unionists are eager to humiliate the employer instead of being satisfied with gaining the end sought.

On the morning of the day following all hands on our shift in the Ryan's Junction Company's mine were in the act of changing to go underground when one of the shift named Tom Ryan came rushing into the changing house, saying in an excited tone,

"It's now or never, boys; they are sending the police to force the men down at the Ristori mine. We must go and stop them."

I said, "Go and see if Dyke's men will go with us."

This mine was only a very short distance away, and within the space of half a minute after Tom had entered their changing house he emerged, followed by Jack Reid, Ned Russel, and others. Together with one or two others, I at once started off at a run, and nearly ran over our manager, Mr. W. Maughan, who shook his stick at us and said, "Mind

what thool are aboot." He got into his North of
England dialect when excited. The whole shift from
each mine followed us. We had over a mile to run,
and about ten minutes in which to get there before
it was time for the men to go below. We crossed
the paddock of private land and pulled a rail or two
out of a fence as we went, which we threw into a
big sludge drain, and thus got across. The Ristori
mine was just opening up, and the only wages man,
a Mr. B. Q. Richards, went on strike against the
reduction of wages. The company called for public
tenders for driving, and in spite of our warnings
miners from Ballarat had tendered at a price we
considered too low to make wages. The president
of the association, Mr. John Sampson, had been
deputed to attend before eight o'clock that morning
to try to persuade the new contractors not to enter
on the work. The management had sent for the
police, and two mounted constables were on the
ground. All the mines were on private property.
President Sampson had been parleying with the
manager ere our arrival, and the latter had asked
the police to arrest him, only to be informed that
they had no power to do so, but that he (the manager) could sue him if he liked. The whistle blew
for eight o'clock just as we rounded the corner of
the engine house. In a few minutes there were three
hundred men on the ground, and the manager
changed his tone. We put the mine on strike, and
he begged permission to allow enough to go below
to make things safe for standing idle. We took
care that none of the new men did so, as we marched
them out into the road, where I mounted the stump

of a tree—for, I think, my first time—and addressed
the men. We picketed the mine night and day, providing a tent for the men to stay in, and within a
week the directors gave way and we won all
along the line. We got back to our work that morning in less than two hours, and what with the excitement and the fact that we had a good boss, we put
our best foot first and did as much work in the six
hours as we usually did in eight. This fact, although
admitted, did not stop some of the shareholders from
trying to get us severely punished. First they tried
to get all hands discharged, but when informed that
this meant stoppage of every mine in the district
out of sympathy, they asked for the discharge of
myself and a couple of others, but especially myself
as secretary. They were informed that this would
have the same result, so we were allowed to keep
our employment.

Creswick miners made a departure in organization in this respect. Experience had shown that
something was needed to keep members in the union
after the first excitement was over. Hence the
organization was made an accident society as well
as a trade union. The companies had previously
adopted the practice of enforcing payment to an
accident fund in each mine. Of course this saved
their pockets. We made use of this by taking over
the existing funds, and making provision for benefits on a more liberal scale. It also gave us an
excuse, if one were needed, for compelling every
man who worked in the district to join the A.M.A.
Owing to the accident benefits saving so much to
shareholders' pockets there was less opposition to

the principle of refusing to work with non-members. Almost at once we enforced this rule, and it has been maintained successfully in that district for nearly thirty years. The Creswick miners were practically the organizers of the A.M.A. We became aggressive, and opened new branches in Ballarat, Egerton, and other places, the Creswick rules, system of account, accident pay, etc., all being adopted by the others. I became General Secretary in 1882.

Holding the view that organization is the first step essential to social salvation, I worked for the extension of the movement. The organization soon added to its strength in Victoria. We sent an officer to resuscitate Bendigo, where, with four thousand miners, they had a membership of fifteen. Believing then, as I do still, that Labor is one in aim all over the world, my ambition was to unite all miners— gold, silver, copper, and coal—in one body, with an Intercolonial Council to deal with large issues and arrange for financial aid in case of need, leaving each colonial district self-governing in its own sphere. It took four years, however, to break down the conservatism of delegates to our annual conferences. After eleven and a half years' hard work my ambition was gratified. Branches of the A.M.A. were established in every colony, including Tasmania and both Islands of New Zealand, and all those engaged in any form of mining were united, with a total membership of about 23,500. I regret to say that after my retirement the conservatives who had always opposed uniting with any other than gold miners, and only with them if in Victoria, once more secured power, and broke up the intercolonial

C

organization. The same element is responsible for the A.M.A. holding aloof from the political movement.

We had uphill work in organizing. The first nine branches had to fight for their bare existence. Members locked out or on strike were paid £1 per week. This involved levies and a strain on the finances, but it was good training for those called upon to levy themselves, as it forced them to take a wider interest in a movement in which selfishness should have no part. During the eighteen years, 1872 to 1890, there were 29 cases of strikes, eight of lock-out, and six other serious difficulties. The lock-out was in all cases an attempt made by the employers to stop workers from joining the union. There were thirteen attacks on unionism. In addition to these, our industrial battles were for shorter hours, three; to resist reduction of wages, thirteen; to resist attempts by employers to increase hours, two; against Chinese, two; against non-unionists, four. In most cases the A.M.A. won. Some were settled by compromise, and one by arbitration. After a time mine-owners readily met us in conference, and friendly settlement took the place of industrial war. In 1882 the Creswick Branch asked for an increase of wages of sixpence per shift. A conference was held between delegates from both sides, the result being that the increase was conceded, as well as some other advantages. The agreement, though not in writing, has been loyally observed by both sides, and was only varied by a similar conference held a number of years later.

Creswick miners do not allow a member to fall into arrears. If he owes over a month's contribu-

tion he is called upon to pay up, or the members will
not work with him, nor will the engine-driver lower
him underground. There is no interference with
men seeking employment, nor with the choice of the
management. When a newcomer appears he is asked
by the steward of the shift if he is a member. If he
is he produces a clearance certificate. If he is not
he is asked to join, and if he has not got the cash
it will be lent to him so that he can become entitled
to benefit in case of meeting with an accident.
Should he refuse to join, then the steward quietly
informs the underground manager or captain of
shift, as he is termed, and he gives the man his
choice of paying or leaving the mine. I can only
recall three cases in fifteen years where it reached
this stage. In one or two mines the management
gave authority to stewards of the association to send
about his business a man who made any bother
about paying into the A.M.A.

The experience of the A.M.A. has shown that
whilst the benefit system undoubtedly tends to keep
up membership, and also to lessen the opposition of
the employers, on the other hand it hampers the
distinctly union side. There is a tendency to increase
benefits without increasing contributions, and thus
leave finances short for bona-fide union work.
Members come to look upon it as a purely accident
relief society rather than as a union. Good leaders
may counteract this to a large extent by vigorous
propaganda, but good leaders are not plentiful. The
miners' organizations have done splendid work for
their members and for the mining industry, not only
in Victoria, but in all the other States. They have

influenced legislation to a considerable extent; though they have been slow in Victoria and in Newcastle, N.S.W., to officially join with the other unions in the political movement.

A very important series of amendments of the Regulation and Inspection of Mines and Machinery Act was made in 1883, and it is worth recording how these were secured. An election had been held and a new Ministry had taken office. The gentleman appointed to the office of Minister of Mines (Mr. J. F. Levien) was a grower of onions, and had no connection with or knowledge of mining. A storm of protest was raised in the press of the mining districts of the colony, and it is hard to say what might have come of it but for our action as officers of the A.M.A. Three of us went to Melbourne to wait upon the new Minister. At his invitation, the night before the day for officially meeting us we met him in a small room in the Library of Parliament House, and there we coached up the Minister on various phases of mining matters of which he was previously utterly ignorant. He was an apt pupil, and was very affable. As we parted he remarked that next day we must remember that he would have his official cap on. Next day we solemnly laid our requests before him, the press being fully. represented; and the papers commented afterwards on the highly intelligent grasp of mining matters the Minister evidently possessed, as indicated by his reply to the deputation. All opposition to his filling the position was killed, and we got our amendments put through, and they are still the law of the State.

CHAPTER IV.

" HE VOS COME BACK NO MORE."

ABOUT 48 years ago, rich copper deposits were found on a part of York's Peninsula, S.A., now called Wallaroo and Moonta. It was so rich that something like £1,500,000 has been declared in dividends without investment of any outside capital to develop the mine. To work it a large body of miners were brought direct from Cornwall, England. For many years they lived isolated from the rest of the colony, remaining more Cornish than Cornwall itself. Eventually the iron horse reached Kadina and Wallaroo, twelve miles away. The discovery of silver at Broken Hill drew away some of the young men, and so it came about that the sons on their visit home told the older men of the advantages of Unionism. It caught on like a new gospel, and a strong branch of the A.M.A. was organized. The Cornish miner is generally a man who can do his share of grumbling, and frequently reckons he knows how to run a mine better than the manager, so when Unionism caught on they realised that many injustices might have been remedied years ago had they been organized and pulled together instead of merely growling as individuals. This feeling led to concentrating, as it were, all the grievances of a quarter of a century into the living present. There were enough genuine grievances without that, but the strong feeling so common when " strike " is in the air partakes of memories of the past as well as

37

exaggerations or misconceptions of the present. Certain concessions were asked for, which the company refused, and so a strike was threatened. This was in 1889. The rules of the A.M.A. prohibited any strike being entered upon without the authority of the Executive Council, who had first to exhaust all means of amicable settlement. The President, Mr. J. B. Burton (since a Minister of the Crown in Victoria) and myself at once visited the district.

Moonta mine had, owing to its isolation, made provision for almost every requirement, and had extensive surface works, such as a foundry and other large workshops. It had its own little railway over the works, telephone and telegraph, etc. Until the railway came to Kadina it was, in fact, a self-contained community. To get at the facts, we wired ahead asking that representatives of all the various departments of labor on the mine above and below should meet us. They did so, and we had a few hours of cramming with the grievances of all and sundry. Moonta miners are a fine body of men, and they selected intelligent men to state the case to us. It was after closing hours when we reached our hotel, but we had no sooner said good-night to our friends and got inside when we were informed that four men wanted to see us privately. We met them in a parlor, and after seeing that the door was locked, they introduced themselves. They were four sensible miners, past middle age, and after satisfying themselves of our privacy, one of them said:

" See here, we do know that thee two be'est come here to do a fair thing by us miners, so we just come to tell 'ee that things ain't so bad for we

underground: men as some 'ov 'em do make out.
Some ov 'em got nice little bit in the bank yon. It's
they surface men wot's worst treated."

We found out afterwards that there was truth
in what the old chaps had told us, and that and
other information proved very useful. On retiring
to our room after seeing them out we overheard a
dialogue in the adjoining room. Two men, one of
whom was a German, were loudly discussing the
threatened strike.

" Ach, you vas vant to do like dey did in my
gountry vonce."

" What was that?" asked his companion.

" Vell, ve try all vair means. Ve ask dem to
meet mit us und dey say no. Ve find de boss he act
de tyrant, and vill not do away mit de injustice. So
von night, bretty late, ve march oop, a goot many
oondreds, to de hose of de manager, and ve say,
' Come oudt,' undt he come oudt. Ve ask if he vill
give us justice, und he tell us go to 'ell; so ve
surround him and march avay mit him into de bush a
long ivay. Den ve all come back but dot manager;
he vas come back no more."

Next morning we had arranged to see the
general manager, Captain Hancock. Representatives
of the branch had been appointed to go with us; but
the Captain objected to seeing them if they retained
as one of their number a man who had led in some
trouble some time before, and who had since been
boycotted by the company. He still had the confidence of the men, and they stood by him. Fault
was found with us for not taking up their attitude,
until we explained that we were there to steer clear

of local heat or difficulties, and to get the true hang of things so as to advise our Executive. We found in Captain Hancock a rather nervous, elderly gentleman, but we readily got all the information he could give us, and then we decided to go to Adelaide and meet the directors. On our return to the hotel the landlord told us that a big Cornishwoman had just been there to borrow his stable broom because, as she said, "it had plenty of wood in en" and she "might want en to sweep Captain Hancock out." It appears that the Captain's predecessor had been swept out of Moonta by the women, carrying a broom each. The German's remark of the preceding night, "Dot manager he come back no more," was given a new significance, and fully explained the very evident nervousness of Captain Hancock. We met the directors, and put what we felt was a strong case before them. Their reply was not a denial of some of the grievances, but simply that at present prices of copper they could not grant the requests; as the mine would not pay them, and if the men persisted they would have to close the mine and let it stand idle. They said, however, they realised that we only wanted to be fair, and so they did not ask us to take their assertion as to whether the mine would pay, but had given their secretary instructions to allow us to examine and inspect the company's books and ascertain for ourselves the exact cost of the production of a ton of copper. We accepted the offer, and by that means were enabled to explain away several errors which the officers and members of the branch had quite naturally fallen into.

HON. T. PRICE, M.L.A.,
Labor Premier, South Australia.

Died 31st May, 1909.

If the example set by that board of directors was followed by others, many a serious strike would be prevented. Troubles arise from a want of frankness on the part of employers. They make the mistake of ignoring the workers as if they had no interest in the industry or its success. At the same time the employers are often loud in their complaints that the workers do not consider the losses. If the workers make a suggestion they are charged with wanting to dictate to the employer how he shall manage his business, whilst the employer assumes a dictatorial attitude all the time. Instead of treating the worker as a partner, he is looked upon as one who constantly wants to take advantage of those who stand in relation to him as owners of the industry upon the success of which his living depends. We had an interview with the directors of the Wallaroo mines before returning to Moonta, and gained some slight concessions from both companies, but failed to secure what the men were asking.

The delivery of our report and ultimatum to the miners was a scene never to be forgotten. Excitement ran high. The brooms were ready, and their plucky owners equally so. No sooner had the signal bell rung for knock off work at 5 p.m. than the men assembled around the platform of the tramway, from which we were to speak. All hands came just as they were. The women stood generally in the outer circle of the crowd. They left the work of decision to the men, but were prepared to loyally carry it out whatever it might be, even if it meant going hungry in order to secure justice. About 2000 persons were

present, and ere the meeting ended torches were lit,
giving the gathering a more varied hue and more
intensity. Mr. Burton and I had an unpopular
report to deliver to them. We had to explain away
many exaggerations. We had to give them solid,
hard facts. We had sifted every grievance. Most
were genuine; in fact, generally those touching
wages were so. We had to show that in many
things they had wrongly blamed the manager, as we
had seen the press copies of instructions sent to him
by his board. Having gone through the books, we
had ascertained for ourselves the exact cost of
production. Having secured certain concessions, with
a better understanding and recognition of the men's
claims, we recommended that no strike should take
place. Others spoke, and amongst them one who,
with fine voice and elocution, delivered an oration
in rhyme. I think it was a parody, but it was a good
one. He had put it together, and there must have
been about thirty verses. It was expressive of the
idea common to most—namely, that we were bound
to have gained for them all or nearly all that they
were asking; so it was a song of victory, and likened
us to Moses and Aaron, who were to lead the miners
of Moonta out of, the bondage of slavery, and our
names were to live when those of the "tyrant directors had sunk in the dead sea of forgetfulness."
The meeting fully accepted our recommendation,
expressed confidence in us, and later were specially
glad that no strike had eventuated, and that there
had been no need for that broom with "plenty of
wood in 'en."

In the detail of the Moonta trouble several instances came under our notice typical of what will be found in all industries where men are not organized. We found grown-up young men working for from 2s. 6d. to 4s. 6d. per day, and in more than one case they were married. Starting as boys, it was apparently forgotten by all concerned that they had grown older as time went on. As their producing power increased so their share of wealth decreased. It was only when unionism came and the body took up their cause that their wages were increased. We found in charge of pattern-making in the foundry a first-class tradesman working for 7s. per day. He was a very superior tradesman, with considerable genius for invention. He was of the type who take a keen interest in their work for the work's sake, and but little in what they receive for it. Quiet and unassuming, and content with a living wage, his only ambition was to excel in the quality of his workmanship. At an exhibition in Adelaide the manager of the mine had been accorded great credit for a rock drill with improved jacket. The drill was the unacknowledged patent of a Victorian, and the improved jacket the invention of the workman paid 7s. per day, while his market price anywhere else was at the lowest 12s. per day. Naturally we made a good deal of this man's case, and as it was published in the press it came under the notice of a big firm at Gawler, whose manager was waiting on the railway station at 6 o'clock in the morning to intercept us and offer the man 12s. to come to their firm. We declined to give his name at that stage, but promised to tell the man himself of the offer. Some time after this I met the man referred to at Waukaringa, earning double the wages he had been paid at Moonta, and of course more highly appreciated. Union officials should be careful to be thoroughly honest and just in their dealings with the other side. It always pays, to put it at the lowest. In the Moonta case Captain Hancock sent his second in command all the way to Kadina to thank us for clearing his name, and to ask our advice on a certain matter connected with the mine and the men. He honestly carried out our recommendation.

CHAPTER V.

THE KING OF THE NORTH-EAST.

A STRONG and well-known personality in the North-East of Victoria was the late Hon. J. A. Wallace, M.L.C. He owned mining. leases all over. the district, and had big influence in the Mines Department—in fact, was quite a petty king in his way. When the miners at Bethanga began to organize in 1885, his manager posted an intimation that anyone joining the A.M.A. would be dismissed. The men joined in spite of it. A lock-out resulted, and it cost the A.M.A. £100 per week for some weeks to support the miners. The engine drivers stood by the employer, and hence I sent a circular letter to each, appealing to them to join with their fellow-workers in the fight for freedom—to unite for the purpose of improving the conditions of life. These letters were published, and Mr. Wallace and the local secretary had some controversy in the press. One day a constable called on me in my office, and asked for and obtained a copy of my signature. A day or two later I was telegraphed for to go to Melbourne at once. This was by order of the late Mr. (afterwards Sir Graham) Berry. On arrival at his office, the Chief Commissioner of Police (the late Mr. Cholmley) was sent for. The Chief Secretary (Mr. Berry) had just discovered that under an old law of George the IV., then in force

in Victoria, proceedings had been initiated by the
Commissioner against me for intimidation.   This
meant a minimum penalty of six months' imprisonment.   The late Commissioner, did not look comfortable.   When asked by 'Mr. Berry upon what
authority he had acted, he could only produce
newspaper clippings containing copies of my letters
to the engine drivers and Mr. Wallace's letters to
the same papers.   Chief Secretary Berry was very
severe on Mr. Cholmley.   He said :

"I am astounded at your action.   You consult
me on the most trivial matters, and yet here you
take action involving serious political consequences
without consulting me at all.   You send a constable
to worm the signature out of this man" (pointing
to me), "and act without saying a word. If such
a thing occurs again I shall take steps to secure a
new Commissioner of Police."

A special meeting of the Cabinet was held, and
in the afternoon I was informed that it was "all
right."   Subsequently I learned what had taken
place.   The king of the North-East had moved the
Commissioner to take proceedings against me. The
constable stationed at Bethanga, when asked to take
action, reported that he saw no grounds for action
against anyone unless it was Mr. Wallace himself.
This did not suit, so it was found that under the old
law—long since repealed in England—a case could
be made; and the constable was ordered to proceed
by criminal summons.   At this stage the Chief
Secretary heard of it through a member of Parliament. He at once saw that such a case would turn
popular feeling against the Government ; hence he

moved at once. When the wires were set in motion,
however, it was found the summons had been made
out and posted to the police at Creswick for service
on me there. The Cabinet were in a dilemma, as no
Government could interfere with law at that stage,
and what they wanted was to avoid anything coming
out. It was got over by the Minister for Mines
hunting up the Hon. J. A. Wallace, and, under threat
of forfeiture of his leases, he who had initiated the
proceedings had to withdraw them. They were only
just in time, as about one day will carry the mail
from Bethanga to Creswick.

One of the drawbacks to mining development is
the evil of "shepherding." Mining leases are
granted subject to certain labor covenants ; that is,
so many men per acre must be employed or the lease
can be forfeited. Syndicates and companies evade
this by securing suspension of labor covenants on
various pretexts. The A.M.A. very early took a
hand in seeing that all suspensions were granted on
some reasonable ground. They did not object to
time being given to those who had laid out capital
in opening up a mine, and who met with difficulties,
such as influx of water necessitating new machinery.
They opposed the " shepherd "—the man or company who took up a lease and did nothing but merely
await a chance to sell and take advantage of the
efforts of other men who had proved adjoining
country... We had a long fight with the Department.
and the late John A. Wallace over his Bethanga
leases. The Ministers were getting tired of giving
him concessions; and at last we were to meet him
before the Acting-Minister for Mines (the late Hon.

Duncan Gillies). The appointment had been made
for 11 o'clock on a Wednesday morning at the
Treasury, but on arrival in Melbourne we received
a message to the effect that the interview was postponed until next day on account of the indisposition
of the Hon. J. A. Wallace. However, we went to the
Department at 11 o'clock, and were in time to catch
our friend Mr. Wallace on his way to see the
Minister. He was surprised to see his ruse a
failure, and we all went in together, and after much
haggling Mr. Wallace was forced to agree to putting
on at least ninety men at once or have his lease
declared forfeited.

The anti-Chinese movement was one of the early
developments of democratic feeling in Australia.
So strong was it that in 1861 it led to riot amongst
the diggers at Lambing Flat, Burrangong, New
South Wales. They drove the Chinese off the
field, some of the pig-tailed heathens losing their
lives. There were at that time 38,000 Chinese in
the two colonies of New South Wales and Victoria—
12,988 in the former, and 24,732 in the latter. But
for the action of the gold diggers and restriction of
Chinese immigration by a poll tax and otherwise,
Australia would have been practically a Chinese
possession. The same strong feeling that caused the
Lambing Flat diggers to revolt actuated the miners
of Clunes, Victoria, in 1876. The directors of the
Lothair Gold Mining Company decided to introduce
Chinese labor. The miners, who were all members
of the A.M.A., determined to resist. The Chinese
were to be brought from Creswick, eleven miles
distant. Two coaches were filled with Chinese and

placed under police escort. The miners had mounted
pickets out, and were informed of every move.
There are two roads to the town, and that on the
west side, where the mine was situated, was
blockaded by the miners. On discovering this the
coaches were turned, and, crossing a deep creek,
they made for the town by the other road. The
miners rushed across, having about a mile to run,
and hastily improvised a barricade, effectually
blocking the way so far as the coaches were
concerned. The excitement and cheering were great,
men, women, and children joining in the resistance.
Near by was a heap of road metal, and arming
herself with a few stones a sturdy North of Ireland
woman, without shoes or stockings, mounted the
barricade as the coaches drew up. As she did so
she called out to the other women, saying :

"Come on, you Cousin Jinnies ; bring me the
stones and I will fire them."

The sergeant in charge of the police presented
his carbine at the woman, and ordered her to desist.
Her answer was to bare her breast and say to him:

"Shoot away, and be damned to ye ; better be
shot than starved to death."

With the words she threw a stone, cutting the
cheek of the officer. After that stones flew rapidly ;
the horses began to plunge, and the Chinese to yell ;
whilst the terrified director (by name Solomon)
in charge crawled into the boot of the coach for
safety. In less time than it takes to tell it, the
horses were turned and driven off whence they had
come, the Chinese invasion was repulsed, and no
Chinaman has ever gained a footing in Clunes even

D

unto this day. Needless to say a fuss was made by the authorities, but no one was punished. The mayor of the town at the time—a fine old man named Blanchard—was an officer of the local A.M.A. Those who put law and order as superior to the welfare of men, instead of being considered as a power to be used for good, of course found fault with the mayor for not reading the Riot Act and tried to get Blanchard into trouble, but wiser counsels prevailed. Clunes residents were and still are proud of their fight against capitalistic greed and Chinese. A few years later, through the influence of the A.M.A., the Mines Department agreed to insert a clause in every mining lease issued providing that Chinese labor would not be recognized as fulfilling the labor covenants.

CHAPTER VI.

CAPITALISTIC INTRIGUE.

NOTHING so manifests the unfairness of the press generally as the way they hide or condone offences committed by capitalists whilst they invariably exaggerate any mistake made by Unionists, and too often invent an offence in order to cause public opinion to be in favor of the commercial classes, in whose interests most newspapers are run. One of the most cruel means adopted by employers is that known as the "boycott." I early had my first personal experience of it, and of the bitter hatred employers feel towards one who takes an active part in inducing his fellow-workers to seek justice. As I have said, I was working in a gold mine at Creswick, Victoria, when we organized the Miners' Association. Shortly afterwards we took the mine on tribute under a three years' agreement. Thus we could not be treated as ordinary wages men. So soon as we finished our term, however, there was no more work for me in any mine. The boycott was enforced, and I had to seek a living for myself and family as best I could. It turned out a good thing for me, however, as I have not done any mining work since ; and it really gave me greater freedom to become a bigger thorn in the side of capitalism by

my being able to devote my whole efforts to
organizing work and extending Unionism. Our first
president of the Miners' Association at Creswick
(Mr. J. Sampson) was also boycotted as soon as he
got out of the job he was working at. Another of
our presidents (Mr. T. Phillips), a very fine, quiet,
decent, and moderate man, with a big family
dependent upon him, was boycotted; because of a
remark wrongfully attributed to him by the press in
reporting one of our general meetings.   He was
driven out of the district, and it was over a year
before he could get back to his family. Several
active members of our committee were treated in the
same way, and had to leave to seek work elsewhere.
At last, when the employers came to realise that
many of these men were getting into something else
much better than mining, they eased off the persistent boycott. They found also that there were
others ready to take the places of the men who were
put out of office, and that they could not kill
Unionism that way.

Shortly after we organized the miners of Broken
Hill in 1887, a black list, containing the names of
eight men, was sent round all the mines in that
district by the Mining Managers' Association. The
eight men were not to be employed in the district.
No reason was given, nor were the men informed.
They were allowed to go from mine to mine seeking
work, always hoping to get a chance, but always
meeting with the reply that they had "no room for
more hands."   These are only illustrations of a
practice quite common. In some cases where it was
clear that men were spotted because they were

Unionists strikes eventuated ; but this only made the employers more careful in the method of boycott'; it did not stop the evil.

The Pastoralists' Union is without doubt the most bitterly unscrupulous organization in the world, hence we find them carrying out the most complete system of organized boycott it is possible to conceive of. Under the guise of giving references as to character and ability, they have extended over a whole continent a huge system of organized boycott intended, not to weed out incompetent workmen, but all Union men who had the courage to ask for a reasonable measure of justice. The system was first introduced into Queensland after the industrial war of 1891. At the finish of shearing work in each shed each workman was handed a reference, giving name of station, classifying the man as "good," or "very good," etc., under the head of ability; also stating how classed under head of character. The document was signed by the employer or his manager, and so far as appeared on the face it was a genuine document. Each reference was numbered, and exceptional type and paper were used to prevent fraud. As it is well-known that Union men are invariably the best workmen; they thought they had nothing to fear from honest references, and so accepted them. They soon found out, however, the real object. Two men, each holding a reference filled up exactly in the same way, present themselves at a station, and ask for work. They are asked to produce their reference. One is put on ; the other is refused employment, although the station is short-handed.

The plan adopted by the P.U. is this. A confidential list is sent in by each station manager at the end of each shearing season to the P.U. office. This list contains the men's names and the number of their references. Under the head of " remarks " it is indicated as to whether the man is " desirable " or no, and " agitators " and " staunch Union " men are specially noted. The man's ability as a workman is quite a secondary consideration. (As a matter of fact, a man may be considered a good workman by one manager and inferior by another, so that it is often merely a matter of opinion.) Prior to next season a book is made up for each district and a copy sent to each station, and hence when a man presents himself and his reference, or when he writes applying beforehand and encloses his reference, the employer or manager simply looks at the list in the book and decides accordingly. The good man from the Union point of view is sent away, or refused work by letter in case of writing. By this system they drove all the active spirits of 1891 out of Queensland.

The A.W.U. in the Southern States fought against the system for some years, but eventually had to give way, though steps were taken in other ways to counteract its effect. The system is still in force. Some of the references acquired a money value, and £1 each for those given by a certain station manager was readily paid. It has been reported that as high as £5 has been paid for one of the references issued by Mr. Chase, of Lanillo Station, in 1894. The possession of one of these was certain to secure a man a job, because it had

originally been issued to one who had taken a
striker's place. The man who bought the reference
simply assumed the name for the time being.

Change of name in dodging the boycott became
so common that it is alleged that some men forgot
what their right names really were. One man who
had bought one of Chase's references for £1 did not
get through with it. It was in the name of Cohen,
and that name suited the buyer with his Irish brogue
well enough. But it just happened that the original
holder of it was a Jew with somewhat broken
English; so when the Irish " Cohen " presented
himself Chase remembered the peculiarity of a Jew
shearer, and so he impounded the reference and the
£1 deposit, and " Cohen " lost his job as well.

Other means of using the boycott were adopted—
such, for instance, as punishing the local storekeeper
or butcher if he supplied a strike camp with
rations or meat. They could make it uncom-
fortable for the butcher by refusing him agistment
for his horses or cattle, and as the squatter held
nearly all the country it would prove effective
enough to close up his shop. They also controlled
the Bench, as the squatter is always a J.P. Then
there were the many methods taken to block the
Union organizer from getting near the men. In
many cases they ordered them off the run, and if
they refused had them fined for trespass.

Organizers have been fired at and Unionists
have been shot by non-Unionists without any action
being taken by the authorities. All the old musty
laws which, though repealed in the land of their
origin, are found to be in force here were dug up

against Unionists. Since the advent of Labor in politics, however, these things are disappearing fast.

Experienced Trade Unionists know that many strikes have been secretly organized by the employers for trade purposes, and with a view of affecting the prices of either commodities or shares. One such attempt, of which I had experience, will prove of interest. Briefly, the circumstances were these: The Amalgamated Miners' Association included in its membership every person employed in or about a mine, and in Creswick included the engine drivers. The engine drivers in Victoria formed an organization of their own, and a branch of it was opened in our district. Those who joined it remained members of the A.M.A. as well. There was much discussion, however, as to whether they should not cease to do so, and it was then that a few schemers who did much mining speculation saw their opportunity.

The plot was laid by the Board of one mine, and they arranged to call a meeting of mine directors. The meeting was duly held, close upon 40 being present. No one who was known to be favorable to the miners was invited. An understanding was arrived at that in the event of a strike taking place there was to be united action on the part of all the various Boards, and all the men were to be locked out. But stoppage would save calls upon the pockets of the directors and shareholders. The mines were all on private property, and those in the call-paying stage could not be stopped without an excuse of this kind or the landowners would come down on them under the agreement. The other dividend-paying mines chanced to be in a good position just then for being allowed to stop without much damage occurring underground.

If a strike took place over a quarrel amongst the members of the A.M.A. a lock-out would be popular amongst directors, and the stoppage of all work would send the price of shares down with a run, When they had got to the lowest the directors in the know would quietly buy up, and when they had got possession they could start the mines going again, either at reduced wages or even at the same rates; the shares would jump in value, and the buyers would steadily unload and thus quietly pocket thousands of pounds among them.

Thus was the plot made, and everything was ready, even to the man who was to make the trouble. The secretary of the newly-formed Engine Drivers' Association allowed himself to run into arrears. He persisted in his refusal to pay, and so it was decided that the men were to refuse to go underground until he paid up. He was on afternoon shift, which starts work at four o'clock.

As secretary of the A.M.A., I went to the mine. The men were all ready to refuse to go below unless he paid up. I had found out the plot by this time, but could not betray my informants. I wanted to gain time, so I used plausible arguments, flattered the vanity of the weak man who was the tool to be used, and got him to agree to pay up. I pointed out that I was sure he wanted to do the honorable thing, and that was to do as men did in a Friendly Society or other body—they paid up and then sent in an official resignation of membership. He hesitated, and did not give way until he went to the office of the mine manager to consult him. I knew it would be all right when he went there, as I had been there before him.

The matter was staved off for a month, but again it came to the time when a stand was ordered to be made by the same shift of men. I tried hard to induce the committee to take another mine as the test case—one which I knew to be outside the ring—but they were stubborn, and would not believe my forecast of what would result; and of course I could not give my authority. The vice-president of the A.M.A. (Mr. Evans) and myself on the day fixed for the stand to be made visited the private home of the secretary of the Engine Drivers, who had again refused to pay up his contributions. We were admitted to his front room, but I noticed that his wife (they were a young couple) stood behind his chair during the whole interview. He was a weak man. She evidently knew it. My persuasive tongue had won him over once—it was not to have a second chance.

However, we had a mission to fulfil. We pointed out the misery that would happen to the wives and children of the miners if a strike took place. We appealed to his sympathy and fellow-feeling for the women and children, if he had none for men; but in vain. That thin-lipped woman behind him stood firm, and her heart was as stone. We pointed out that in any event his organization was bound to be crushed. If the mine-owners won—as they were likely to do—both Unions of the men would go under. If the A.M.A. won, then they

would swallow up the drivers, the latter being so
few in number. At last, in spite of that cold ruler
of his life behind his chair, we secured a promise
from him that he would call a special meeting of
the officers of his Union for that evening, and that
in the meantime he would not go to work.

We left it at that. I did not go to the mine ;
but evidently the woman did her part, because the
man went notwithstanding his promise not to go ;
and, taking the engine, lowered the men to their
work. They were prepared to stand out, but were
too well disciplined to act without orders, so his
effort to bring on a strike failed ; and the letters
lying in the drawer of the mine manager's desk—
ready to send to the other mines—were not sent,
nor was the horse which was ready in the stable
needed to carry them. Had I carried out my
committee's instructions there would have been a
strike, followed by a lock-out, to the ruin possibly
of a very fine organization. However, we met the
executive of the other body that evening. They
were all straight Unionists, and a mode of settlement
between the two bodies was arrived at; and thus
the plot of the schemers failed ; and that wife's
ambition, whatever it may have been, was not
gratified.

No sooner had the Arbitration Act become law
in New South Wales than a move was made by the
pastoralists and shearing contractors to prevent the
A.W.U. from securing any advantage under it. They
secretly organized a bogus Union, called the Machine
Shearers' and Shed Employees' Union. This body
they registered, and were allowed to do so owing to

bad regulations under the Act, though the Judge
held that the intention of the Act was clearly that
there should be only one Union representing an
industry.

This bogus organization was backed up by funds
given to it as donations. A conference was held
between it and the Pastoralists' Union, which came
to an agreement for a reduction of wages and rates;
and this agreement was duly registered under the
Act, and became binding under the law. The bogus
Union—the M.S.U.—had but a small membership,
but as employers refused to engage men unless
they could show a ticket in it the membership
naturally increased. It started with a subscription
of 2s. 6d. per annum, but soon raised it to 7s. 6d.
The rules secured the official positions for two years
to those first elected, so as to prevent any scheme of
swamping them out being carried.

The genuine body—the A.W.U.—was thus kept
out of Court after fighting for arbitration for years,
and by the Act itself was prevented from striking for
higher wages. The fear of the law did not prevent
its doing so, however, and a big strike took place in
1902. A Royal Commission was secured to enquire
into the bona fides of the M.S.U., but could get no
evidence from either the officers, the auditors, or
the bank manager. These gentlemen took the risk
of a £20 fine rather than disclose the crookedness of
the bogus affair patronised and supported by the
P.U. The Commission, of course, declared their lack
of bona fides.

Still, their audacity knew no limit, and when
the Federal Arbitration Court became law they

registered under it, but withdrew when the A.W.U. began proceedings to have the registration cancelled. Fortunately, A.W.U. members are too strong in Union principle to allow their organization to be destroyed, otherwise the move would have succeeded in breaking up the Union.

CHAPTER VII.

THE WOOL-KINGS OF AUSTRALIA.

THE biggest industry in Australia is that of wool - growing, so far as value of product is concerned. The labor cost is the lowest. The squatter holds large areas of leased lands, and also owns vast areas of freehold. Over all these he is monarch of all he surveys, and prior to 1887 he did as he liked. He fixed his own terms for labor himself, drafted the agreement which the men had to sign, and so early as 1846 got a Masters and Servants Act passed in New South Wales—the principal wool-growing State—with special provisions enslaving the shearer under penalties of fine and imprisonment, and in addition forfeiture of earnings. When we also remember that the squatter was in most cases the magistrate administering the law, we can see that the unfortunate shearer or other station employee had but a poor show for justice.

The general shearing season in New South Wales lasts from July to December. The custom is for shearers to write beforehand and ask for a " pen " or " stand "—that is, an engagement to shear. (The sheep are placed in a pen, where the shearer catches one at a time and carries it to the shearing floor.) The employer replies, and if he engages he asks for £1 deposit to be sent, which is forfeited if the shearer fails to turn up at roll call. Shearing is by piece-work—or contract, as it is called. Each man engages to shear at so much per 100 sheep, the rate for some time having been 20s., but is now 24s.. The shearer finds himself in shearing requisites and food. They all live in a hut provided for the purpose, and engage their own cook, to whom they pay four shillings or a little more per man per week. Rations are obtained from the station store.

In the pre-Union days not only did the squatter offer low rates for shearing, but he took advantage in many other ways. A favorite method was known as " second price." The squatter would provide in the agreement which the shearers had to sign that he would pay for all sheep shorn to his satisfaction the sum of 17s. 6d. per hundred, but if at any time the shearer failed to do his work in a manner satisfactory to the employer or his agent he would be paid at the rate of 15s. per hundred—not only for the sheep alleged to be badly shorn, but for all those shorn previously and already passed as well done. Under this clause many men have had their work condemned during the last few days of the shearing, and have been victimised to the amount of 2s. 6d. per hundred on thousands of sheep, which had been shorn satisfactorily.

Another scheme was known as " raddling." This meant that a whole penful of sheep would be marked and not paid for because the last one or any other one was not done to please the boss. As the employer was sole judge, he had the men at his mercy. The greatest of all schemes for robbing the shearer was the almost universal practice of charging exorbitant prices for rations. For instance, £2 10s. per bag has been charged by the station for flour, though it could be bought at a store a mile away for £1. Men have had to pay 3s. per bar for soap which could be bought for 8d. in the shops. Everything was from 20 to 100 per cent. dearer than ordinary store rates in the same neighborhood. To make sure of securing these prices they would insert a clause in the shearing contract agreement binding the men to purchase everything at the station store. Further, many of them prohibited hawkers from coming near the shearers' hut.

As the cook had to obtain the supplies when required, the cost would depend largely not only on his ability as a cook, but his attention to the weight and quality of goods. Some squatters insisted on having a voice in the appointment of the cook, though they had nothing to do with paying him. In the new agreement put forward by the Pastoralists' Union in 1894 they had a clause claiming the privilege.

It is not hard to understand why they wanted to have their own man appointed. Once a shearer or shed employee signed on he was a prisoner till the work was done. He could not leave, but could be discharged at the sweet will of the employer or his agent, and often the conditions of agreement made it to the advantage of the employer to discharge him. Needless to say, all classes of labor on stations were treated in a similar way so far as circumstances would permit. It is not claimed that all pastoralists acted unfairly, but nevertheless the great body did so. As might be expected under such provocation,

Monument to Wm. McLean, shot at Grassmere, 1894.

it was not every worker who treated the employer with due consideration.

. The accommodation provided for the workers at shearing time was something awful. Mostly it was unfit to put human beings into, and consisted of long, draughty· buildings without windows, the timber·often being so open that you could put your arm through. Two and often three tiers, of bunks, one above the other, would be ranged all round the walls of the narrow hut. The table at which the men ate their meals ran down the centre. The cooking was done in a huge fireplace at one end, with the oven at its side. When the cook wanted to grill chops he spread burning coals on the earthen floor in front of the fireplace and laid his gridiron—a frame about three feet square—on the coals, the smell of the burning fat filling the hut where the men had to dress and undress, eat and sleep, all in one room.

The bunks for sleeping in were made of rough boards, neither mattresses nor even straw being provided. They were only a bare six feet in length over all, and as Australians are mostly tall men— from five feet ten inches to six feet seven being not uncommon—the closeness of your neighbor's feet to your nose can be pictured. The odor of clothing saturated with the yolk of sheep's wool, mixed with perspiration, is anything but pleasant. The floor of the hut was earth, frequently worn lower than the surface outside, thus being full of stagnant water when unused between shearing seasons.

The surroundings of the hut were insanitary, the men being left to make provision for themselves. Frequently the drainage of the hut and its insani-

E

tary surroundings ran into the only water supply available to the workers. In more than one station typhoid fever appears almost annually, and many deaths occur from this and other ailments distinctly traceable to the want of reasonable provision on the part of the employer for the comfort of his employees. As a matter of fact, the horses and dogs of the pastoralist were better housed and cared for than the workmen out of whose labor he made enormous profits..

Shearing is very hard work, and is inevitably done under severe conditions as to temperature. Men try to out-do each other in their ambition to be the " ringer " of the shed. The stooping position, the handling of sheep sometimes wet, inhaling impure air under a low roof of galvanized iron in a hot climate, are all conditions which entitle the worker to high wages. Further, there is no industry in which the value of the product is more readily and seriously affected by inefficient workmanship.

Then, again, men who follow shearing must travel long distances prior to starting. The average would probably amount to 300 miles. Very rarely can this be done by rail, and in any case some means of travel is needed between stations, as men must have more than one shed or it will not pay to go out at all. The inevitable lost time is never allowed for by the pastoralist.

At one time there was work during the off season on the stations—tank-sinking, fencing, etc.— but that is done away with; and the pastoralist must now depend on many thousands of men leaving other occupations to furnish the labor required in the shearing season. He is very slow to see that he will have to give better terms or he will fail to get it. The evils here referred to, and an attempt to reduce the shearing rates by 2s. 6d. per 100 sheep. led to the organization of the Amalgamated Shearers' Union in 1886.

CHAPTER VIII.

ORGANIZING THE SHEARERS.

THE organization and work of the Shearers' Union (now the Australian Workers' Union) have had a very decided influence on the Labor Movement in Australia, therefore some details as to its history are excusable. Quite a number of attempts had been made to organize the workers in the pastoral industry prior to 1886, but all had failed. Those who had moved in the matter lacked experience, and confined their efforts to a limited area. With a nomadic class who only worked at the occupation a portion of each year, and many of whom had thus no settled abode, the work of organization was naturally difficult.

In all such work it is essential to choose the right time. It came in 1886. A reduction in price had been notified, and those who usually went out shearing were indignant and ready for concerted action if some one in whom they had confidence, and who was widely known, would take the matter up. A young man named David Temple was working in the gold mines at Creswick, in Victoria. He and his brothers usually went shearing each year. He was a member of the A.M.A., and knew of the good work it had done. When the notice of reduced shearing rates appeared he said to his brothers that it was not worth while going out shearing unless they had a union like the A.M.A. The young man's mother, a practical Scotchwoman, said to David:

" Why don't you start a union, then?"

He said he did not know enough of such work, and all previous attempts had failed.

His mother replied, "Why don't you go to Mr. Spence? I am sure he will help you."

He took his mother's advice and called on me. We talked matters over until I got a grip of things, and then we made a start.

I at once wrote a letter, which appeared in the "Ballarat Courier" on the 27th May, 1886, urging shearers to become organized if they wished to prevent a reduction of wages, and offering to assist. Three letters from shearers approving of the suggestion appeared on the 29th, and two others, with one from myself, on June 2nd. On June 3rd Mr. Temple opened an office at 30 Armstrong Street, North Ballarat, and commenced to enrol members. I gave him a letter of introduction to the late Mr. Bateman, editor of the "Ballarat Courier," who wrote a leading article setting out the grievances of shearers. This appeared on the 4th June. In it he said:

"The effort was originated by Mr. Spence, secretary of the A.M.A., whose abilities in such organizations could not be overdrawn or overpraised, and his proposal has since had warm support in other letters which have been published since."

The following advertisement appeared in the "Courier" of June 12th:—

"IMPORTANT TO SHEARERS.—A meeting of Shearers will be held at Fern's Hotel, Sturt Street, this (Saturday) evening at 8

o'clock. Business—Re establishing a Shearers'
Union. All shearers particularly requested to
attend. David Temple, Sec. pro tem."

The meeting was held, Mr. Temple reported 40
on the roll, and about 100 in all when returns came
in. Objects and rules were adopted. I was elected
chairman, Mr. Temple secretary, and a committee of
nine was chosen. Thus in a small way was launched
the Union which now numbers 44,000 members.

A Union was started at Bourke, N.S.W., which
had 21 members at its first meeting held in Dugan's
Shakespeare Hotel on Saturday, October 2nd, 1886.
Shortly before that date a similar Union had been
started in Wagga Wagga, N.S.W. Both these joined
the A.S.U. in January, 1887, and became branches of
the amalgamated body. Bourke has continued as a
branch, but Wagga became merged in a larger
district.

After our first meeting in Ballarat in June, not
much was done until the start of shearing in August,
but finding from Mr. Temple and others who had
gone out shearing that the time was opportune I
sent out three organizers, who volunteered for the
work—Messrs. D. Temple, J. A. Cook, and J.
Slattery. These men went from station to station
enrolling members. The entrance fee was half-a-
crown, and the contribution for the year five
shillings.

Near the end of shearing I sent the three
organizers to New Zealand, and they organized the
shearers in that colony also. We had the rules
translated and printed in Maori. We enrolled a
considerable number of that race and found them

staunch Unionists. Acting as president, treasurer, and general director of the movement, I enrolled close upon a thousand in the office. As a result of our work we came out at the end of the year with over nine thousand members.

All through the history of the Union the plan was followed of trying to conciliate the employers. In taking up a new district, circulars, copies of rules, etc., were posted to each squatter, inviting him to reply or to join in arranging for a conference at which conditions mutually satisfactory might be arranged.

A new shearing agreement was drafted by the Union, admittedly one which fully protected the employer, and in 1887 we commenced to enforce it. We had £740 with which to begin a fight against the wealthiest and most powerful class of employers in Australia. The men won, and the next two years saw an amicable settlement and recognition of the Union in some districts, whilst there was still fighting to be done in the new portions of the colonies taken up for organizing.

Queensland had in the meantime also organized a Shearers' Union, whilst the A.S.U. extended until it covered New South Wales, Victoria, and South Australia. At the start the station labor other than shearers was also enrolled, but as these workers did not come in very readily it was made a distinctly shearers' organization. The shed hands, however, were organized in 1890, but both Unions became one body in 1893 under the name of the Australian Workers' Union. In 1904 the kindred body in Queensland joined, so that the A.W.U. is now one

organization, covering practically all the States, and
with a membership of 44,000.

From the beginning the Union has been Federal
in spirit. In its allotment of districts to branches·it
ignored the political boundaries of colonies. It also
ignored all class or sex distinctions, and admitted
all who had no other union which · they could
conveniently join. Owing to the effect of the
Arbitration Act under which the A.W.U. is registered the rules had, however, to ˙be narrowed in
respect to those admitted, and it is now confined to
those engaged in pastoral work. The Union draws
the line at colored aliens, as,—"No Chinese,
Japanese, Kanakas, or Afghans or colored aliens
other than Maoris, American negroes, and children
of mixed parentage born in Australia shall be
admitted to membership." That the Union is broad
in its aims the following quotations will show. The
first is Rule 3, in which the objects of the Union are
set out, and the other is the preface to the Rules,
which indicates the spirit in which the Rules are to
be interpreted:—

OBJECTS.

3. The objects for which the Union is
established are, by the provision and distribution of funds and by all other lawful means,
whether industrial, political, municipal, or
otherwise;

(a) To regulate and protect the conditions
of labor, the relations between workmen and
employers and between workmen and workmen;

(b) To impose restrictive conditions on the conduct of the trade, business, or industry of the members;

(c) To promote the general and material welfare of the members and to improve the relations between employers and workmen;

(d) To gradually replace the present competitive system of industry by a co-operative system;

(e) To provide legal assistance in defence of members' rights where deemed necessary;

(f) To establish and maintain a Funeral Fund for the burial of deceased members;

(g) To endeavor by political action to secure social justice;

(h) To establish and maintain Labor journals;

(i) To assist by federation or otherwise kindred organizations in upholding the rights and privileges of workers, and generally to assist in the emancipation of Labor.

Disbursements in furtherance of any of the above objects shall be deemed to be part of the ordinary expenses of the Union within the meaning of Schedule B of the Commonwealth Conciliation and Arbitration Act.

PREFACE.

" Daily, as the various and widespread sections of the human family are being insensibly drawn into closer touch with each other, it becomes clearer that men should become co-operators—mates—instead of antagonists. ' No

man liveth to himself.'. We are all mutually
dependent one upon another. . Under the existing order of things, however, each is forced into
warfare with his fellow, and life is made a
struggle in which the success of the winner
means that those whom unjust conditions have
forced. into a fight are crushed back into hopeless misery. So long as man depends upon his
fellow man for leave to toil, so long will the
lives of the great mass be one continuous
struggle, rendered more keen and uncertain by
every scientific and mechanical appliance
brought in to facilitate wealth-production.
Nature's storehouse holds ample supplies to
gratify the needs of all; but so long as the few
are allowed to hold possession the many must
starve. The doors of the storehouse must be
thrown open to all and the toll-bar of monopoly
be broken down ere justice can be done. Production must be for use and not for profit
before robbery of Labor will cease and the fear
of poverty be for ever banished. With the
disappearance of enforced poverty, crime will
gradually cease. With machinery put to its
proper use—that of contributing to the happiness of mankind—the increased leisure will give
opportunities for the cultivation of all those
higher faculties latent in man, but now repressed
by the pressure of a social system which makes
the satisfaction of mere material wants an all-
absorbing struggle.

"It is evident that the changes so essential to the true progress and development of all

that is best in humanity can only be effected by setting up its accomplishment as our aim, and working towards its realisation. Experience has taught us that no great reform can be secured otherwise than by systematic organized effort. Alone, we can agitate; organized, we can compel. It is by the organization of Unions that the conditions of life for all have been prevented from becoming worse than they are. To continue, however, upon the lines of old Trades Unionism alone will but stave off the crash that now threatens our civilisation. To narrow the fight to a mere question of employers and workmen is but a waste of energy, and can never secure that reconstruction which will leave one no longer dependent upon another, but under which all shall have equal opportunities.

" Realising, then, that we must attack a system, and change it so that there will no longer be room for conflict between interests— no room for narrow selfishness to govern men's actions—the Australian Workers' Union starts with new aims. Realising that all workers, no matter what their occupation or sex may be, have a common interest, the A.W.U. aims at embracing all within its ranks. Whilst it of necessity uses that power which combination and that alone gives for protection of present material interests, the A.W.U. looks to education and such social and political reforms as strike at the root of the injustice from which the masses now suffer. By loyalty to principle,

.unity of purpose, aim, and method alone can we succeed. Rules are but a means of securing unity of action; nevertheless their observance and recognition are essential to success. We trust, therefore, that each member, of the A.W.U. will strive to understand the high and noble aim this Union has in view, and become an active unit in the great army of Reform— active as an agitator and true to his comrades, as a Unionist always is—and success is certain."

The A.W.U. was the first to introduce the idea of applying Trades Union methods to secure political and social reform. It teaches its members that to vote straight for Labor candidates is as necessary as to act straight in regard to Union rules and conditions industrially. The working man who supports any candidate for Parliament opposed to a Labor candidate is considered as politically blacklegging on his class. The effect of this teaching has been such that wherever the A.W.U. holds sway the representatives in Parliament are all Labor members; and if there be any member of the Union who votes for any other he is unknown and unheard of.

The Union has recognised that it is not by hoarding money, but by the judicious expenditure of its funds, that success comes. To secure an educated membership is its aim rather than the building up of big funds. It is men rather than money who will win the fight for social justice. Every year the Union sends out organizers, and last year it had twenty-eight working at one time, all of whom are paid, and whose duty it is not only to enrol members, but to educate them industrially and politically. A certain sum is spent in literature, and one shilling per member per year is set apart in a Parliamentary fund for paying the expenses of candidates.

The annual contribution is fifteen shillings for shearers and cooks, and ten shillings for others. From each of these subscriptions the sum of five shillings is paid to " The Worker " newspaper, published in Sydney, which entitles each member to a copy of the paper free of charge posted weekly to his home. The Queensland members pay a subsidy of 3s. 6d. to " The Worker " published in Brisbane, and get a copy in the same way.

The Southern " Worker " is entirely owned by the branches in the three Southern States. The paper was started at Wagga Wagga, N.S.W., as a small sheet called " The Hummer," and was first issued on the 19th October, 1891. The name was changed to that of its Queensland predecessor, " The Worker," in 1892, and in 1893 it was removed to Sydney. Since then it has gone through troublous times, but kept alive; and is now practically the largest union-owned paper in the world.

For some time past all profits from the journal and from job printing have been devoted to enlarging and improving the paper. It has the largest circulation of any weekly in Australia giving news of the day to its readers. It has a special correspondent in Melbourne and another in Adelaide, and keeps its readers in touch with Federal and State politics. It owns a fine five-storied building in

Bathurst-street, ·Sydney, with an up-to-date plant, including the latest and most improved machinery.
. . The Queensland " Worker " was the pioneer in Labor papers in Australia. It is owned and controlled by an Australian Labor Federation of that State, and has done splendid work. The paper is on the up-grade, and exerts a powerful influence on the Labor movement in that State.

. Unionism came to the Australian bushman as a religion. It came bringing salvation from years of tyranny. It had in it that feeling of mateship which he understood already, and which always characterised the action of one " white man " to another. Unionism extended the idea, so a man's character was gauged by whether he stood true to Union rules or " scabbed " it on his fellows. The man who never went back on the Union is honored to-day as no other is honored or respected. The man who fell once may be forgiven, but he is not fully trusted. The lowest term of reproach is to call a man a " scab."

Experience has taught that the man who sells himself to the employer at a time of strike is a man of weak character, if not worse. At many a country ball the girls have refused to dance with them, the barmaids have refused them a drink, and the waitresses a meal.

Unionists have starved rather than accept work under other conditions. Hundreds of men have worn their boots and clothes to tatters seeking work upon Union terms; and not finding it, have gone without for a year—remaining penniless, but inde-

pendent and proud that they had not degraded themselves. It was such men who made the Union a
success, and enabled it to hold its own against well-
organized Capitalism aided by friendly Governments.
Men imbued with such a spirit put the cause above
personal self-interest. They needed no prompting—
no exciting by fiery orators—but stood loyal to
principle, no matter what the consequences might
be. Rough and unpolished many of them may be;
but manly, true, and " white " all the time, and the
movement owes them much.

CHAPTER IX.

A FIGHTING UNION.

SHEARING sheds employ a varying number of hands, ranging from half-a-dozen to upwards of 200. Each shed, therefore, can be likened to a factory. Generally it is far from any centre of population, and is only used at shearing time, being locked up during the rest of the year. Counting each shed as corresponding to a factory, it is safe to say that more strikes have taken place in connection with shearing sheep than in all the other industries combined. Probably 10,000 cases since 1886 would be under the number. These lasted from one hour to eight weeks. But one hour meant that the Unionists were prepared for a much longer term if necessary.

Sometimes the employer would be merely trying the men, and if they gave in he profited; but if they held out he was not prepared for the risks and delay, so would come to Union terms. Up till 1890 there was no collective unity amongst pastoralists except the natural class feeling. Each had been so accustomed to having his own way that he took any interference unkindly, even though he admitted that the Union demands were quite reasonable. Some came to terms at once, and did well for themselves, as they got the pick of the men, who on their part showed their appreciation by more carefully looking after the Union employer's interests.

Twenty-third Annual Conference

The majority put up a fight, however, objecting either to paying Union rates or using the Union agreement. The latter contains the specifications as to how the work is to be done, although many prefer a verbal agreement only. If the men failed to get their terms at roll-call they would either go away and look for another shed, or, when so directed by the Union, retire to some reserve near at hand and form a camp. In the latter case a cook would be appointed, rations obtained from the nearest store, and a complete system of picketing adopted. The shed would be surrounded, and any man looking for work would be brought into camp and fed with the rest, the Union paying the accounts. In all sheds the men select one of their number to act as spokesman, and also a committee to help him look after mess accounts, etc.

This training rendered it easy to fall into line when in camp. Strict discipline was maintained, and good behaviour insisted upon. No one was allowed to bring any drink into camp. In dry seasons the grass seeds ripen and get into the wool, so the pastoralist cannot wait, or the value of his wool will be lessened. This fact helped the Union to win many a shed.

In many cases, when a Union organizer called at a shed he found it had started, and after he had addressed the men they not infrequently struck and demanded that the agreement they had signed should be cancelled and Union terms conceded. This gave the pastoralist an opening under the " Masters and Servants' Act," and he sometimes sued the men. The Union in such cases provided for defence, and

F

also paid the fines, often making good the wages forfeited as well. However, law was not much good to the squatter, as he had to get his sheep shorn in any case, and so he had often to give way with the best grace he could.

Sometimes the men at work were non-unionists, who refused to make a stand, but worked on. On many occasions their hut was rushed at night, and they were taken away to a Union camp, where the employer would come next day and interview them. They generally assured him that they were in camp of their own free will, and intended to stay there until he gave them Union terms. This would be said in the presence of the police, and it is not easy to ascertain how much the non-unionists were influenced by fear, as many of them remained true to Union principles afterwards, although at first brought into it by compulsion.

The years 1887 to 1889 inclusive saw a great deal of fighting of this kind. Penalties were imposed on the shearer who stood out against the Union. He was made to pay up sums equal to the total paid by those who had joined at the beginning. Then fines were imposed, and some had to pay as high as £10 each in cash in order to be placed on the right footing with their fellows.

Organizers were kept very busy, often knocking up several horses during the season in rapid riding to get from one shed to another in time to be at roll-call. One man had thus nine changes of horses in a season. Owing to the pastoralists ordering them off the run, the organizers and leaders had to obtain maps showing the roads, reserves, etc., and as these had been in many cases fenced in and made use of by the squatter, he was often surprised at finding the men simply camping within a few yards of his hut and setting him at defiance. He himself had forgotten where the road or reserve was till the Union found it.

Up till 1890 the struggle had been with the individual pastoralist, and the Union had won pretty well all along the line, and had come to friendly arrangements with some sections of the pastoralists who had become organized in different districts. The year 1890 saw the federation of the Pastoralists' Union, and their unity with the Employers' Union. It altered the methods of fighting.

The P.U. began to systematise the work of getting anti-union Labor. They raked the cities, offering work to any kind of creature in the semblance of a man. Professional thieves and burglars who were well known to the police were engaged, and under police escort were taken on free passes on the people's railways to the sheds to fill the places of respectable workers.

Higher pay than that asked by Unionists was given these creatures, who enjoyed the change and the good things provided on the road. They were taken from Tasmania and from New Zealand, by steamer, first to Queensland and afterwards to New South Wales and Victoria. This was in 1891 and again in 1894. The A.W.U. was of course alert. Boats were watched, and Pastoralists' Union offices picketed. We used a secret code of our own for telegraphing, and often sent a man with the crowd in the steamer or train, as the case may be. Once these men started on their journey they were practically prisoners, as they were locked in the railway carriages, the man in charge of them having the tickets.

The Government of the day sided with the capitalists, and gave them the use of the police—ostensibly to keep the ring clear, but in reality to try to crush Unionism. The squatter was at first called upon to pay for any police sent to his station, but if any disturbance took place the cost was then thrown upon the country. It was not difficult to have a disturbance, especially as the press was strongly anti-Labor. The fight was a costly and unsatisfactory one to the pastoralists.

One station owner, who was notorious as anti-Union and as an employer of Chinese, engaged a body of non-unionists in Melbourne for his shed on the Darling River, N.S.W. He had to take them over 1000 miles by rail, and then drive them by coach to his shed. They were a lively lot, and made him treat them handsomely on the way. They had, in fact, a really good spree. The Unionists were on the look-out for them at the place where they had to leave the train, and interviewed them on arrival, the result being that they left the squatter to pay all expenses of their trip and then go and look for another team to do his work.

Those who did succeed in getting non-unionist labor lost severely, owing to the inferior workmanship causing deterioration in the price obtained for the wool. Some of the squatters' homesteads suffered also, as the family's jewellery sometimes disappeared. In 1891, for the first time in the history of Bourke, N.S.W., big firms in that town had to put on night watchmen, on account of the thieves brought into the district by the P.U.

Nothing was too hot or too heavy for these new-found friends of the lordly squatter. One young fellow—a Sydney larrikin—brought back with him a huge bunch of door keys which he had collected on his travels out back. Unfortunately a certain number of the same class have gone out ever since under the P.U. engagement system, and shearers find it unsafe to leave a watch or any other valuable in the hut, as it was at one time reasonably safe to do.

The fight against the Bushworkers of Queensland in 1891 proved so costly to the P.U. that they came to terms with the Shearers' Union in August, 1891, in time for the major portion of the shearing. It was understood that the agreement then signed between the two bodies, representing New South Wales, Victoria, and South Australia, would hold good until altered by mutual consent. The A.S.U. had conceded the point of refusal to work with non-members owing to a blunder made by one of the branch secretaries, but the A.W.U. loyally carried out the agreement arrived at, and for three years work went on smoothly.

In 1894 the Annual Conferences of both bodies sat in Sydney at the same time, and some communications passed between them. Without warning or consultation the Pastoralists' Union broke its shearing agreement, and issued a new one, containing, amongst other objectionable clauses, one declaring the employer or his agent sole judge in any case of

dispute as to breach of agreement. This was
actually contrary to law, but as the squatter is
mostly the magistrate, its illegality did not matter
much.

This action on their part brought on the strike
of 1894—by far the biggest fight any Union has
had to put up in Australia. The P.U. were favored
by the bad times which had followed the financial
disasters of 1892-3, and which left a mass of unemployed. In spite of that fact the A.W.U. won in the
great majority of the sheds. The years 1895-6 saw
the A.W.U. considerably weakened, but quietly
re-organizing and recovering the losses of 1894.
From the year 1897 it has been on the up-grade.

Ever since 1891 the Pastoralists' Union has
persistently refused to meet the A.W.U. in conference; and, being tired of asking, the latter in 1902
made a demand for increased shearing rates. This
was resisted by the P.U., and a number of strikes
took place. In many cases the increase asked for
was conceded, and probably further fighting would,
under the old conditions, have enlarged the number.

But now we met with a new experience. The
decisions in the Taff Vale and other cases in England
had given a new interpretation of the law as it
affects Trades Unions, and hence, when a camp was
formed at Coonamble, an injunction was applied
for and obtained against the officers of the A.W.U.,
which forced the breaking up of the camp and
rendered it unwise to continue the struggle on those
lines.

The action in this case was taken by Mr. Keogh,
who, it is alleged, was not a member of the P.U. He

was bringing a body of non-unionists, hired in Melbourne, to his shed at Warrana. Suspecting trouble, he hired five professional pugilists in Sydney to come with them, whose duty it was to punch any Unionist who came interfering with his team.

The non-unionists were travelling in coaches after having left the train, and were being taken across a paddock so as to avoid the town and the crowd. It was necessary to cut the wires in the fences in order to get through, but ere they had time to do so a number of men from the Union camp—about one-half of whom were not members of the A.W.U.—arrived on the scene and interrupted proceedings. The hired pugs were expected then to do their duty, and each to earn the " fiver " which he was to get. One of them, eager for the fray, issued a challenge, which · was immediately taken up by a young man—a Union shearer—who looked a quiet, simple chap. A ring was formed, and they took up positions facing each other in proper style.

The first round ended the fight, as Mr. Keogh's professional pugilist had found more than his match in the quiet young man, who was quite prepared for any of the others if they wanted it. They did not " care about any " just then, however, and, instead, joined the Unionists, and all hands marched off to the Union camp. It was following this that Mr. Keogh took legal action, and proved that the law is once more in favor of the employer and against organized Labor.

The organizers of the Union have had to resort to many schemes to gain their ends. Some of them became clever strategists,. and would make splendid officers to lead an army. The Union was anxious to get a small station owned by a big Scotchman named Graham, and situated close to Kingston, in Victoria. The Union organizer (O'Brien) was amongst the men who were camped in Graham's hut waiting for roll-call. Of course it was not known that he was a Union organizer, but when he stood out as spokesman for the men when roll was called, Graham found him out and ordered him off the premises. O'Brien got nearly all hands away with him, however, as he had not been some days amongst them for nothing. The shed was declared on strike, and the men camped in the town.

Graham secured another team of men from Ballarat, some 16 miles away, and was driving these to his place when he was met by O'Brien, who rode alongside trying to talk the non-unionists 'into coming away with him. Graham was driving a pair of horses, and whenever be got a chance he would cut at O'Brien with his whip. The latter kept alongside, however, until they got into Kingston, near the Union camp. He then rushed his horse in front of the heads of Graham's pair, and blocked them.- It was dark by this time. Meantime the men from the camp and others came up, and the non-unionists were lifted out of the vehicle just as the constable came along on horseback and dispersed them.

A friendly landlady planted O'Brien until we should find out how things stood. The press, of course, had a sensational account of a riot, and of stone-throwing, and other things. The Union secretary (Mr. Temple) and myself drove out to see about matters. As Graham did not know Temple, I sent the latter down to interview him on behalf of the press, and Temple had the pleasure of dining with Graham and of getting the full strength of things. He was shown over the shed, and was able to see how many were there, and to obtain other details. Graham also told him that he did not intend to prosecute, as he could not swear to any of the men; though he said, of course, that he wanted the press to say that he intended doing so, in order to frighten them. That was all we wanted, and we were back in time to meet the head of the police, who had called at the office to inquire about the disturbance.

Graham was stubborn, but got along badly with a poor team of men. Finally, to get to know how many he really had, we sent for another organizer—Jim Cook—whom he did not know, and got him to engage as a non-unionist. He came by train, and the play was beautifully acted on his arrival, as the men from the camp were there, and in loud tones were trying to persuade him to be a man and join the Union, Jim giving the usual and well-known answer of the non-unionist that he had a sick wife, and was not going to let his kiddies starve. Near the gate there was quite a " tussle," and as Jim did not want to carry his leggings with him he gave them to one of the men from the camp.

The press made a great deal of that incident, and related how the shearer had been hustled and actually robbed by the Unionists on his way to earn an honest living. Of course, the boys in camp knew all about it; but their acting was good enough to deceive Graham and the press as well. When Cook saw how things were he left, and the strike was declared off. The constable, in commenting on the O'Brien incident, complained of his not stopping the buggy further out instead of directly in front of the police station. Said he:

"How the divil could I stay indoors whin the row was forninst me. I got me horse so as I could gallop about and not see anny of them, so divil a one o' them could I identify."

Some of the Unionists were great believers in immersion as a cure for "scab." One experienced organizer said he had only known one case which required more than one dip. That was in Western Victoria. He was on picket duty, and caught the "scab" creeping across a bridge over a stream at three o'clock on a frosty morning. He tried moral suasion without avail, and finally he dropped the "scab" from the bridge into the cold water. The poor fellow came out still loyal to his desire to oblige the employer, so he was again pushed in. He came out the second time still a hardened sinner, and after some further parley was again dipped under the cold water. He repented this time, and came out a convert to Unionism and a monument to the efficacy of cold water in judicious quantities properly applied.

This was at Barwidgie, where Mr. Arthur Rae, whilst travelling organizer, got in as a shearer and worked amongst the non-unionists a while ere the boss (Mr. Ware) found it out. Rae had just time to get away, and Ware got out a summons for him for leaving his hired service. Of course Rae was under an assumed name. That summons was all over the country, and mostly in a direction where Mr. Rae was not expected to be found. It was once handled by Mr. Rae himself, who was unknown to the constable, who was asking for someone not of the name of Rae. Ware got a renewal extending the time, so anxious was he to get at the Union agitator; but he didn't get him, and after nearly wearing the summons out he gave up.

The writer has been President of the Union since its inception, with the exception of three years, when he was the General Secretary; and, in closing this chapter reviewing some of the achievements of a fighting Union, in which he necessarily played an important part, cannot refrain from quoting an excellent caricature of the malicious misrepresentation to which he has been subjected. The verse is from the pen of a Union shearer, and appeared in " The Worker " some years ago:—

SPENCE'S STATION.

[In the old Union days it was a favorite gag with squatters to tell Union men that Spence was making a good thing out of them. In New South Wales I've heard them say Spence had a station in Victoria; in Victoria they'd say he had a run in New South Wales. Have known Spence many years,

and have travelled Australia from the Territory to
the Bight, but could never locate Spence's Station.]

Beyond the furthest far-out-back, beyond the setting
 sun,
Beyond the Western desert plain, where rivers never
 run;
Away beyond the border fence, 'neath azure summer
 skies,
Where droughts and floods are both unknown—
 there Spence's Station lies.

He owns five hundred million sheep of Lincoln-
 Leicester breed,
That's crossed with old Merino strain, true type of
 squatter's need;
His stud ram weighs ten thousand pounds, of wool
 he cuts a ton;
He's three weeks' shearing with the blades for
 Howe, the Queensland gun.

His shed is roofed with beaten gold, brought from
 the planet Mars;
From huts to shed the shearers ride in cushioned
 motor cars.
The drummer shears two hundred sheep and never
 turns a hair;
No cuss words on the place are used, all work doth
 start with prayer.

He got eight million pounds, we've heard, by
 pinching Union funds,
And purchased houses in the moon and many station
 runs;

And when he's made his pile they say he'll give the
    Union best,
And live in regal style while we are tramping in
    the West.

I've toured this land from north to south, from
    westward to the east,
In times of flood, in times of drought, of famine, and
    of feast;
I've tramped it when the plains were dry and when
    the plains were wet,
But never crossed the boundary fence of Spence's
    Station yet.

F. J. MURRAY.

CHAPTER X.

THE EMPLOYERS' UNION AND FREEDOM OF CONTRACT.

THE following is said to be a programme laid down and agreed to by a private meeting of the capitalistic combination of New South Wales, comprising shippers, pastoralists, merchants, members of Parliament, and other large employers of labor:—

"1. Plan to overthrow the combination of labor and unionism, and the universal advancement of the workers.

"2. To obtain co-operation of the various Australian Governments with a view to enable the Australian employers of labor to enforce all or any agreed terms of the employers by force of arms.

"3. To enforce, through Government. freedom of contract by the force of 'law and order.'

"4. The maintenance of a high standard of wages as applied to shearers and others until such time as the unions agree to receiving freedom of contract under any conditions.

"5. The disbanding of unions by means of freedom of contract, and then the rapid reduction of wages at once (25 per cent.) for all employment.

" 6. The Pastoralists' Union, in conjunction with the Employers' and Shippers' Unions, to agree to the conditions and act as a body when either party's interests are involved.

" 7. The Shipping Union to arrange as part and parcel of capital to introduce German, Italian, and Coolie labor by the importation of 5000 men per year.

" 8. That arrangements be at once made to secure the adoption of General Booth's emigration scheme—the flooding of the Australian labor market with men of all sorts and conditions.

" 9· That free passes be granted to all men desirous of leaving the city in time. of metropolitan strikes, or vice versa, to enable men to come from the country districts.

" 10. The arming of all free labor in self-defence.

" 11. To discharge gradually all union labor from shipping and other circles of employment. The prevention at all hazards of one-man-one-vote.

" 12. The Labor candidates to be opposed by good local men, or where no local men, to put up a Labor candidate favorable to capital, all his expenses to be paid by the Association.

" 13. That the representatives of shipping commerce, and pastoralists combine to make the combination of labor illegal."

The original of the above was given to me by one who said he was present. He gave me at the same time a good deal of verbal information which I have since verified. We have had evidence in various ways of efforts made to carry out this plan, and whether it was laid down or not on the date mentioned (24th April, 1891) by the 65 alleged to have been present, we have other and ample evidence of a combination amongst Australian capitalists to accomplish the objects set out in the foregoing list of proposals.

To anyone acquainted with the history of the Trade Union movement and its wonderful achievements in the face of the most powerful forces brought against it, it would seem incomprehensible that any body of intelligent men in this age should dream of attempting to crush it out of existence. The fact is that the leaders in the employers' organizations were ignorant of the real strength of Unionism, and knew nothing of the spirit underlying it.

The workers are rapidly awakening to the fact that they are being taken advantage of, and are no longer willing to be treated as so many wage slaves willing to accept just what is offered them by a fellow-man who is termed an employer. The trade union introduces the collective bargain; and, to secure this, conferences between employer and representatives of the workers are necessary. Where unions stood alone the employer met his own employees as delegates representing the rest of the workers. The fear of the boss's displeasure and of the resultant loss of employment were always over them, hence the employer had not so much to fear.

· As the number of unions increased, and those in one industry became one body with a paid secretary. the circumstances were altered. Often the employer refused to meet unless the delegates were all his own employees. The most outspoken would often lose his position, and as a consequence a strike would result until his reinstatement was secured. Employers termed this an interference with the management of their business. If a conference resulted in improved conditions in one industry it inevitably led to a demand for improvement in others.

The greedy unscrupulous employer would reduce wages, and a strike would take place. Other unions would be drawn in, and in any case they would support the one in trouble, realising that injustice to one should be the concern of all. All these influences combine to force organization and federation on both sides.

At a banquet tendered Mr. E. M. Young, President of the Employers' Union, on the 26th February, 1891, that gentleman, after referring to the necessity for unity said that " with that intent he invited all who were available at the time to meet him, and from that small beginning arose their Pastoralists' Union. But he had dreams far greater than the Pastoralists' Union. He dreamt of uniting the vast Western Plains of New South Wales and the distant West of Queensland; and he thought recent events had shown—in view of the scheme of federation which he had recently successfully carried through, and which had bound all together—that he

G

was justified in dreaming thàt the scheme was possible.''

The attitude assumed by this federation of employers is clearly set forth in another portion of the same address as follows :—

'' The working men here were simply asking for control. There was no question of wages, of hours, nor of terms in any shape. All that the employers insisted on was that they should be allowed to conduct their business as they pleased, and to employ whom they pleased, whether the men were in unions or not.''

This sets forth two extreme views. Firstly, that the workers' unions ask for control of the industry— a statement entirely devoid of any foundation. Secondly, that there was no question of wages and conditions, when the facts were and still are that wages, hours, and terms are the only questions about which troubles are made, the question of who is to be employed being rarely raised. Experience has shown that ever since its establishment the Employers' Union has set itself against conferences with the workers' unions, and has fought for freedom of contract. It seeks to ignore collective bargaining, and tries to force into practice individualism between employer and employee.

In an age specially characterised by the disappearance of the private employer and the growth of corporations, public companies, combines, trusts, and monopolies on one side—necessitating as it does the organization and federation of labor on the other—to attempt to introduce something so foreign as freedom of contract was not only bound to cause trouble, but was certain to be found practically impossible. Mr. Young and his federation certainly made a great effort. · ·

The P.U. was first organized in 1889. In 1890 it began on the Darling Downs, Queensland, to employ non-unionists only. This was by a collective understanding amongst pastoralists, as admitted by Mr. Williams in conference in May, 1890. To checkmate this the Australian Labor Federation of Queensland took action. They selected the Jondaryan Station, and refused to allow the wool to go on board the s.s. Jumna unless the pastoralists agreed to employ unionists. The P.U. gave way, for the time being only.

This was in May, 1890, and in June an attack on the Shearers' Union in New South Wales was proposed at a meeting of pastoralists held in Maitland, New South Wales, and a leading pastoralist in Sydney offered £5000 towards a £50,000 fighting fund. The Amalgamated Shearers' Union, covering New South Wales, Victoria, and South Australia, took action at the same time by issuing a manifesto on the lines so successful in Queensland, and would have met with similar success but for the action of the Employers' Union. That body precipitated the Maritime Strike of 1890.

The year 1891 saw the war carried into Queensland, and it extended from there into New South Wales, but owing to the cost having proved too much for the pastoralists they came to terms with the A.S.U. in August of that year. Next year the miners of Broken Hill silver field were attacked. The big mine, which has paid over £11,000,000 to its shareholders, had during the trouble of 1890 stopped, on the paltry pretext of not being able to get supplies, but in reality to cut off supplies of cash to the strikers on the coast. The miners had sent on £700, and had struck a levy of 2s. 6d. per week. The mine-owners had an agreement with the Miners' Union, arrived at in 1889, which runs as follows:—

AGREEMENT OF NOVEMBER, 1889.

"It being distinctly understood that the only question at issue is the employment of union or non-union men, it is hereby mutually agreed between the officers of the A.M.A. and the Broken Hill Proprietary Company, Limited, the British Broken Hill Proprietary Company Limited, the Broken Hill Proprietary Block 14 Company Limited, the Broken Hill Proprietary Block 10 Company Limited, and the Broken Hill North S.M. Company Limited—

"1. That the A.M.A. will as early as possible take means to have the Barrier District made a colonial district so that the executive may control their own affairs, and draw up such rules as will be approved of by a committee of managers.

"2. Shift bosses and foremen are not to be compelled to join the Union, but may form a union for themselves.

"3. The surfacemen and furnace hands may form a union of their own, and may be affiliated with the A.M.A.

" 4. Tradesmen and mechanics already members of recognized societies are not to be compelled to join the Amalgamated Miners' Association.

" 5. The companies undertake to collect the dues for each of the unions on pay day and hand the same over to the duly appointed officer of the Union, who will be present on pay day.

" 6. Work to be resumed on the mines forthwith—that is, as far as practicable.

" 7. It is understood that no local union will be recognized by the employers unless exceeding the number of one hundred; if below that number, permission must be obtained from the A.M.A. executive and Managers' Association before it can be formed.

" 8. All past differences to be forgotten."

It will be seen from the reading of clause 1 in the agreement that the officers meeting the representatives of the mine-owners had given way a great deal when they allowed the managers to have a say in the approval of the rules. I was so strongly opposed to it that I immediately, as general secretary of the A.M.A., wired to the secretary at Broken Hill objecting to the clause, and followed it by letter, giving my reasons. There was no objection to the miners of the Barrier forming themselves into a separate district, as that had been agreed to by the A.M.A. as a body.

When the stoppage of the big mine took place in 1890, a conference was arranged for and was held in Melbourne, at which all difficulties in the way of

carrying on the mine were removed and a new
agreement arrived at which reads as follows:—

THE AGREEMENT OF 1890.

" 1. That in the event of any future trouble
existing, the point or points at issue shall be
referred to a Board of Aribtration of équal
numbers of either side, say three; and failing
their being able to agree, that an umpire be
appointed, who shall be either a Chief Justice or
a Judge of the Supreme Court or any of the
Australian colonies. In the event of the Board
not being able to agree, the Judge shall be
chosen as umpire; or upon his declining to act,
the selection shall be made by lot out of the
list of Judges of the various colonies. The
decision when given to be final and binding on
both sides. The award to take effect from date
of notice of arbitration on either side.

" 2. That until the said Board, as provided
above, shall have been appointed and delivered
its decision, work in every branch of the mine
shall continue as is usual without let or
hindrance.

" 3. That the A.M.A., Barrier Colonial
District No. 3, agrees that no question of any
kind in connection with any other Labor
organization shall form the basis of dispute, and
only a question affecting the mines and the
employees is to be considered a matter on which
arbitration shall be resorted to when trouble
takes place. The meaning of this being that in
the event of a Trades Council or any Labor

body outside the A.M.A. of the Barrier Colonial District No. 3 calling the latter out for a dispute foreign to the mine, they will refuse to come out and will not raise such questions as between the mines and themselves.

"4. That contracts other than stoping of ore shall be allowed as heretofore.

" 5. That on the foregoing being agreed to, work shall be resumed at the earliest date possible on the various mines represented by this conference; the same rate of wages as before the present cessation of work to obtain, and the week's work underground shall consist of an average of 46 hours arranged as follows : Day shift eight hours, the afternoon shift on Saturdays to work only from 4 to 10 p.m., and the morning shift on Monday to start at 4 a.m. and work till 8 a.m. All other days than Mondays and Saturdays to be full time.

" 6. That the November, 1889, agreement as it stands shall hold good as heretofore, and the conditions thereon be upheld by all the companies represented at this conference.

" 7. That the foregoing shall come into force on the Port Pirie Working Men's Association agreeing to ship by ocean-going steamers without further trouble the bullion now at the Port, and hereafter to be produced when work is resumed at the mines; also to handle and receive timber now afloat or to be shipped in sailing vessels as required. This clause to apply only until the maritime strike is

adjusted, when the decision come to will apply
to Port Pirie as a natural consequence.

" 8. On the above undertaking by the Port
Pirie working men being supplied in writing
orders to be given to resume working forthwith,
and the men employed as rapidly as the
circumstances will admit.

" 9. That even in the event of a delay at
Port Pirie on the signing of the agreement it
is understood the managers be instructed to
start all dead work forthwith, also the pumps,
and that the necessary men to do so be put on.
This clause only to be subject to the approval of
the Labor Defence Committee of Broken Hill.

" 10. That all past differences are to be
forgotten."

This agreement provided clearly for the
settlement of all future differences and also
narrowed down the area, as it prevented the miners
taking up any other organization's troubles. It was
loyally observed by the A.M.A., but the mining
companies broke away in several matters without
the Union making a noise about it.

In 1892, however, the mine-owners were ready,
and having saved up a quarter of a million of a
reserve fund they took up their share of carrying
out the policy of the Employers' Union, and
deliberately forced on a strike. The first step was
taken by Mr. Knox, the mine-owners' secretary, who
wrote to the A.M.A., stating that the companies
wanted to introduce the competitive contract system
into the stopes of the mines at Broken Hill. The

officers of the Miners' Union replied, asking for more particulars as to what was proposed. Mr. Knox answered that the Board did not consider it necessary. The miners asked for arbitration as per the agreement of 1890. No reply was vouchsafed, so they wrote again. This time they were met with a refusal and a notice that the agreement was determined. The mine-owners' manifesto stated that they wanted "freedom of contract." The miners, after exhausting all means of avoiding trouble, came out on strike. This lasted from July 4 to November 6, 1892, and the arrest, trial, and jailing of the leaders of the miners provided enough excitement and gratification for the Employers' Union for 1892-3.

In 1894 the next move was made. When the conference of 1891 was being arranged for between the pastoralists and the Shearers' Union a blunder was committed by one of the branch secretaries, and the Union was committed to agreeing to work with non-members. The press in general, and the president of the P.U. in particular, constantly asserted that men were only members of the Shearers' Union by coercion ; hence when the concession was made they fully expected to see vast numbers refusing to pay up their subscriptions.

Three years' experience had shown the fallacy of this idea, as the Union had become stronger than ever, and had organized the shed hands as well. Men had been coerced into remaining outside the Union, but the settlement had allowed these to join. The P.U., therefore, in 1894, without notice, broke its agreement of 1891. The Australian Workers' Union had no alternative but to fight. With an over-crowded labor market and Government aid to the employers, the fight was a bitter one. It cost the A.W.U. over £12,000, and proved a big loss to the pastoralists. The A.W.U. was temporarily crippled, and the P.U. was enabled to reduce wages and shearing rates for a couple of years.

The action of the P.U. proves that there is more than what the Employers' Union terms "freedom of contract" behind the actions of that body. The Shearers' Union (now the A.W.U.) had agreed to work with non-members, and had consented to the shearing agreement bearing the P.U. definition of what they meant by freedom of contract. This was printed at the top of every agreement signed by the men, and read as follows:—

"Shearing Agreement for New South Wales adopted at a conference held in Sydney on the 7th and 8th of August, 1891, between representatives of the Pastoralists' Federal Council of Australia and representatives of the Amalgamated Shearers' Union, at which the following was agreed to: That employers shall be free to employ and shearers free to accept employment, whether belonging to shearers' or other unions or not without favor, molestation, or intimidation on either side. (This is the definition of freedom of contract of the Pastoralists' Union of Australia.)"

The heads of the P.U. expressed themselves as well satisfied, and promised to use every endeavor to see the agreement carried out. Their break-away, therefore, can only have one interpretation. It was simply carrying out the plan of the Employers' Union, whose ambition was to crush the workers' organizations throughout Australia. The persistent refusal, either straight out or by subterfuge, to meet the organized workers in conference proves that they did not wish to recognise unionism amongst the workers. All mediation, however influential, was refused, and in some cases snubbed.

In 1894 Sir George Dibbs, as Premier of New South Wales, sent a telegram, drafted by myself, to the Premiers of all the other colonies, soliciting their aid as mediators. He also asked the managers of the various banks to meet him. They at first refused, but a peremptory message brought them, and he then asked them to use their influence with their clients to prevent trouble arising in the big industry of wool-growing. They agreed to submit his request to the Associated Banks. They did so, but that body refused, thus showing that they were all behind the Employers' Union in its aggressive attack on Labor.

Australian employers acting collectively will not avoid conflicts with Labor. They will not settle either by voluntary conciliation or arbitration, nor will they keep to any agreement they make with the workers' organizations any longer than suits their pockets. They have absolutely no sense of honor when acting together. The only exception to this has been the Mine-Owners' Association of Victoria. The Broken Hill mine-owners broke their agreement of 1889. The P.U. of South Australia came to terms with the A.S.U. in 1891, but failed to keep the arrangement, as they were over-ridden by the Federal Council of their own body. The Federal Council's agreement with the A.S.U. in 1891 was broken in 1894. In 1902 an agreement was arrived at with the Victorian section of the P.U. The South Australian section followed suit, but only kept it one year. The Victorians broke away again in 1906. The experience of the Coalminers' and the Seamen's Unions has been somewhat similar.

It was such experiences as these which led to the strong desire on the part of the workers for a Court of Arbitration, with powers of compulsion, not only for settlement of disputes, but for the enforcement of awards when made. Employers do not like this method of securing industrial peace, but the system of compulsory settlement has come to stay, and the employers themselves have been the cause of the demand for such Courts.

After all, why not settle matters in this way? The State provides courts with highly-paid staffs for the collection of private debts, the enforcement of private contract, and the settlement of every quarrel no matter how trivial. Two persons are not allowed to resort to fisticuffs to settle their differences without the Court interfering, yet no provision was made anywhere until recently for the settlement of disputes involving serious consequences or for the enforcement of agreements voluntarily entered into between employers and organized workers. Compulsory Arbitration must be preserved as a better expedient than any other so far put forward, and, with all its drawbacks, can be put up with until the disappearance of the competitive system with its natural corollary of wage slavery.

Time has not changed the Employers' Union. In November, 1906, the building trades of Melbourne demanded a reduction of hours from 48 to 44 per week. The contractors by whom they are mainly employed were on the point of giving way when the Employers' Union took a hand. This body put the screw on them by calling upon all firms from whom they purchased material to decline to supply them if they gave way. The combine of brickmakers refused bricks, and so this body, which did not believe in dictation as to how a man should manage his business, used all its powers to prevent employers doing so.

A large proportion of the Unionists, however, were able to keep at work, and thus support came for the rest. Contractors secured supplies from the back doors of firms who had their front doors closed, and who belonged to the employers' combine. The men were winning when the matter was remitted to Justice Cussen, who gave an award raising wages but leaving the hours as they were. The strike lasted eleven weeks. It was the beginning of a demand for shorter hours than 48 per week, which is spreading and growing.

The Employers' Union has a paid secretary at £1000 per annum, and he goes around preaching the economic gospel of the organization. In a speech delivered at Lilydale, Victoria, in April, 1902, he set forth their creed very neatly. He said:

"Marriage·was a luxury·for the workers, as were also long sleevers, attending theatres, and the like; and it was not fair to compel employers to pay for·such things."

This gentleman's name is Walpole, and he has recently been on·a trip to America to pick up points to be used in resisting every demand for improved conditions put forth by Australian Unionists. He makes much trouble for the employers, but really helps the Labor organizations; and we are sorry that the Employers' Union does not employ about a score of such men. The more that body intrudes itself the more clearly its character and aims become understood. The more apparent it makes its opposition to the masses, the more it weakens in power and influence.

CHAPTER XI.

THE TURNING POINT.

THE great turning point in the history · of Australian Labor was undoubtedly the maritime strike, as it was termed, in 1890. In reality it was a lock-out, and came about in this way. There had been a boom in land speculation, good seasons in pastoral pursuits, and capitalists had somewhat lost their heads. On the Labor side there had been steady advance, and quite a number of requests of various kinds had been submitted to different sections of the employers. Labor was considered too aggressive.

The year 1889 had been full of trouble. There had been a big strike at Broken Hill in November of that year, a strike of miners in Ballarat, and strikes in the building trades of Sydney, in the collieries of New South Wales, and amongst the waterside workers in Queensland. The Seamen's Union had one or two matters which they asked should be adjusted; whilst the shearers in Queensland, backed up by the Labor Federation, were asking for full recognition of Union men and the withdrawal of the boycott. The shipowners were then, as now, more or less closely associated with the pastoralists.. The former were organized, whilst the Pastoralists' Union had just come into existence: Both were intercolonial bodies.

Early in 1890 a meeting of representatives of employers' organizations of each colony was held in Melbourne, and it was determined that steps should be taken to stop the aggressiveness of Labor Unionism. A Federation of employers' organizations was formed, known as the Federated Employers' Union. A strong feeling against Unionism soon developed, and it was argued that the dictation—as they termed it—of trades unions and their " irresponsible " leaders must be put a stop to. The term " freedom of contract " was adopted as if it were some great and sacred principle. They gave no definition of it, but as time went on what they really meant came out. At a conference in Adelaide between the bakers and the employers, the President of the Master Bakers gave the following definition of the term :—

" 1. That they have the right to discharge any man without being asked the reason for so discharging.

" 2. They shall have the right to bring a man into their shop without being questioned whether he is a union or non-union man.

" 3. They shall have the right to employ whom they please.

" 4. They shall pay what they choose without being questioned on the matter by anybody."

Mr. E. M. Young, then president of the Employers' Union, gave the following statement of its meaning as reported in the Capitalists' own

HON. J. C. WATSON, M.H.R.,
First Labor Prime Minister of Australia.

official organ, the Melbourne "Argus," of the 27th February, 1891:

"All that employers insisted on was that they should be allowed to conduct their business as they pleased, and to employ whom they pleased, whether the men were in nuions or not."

Practical proof of what they meant was given by the following notice posted by Messrs. Flood and Co. in Sydney on the 19th August, 1890:—

"Let it be understood that for the future all men working for us will be expected to do such work on such terms and arrangements as may be required by us."

Some time prior to this the "South Australian Register," when engaging compositors, compelled them to sign a thirty-six months' agreement containing the following clause:

"The employee shall not, during the service aforesaid, be or become a member of the South Australian Typographical Society or any of a similar nature or having similar objects."

It was clear that the employers, though becoming organized themselves, set up the aim of refusing to recognise the right of the worker to organize. They wanted to revert back' to the days of the iron law of wages and unrestricted competition by workmen for work on such terms as the selfish, greedy employer might choose to fix. Whilst the capitalists were nursing this grand idea of freedom of contract the workers' unions kept steadily on in their own way, and no doubt by some

H

of their actions helped to add fuel to the fire of hatred burning in the breasts of capitalism.

Finally, in 1890, the Employers' Union conceived the ambition of wiping out Australian Unionism at one blow. They first had the idea of a universal lock-out. With this end in view the co-operation of certain bodies which had hitherto held aloof from the Employers' Federation was sought. The Mine-owners' Association of Victoria, whose head-quarters were in Ballarat, were asked to join in this grand coup. They, however, declined, as they were on good terms with the Miners' Association. The mine-owners of Broken Hill were sounded, but mainly through the influence of two of the directors, support in that direction was declined. The heads of several large firms in the cities were also humane enough to decline to be a party to such a plot. These rebuffs caused a change in tactics, though not in design; and it was decided to take the unions in detail.

Meantime, in pursuance of the policy of ignoring Unionism, the pastoralists in Queensland had instituted a boycott of union men, and the Australian Labor Federation determined to bring things to an issue. The Darling Downs pastoralists were the aggressors, and, as stated in the last chapter, the Waterside Workers' Unions were asked to refuse to load non-union shorn wool from the Jondaryan Station unless the pastoralists agreed to recognise Unionists. A big demonstration was made, and the co-operation of all the southern organizations of Labor was readily granted. The waterside men refused to load the s.s. Jumna with the Jondaryan wool, and when it was seen that Labor was determined the pastoralists gave way, a conference was held, and an agreement arrived at in Brisbane on the 17th May, 1890.

In the meantime keen interest had been taken in other parts. Careful enquiry had shown that in a large part of New South Wales pastoralists had become tired of an unsuccessful fight year after year with the Shearers' Union, and were in an unsettled state of mind as to the best course to pursue. On ascertaining this we felt that some movement on our part was necessary to make them decide one way or the other prior to the beginning of the shearing season. Following the lines of Queensland, the A.S.U. issued a strong manifesto appealing to the other unions, and especially to the waterside and maritime workers. At the same time we appealed to the Pastoralists' Union to meet in conference and settle matters amicably.

The move was so far successful that several sections did meet us, and agreed to leave the matter in the hands of their executive. The latter also agreed to meet us, and everything was working smoothly, when suddenly the maritime trouble was sprung upon us owing to the action of the employers, who put into force the new policy laid down in secret, namely, to take the Unions in detail. The marine officers were an organized body, and in Melbourne they were affiliated with the other maritime bodies. In Sydney they were not affiliated with any other section of Unionism. Communications had passed between them and the shipowners in both colonies, and their Union was fully recognised, as also was the fact that they had reasonable grounds for increased pay.

No considerations of fair-play actuated the Employers' Union, however. They, like the Zulu chief, tackled the weakest Union first. They placed the matter in the hands of the late Mr. Alfred Lamb, of Sydney, who acted promptly by ordering the refusal of a conference to the marine officers. The latter, acting without consulting anybody, refused to sail; and when others took their places the seamen refused and stood by the officers, and thus the whole trouble was precipitated. The president of the Employers' Union (Mr. E. E. Smith), when responding to a toast at a function in Victoria, said:

" They had to thank the executive of the Employers' Union for the way in which the strike had eventuated, as well as the secretaries and the other gentlemen who had worked so amicably with the executive through a difficult and trying time. The late Mr. Alfred Lamb, of Sydney, was the man who had really brought the thing forward. He knew it was the intention of the Labor bodies to postpone the difficulty until the height of the wool season, and he thought it was better to bring it on sooner. He was very sorry that the country should have lost over a million of money in proving to a section of the community that it could not coerce the whole. This was now, however, laid down, and it would be difficult to disturb the position which matters had assumed."

The statement that Labor intended to postpone the difficulty had no foundation in fact. Labor had no desire for trouble, and as it had no executive or other head managing affairs in the way the employers had, each union was simply dealing with its own affairs in its own way. The only threatened action was with regard to non-union shorn wool, and this was only a factor in Queensland· and New South Wales, and would have been out of the way had the promised conference between the P.U. and A.S.U. taken place.

In Melbourne the shipowners' excuse for declining to meet the officers was that they objected to their being affiliated with any other body. In Sydney they had no excuse of this kind, and so simply refused straight out without any reason being given. After the seamen and cooks and stewards had refused to sail under blackleg officers, some creatures were obtained to take their places, and a steamer called at Newcastle for coal. The miners in the mine from which coal was being obtained at once dropped their tools and went out without any orders from their union. This excuse was eagerly taken advantage of by the mine-owners, as next morning the white flag was up, and all the miners were locked out.

When the trouble was precipitated there was no organization to take charge on the Labor side, so I at once called together representatives from the Trades and Labor Council, the Maritime Council, and such unions as were directly concerned in the matter. In addition to the councils mentioned there was also in Sydney at that time a Builders' Trade Council, and many unions were not affiliated with any of the Councils. The Committee organized by myself was called the Committee of Defence, and took charge of affairs so far as Sydney was concerned. In Melbourne a Committee of Finance and Control was set up, whilst in other colonies the local councils dealt with matters as they cropped up.

The principal centre was Sydney, and there the burden of supporting over 30,000 men, most of whom were married, became a serious problem. Throughout the continent the loyalty of the Unionists was wonderful, and astonished the employers. Unionists employed on buildings in the city of Sydney, and entirely unaffected by the strike, came to the committee begging permission to come out also, and it took all the efforts of the committee to prevent a universal strike taking place. The committee had promised the mayor and the people of Sydney that the city would not be put in darkness, and had great difficulty in inducing the gas stokers at the gas-works to continue work. As a matter of fact, they refused unless a written order was served upon them showing that they, as individuals, were not blacklegging, and not responsible for handling coal which was " black " from a union point of view as well as by nature.

Out of all the hundreds of unions in Australia, but one was found to side with the employers. The Marine Engineers held the key of the position. Every possessor of a certificate was a member of their union, and under the law no ship could sail without a certificated engineer in charge. Every influence was brought to bear to induce them to throw in their lot with their brother Unionists and thus end the trouble with a win for organized Labor. Not only did they refuse, but they took a selfish advantage by accepting a bribe of better terms from the shipowners. As might have been foreseen, they have had to accept a reduction since. Fortunately for the credit of Australians, this was the only exception, but, together with the luck of fine weather, it had the effect of enabling shipowners to carry on in a rough sort of way.

The trouble having extended around the coast, it was found necessary to have a committee to deal with intercolonial affairs, and so, on the 12th September, delegates from each colony met in Sydney in conference. This sat continuously until the end of the strike. As the official records of this conference were very foolishly destroyed since —though they contained nothing which might not have been published—some particulars from my own notes taken from the minutes ere handing them over may prove of interest.

The conference met at noon on Friday, 12th September, 1890, in an upper room in the Protestant Hall, Sydney. There were present Messrs. J. Finch. G. Herbert, R. McKillop, W. A. Murphy, P. J. Brennan, and T. M. Davis for New South Wales; J. A. Thomson, Newcastle miners, N.S.W.; J. B. Nicholson, Illawarra miners, N.S.W.; W. Trenwith, C. Cox, F. Hall, C. E. Parkin, J. M. Mansfield, and W. G. Spence for Victoria; R. S. Guthrie, G. Mellor, and J. MacGillivray for South Australia; A. Hinchcliffe, H. Turley, F. E. Holmes, and C. Seymour for Queensland. Messrs. Davis, Mansfield, and Seymour also acted for New Zealand. Messrs. J. H. Cann. R. Sleath, and P. Quinn, from Broken Hill, attended

on the 27th.   Mr. P. J. Brennan was appointed
chairman, Mr. G. Herbert vice-chairman, Mr. W. A.
Murphy treasurer, and Mr. W. G. Spence secretary.

Reports were obtained from the representatives
of each colony, giving cause of trouble, number of
men affected, and funds in hand.

In South Australia the trouble was over the
marine officers only.   They had 500 men out; had
received £800, and spent £400.

In Victoria it was marine officers only.   There
were 3500 men out, and they had £4000.   Had
expended about £500.

In Queensland there was the Corinna case, the
marine officers, and the non-union wool.   There
were 2000 out; they had spent about £1000, and had
about £500 in hand.

New Zealand had 5000 men out.   No report as
to funds.

In New South Wales it was marine officers first
and non-union wool question second.   In Sydney
there were 4748 out.   They had expended £2253, and
had a balance in hand of £5553.   Newcastle men had
been locked out because a few men in one mine had
refused to supply coal for a blackleg crew.   There
were 4500 men idle in consequence, and they had
£7000 in hand.   Illawarra reported 1600 men locked
out.

Summed up, the reports showed that there were
28,500 men idle, with about £20,000 at their back.

The first resolution was one asking the
employers for a conference, and appointing delegates to meet them.   These were given a free hand
as to terms.   The representatives of the employers'

organizations were sitting at the time in an intercolonial conference, and we sent on the appeal to
them at once by letter. They refused to meet
us, and at once closed up their conference and
cleared out of Sydney. Every effort was made to
induce them to meet in unconditional conference,
but without avail. Lord Carrington (then Governor
of New South Wales), Mr. S. Burdekin (Mayor of
Sydney), Cardinal Moran, the Chief Justice, and
others all tried hard to get them to meet us, but in
vain.

The fight became more severe, and on the 15th
the miners of Lithgow and Broken Hill were asked
to cease work, and the stevedores and others at
Melbourne and Adelaide were asked to block vessels
in those ports. It was decided to allow coal to be
supplied to the various Governments. We tried to
arrange for running a steamship in opposition to
the steamship owners, but the miners objected to cut
coal. By the 18th everything was at high pressure,
and it was felt that some decided and strong step
must be taken so as to help on the efforts of those
who were still trying to secure a conference.

Early in the struggle the shearers had been
asked to stay at home and not accept engagements.
It must be remembered that the Pastoralists' Union
had in the beginning thrown itself into the struggle
by uniting with the shipowners. The call to stay at
home did not affect many, as shearing was in full
swing in New South Wales and in parts of Queensland. On the 19th the following telegram was sent
to every shearing shed where men were working:—

" Instruct all shearers, laborers, and carriers to cease work after Wednesday night next at all hazards. No man to go to work till further notice. This step absolutely necessary to protect Australian Unionism."

This notice had splendid effect. It brought some of the big squatters to the city, and caused them to throw their influence on the side of a conference. Unfortunately, the press ridiculed the idea that men would forfeit their earnings and lose employment for the sake of the marine officers and at the behest of an irresponsible body. Writing daily in this strain had some effect on the employers. On the 23rd a motion was proposed, delaying the call-out till the Monday following. There was a long discussion, lasting until the afternoon of the 24th, when it was defeated, the only two voting against the call-out being Mr. (now Senator) Trenwith and myself.

I was president of the Shearers' Union at the time, and that fact no doubt added to the loyalty of the shearers, as the wires were sent in my name— though in my capacity as secretary to the strike conference. The wires were sent, and the result proved the press to be false prophets, for 16,000 men ceased work at once on the day fixed. Their loyalty stands out as a magnificent monument of what true Unionism means. They asked no questions, took all risks, and left their work, in most cases penniless and not knowing where their next meal was to come from. Before the end of the month the effect on the employers was such that they promised Mr.

Burdekin (then Mayor of Sydney) that if the shearers were sent back they would meet us in open conference.

A resolution that the shearers be sent back to finish their contracts had been discussed for nearly three days, and was carried late on the afternoon of the 2nd October. The men were ordered back; and though on that very day the employers had definitely promised Mr. Burdekin that they would meet us in open conference, they failed to keep to their promise. Had they kept their word the call-out would have been a success, and those who voted for it would have been lauded amongst Unionists. As matters stood, it proved a mistake, as it had cut off supplies and involved the men and their union in serious loss. It cost the A.S.U. about £9000 afterwards to pay for fines and forfeited wages.

Though the men had only been out for a week, most of the squatters refused to let them go back, and so wires daily poured into the conference asking what they were to do. Delegates at conference, in the face of this demand, frankly owned up that they had more than they could manage, so on the 4th October they passed a resolution that the question of dealing with the shearers be left entirely in the hands of Mr. Spence. Conference saw that Labor was defeated—not from lack of loyalty, but from want of funds. On the 9th it adjourned sine die, leaving the executive to wind up affairs, which they did on the 13th.

Twelve of the delegates were subsequently elected to Parliament as Labor men. Two of these have since died, and seven are still members—four in the Commonwealth Parliament, two in New South-Wales and one in Queensland State Houses.

During the sittings of Conference a good deal of information was supplied to us by an anonymous writer, of whose reliability we had evidence. He was in some position in close touch with the Government of the day, and we found his hints useful. In one letter he stated:

"Your bitterest enemy is Lamb; your best friend Lady Parkes—she has the curb on Sir Henry."

In Donnelly's " Caesar's Column " the clever schemer is a Jew with a crooked neck. During our sittings a Jew, a man of independent means, came to me with a scheme which had much merit in it. This particular Jew had a crooked leg. He said he knew there would be no freedom if the capitalist won, and his race were ever lovers of freedom. His scheme was that we should arrange that a large body of the miners of Newcastle, who were idle by reason of the lock-out, should commence to march to Sydney, carrying their tools, or at any rate a pick each. They were to walk, and not to hurry.

Meantime, secrecy as to why they were coming to the city was to be maintained. As they came nearer, arrangements could be made for bringing the shearers down from inland, and the city Unionists were also to be in readiness. It was the mystery of the procedure that was to tell. The reporters would be busy; they would interview all and sundry; but as nobody could tell them anything the effect would be to frighten the wits out of the capitalists, whose whole life is bound up in property and business. The chairman of the Defence Committee and I were prepared to act on the suggestion, but we could not get the representative of the Newcastle miners to agree, and of course we could not do anything without his consent.

During the sittings of the conference the first post one morning brought a letter addressed to Messrs. Brennan and Spence. Mr. P. J. Brennan (chairman of the conference) having arrived first, opened the letter and got somewhat of a shock when he found it to be a notice of doom, with a rough drawn coffin and cross bones at the bottom. There was a warning to both of us, and a note to each couched in similar language. That to myself read as follows:—

" Mr. Spence,—We have had enough of this game. I and a few others have stuck to the cause, but you and the cause have not stuck to us. Our wives and children are starving, and we see misery everywhere. You and your mates have ruined us all for the b—— cause—what cause? Curse the delegates. We had a meeting and drew lots, and you are a marked man. So your b—— life is not worth much. We have sworn to do it. You have ruined us. You are to be followed; prepare to meet your God. It is our rule to warn our victims. God help you. It is to be done."

It was handed to me on my arrival, and I could see that Mr. Brennan, who was somewhat emotional, was upset and took it rather seriously. I laughed at it, as possibly some trick. That evening Mr.

Brennan was on his way home just after dark, when by some peculiar accident a portion of a brick fell from the top of a building as he passed it, and striking him on the head caused him a slight injury but a worse fright, as he thought it was the threat of the letter-writer being put in force. He was laid up three days through it.

The manifesto issued at the close of the intercolonial conference read as follows:—

" TO UNIONISTS AND GENERAL PUBLIC.

" We have the honor to submit the following brief report:—This conference of delegates from the committees, having the management of the strike in each colony, was convened by the Labor Defence Committee of New South Wales as quickly as possible after the Intercolonial Conference of employers had met in Sydney. It was felt that in view of the disastrous effect produced upon the community by long continuance of a strike it was the duty of both sides to endeavor to arrive at an honorable and amicable settlement as early as possible. Delegates met in the Protestant Hall, Castlereagh Street, Sydney, on 12th September. The first act of the conference was to pass the following resolutions:—1. ' That this conference requests the conference of employers, now sitting, to appoint six of their number to meet six members of this conference with a view to (if possible) deciding upon a basis of settlement in connection with the present Labor struggle. 2. That a copy of the foregoing be forwarded to the employers' conference, with a request that, if approved of, they will meet our representatives at 2 p.m., at the Town Hall, on Saturday, the 13th instant.' This was sent at once to the secretary of the employers' conference, but, we regret to say, was not dealt with by their body, who, we were informed next day, had dissolved on the afternoon of the day of our first sitting.

" A manifesto was issued to the public by the employers' conference, containing the following statement of the position assumed by them:—1st resolution—' That this conference re-affirms the principle of " freedom of contract ". between individual employers and employees, and asserts that any infringement of that principle is not only destructive to commerce, but is also inimical to the best interests of the working classes.' 2nd resolution —' That any attempt to apply force, or the threat of force, or any persuasion, other than that permitted and defined by law, to men who are not Unionists, or any other form of boycotting, should, in the opinion of this conference, be resisted by united action.' 3rd resolution— ' This conference is of opinion that employers should declare that they will not be coerced in the dismissal of any labor that has taken service with them in the present emergency, and in the event of any attempt being made to coerce such labor to join any trade organization, or to interfere with them in the discharge of their daily work, the combined associations represented at this conference will take all possible means to

insure their personal safety.' 4th resolution—
'That this conference declares that to maintain
discipline, and thus protect life and property,
owners of shipping in the coastal and intercolonial trades should not engage or retain in
their employ any captains or officers who may
be members of a union affiliated with any
Labor organizations.' 5th resolution—'That
with a view to the extension of the various
employers' unions, it is desirable to encourage
employers and others connected with all trades,
businesses, and interests to join existing
employers' unions, and form other unions where
necessary for mutual protection and defence
upon the basis of resolutions passed; that such
unions form federal councils for each colony;
that all such federal councils be affiliated and
confederated. This conference desires a speedy
termination of the present unsatisfactory state
of affairs, and to facilitate a resumption of work
employers are urged to proclaim as soon as
possible the terms upon which engagements will
be made.'

" Our conference at once prepared a reply
and set forth the position taken up by Labor in
the following resolutions:—1. ' That this conference agrees with the principle of freedom of
contract between employer and employees, but
holds that combination is absolutely necessary
in the best interests of the people, and that
trades unions, being legal institutions, are
entitled to the recognition of all classes.' 2.
' The basis of Unionism being voluntaryism, it

is against their principles to use coercion of any kind, and they therefore use moral suasion only. They claim that every workman should have freedom to join any organization he may choose, and deny that employers have any right to use any influence other than moral suasion to prevent his doing so.' 3. ' This conference claims that it is absolutely necessary in the interests of the working classes that they shall have the right to refuse work when the conditions under which they are asked to continue work are such as to be detrimental to their interests.' 3. ' This conference is heartily in accord with the general principles contained in the proposals of the Employers' Conference as set forth in their fifth resolution, and on similar grounds claims that the workers should have absolute freedom to affiliate their various organizations.' It will be seen that there is evidently considerable difference in the position taken up by each side as set forth, and that to arrive at the real meaning of each resolution some explanation was required before either side could reasonably be expected to accept the principles involved therein. We deemed it best for both parties to the dispute to meet in conference without any conditions ' a priori,' and made a proposal to that effect.

" During the whole of the 20 days' sittings of our conference we have used our best endeavors to bring about a settlement by conference with the other side. The Most Worshipful the Mayor of Sydney (S. Burdekin, M.L.A.), and a number of other gentlemen, have also done all they could to induce the employers to meet us in conference, but without avail. The Employers' Union have during the whole period evaded the question as much as possible by shuffling and delay, putting forth the excuse that they must await the issue of negotiations going on in Melbourne; the Employers' Union in Melbourne acted on similar lines there, by putting forth the plea that they must consult the Employers' Union in Sydney. No definite reply as to whether they will meet us or not having been obtainable, we regret that we have been compelled to adjourn. Before doing so we make the following recommendations:—'We are of opinion that no settlement of a satisfactory character can be arrived at except at an inter-colonial conference of both sides.' 'In the event of the employers being at any time prepared to meet us in any of the colonies, we recommend that the delegates be at once called together by the committee having control of strike matters in the colony the conference is proposed to be held in.' 'That no terms of settlement be accepted by any strike or defence committee in any colony without first consulting kindred committees in all the other colonies interested; also, that no single society accept terms of settlement without first consulting the committee having control of affairs in the colony in which such body is situated.'

"The refusal of the employers to even meet and discuss matters, can only be construed as an evidence that they prefer to let the strike continue, in hopes that they may crush Unionism; hence it becomes necessary to close up our ranks, and loyally resist this unwarrantable attack on the rights of Labor. We recommend that each union, and every friend of humanity, be appealed to, so that full financial support may be secured. We suggest to each committee the desirability of directing their energies in the direction of a systematic collection of funds. We would also call attention to the actions of the Governments of each colony in regard to the strike, and recommend active, energetic work throughout all Labor organizations in preparation for taking full advantage of the privileges of the franchise by sweeping monopolists and class representatives from the Parliament of the country, replacing them by men who will study the interests of the people, and who will remove the unjust laws now used against the workers and wealth-producers, and administer equitable enactments impartially. We are pleased to be in a position to congratulate the unions on the splendid loyalty to the cause displayed throughout the strike. Every effort has been put forth by our opponents, assisted by their agents, the Governments of at least three of the colonies, to provoke breaches of law and order. We are proud to say that everywhere their efforts have failed. The workers of the colonies have demonstrated their powers of self-government, and proved that it is the discipline of Unionism, and not the power of armed force, which has guided their behaviour under most trying circumstances. We look forward with confidence that the loyalty and unity of our members will be maintained, and that in a short time victory will be on the side of humanity and progress.

(Signed) " P. J. BRENNAN, Chairman.
" W. G. SPENCE, Hon. Sec.
" Sydney, N.S.W., 8th October, 1890."

In Melbourne the only question involved was that of the marine officers, and so far as the public and official statements of shipowners were concerned they only objected to the officers being affiliated with the Trades Hall Council. It will be remembered that in Sydney they were not affiliated with any other body, yet they were refused a conference just the same. However, no sooner had the trouble arisen in Melbourne than the Hon. James Service, M.L.C.—himself a shipowner—mediated between the parties, and on the 14th August the shipowners, by official letter to him, agreed to meet the representatives of the marine officers in conference. Mr. Service communicated with the Committee of Finance and Control at once, a meeting of the marine officers was held, the offer was accepted, and delegates appointed.

An official letter so informing the shipowners was sent direct so as to save time. No reply coming next day inquiries were made, when it was found that the shipowners, who had loudly objected to dealing in any other way than direct with their officers, had suddenly brought up a question of etiquette, and said that the letter should have been sent through Mr. Service, and without explanation they failed to meet or keep the promise officially made. The Hon. James Service said in the Legislative Council afterwards that "it was the refusal of the shipowners to meet the Trades Hall delegates that had precipitated the catastrophe."

The fight in Melbourne went on; and, as in Sydney, quite a number of influential men tried to mediate, always to find the employers obdurate. They met with the same shuffling and lack of honesty as was our experience in Sydney. Of course, we could understand it later, when we found out the secret plot of the Employers' Union, but at the time no one could understand why men supposed to be reputable citizens should so far fall short of honorable dealing as to fail to keep official promises. Public opinion in Victoria was considerably aroused by their action, and leading men expressed their sympathy by monetary aid. That grand democrat, the late Chief Justice Higinbotham, sent the following letter:—

"To the President of the Trades Hall Council.

"The Chief Justice presents his compliments to the President of the Trades Hall Council, and requests that he will be so good as to place the amount of the enclosed cheque for £50 to the credit of the strike fund. While the united trades are awaiting compliance with the reasonable request for a conference with employers, the Chief Justice will continue for the present to forward a weekly contribution of £10 to the same object.

"Law Courts, Melbourne, September 29th."

Another letter appeared in the "Age," as follows:—

"To the Editor of the ' Age.'

"Sir,—Enclosed is a cheque for £50 in favor of the treasurer of the strike fund, which sum I intend to give weekly so long as the struggle continues.

"Yours, etc.,

"JOHN ANDREW.

"383 Latrobe Street, 3rd September, 1890."

The Victorian committee were in a much stronger position for carrying on the fight than that of Sydney. They had only 3700 on the strike list. Of these the marine officers numbered but 150, and yet they were the men the whole of Australian Labor was fighting for. The strike, so far as Melbourne was concerned, was suddenly ended by the marine officers giving way without consulting those who had put up such a brave fight in their support. On the 30th October, 1890, Mr. C. E. Parkin, their secretary, sent the following telegram to all concerned:—

"Shipowners have agreed to recognise the association. We have agreed to forego affiliation. Settlement shortly."

Whilst there was no doubt about the loyalty of the unionists, and whilst all concerned did their best, the event brought out the fact that if Labor was ever to go into such a struggle again it must be better prepared, and must have some governing head of an intercolonial kind. The calling together

of the Intercolonial Conference on the 12th
September was an attempt to provide this, but
there was still lack of a recognition that only one
central authority could properly deal with the
whole trouble in the large sense.

For instance, the very day before the meeting
of the conference in Sydney the Committee of
Finance and Control in Melbourne had taken action
by placing in the hands of Mr. Andrew Lyell, of
Melbourne, proposals for settlement without consulting other bodies concerned. The first that our
conference knew of it in Sydney was through an
outsider, in the person of Mr. Champion. Three
of us, as delegates from the Intercolonial Conference, were by appointment having an interview
with the Mayor. Whilst there, Mr. Champion
walked in and produced the document marked
" private and confidential " which had been given
to Mr. Lyell, and which contained proposals we
did not agree with.

In Sydney we had been negotiating for an open
conference without any beforehand restrictions,
whilst in Melbourne proposals in black and white
had been made without our knowledge, and which
an unauthorised person brought to Sydney, and
for all we knew might already have been submitted
to the employers. The whole face of things has
altered since, and hence it will not be necessary to
make provision against any such thing again
occurring.

Even with more perfect organization, the
employers would have had the advantage. The
question of whether it has paid them is one they

may not care to answer, as it is pretty clear that
they have placed themselves in a worse position
owing to the fact that they aroused a sleeping, all-
powerful giant, and by the peaceful method of
straight voting for straight men of his own class,
giant Labor is going to rule shortly over shipowners
as well as shearers. The monetary cost to Labor,
exclusive of loss of wages, of the various troubles
the Employers' Union has brought upon the
community by its secret plot of 1890, I estimate
to be in round figures about £190,000. If we could
estimate the good resulting to Labor it will be
found to be cheap at the cost. The Employers'
Union has no gains to count.

CHAPTER XII.

INCIDENTS OF THE BIG STRIKE.

CAPITALISTS are great believers in law and order so long as they can control its administration. Having so long held the ruling power in every country, they rush to coercion whenever the workers show a determined front. During the maritime strike they were very anxious in Sydney to find an excuse for having the military called out. There had been no interference with the procession of 10,000 unionists who marched through the streets of that city on 6th September, 1890. Everything passed off in an orderly manner. This good behaviour on the part of the strikers did not suit the employers.

The Trolly and Draymen had joined the strikers, and had refused to carry wool or goods to be handled by blacklegs on the steamships. A number of squatters and their friends therefore arranged to drive the teams themselves from Darling Harbor to Circular Quay. They laid their plans in such a way as would, they hoped, provoke a riot and provide an excuse for having the military called out. Those who took on the job were the Hon. W. Halliday, M.L.C., and Messrs. Vincent Dowling, Harry Graves, H. Doyle, H. C. White, W. Cope, H. Cunningham, Irving Winter, George Maiden, Solling, and Allister Lamb.

On Friday, 19th September, 1890, these valiant men, safely guarded by special constables and

mounted police, paraded the streets of Sydney in a
lengthy procession of teams loaded with bales of
wool. When they reached Circular Quay there were
60 mounted police, 200 foot police, and 200 special
constables on the spot, selected for the hoped-for
riot. Mr. Nugent W. Brown was in waiting to read
the Riot Act, and at a given signal he came forward
and is alleged to have read it. It was not clear to
listeners whether. he was too drunk or too nervous
to make understandable what he was trying to read.
He had no sooner collapsed, however, than there
was a rush made by the police, and those who, out
of pure curiosity, were quietly looking on, were
surprised at being suddenly hustled about and
charged by the troopers. There was no riot nor
semblance of one, in spite of the efforts to produce
one.

Following this up, the employers by deputation
waited upon Sir W. McMillan, who was Acting
Premier during Sir Henry Parkes's illness. They
urged that more extreme action should be taken by
the Government, and that the military should be
called out. Sir William was entirely sympathetic
with them, and would certainly have had the
military brought into requisition had not Sir Henry
Parkes at once intervened and disclaimed all
sympathy with the utterances and promises of
McMillan. The latter was hit so hard that he sent
in his resignation as a Minister. It was not, however, accepted.

An incident occurred at this time which is
known only to a few, and is worth recording. A
fine, strong-charactered member of one of the unions

concerned felt annoyed at the very evident desire of the employers to use force, so he said to some of his mates:

" D—— them, if they want a riot, let them have it."

The P.U. members had publicly notified that on the Monday following they were going to take the wool to Circular Quay in spite of everything. Our friend practically accepted this challenge, and carefully and with the utmost secrecy picked out about 100 men upon whom he could rely, and all of whom had been drilled in connection with the volunteer movement. These men were to muster at 6 a.m. on the Monday at the spot where the wool teams were to start from. They were to arm themselves with a keen-edged knife each. The knife was to be used to hamstring the horses in the wool teams, and those of the troopers likewise. This was to be done on a given signal from the leader.

The plot was only found out by one of the officers of the Seamen's Union late on the Sunday night. He came to me with the information, and I took steps at once by getting together the executive heads of the various unions and arranging for a demonstration to be called for in the Domain so as to draw off the union men. I inserted advertisements in the newspapers accordingly, and at the same time the leader in the hamstringing movement was persuaded to call his men off the job.

Our move was successful, as on the Monday morning the streets were practically deserted when the procession of wool teams paraded the streets,

escorted by specials and foot and mounted police as
before. The specials, being in plain clothes, and
marching next the teams and between uniformed
constables, had the appearance of being prisoners
on the way to a lock-up. Some of the big squatters
again made a display of themselves by driving the
teams. The cavalcade proved a source of amusement to the few onlookers, and the girls in upstairs
workrooms had an especially good time jeering the
" Johnnies " who acted as special constables by
asking them what they were " in " for. The
drivers this time were Messrs. J. L. Hayes, W. L.
Thompson, C. Brown, H. M. Deakin, Byron Baily,
W. C. Jones, S. F. Walker, H. A. Podmore, and
M. McMahon.

The Sydney " Daily Telegraph " said of it:
" The whole affair, as it passed solemnly out of the
station and marched slowly along the wretchedly
muddy thoroughfares leading into George Street,
looked more like a section of a State funeral than a
purely commercial or business operation."

In the city of Melbourne there was not so much
cause for excitement. The numbers affected were
very much fewer, and owing to the difference in
the topography of the two cities were much less
congested than was the case in Sydney. Nevertheless, the Government of the day took the most
extreme measures, and did what was calculated to
promote disorder rather than to prevent it. A
special meeting of the employers had been held in
the Atheneum on the 26th August, 1890, when a
very strong attack had been made upon the workers

and charges of boycotting levelled against them. The Committee of Finance and Control decided to call a mass meeting for the afternoon of Sunday, 31st August. They applied for the use of the Friendly Societies' Gardens, which practically belonged to the workers. A member of the Government (Dr. Pearson) blocked them, however, as he had some power as President of the Board of Land and Works. The Committee then arranged for the use of Flinders Park, adjoining.

The mere announcement of the intention to hold a public meeting of Victorian citizens struck the Government with panic. A special meeting of the Cabinet was held on Friday, the 29th; proclamations were issued; Mr. Shuter, police magistrate, was commissioned to read the Riot Act; and orders were wired to the different centres to call out the Mounted Rifles, the Horse Artillery, the Cavalry, Permanent Artillery, and Victorian Rangers. The city was placarded with proclamations and copies of the Unlawful Assemblies Act.

By Saturday evening there were about 1000 military in barracks. On the evening of that day Colonel Tom Price formed the Mounted Rifles into a hollow square and addressed them as follows:—

" Men of the Mounted Rifles: One of your obligations imposes upon you the duty of resisting invasion by a foreign enemy, but you are also liable to be called upon to assist in preserving law and order in the Colony. This latter task is now asked of you in the event of circumstances requiring your aid. Should the necessity arise, I have no fear that you will do your duty like men and soldiers.

I do not think that your aid will be required; but if it is, let there be no half measures in what you do. To do your work faintly would be a grave mistake. If it has to be done, let it be done effectively. You will each be supplied with forty rounds of ammunition and leaden bullets, and if the order is given to fire don't let me see one rifle pointed up in the air. Fire low and lay them out— lay the disturbers of law and order out, so that the duty will not again have to be performed. Let it be a lesson to them. Treat any comment that may be levelled at you in the street with the silent contempt which it deserves. Don't lose your heads or your tempers. That you will do your duty faithfully and well I am sure of."

Next morning the men were paraded in Victoria Barracks for divine service, and the blessing of the God of Battle invoked to help a set of warlike armed citizens to lay out another set of peaceful and unarmed citizens who dared to attend a public meeting. If certain statements made to me by members of the Mounted Rifles were true, it was a lucky thing for Colonel Price that he did not get a chance to give the order to "fire low and lay them out." Knowing that a moving crowd is more orderly and more under restraint when in procession, the Committee of Finance and Control had intended to march from the rendezvous at the Burke and Wills Monument in Spring Street. The authorities, however, prohibited a procession, so we simply strolled along to the Park.

There was an immense gathering of 60,000 people—men, women, and children—well-dressed, orderly, and peaceful, but intensely interested in the utterances of the several speakers. A slight shower fell during the proceedings, calling up umbrellas, but not one person moved away. The vast sea of faces, as seen from our raised platform. was something to remember. Mr. W. T. Carter, M.L.A., occupied the chair.

Mr. (now Senator) Trenwith moved, and Mr. T. Porter, of Ballarat, seconded the first resolution, as follows:—

" That this meeting desires to express its indignation at the action of a section of the employers of labor throughout Australasia who, by their unjust and arbitrary action, have precipitated an industrial crisis which must necessarily entail a large amount of suffering and inconvenience on the entire community."

The second resolution was moved by the late John Hancock, and seconded by myself:—" That this meeting expresses its surprise that the members of the Employers' Union, at their meeting at the Atheneum, should have declaimed so vigorously against the principle of the boycott, in face of the fact that they practise it daily."

A third resolution pledging support, and a fourth conveying thanks to the workers of Britain, were also carried unanimously and amidst much enthusiasm and the waving of the British and Australian flags crossed.

Public feeling was at fever heat, but again it was proved that the best outlet for excitement is the right of free speech and public meeting—that the right to voice their grievances is the safety

valve of the English-speaking race.   Any interference is resented strongly.

The late John Hancock and. myself had been
specially asked to deal with the question of the
boycott.   We had such a fund of facts and details
of typical. cases showing how systematically and
cruelly the employers had always used it, that we
silenced the other side and. turned public ·opinion
against them.   From that day to this they have not
had a word to say about the boycott.   It was one
of those occasions where, by means of ·the press,
public opinion was affected, and many previously
adverse to union methods modified their views.
Meetings similar in aim were held in the country
towns afterwards, so that the attitude of the
unionists could be placed before the people.

CHAPTER XIII.

THE INDUSTRIAL FIGHT IN QUEENSLAND

THE attack on the Labor organizations of Queensland in 1891 was but part of the great scheme of the Employers' Union, referred to elsewhere. The banks controlled the squatters, the latter formed a Pastoralists' Association, and the Government were but a committee for carrying out the behests of employers. All the powers of the colony were used against the workers. The public service was terrorised into helping the Government. Railway men were ordered to leave their union, and if one of them was reported as giving any assistance to the shearers he was dismissed. Every magistrate and officer of police knew that promotion depended upon his activity in getting unionists jailed on any pretext.

Pastoral employees had made no new or unreasonable demands. The squatters had cut wages. This was bad enough, but when they were going to fill white men's places with Chinese, and further insisted on "freedom of contract," shearers and shed hands had no alternative but to go on strike. Even Sir S. Griffith admitted to a deputation that the request of the Union for open conference was reasonable. He did nothing to help, however; but on the contrary put his great ability at the disposal of the employers. He was one of the Cabinet at the time.

Every effort at conciliation was made by the workers without avail. It has become clear since that the ruling authorities had never intended to give fair play. They laid their plans to crush the men, and it stands to the credit of the workers that in spite of all the powers of State, of suffering and imprisonment, they stood true to the cause they fought for, and proved themselves worthy sons of the great white race. Their Union was registered under the Trade Union Act, which they understood would protect them from the old law of conspiracy, but how they were deceived is explained in the remarks of Chief Justice Lilley in the appeal case of George Taylor. He said:—

" I think the Trade Union Act is something like a sham; it is a delusion and a snare. It does away with the old law of conspiracy to some extent, and provides that you may call yourself a trade union, and that shall not be a conspiracy. The fact is that all through the history of trades combination the law has been made to help the master and not the man. The present statute is a milk and water Act. It is, so to speak, simply a sprinkling of rosewater."

(The Shearers' Union was registered in Victoria, but, in spite of the fact, a member named Waters was sent to jail for twelve months on the charge of conspiring to raise wages. He was in a camp of men who were on strike for union rates and by union orders, but it did not save him.)

The fight was bitter. It could not be otherwise. The marvel was that it did not result in civil war. The efforts of the leaders to try to effect

settlement on reasonable lines, and the fixed idea of
the men that' they were engaged in an industrial
strike, alone saved the country from civil war. At
one time it was feared that it would come to that,
and to prepare for such a contingency one of the
leaders of the A.L.F. and myself held a private
conference at three o'clock in the morning, whilst
travelling on the Adelaide express to Melbourne,
and came to an understanding as to certain action
to be taken by myself in the southern colonies. The
men were becoming very exasperated at that time,
and had they gone to extremes they would have
taken possession of the country.

The Government had an idea that they maintained law and order by the force of military and
police, but such an idea is an illusion. The Governments admitted breaking the law in their treatment
of unionists. They did all they could to tempt men
to break the law, so as to have an excuse to lock
them up. Spies were sent into every camp. The
scum of the cities of Australia was raked up to
take the work from decent workmen. The use of
the railways was given the squatters. The '' scabs ''
were armed, and if they shot any union man they
knew it would be to their advantage.

The police magistrate at Barcaldine (Mr.
McArthur) was a fair man, and had an influence
for good accordingly. He had reported that the
unionists in camp there were law-abiding. He was
removed to Muttaburra, which is known as the
'' Siberia '' of the service. Mr. C. A. M. Morris,
P.M., was put in his place with a promise of promotion if he '' did things.'' The P.M. at Rockhampton

(Mr. R. A. Ranking) was put in charge of the whole affair. The secretary of the P.U. (Mr. Sherwood) stayed in the same house as Morris at Barcaldine, and at least on one occasion a meeting of the squatters was held there. Morris entered into the business of helping the squatters with a zest, and must have pleased them, as he secured promotion. That the Government had placed Morris and Ranking at the disposal of the Pastoralists' Union is clear from the following letters sent to Morris in April :—

"Queensland Pastoralists' Association,
"20th April, 1891.
"C. A. M. Morris, Esq., P.M., Barcaldine.

"Dear Sir,—The twenty specials were engaged yesterday, and will leave here to-morrow by steamer. They should arrive at Barcaldine on Wednesday next, where they have been told they will be met by you. They go up in civilians' clothes, and will require to be sworn in when they reach Muttaburra, or possibly at Barcaldine. See Ranking as to what would be best. Saddles, bridles, four pack-saddles, rifles, revolvers, and ammunition for each man go by same boat, packed up and addressed your care. The men carry their uniforms and blankets in their valises. They must not carry arms till they have been sworn in, and it might not be advisable then either. They are young gentlemen that have been promised treatment as such. It has been clearly explained to them that no one holds position

over another, except that they will have
attached to them a sub-officer and constable of
police. They could be divided into squads of
five if necessary. Sub-inspector White will be
in full charge. Have twenty-four horses with
you ready for them at Barcaldine waiting.

" Yours, etc.,

" F. RANSON.

" Secretary Federal United Pastoralists' Union
of Queensland."

" Darr River Downs,
" Muttaburra, 2nd May, 1891.

" C. A. M. Morris, Esq.

" Dear Morris,—I enclose copy of wire
received by me from Secretary Pastoralists'
Union, which of course explains itself. It is
impossible for me to get down to see personally
to these men. May I therefore ask you to take
the matter in hand for me. I think it will be
advisable to have them sworn in as specials
immediately they arrive in Barcaldine; then,
as there does not appear to be any boss man
amongst them, kindly get police to put an
official over them to conduct them up here with
all speed consigned to care of P.M., Muttaburra. Upon arrival here I will hand them over
to the authorities to guide their youthful minds
in the way they should shoot. I am sending
Messrs. H. Atkinson and Goss down with
twenty horses for the men, and with instructions to report themselves to you and receive

your orders. I fear I am rather adding to your trials just now, but see no other way to get the men put through to Muttaburra without a hitch.

" With kind regards, and hoping to see you soon,

" I am, yours sincerely,

" GEORGE E. BUNNING.

" P.S.—If any hitch occurs, wire Mr. Klugh as to what is to be done."

The following advertisement appeared in the press :—

" The Government are prepared to provide free rations and protection in police or defence camps to all men, union or otherwise, who are willing to return to their work at once. A list will be kept of the names of all such men, and those applying first will receive the first engagement. Plenty of men can find work on those stations where shearing is about to commence, and on all other stations about the central district.

" CHARLES A. M. MORRIS, .

" Assistant Government Agent.

" April 7th, 1891."

One of the Union leaders (Mr. W. Mabbott) called attention to this advertisement publicly, and Boss Ranking at once saw the mistake of Morris, and sent him the following letter :—

"Rockhampton,
"18th May, 1891.

' "Dear Morris,—

"Above is an extract from 'The Courier'
of the 11th May. There is no doubt that
Mabbott. has intended to refer to your advertisement. Lane, of 'The Worker,' who is here,
tells Blair this is so. Of this advertisement
Tozer, of course, is ignorant. We must not
allow Tozer to remain any longer, in ignorance,
or he will commit himself and the Government
unwittingly. However painful it may be to us,
we must, without a moment's loss of time, put
Tozer in possession of the whole facts. Such an
explanation will come better from you than
from me. I rely on you doing it by return mail.
You can easily refer to par. and say you feel
that he ought to be placed in possession of the
facts. Send him copies of your telegrams to
me when at Clermont, and my reply. Dwell on
the fact that we were all expecting his approval
of French's scheme, and let him understand
that immediately you and I met you withdrew
the advertisement. Don't lose a moment. It
can make no difference to you, as you've got
your promotion, and if you do not see your way
to do it I must, in self-defence. I could not let
the Government go to Parliament to have such
a bombshell burst on them unawares.

Yours,
",R. A. RANKING."

"TELEGRAM.

"Rockhampton,
"May 21st, 1891.

"Message for C. A. M. Morris, Barcaldine.

"Send a wire saying that you have by press of business been prevented from answering. I shall be up before Sunday, and you can reply Monday.

"R. A. RANKING."

Of course it was never intended that such letters should become public property, and it fell like a bombshell on the Government when they were read in the House by the leader of the Labor Party. They howled at him, charged him with stealing, etc. Morris was asked to account for their getting into the hands of the unionists, and he said that he had them in a tin box, which was abstracted from his luggage at Rockhampton railway station. This was untrue. By mistake, his luggage was sent with that of another man of the same name. The letters were not in his tin box at all. He did not take them with him from Barcaldine.

Strong effort was made to provoke the men to bloodshed. The Government sent a wire saying: "Don't dilly-dally. Exercise vigor, even if it cause bloodshed." This was supposed to have been sent to Colonel French, but that was an error; it was sent to Ranking. The latter put vigor into his work. He wrote Morris, assuring him that if the leaders were run in it would stop supplies from the south. The Union Committee at Barcaldine was at once arrested by Inspector Douglas and Constable

Malone. Outside, 200 military stood at attention. Secretary Kewley was locked up; a spy was put into the cell with him, and he was supplied with liquor in order to see if he would talk.

The strike committee was tried in private. The members of it were sent to jail in 1891 for three years, and ordered to find sureties afterwards. They served their full term, and did not come out until November, 1893. They were Messrs. H. C. Smith-Barry, W. Fothergill, A. Forrester, J. A. Stuart, G. Taylor, P. F. Griffin, E. R. Prince, W. J. Bennett, D. Murphy, W. Hamilton. Long after the 1891 trouble the Government was appealed to, and urged to release these men. They offered to do so if the men themselves would petition for release. This the men refused to do. They declined to crawl and cringe to such a ruffianly crew as the "continuous Government." Two other men, named Lowry and Heathcote, did petition, and were released. After getting £18 15s. each from the Union Prisoners' Relief Fund they went away south and turned traitors to their fellows.

When the office was taken possession of, all the papers were seized, and any letters which could be used against the unionists were produced, but they refused to allow any in their favor to be read. Everything was glaringly one-sided. A Justice of the Peace was struck off the roll because he had been seen in company with unionists, whilst not a word was said to Mr. Newton, J.P., who wrote to Brisbane "Courier" advocating the shooting of unionists. A number of men were arrested and charged with arson. James Toohey tried to com-

municate with them, and was fined £15 or three
months' imprisonment. The strong bias of judges
is illustrated by the following quotation from the
report of the trial of men for conspiracy:—

" There were 200 men in the crowd at Clermont.

" His Honor: It is a nice, pleasant country this,
where such a state of things can exist.

" Mr. Dickson: How many policemen were
there?

" Witness: Four.

" His Honor: Let me see. They all had six-
shooters. Four times six are twenty-four. That
would have been twenty-four shots. There would
not have been many boohooed the second time if I
had been one of them.

" Mr. Lilley: You cannot shoot men for dis-
orderly conduct.

" His Honor: Very probably they could have
found justification."

The authorities were active in locking up every
man who was a strong unionist. James Martin was
" sent up " for two years in 1891, and for fifteen
years in 1896. Justice Cooper sentenced unionists
Jeffries and Murphy to seven years each for burning
wet grass. Another man, Irwin, also got seven
years. Ranking acted the autocrat. Letters were
opened, also telegrams. A press wire of importance, addressed to " The Worker," was detained
for three weeks. Anything and everything was
justified by the Government which tended to crush
out the Union. which was the only protection the
workers had against the sweating and robbery of
the banks and boodlers.

Looking retrospectively at the events of those years, and the happenings since, the capitalist class which ruled then must see how foolish they were. They gained nothing. On the other hand, Labor was aroused, and has taken up the challenge, and is now almost in possession of the reins of government. William Lane, founder and editor of "The Worker," sitting in the Court House at Rockhampton, wrote the following, which appeared in that journal on 30th May, 1891:—

"In the court-room at Rockhampton. A close, drowsy afternoon. A wearied, listless audience, being lulled into greater listlessness by the droning charge of the judge. For the great conspiracy trial is drawing to its close, and to-night, apparently, the jury will retire and the prisoners will know their fate—or rather Society will know its fate, for it is evident on the face of it that the prisoners are not on trial at all. A paradox, this, is it not? Ah, well, life is full of paradoxes, as you would think if you were sitting here in the Rockhampton court-room and began to ruminate over things as I have just begun to do.

"This is the court-room and the bushmen are here on trial, the judge will say; and the press and the lawyers and the squatters smile cheerily as Judge Harding 'rubs it in.' But it seems to me, sitting here, that they are not on trial. It is Society which is being tried; and the verdict of this jury will not matter, whatever it is. Society is being tried here as a

whole, prisoners and squatters and judge and
jury and lawyers, tried here as it is being tried
wherever the opposing elements of Society are
brought face to face, wherever the upspringing
of Humanity finds an advocate or meets a foe.
And its judge is God—the eternal God which
has no defining and no dimensions, but which
holds the stars in their places and makes Right
Might, and Justice strong, the same God—call
it Law, or Nature, or anything you like, what
do names matter?—the same God that laid
Rome low and shattered Greece, the home of
art and slavery, and that judges our Society
now, weighing it in the balance, as Olive
Schreiner says, to know whether it be wanting.
And it is ' wanting,' indeed it is, as you would
think if you were here—and thought as I do.
For justice here is a farce and Patriotism a
mockery. Here in this court-room the class-
fight is being fought out. Here squatter and
laborer face one another, and the Government
and the judge, and the whole judicial system
chum in with the squatter, and one sees how
hollow the Law is and how useless it is ever
to think of working together, capitalist and
Laborer, for the settlement of our social
troubles. It is boiling over here—class-jealousy,
class-hatred, class prejudice, class-bitterness;
and penned up in this boiling cauldron are the
bushmen, officially said to be standing their
trial, and they have not two friends sitting
together except in the public gallery, and there
—well, there the squatters could not find two

friends, only the public gallery does not count
yet.

" In the prisoners' dock are the bushmen,
rough-looking men, roughly dressed, with
broad, browned hands, with poses that lack the
grace of Vere de Vere and of the squatter who
lounges easily on his bench half a dozen paces
away. They wear moleskin pants, mostly, and
few wear vests ; one or two who are better
dressed, with all the town-bred attachments, are
lost in the general effect. I saw them in a dark,
windowless, ill-ventilated cell, two hours or so
ago, wherein they were awaiting the re-opening
of the court, and they looked a pretty rough
lot.   And so would Judge Harding and his
associate and young Lilley and Virgil Power
and these aristocratic squatters, if they were
dressed in nondescript garments and inducted
in the same conditions. If you were to see
these men out West, as I have seen them,
camping under the starry sky and gathering in
on horseback to the great bush meetings, free
handed and free hearted, open as children and
true as steel and simple in their habits as Arabs,
you would not have said they were ' rough-
looking ' then. You would have said that they
fitted—but they don't fit here.

" For my part I would rather be prisoner
at the bar than any one of them. Foolish some
of those prisoners may have been ; not one of
them but has sought to aid his mates against
the oppressor, not one of them but is being
victimised now on general principles for having

given that aid. They to-day, us to-morrow, you some other day ; under some pretence or other those who love the people are doomed to suffer. And when our time comes, as theirs has come, may we be as they are; patient, courageous, and fearless, ready for the worst that can be done to us, comforting ourselves with the sure and certain knowledge that we prepare the way for those who will triumph in the end. And surely! when the People's Jubilee has come, when Labor shakes off its fetters, when Wrong and Misery and Poverty are rolled away like clouds before the wind, surely then men will give a thought to the martyrs who have made redemption possible, surely here in Australia men will remember those who stood their trial for Labor's sake at Rockhampton in 1891.''

What Lane wrote then is being verified to-day. It was Capitalism on trial—not Labor. It was the beginning of the end of capitalistic misrule. It was not a trial. The men were really sentenced ere a witness was called. It was a farce arranged in order to still further deplete the Union funds. The summing-up was but an excuse to browbeat the jury so that capitalism should have its victims. It was left to Lane and perhaps a few others, whose faith in the great cause never wavered, to see glimpses of the future when some of these very rough bushmen then '' on trial '' would take a place in the country's Parliament. More than one of them have done so. As the world grows older they, and many others of that period, will be placed on the

Roll of Martyrs in the 'cause of human progress and the setting up of Justice.

'In spite of the big cost though little gain in the industrial war of 1891, the P.U., aided by the Government under Nelson and Tozer, had another try in 1894. This time they passed a Coercion Act, which was practically a copy of Buckshot Forster's Irish Coercion Act. Anybody having or suspected of having fire-arms could be arrested without warrant and would be tried privately, no person other than the magistrate to ask any questions.' No one could see him tried unless the magistrate permitted. A witness could be compelled to give evidence, even if he incriminated himself. A person could be kept locked up without trial for 30 days—and, under special warrant, two months—without trial. The bill was rushed through in one night. The Labor members put up a fight, but the gag was applied. Messrs. Browne, Reid, McDonald, Dawson, Turley, Dunsford, and Glassey were suspended for one week from attendance at the House. Mr. C. McDonald, who is now Chairman of Committees in the House of Representatives, shouted out as they removed him from the chamber, " A brutal Speaker and a brutal Chairman."

Not long before a most awful case of gross violation and murder of a woman had taken place, and a reward of £250 only had been offered. Eight or ten men had been murdered up in the North, but scarcely any effort was made to find the murderer. Some men had been out eighteen days in an open boat, and the Government did nothing.

These concerned human life.   When it came to property they offered £1000 reward for the discovery of a fire on a ship, and £500 for conviction of anyone setting fire to a woolshed.   Later £1000 was offered for conviction of damage to property.

The military was sent out West, and had to drag Nordenfeldts, Gatling guns, and a nine-pounder about over the back country.   Colonial Secretary Tozer issued a manual of instructions, and under the heading, "Firing to be Effective," they were told to pick out the leaders and not to fire over their heads, but to shoot straight.   Major Ricardo, when addressing them before they started, said:

"Go forward, gentlemen, and defend your hearths and homes."

In what way they were in danger he did not say, and probably had not the remotest idea.   The officers were all made Js.P.   The soldiers were a huge joke to the bushmen.   They played tricks on them, but the officers seemed to take the business with immense seriousness.   They kept up sentry duty, and turned out on the slightest alarm.   One night a black gin went to the camp.   It was raining and pitch dark.   She only wanted to see her husband, who was a tracker; and wanted to know what they meant when the sentry took alarm and called out the whole regiment.   Another night a pig got loose and kicked over some tins.   The whole army was promptly aroused into action.

The military was only brought out at first through a joke.   A considerable body of shearers were camped outside Clermont, and to amuse themselves a portion mounted and rode through the

Marked Tree, Union Strike Camp of 800
Men, Hughenden, 1891.

town and returned to camp. Later another body would ride through, and so on until, without any inquiry, a wire was sent to Brisbane that over a thousand armed men had passed through Clermont. The military was hurried out West at once, to find on arrival the ashes of a camp fire. The anti-Labor press had worked up a scare. A statement was made by the Colonial Secretary in the House one night to the effect that a homestead had been attacked, and that but for the police using their arms there would have been murder. The real fact was that a ram had wandered round the homestead, and the police had fired and shot it dead.

Amongst the many extraordinary things done by the Government and their pliant tools I can only give space to a few. At Augathella six men were kept on one chain day and night for ten days. Fourteen men were kept in two cells 7 x 8 each. A man named Gavin was kept in handcuffs all night, though it was known that he was suffering from fever and ague. Men were taken long distances on horseback in leg-irons and handcuffs. When the horses knocked up the men had to walk. When Macnamara and Latrielle were arrested out at Augathella, Inspector Stuart covered them with a revolver and threatened to shoot if they did not move faster. Latrielle stopped and said:

"Fire, that's all you are good for—firing on defenceless men."

The inspector then ordered them to be handcuffed, saying,

"Screw them together like dogs."

K

Hughenden woolshed and homestead are about one mile 'from the town of Hughenden. Edward Cowling was taken past the town lock-up and kept at the woolshed for six weeks. They had an idea that he knew something about the burning of Ayrshire Downs, and so they kept him, hoping to induce him to say something. He was offered £1000 and a free pardon, but had nothing to say. He was then paid £3 to sign a document ; was let go, to be immediately re-arrested. He was tried at the woolshed by the manager of the station, and committed to Muttaburra. From there he was taken to Townsville in a first-class compartment. He was then ordered to dress well, and was taken by boat in the saloon to Rockhampton, where he was brought before the famous Ranking. Ranking sent him back to Muttaburra, but, when the train reached Alpha he was taken out there. Cowling, together with James Martin, John Loyola, and D. Bowes, was tried by Judge Miller at Rockhampton on the 8th June, 1896, for burning Ayrshire Downs, and Martin was sentenced to fifteen years, the others to ten years each.

Another severe sentence was recorded by Judge Real in the case of a man named Prior, who was charged with shooting a man at Combe Martin. The evidence was notoriously weak, as the man who was wounded said it was a police officer, and not Prior, who had shot him. Still, Prior was sent up for six years. Six men were arrested and tried, and they decided that Prior was the right man!

To enforce the Peace Preservation Act it was necessary that some complaint should be sent in.

Kyuna was proclaimed, and immediately a man named Finn went to the police and informed them that he had 2500 rounds of ammunition, which he would be glad if they would take care of for him. Inspector Cooper said it was unnecessary, as it was alright where it was. Shortly afterwards the police raided Finn's place, arrested him and two others, and brought them up for trial. They got off, and when Cooper was asked why he did not take the ammunition when offered, he replied:

" Oh, well, old man, it is like this: If we did not make some fuss up here, they would think down in Brisbane that we are doing nothing at all."

Ten' men who were engaged kangaroo-shooting left McKinley when it was proclaimed, but were arrested, brought back 80 miles, and chained by leg-irons to a log in a bough shed. They were fined five shillings, and had their rifles taken from them. These were returned afterwards, as the men were found to be of good character.

Maxwelltown Station was included in a proclaimed district, and four constables called there and began to search the men's huts for fire-arms. Hearing a noise in the shed hands' hut, the shearers came over to investigate. A dispute soon arose, and resulted in the men disarming the police. Jim Martin was shot in the hand, owing to a constable's revolver going off accidentally The men then ordered the police to leave the station. Next morning, seeing that the police had not gone, Martin said:

" How is it you have not gone? Didn't we tell you to clear out?"

At the same time he was approaching the place where the police stood, when the sergeant took aim at him with a rifle, saying:

" If you come any further I will shoot you."

Martin did not pause, but calmly walked up to the muzzle of the rifle, and taking hold of it wrested it from the sergeant. The police were then ordered off, and they went and camped some distance away. Later the station manager came to the men, and urged Martin to return the weapons to the police, pointing out that they would be obliged to report their discomfiture, and would lose their billets. The men admitted that they did not want to injure the police, as their quarrel was not with them. Eventually, to help the police out, Martin agreed to return the weapons on condition that they would arrest such person as he would point out to them, and that afterwards nothing should be said about the matter on either side. This was agreed to, and a quiet man who had taken no part in the affair at all was arrested, and charged with resisting the police. He pleaded guilty, and was fined five pounds.

In another district a number of men were camped in some scrub, when they heard that the police were on the warpath for arms. The whole crowd crept up to the edge of the scrub with sticks in their hands, with which they took aim at the police. The latter did not come close enough to investigate, but rode away out of rifle range as rapidly as they could. Another party of shearers rode out of their way to meet the police, and slung their rifles over their shoulders before riding up and saying " Good day." They were not meddled with. The report of the Chief Commissioner of Police on the 1894 strike states that 78 men were arrested, of whom 44 were convicted for various offences.

One of the actions most characteristic of the Government took place in connection with this report. Colonial Secretary Tozer ordered an alteration in the report so as to make it justify his Coercion Act.

The Commissioner said: " That is the truth according to my light."

Tozer replied: " I want the truth according to my light."

Mr. D. T. Seymour, the Commissioner, had written in reference to the Act : " It was not necessary to enforce any of its provisions." This was erased, showing to what lengths Tozer would go. Oakden, who had charge out West, dared to say that there were faults on both sides. Under the cross-examination of Labor members in the House, Tozer became so notorious for the unreliability of his statements that all over Queensland to-day, when you don't believe a statement, you say, " That's a Tozer."

The Peace Preservation Act referred to was only put into force after the strike was declared off. Evidently the Government was not satisfied that the men had been sufficiently crushed. It quite realised from past experience that men of the stamp of the Australian bushman may be forced to give up a fight for want of funds, but that it makes no difference in his spirit or intention. He only intends to get ready to renew the attack, and will never stop fighting until his reasonable demands are acceded to. The country was saved the disaster of a civil war by the efforts of the Union leaders. If it had come to such a pass the Unionists would have taken possession.

Australians do not carry arms. In a camp of Union shearers and shed hands there would not be two per cent. who have arms, and these are in all cases men who keep a rifle as a tool of trade to make a living in the off season by kangaroo shooting. But the action of the Queensland Government and its grossly unfair administration of justice so provoked men that at one time it was probable at least 800 rifles, with ammunition for same, were in possession of the unionists. The business people of one town subscribed £200 for the purchase of rifles and ammunition, and one hundred rifles were secured in Brisbane and taken from there by rail under the very eyes of the police and detectives and safely landed in the Union camp. These were Mauser and Mannlicher rifles of up-to-date pattern. Men of the resource of the Australian bushmen could have taken possession with ease and without much bloodshed. In the "Sydney Moruing Herald" of September, 1894, the following paragraph appeared, having been wired from Brisbane under the head of news from Winton district:—

"The mounted infantry men sent to the Winton district, with a few exceptions, are unfit for police duty. Several are utterly undisciplined and untrained. Some are very bad riders, with a mixture of plain clothes and uniform. The general impression is that a serious mistake has been made in sending such men to this district."

The correspondent also says that one was charged with sleeping whilst on sentry duty. To take such a body of men prisoners would have been amusement to the organized unionists of the West. Assistance would have come from New South Wales of a very practical kind had such extremes been forced upon the men of Queensland. All along the Australian worker has asked for peaceful methods of settling industrial disputes. It has been the employing class and its pliant tools—who hitherto have had charge of the affairs of Government— who have adopted the coercive attitude. Unionists prefer constitutional methods to the adoption of force, hence the restraint always placed on the extremists. It was a lucky thing for Queensland that union leaders had more influence and more intelligence than the Government, as no Government ever did more to provoke and justify revolt than the Ministry ruling Queensland in 1891 and 1894.

Capitalism has hitherto ruled by force and foolery. The days of force are gone, and the days of foolery are nearly departed, as the worker is awaking to the realisation of his own power and his duty. The press no longer dominates him as it once did. The political dust-thrower can no longer blind the unionist with the foolery of platitudes and promises. Industrial organization and political education run together, and soon in every State and in the Commonwealth the masses will elect their chosen representatives who will make laws for the welfare of all the people; and class misrule and misgovernment, with all its attendant injustice and misery, will have become a thing of the dark ages of the past.

CHAPTER XIV.

LAW AND ITS ADMINISTRATION.

" ALL men are equal in the eye of the law." This
is one of the fallacies common to mankind.
It is not even true in the abstract. It is not true,
to judge even by the reading of the Statutes themselves; much less is it true in fact. The capitalists
of the world claim and enjoy all the good things,
and men have been so perverted in their judgment
that even the masses seem to concede to the rich
rights and privileges denied to others. Not only are
the rich able to succeed at law because of being able
to hire the ablest brains as advocates, but they start
off with the advantage of having all the bias of
administration in their favor.

The worker is told that it is a creditable thing
for him to improve his position in life; but the
moment he attempts to do so by seeking better
conditions, or even when he refuses to be sweated or
put on starvation wages, the view of his well-to-do
adviser is suddenly changed. The striker is put
upon the footing of a man taking part in a rebellion
—one who ought to be shot on sight.

I can only recall one case in a thirty years'
experience where the Government acted in such a
way as to help the workers. That was in Victoria.
The miners of Bendigo were on strike, and the
mine-owners were fighting them. The latter held
leases from the Crown on certain labor conditions—

that is, they must employ a certain number of men per acre or the lease was liable to forfeiture. They applied for suspension of the labor covenants, but the then Minister for Mines (the Hon. Francis Longmore) refused. He took the correct neutral attitude by simply saying that work had to go on. The mine-owners soon came to terms with the workers after that message reached them.

In all our big industrial battles the Government has invariably aided the capitalists. We have not had a Government in power during any trouble which really trusted the people. Australians are a law-abiding people. They believe in law and order, and in good government. Above all, trades unionists are disciplined to a recognition of the principle of the common good being the first consideration. Absolutely without justification the police—and on many occasions the military—have been called into requisition to help degrade the workers and reduce their already small earnings.

Nothing will destroy the love of a people for law and order so quickly as to see its power abused by making it a weapon to do injustice. Where employers are so unreasonable as to refuse mediation or decline to meet delegates from the employees, they should have no consideration or help from the Government. If no police or military were placed at their disposal they could not, in Australia at any rate, get enough non-union labor to count at all in any case of industrial war, and would be forced to come to terms at once.

In mining they have not of late years been able to get men to take other men's places except in rare

instances, and in these it was through the influence
of the Government. In the Newcastle coal field they
do not even now try to fill the men's places. They
have not been fortunate in the past. ¡In 1861 the
employees of the A.A. Co. in the Borehole mine were
on strike. The manager (Mr. Winchip) brought a
number of men from South Australia to take the
strikers' places. These men found that they had
been misled, and refused to go to work. They went
to prison rather than work against their fellows. A
strike took place in the Australian Shale and Oil
Co.'s mine, Joadja Creek, N.S.W;. and the company
brought men from Scotland on a two years' engagement. These men likewise refused to work, and
many absconded when they found out how they had
been misled.

The class of men obtained by employers at
strike time is invariably a low type, and not to be
trusted. They will "take down" the employer
just as readily as work against their fellow-man.
They are always inferior workmen, and would not
be kept on for a day except as tools to crush the
unionist. This is the class the Government has
backed up in the past as against the respectable
honest worker.

If a ship enters one of our ports it is visited by
the health officer, and if there are signs of any
dangerous epidemic disease amongst passengers or
crew, the ship is sent into quarantine at once, and
no one is permitted to land. Every one agrees that
such an extreme step is quite justifiable on the
grounds of public safety, and because to do
otherwise would probably allow misery, suffering,

and perhaps death to come to the people of the country in which we live. Governments profess to desire to see the masses improve their position and set up a high standard of civilisation; yet they not only permit a small minority of the people to introduce that which is worse than smallpox or plague, and which is deliberately directed to produce suffering, misery, loss, and death, but they help them to do so.

To introduce blacklegs and " scab " labor is to degrade the workers upon whom the prosperity of the country depends. " Scab " should be treated in the same way as smallpox. The Commonwealth Parliament has vaguely recognized this, as in the Immigration Restriction Act certain clauses prohibit bringing in labor under contract when any labor trouble is on. The principle should be adopted by the States and applied generally, unless they take the other method of providing proper tribunals to settle matters of industrial difficulties, and prevent strikes or lockouts taking place at all.

There is also the evidence of strong bias on the part of judges and others who administer the law. In 1894 some " scabs " were being escorted through Walgett, in New South Wales. As it was customary for unionists to interview all such in order to post them up as to the situation, a number of union men rode alongside the coaches as they passed through the town. Along the street a man standing on the footpath threw a stone at the coaches. He was caught in the act, arrested, and brought before a police magistrate the next day, and was fined £1. Thus the opinion of the magistrate was that a penalty of twenty shillings met the case. During the trial the sergeant of police was busy getting the names of the men who had interviewed the " seabs." He then arrested them, and after being committed they were tried before Judge Docker, and twelve out of the thirteen were sentenced to terms of imprisonment of from ten to eighteen months. They had made no disturbance; but they were all union men, whilst the man who had thrown the stone was let off with a twenty-shilling fine because he was not a member of the Union.

In one place in Queensland in 1891, 200 men had assembled. There were 60 armed military in charge of a number of non-unionists. There was no disturbance, but a Justice of the Peace who was in readiness read the Riot Act. The unionists kept calm, and asked permission to interview the non-unionists. They were allowed to do so, and sixteen came away with them. Next day the six who had carried out the interview were arrested, and five of them were sent to prison for three months for intimidation. During that year some scores of unionists in Queensland were sent up for periods ranging from three months to three years.

In 1894, in New South Wales, 87 men were sent to jail for periods of from fourteen days to seven years. It was not necessary to have done anything—it was enough to be in a camp, and above all to be a unionist. Chief Justice Darley, when passing a sentence of seven years on a union man, (C. Murphy), said that it did not matter if the man was 100 miles away when the offence was committed; so long as it was proved that he had been in the camp

it made him guilty. At all times it is a common
practice for men to form a camp when waiting for
shearing to start, so clearly there was no offence in
that.

Another man—a very quiet decent fellow,
named Richardson—who took no part in anything,
and did not know anything about it, stayed at the
camp and was arrested. He was sent up for four
years. He could easily have gone away, but very
naturally thought that the courts of his country
were courts of justice and would only punish the
guilty, and that therefore the innocent had nothing
to fear. In this particular case the real offenders
were never caught.

In another case a very fine young man, named
Wm. McLean, was shot in the chest by a " scab."
McLean was one of a party of unionists who went
out to interview some non-unionists who were
working at Grassmere Station, some 40 miles from
Wilcannia, N.S.W. The unionists were approaching
the hut to speak to the " scabs " when they were
fired upon. McLean was shot in the chest, the lung
being pierced; another unionist (J. Murphy) was
shot in the shoulder; and a third man in the foot.
The unionists were unarmed, as was usual, and had
given no provocation. They hurried away so as to
have the wounded attended to in the hospital, and
on the way were arrested by the police. McLean
was sentenced to three years' imprisonment. The
wound and the coldness of the prison cell killed him.
He was released in time to go home to his good old
mother to die. No action was taken against the
scoundrel who shot him—indeed, the president of the

P.U. (Mr. W. E. Abbott) sent him his congratulations and a medal.   He was also given a considerable sum of money.   I have heard the same Mr. Abbott on a public platform boast that he had armed his non-union shearers with rifles and ordered them to shoot any unionist who came on the board.

It is not denied that many things were done which were wrong.   Those men not only had no sanction from the Union, but they were strongly condemned.   What the unionists complained of was the panic manner in which law was administered, and the evident bias against union men.   They were placed on the footing of persons entering on a civil war against the State.   Everything the employers did was right; everything the unionists did was wrong.   Any interference was called "hindering."

"Riot" and "unlawful assembly" were real dragnets.   Any shearers' camp could be called an unlawful assembly.   For these alleged offences thirty-two members of the Australian Workers' Union were sentenced in 1894—one to 15 months, five to 18 months, seven to two years, three to two years and a half, four to one year, one to two years and three months, nine to three years, and one to four years.   For setting fire to station buildings four were jailed for seven years, and one received a like sentence for setting fire to a steamer.   In all about fifty were sentenced to over a year's imprisonment each.   Many of the disturbances were first of all started by city larrikins who were not union men at all.   The plan of holding all responsible who were assembled in a camp gave a fine opportunity to pick out all well-known unionists—or, as in some eases, the most innocent and well-behaved members.

In 1890 the Defence Committee and the members of the Intercolonial Conference, sitting in Sydney would have been arrested. but, for leading counsel advising the Government that the employers would also have to be arrested. The idea of locking up "leading" citizens was too shocking, so we escaped.

At Broken Hill, during the strike of 1892 the strike leaders kept splendid order. There were a large number of Italians and other foreigners amongst the strikers. One night these men held a meeting, and after discussion sent for the strike leaders, who were the officers of the A.M.A. On the arrival of the latter, the chairman of the meeting explained that the large body of men present were all trained soldiers who had seen service, and they were at the disposal of the strikers. If the Union said "Keep out the blacklegs," they would do it. They were armed, and knew how to use their weapons, and would take the risk. If, on the other hand, they were told to maintain law and order they would do so. The union leaders said, "Maintain law and order, and do no violence"; yet five of those leaders were sentenced to terms of imprisonment of from three months to two years.

"SHEARERS' TROUBLES AT BROOKONG.

"A State of Siege.

",Brookong Station, Urana, is in a state of siege by the shearers. Police have been telegraphed for, as the local force are powerless to prevent outrages. The servants on the station have been dragged from their beds and ill-treated. The Hon. W. Halliday, the proprietor, has wired for forty Colt's revolvers, and one hundred rounds of ammunition for each. He intends to fight the shearers to the last."

The above appeared in the columns of the " Wagga Wagga Advertiser " on the 16th August, 1888. It was the second year of enforcing the rules of the Shearers' Union. At first about 25 men were camped on a reserve near Brookong Station, N.S.W. By the date named in the paragraph the numbers had increased to about 150. Two union organizers were there, who, on behalf of the men, tried to induce the manager of the station to grant union terms. He refused, as he reckoned he had enough non-union labor. Shortly afterwards some of the wilder spirits left the camp at night, and entering the shearers' hut near the station, took away the men who were there, and who had engaged to do the shearing. They took them into the camp. The manager, together with the sergeant of police and two constables, visited the camp next day, and some of the " scabs " tried to leave with them, but were nearly all prevented by the men in camp. Some of them were roughly handled, but no serious injury was done to any. The servants at the homestead were not interfered with in any way. 'All that was done took place under the eyes of the police. The Union organizers took no hand in the matter. These facts are taken from the sworn evidence. Nine men were arrested, and on being tried before Judge Windeyer were sentenced to terms of imprisonment as follows:—Three to one year each; four to two years; and the two Union organizers, John Parker and Brian Lee, to three years each.

When one compares these sentences with those meted out to city " pushes "—bands of low ruffians who rob and ill-treat helpless old men and women— an idea is gained of the strong bias ruling on the Bench. The trial took place at Wagga Wagga, and, curiously, Windeyer had just been put on that circuit. The office of the local branch of the Union was in Wagga Wagga. The secretary (Mr. W. W. Head) and myself went to the court to hear the trial. We found a cordon of police round the court-house and the gates well guarded. Business people and squatters were admitted, but unionists were shut out. However, we managed to get in. I was president of the organization at the time. We had engaged counsel to defend the accused, and Mr. Head and myself were pushing our way to the front when I was rudely pushed back by a constable, whilst Mr. Head was rushed with rapidity into the dock and placed on trial with the others.

The dock in New South Wales is a remnant of the convict days, and is made of enormous iron bars with spiked tops about six feet high. It is more formidable looking than the tiger cage in any menagerie. To place men in the dock is to prejudice their case at once. When you look at them you feel instinctively that they must be dangerous to society, and unconsciously the jury finds each guilty before it hears the evidence. The judge was on the Bench when we went in. He had a look on his face which indicated that he meant business this time. It was he who had ordered the arraignment of Head. No doubt he felt sorry that he could find no excuse for running me in also. Mr. Head was given no warning. The others had been tried in the lower courts and committed for trial, so there was time to prepare a defence. No such chance was given branch secretary Head. He was not permitted to instruct counsel nor arrange for his office work, nor to say a word to his wife. All that Head was guilty of was that he had ridden ont to the camp to see Mr. Halliday and the Union organizers. He had not stayed at the camp any length of time. Nevertheless, Windeyer tried hard to convict him, saying in his summing up:

" If a man came in and took a hand, so to speak, for ten minutes, that was quite sufficient to make him guilty, though perhaps not so guilty as some others."

The jury, however, were not so biased as the judge, and Head was acquitted.

In commenting on the severe sentences given in this and other cases of a similar kind, we must remember that many of the men were persons of strong mentality, and of such character that they felt punishment much more than men of the low criminal type. A sentence of three years in New South Wales carries with it the awful cruelty of solitary confinement. So notoriously evil is this in effect that at least one judge (Simpson) has refused to give a three years' sentence in any case, no matter how bad the crime may be. Several of

our unionists who served the longer sentences came
out mental wrecks and ruined for life through the
solitary system. As further illustration of law and
its administration I make the following extract
from my official report as President of the Shearers'
Union issued to members at the close of the
maritime strike in 1890:—

"In connection with the actions at law,
the most extraordinary decisions have been
given and strange courses followed by the
administrators of our laws. Full advantage was
taken of that unfair old fossil of a statute, the
Masters and Servants Act. The fact that the
maximum penalty under the Act is £10 was
quite ignored. In the cases tried at Louth, one
man who had been stinting himself in order to
save his hard earnings to clear off a debt, had
£35 wages due forfeited. Another man, who
had put his earnings in various articles, had
only 10s. to come. Both had committed the
same act—one was fined £35, the other 10s., the
decision being forfeiture of wages in each case.
In a number of cases at Narandera, members'
wages to the amount of £25 each were forfeited. Take two cases again as an illustration.
One man was £2 in debt to the station, another
on the same board had only 10s. to his credit.
The latter was let off by forfeiting his 10s., but
the former, not having a farthing to his credit,
which would have saved him, was fined £10 or
fourteen days in jail. Take, again, the following facts:—Sixteen members who had been

fined elected to go to jail, as they had no
money. They went to the lock-up, but the
authorities declined to put them in. It was on
a Saturday, and they were told to call on
Monday. They accordingly did so, but were
again refused, and told to go about their
business for sixty days.

" Another peculiar case is that of the Union
agent, Mr. Arthur Rae, at Hay. As agent, he
gave a letter to the shed representative at
Mungadel, and another to the shed representative at Toogimbie, notifying the men to come
out. Rae was summoned by the owners of the
sheds (named Messrs. Simpson, Parsons, and
Dill respectively), although he had only done
his duty, yet under that peculiarly elastic Act
of our capitalistic Parliament sixty-one cases,
one for each shearer, were taken against him.
One set, that of the Mungadel cases, was taken,
evidence being heard in one case only, that of
the shed representative, which, although totally
unlike all the others, was enough excuse for the
individual who, unfortunately, has been made
a magistrate, instead of being put in some
position more suitable to his intelligence. He
was dealing with a union man and an agent,
and, after showing a bias sufficiently strong to
have him kicked out of office in any country
not ruled by wealth, he fined Rae £5, or
fourteen days' imprisonment, for each of the
twenty cases, costs added. He thus had to pay
£155 12s. 8d., or go to jail for over twelve
months. The other thirty-two cases had yet to

be tried, as part of the evidence was taken and cases adjourned. As the magistrate must follow the same decision, Mr. Rae, for carrying out instructions—for doing his work honestly —must serve nearly two years and a half in jail, or pay over £320 fines.

" Another point is worthy of notice in this case. Mr. Rae stated in Court that he would not pay the fine, but would go to jail. Whether the gross injustice of taking away a man's liberty merely to gratify the spite of a squatter struck the magistrate or not, he would not let Rae go to jail. He first suggested bail, but, on being reminded by someone in Court that he could not let a man off on bail who had been convicted, he fixed it up by accepting Rae's cheque for £155 12s. 8d., same not to be payment of the fines, but to be held by the C.P.S. until Mr. Rae elects to take out his term. Mr. Rae did not know how much was to his credit at the time, and the fact was there was not sufficient to meet it, so that the cheque was practically valueless. This is one out of many samples of the free and easy style in which law is administered in New South Wales.

" As you are aware, we consulted counsel, and took the very earliest opportunity of bringing a test case before the Supreme Court in Sydney, where subsequently the decision of the Full Court was adverse to the A.S.U.

" We intend to see that every member who lost his wages by the call-out shall be paid. A large number of those pastoralists who had taken action, and even secured verdicts, have already paid shearers, as your officers took steps to induce them to do so, and members very properly refused to work for them until they agreed to pay.

" In Deniliquin district, a number of pastoralists have been mean enough to retain the hard-won money of the shearers, without even securing the co-operation of the magistrates to take possession. If these men do not give up that which is not theirs, it is probable that they may have to do their own shearing in future, as no one will work for them. We are collecting a list of amounts due, and will see that they are made good as early as we can, although we are not sure yet as to the amount; and if it is very large, the more fortunate will, we are sure, be willing to help their fellow-workmen who have suffered in upholding the principles of unionism."

Payment of forfeited earnings and law costs put the Union to an expenditure of about £9000. In all cases where men were imprisoned the Union maintained their wives and families, and also raised a fund to give them a start of a few pounds when they were released. According to law Mr. Rae, as medium for inducing men to leave their hired service, was liable to two and a half years' imprisonment. Under the same law I am liable to over 643 years. I issued the order for the shearers and others to cease work, and over 16,000 men ceased work in consequence. So far the Government have shown no desire to start me on this long term. They have apparently seen the foolishness of applying a law made for one set of conditions to circumstances to which it was never intended to apply. Mr. Arthur Rae afterwards became a member of Parliament for the very district in which the farce of his trial was enacted.

The big strike forced on the Broken Hill miners in 1892 was full of incident, as showing how professedly democratic Governments attack Labor when it needs protection instead. The police magistrate in charge acted in the most glaringly partial manner by using his powers to help the wealthy mining company. The Government of the day helped them by suspending the labor covenants, and, when one extension was not enough, by giving them another. Further, they sent up a Crown Prosecutor to make doubly sure of getting hold of some of the men's leaders. The strike lasted from July 4th to November 6th, 1892.

After it had gone on for some time and good order had been maintained, it evidently did not suit, so eight men were arrested, including the leaders of the union. With well simulated sympathy the Government, on the pretence of getting the men a fair trial, had them sent to Deniliquin, where a jury of farmers might be got. Further, they specially sent up Judge Backhouse to try them, letting it be known that this was because he was not only unbiased against Labor, but rather the other way.

All this was sham and hypocrisy, and was said simply to mollify public opinion, which was against the Government. Usually persons out on bail are tried last when a Court sits. On that occasion there were seventeen other cases set down for hearing; but they had to wait and rot in jail, owing to the hurry of the Crown to run in the Labor leaders. The trial began on 24th October, and lasted six days. At its close the wonderful jury which they had been brought so far to be tried by declared all hands except one guilty of conspiracy. All of the accused were coupled with somebody excepting one, whom this marvellous jury wanted to convict of having conspired with himself. The judge pointed out the impossibility of such a thing, when they calmly asked if they could couple him with a certain other whom they named, but were informed that there was no evidence of his having had anything to do with the man mentioned.

Evidence mattered not to this jury, just as it did not matter to the Crown Prosecutor who acted for the Government in ordering the arrests. However, the man had to be discharged. As a reward for maintaining order the officers of the union were sent to jail—the leaders for two years each, two others eighteen months each, one nine months, and one three months. Two out of the eight were discharged, as there was not a tittle of evidence against them.

The sham of the whole thing was fittingly completed by the jury expressing surprise at the severity of the sentences, and saying that they had been misled by the judge, who had indicated in his summing up that he was not going to give them seven years even if they were found guilty. If he

had not said that apparently the jury would have
let them off altogether, which is only in keeping
with most of what occurred.   The best proof of
how the public looked at the matter lies in the fact
that both the two years' men (Messrs. Sleath and
Ferguson) were sent into Parliament for some
years afterwards, and by more than one constituency.

The trades unionists of Australia have received
far worse treatment than those of the old world.
The Governments have been more cruel and unjust,
and judges have displayed a bias which can only
be characterised as class hatred.   Whatever judicial
capacity may have been exercised in other cases,
unionists met with neither justice nor mercy.
Whenever a report appeared in the press of an
alleged union outrage the authorities demanded
that some one should suffer for it.   A number of
men were arrested for the burning of the steamer
" Rodney."   There was no evidence against them,
and when the Court adjourned for dinner it is
alleged that a telegram was sent to headquarters at
Sydney to the effect that the men were innocent.
The reply was that some one must be punished for it.
A victim was eventually found and sent to prison
for seven years, though he was 200 miles away when
the steamer was burnt.   The real culprits were
never punished.

If the advice of the judges before whom some
of our unionists were haled had been taken, it would
have led to the practice, so degrading to the masses
in Western America, of being ever ready to shoot

on sight—a practice hitherto unheard. of in Australia. The great majority of the " scabs "' were notorious criminals, well known to the police. Many of them were bullies and larrikins who in dark city lanes " dealt it out," as they termed it, to weak old men. This was the advice Justice Stephen went out of his way to give such characters :—

" He had often been surprised that free laborers did not arm themselves and resist the outrages that were perpetrated against them. They were, of course, entitled to resist—and to resist, he maintained, with fire-arms—if they had a reasonable idea that their lives were in danger. . . . If Baker had to stand his trial for killing one of the men, he would go so far as to say that the jury might well have returned a verdict of justifiable homicide."

The above is from the report of the trial of the Grassmere case at Broken Hill on the 18th October, 1894. Baker was the " scab " who shot McLean, referred to elsewhere.

Look also at the remarks of Sir George Innes when trying the cases of alleged riot at Weilmoringle :

" . . . . The case tried before me yesterday, in which the jury unhappily have not been able to agree, presented features of worse and more revolting barbarity; and serves to illustrate still more forcibly the fearful menaces to liberty and order which are now rampant."

The case he commented on had to go before a fresh jury at Sydney, and his remarks were calculated to give that jury an unfair bias. The

same judge, in the case before him, spoke as
follows:—

"Possibly you are to some extent misled by
the leaders, who are well paid, and who for their
own sordid and selfish ends and purposes—under
the guise of pretended sympathy with the poor and
suffering—fan the flame of discontent and thrust
you and others into the forefront of the battle,
taking very good care to keep themselves comfort-
ably out of the meshes of the criminal law. But it
is to be hoped that justice will yet overtake these
designing and unscrupulous men. In the meantime, the law must be vindicated and order maintained."

The reckless way in which this judge slanders
the leaders only shows how strongly he is influenced
by the views set out in the capitalistic press. He
had no evidence that any union official was paid
at all. As a matter of fact, the highest officials of
the organization were at the time and are still
unpaid. The most bitter and unfair of the whole
bench was Chief Justice Darley, before whom the
Kallara men were tried—it would be more correct
to say sentenced.

The camp was some three miles from the
woolshed on the opposite side of the river. Some
of the men, quite unknown to the rest, went across
to the woolshed and came to the men's hut, which
contained some "scabs" and police constables.
The attacking party got close up against the walls
of the hut, and when a constable put his arm over
a wall and tried to fire on the men his revolver was
quickly knocked out of his hand with a stick. The

leader of that gang always used a stick. No damage was done, and the men returned to camp. Of course, those who had taken part knew the risk, and they left. The leader was an able man. The police looked for him towards Queensland. He expected that, so he rode the other way, and came right into the heart of the enemy, taking up his residence in Sydney for months after.

The police never arrested anyone who was really in the affair. A man named Murphy, who had been spending his time at the Kallara Hotel, step-dancing and drinking, and who had nothing to do with the so-called riot, was arrested, however; and, after being bashed about in a most disgraceful manner by the police on the banks of the Darling River, was locked up. He, with another innocent man named Richardson, had the bad luck to come before Darley, who spoke of unionists as " a closely knit band of criminals with commissariat arrangements, with waggons and fire-arms and ammunition, devastating sparsely inhabited country, holding the few inhabitants in terror, and compelling honest laborers to desist from work." He also said they ought to be shot down like dingoes, or something to that effect.

His remarks not only show gross bias, but they are absolutely untrue as to fact. Waggons, for instance, are unknown and never seen in a union camp or on the road. Neither do unionists, as has already been pointed out, carry arms and ammunition. No evidence was given in that case that they had done so, hence he went out of his way to influence the jury. If the advice of these judges

of New South Wales had been acted upon it would
have led to men becoming armed, and as unionists
are in the majority, and are braver men, there
might have been a civil war, and the ". scab " would
have been annihilated. Fortunately, the Australian
working man has more knowledge and more sense
in these matters than the judges, so their advice
was not acted upon.

It is a noticeable fact that whenever public
opinion got a chance to express itself it was always
against the action of the judges. Peter Lalor, the
leader of the great strike of gold diggers which
culminated in the fight at the Eureka Stockade in
December, 1854, and for whom the Government
offered a reward of £200, was sent to Parliament
the following year, held the position of Speaker for
four Parliaments, and when he retired was granted
£4000 honorarium. Of unionists who suffered
imprisonment in the years 1891-1894, over, half-a-
dozen were returned to Parliament so soon as an
election came after their release. Several who are
in Parliament to-day suffered justice's injustice for
being unionists.

It may be urged that, as unionists were tried
before a jury of their fellow-men, they had no
reason to complain. But the juries were mostly as
biased as the judges. The jury list is a limited
one at best. When the Crown challenged it they
weeded out working men likely to favor unionists,
the other side challenged capitalists; and generally
the result of the weeding out was to leave a jury
mostly composed of shopkeepers or other men with
little intelligence and no force of character.

This story of the jury-room will illustrate this:
Away back in the eighties, there was a serious
industrial trouble at Newcastle, N.S.W. It was the
time that Henry Parkes sent up the military with
Nordenfeldt guns. A number of men were arrested.
Several were sent to jail for fairly lengthy sentences.
One lot was sent for trial before a Sydney jury.
Both sides challenged freely.

One juror who passed was a young man who
was then a builder and contractor. He took very
full notes during the hearing in regard to the
evidence as it affected each of the accused. There
were eleven men on trial. On the conclusion of the
evidence the jury retired to consider their verdict.
Of course, our friend who had taken notes naturally
expected that they would take each man's case on
its merits, but soon found, to his consternation, that
ten out of the twelve had no such idea. They held
that their duty was to find all hands either guilty
or innocent.

Our friend was stubborn, however, and at last
they agreed to ask the judge. They retired again,
and our friend decided to leave them alone for a
while. They took the list; and, as it chanced, the
first name was that of the worst case of all. If any
were guilty it was this man. They found him not
guilty. The next was treated the same way, and
so they went on until about six had been found not
guilty. They then reckoned that the rest ought to
be brought in guilty, as it would never do to let
all of them off.

It was here our friend took a hand. He had
notes, the others had none; for, though a few had

begun well in that respect, they had stopped after a few men had been dealt with. Our friend argued, and read from his notes to show that the men then under consideration were innocent—and especially when compared with those already let off. His notes were disputed, and eventually, at about eleven o'clock at night, the judge was called into Court, as was also the accused, and His Honor was asked to read his notes for the benefit of the jury. Again there was argument, and finally the jury went to bed. ·

The leader of the ignorant section of the jury was a suburban alderman with a big sense of his own importance, but without an atom of sense of justice. Our friend started on him at four in the morning, flattered his vanity and self-importance to such an extent that he got him to agree to let off two men, and disagree on the other three. He followed·up by seeing another of the leaders of the party who held that it would never do to let all go unpunished, and by 8 o'clock in the morning he had his way; and so the eight who were most guilty—if any were—were found not guilty, and the jury reported disagreement in regard to the others. Needless to say, the latter were never tried again, and, further, owing to the verdict in the case of the others, the men already in jail had the remainder of their sentences remitted. The man who so successfully fought for fair play for each of those accused unionists is now a member of the Labor Party in the Commonwealth Parliament. ·

· Here is an incident of another kind: After the English decisions in the celebrated Taff Vale and similar cases, the law was made use of in the new form in Australia so soon as opportunity offered. The A.W.U. conducted a big strike for an increase in shearing rates in 1902. It had a large camp at Coonamble, just outside the town. An injunction was obtained against us, and the camp had to be broken up. The first case connected with this camp had been heard in the Equity Court by Justice A. H. Simpson, and resulted in our favor. A second case was to come before the same judge, but by some means it was called on before Justice Walker. From the opening of the case it was evident that his mind was made up, and the Union would get no consideration from him.

The case was argued on affidavits, and we wanted a trial, so that we could cross-examine and compel some of the " scabs " who had made false affidavits to admit having been paid for doing so. Our funds had been drained, and apparently the judge knew that, because he insisted upon our paying the full amount of costs claimed—over £1500—into Court at once. We asked that costs should be made costs in the cause, and offered to pay in £1000 at once; but the judge was adamant, and it was with difficulty that our counsel (Sir Julian Salomons) could get three days' grace for this. We of course managed to raise the money in time, but it was clear that the pastoralists thought they had a chance to come down on the Union and take possession of " The Worker " newspaper, and also force General Secretary Macdonell and myself into insolvency and thus out of Parliament. When the costs were taxed afterwards the Taxing Master

M

reduced the amount to about £800, so that our offer of £1000 was ample security.

The dodge of getting a favorable judge sent to try a case is a favorite one with those who have any influence with the men in authority. If an Attorney-General wants to get a man off he has him charged on a count on which the evidence is weak. Under capitalism the rich wrong-doer escapes in quite a legal way; the poor man has all the legal forces arrayed against him, backed by prejudice and class bias.

CHAPTER XV.

THE PRESS.

THERE is an old song, the refrain of which runs "It must be true because it's in the papers." The majority of people believe what they see in cold type if it does not conflict too strongly with their own opinions. Only those who have had an opportunity of getting behind the scenes realise how unreliable the ordinary newspaper is. Part of the blame rests upon the system. Take ordinary news, which may be classed as the gossip and scandal of the community put into print. The reporter does his best to give a correct report of a public meeting or some other incident, but owing to the exigencies of space the sub-editor cuts slabs out of it, and alters the whole tenor of the report.

Again, every paper has a policy laid down by its proprietors, and the man whose brains are hired to act as editor must build according to design and specification. The paper caters for a certain class of readers, and only prints what makes the paper sell, and thus secures advertisements. Readers like an organ which clearly puts ideas that are floating more or less vaguely in their own minds, and throw down in disgust any paper which exposes the falsity of long-cherished opinions. The people generally are not seekers after truth. They like what panders to their own vanity, and they get it.

The big, well-established newspaper is a money-making concern. Its income is mainly derived from advertisements, and it will not get these unless in its policy it favors the commercial classes. All advertisements are not found in the regular advertising columns, nor are they even denoted with an asterisk or the abbreviated " advt." at the bottom. The American system has already secured a place in Australian journalism, and in ordinary news items, if the name of a company or firm is mentioned, it is nearly sure to be an " ad." The reports of the half-yearly meetings of banks and the annuals of insurance companies are mostly paid for as " ads." The report of an alleged street accident, in which a hotel is named, is an advertisement. The accident has not occurred, and the account of it was pure fiction.

As for the cable news, there is probably a substratum of truth sometimes, but how much no one can tell, because it is amplified in the office of the paper which publishes it. Only one cable comes to Australia, and it is controlled by a ring composed of the leading dailies in our cities. · In honest amplifying, the way it is interpreted depends on the acquaintance of the person doing it with old world movements. Boiled down, it is safe to say that the average man who depends for his education upon newspapers will be a very misinformed man, to say the least. He would be better informed if he only read novels.

Then the system of getting country news is bad, and invariably leads to the coloring of " facts," if not to their creation. The country correspondent is paid by the line, generally a penny half-penny. He is not allowed to wire news unless it is important and sensational. He is only paid for what is published, and he may lose his connection with the paper if he telegraphs matter not, in the opinion of the editor, good enough for publication. Hence the correspondent, if he has a vivid imagination, takes care that the matter wired is such as will make good reading.

One or two illustrations out of scores known to me will do. During strike time news is eagerly looked for. In Queensland, in 1891, a shearer who was a bit of a wag rode into a town and was at once pounced on by the newspaper correspondent of one of the Brisbane dailies. He was asked if there was any news. He replied:

" Oh, haven't you heard of the riot and burning down of —— woolshed?"

Pressed for further particulars, he gave them splendidly out of his own lively imagination. He reckoned he was doing a good turn to the poor correspondent. The shed named was thirty miles out, so the correspondent had no time to visit it. He telegraphed a graphic account of the alleged disturbance to his paper, and it was published under big cross-heads next day. As all the papers are associated, the same account was sent south, and every reader in Australia next day had the excitement of reading about the alleged outrage, and doubtless many joined in denunciation of unionists who would do such things. Probably the item was also cabled to the old world also. What happened to the correspondent is not known.

In another case a shed was reported as having been burned to the ground by unionists, while as a matter of fact there were two feet of water all around it at the time, and no one near it, unionist or otherwise. When we remember that the leading press is bitterly hostile to Labor, we can understand how eagerly it circulates lying statements of this kind. The press is therefore utterly unreliable to take as an authority on any industrial dispute. Press inaccuracies have been exposed in the official reports of police inspectors, but of course the papers carefully suppress anything calculated to destroy or weaken that superstitious faith which the average reader has regarding his favorite journal.

Practically all the big daily papers in our cities are against Labor. In 1890 more than one editor gave up his position on leading Sydney dailies because he was ordered to write down Labor. As a matter of fact, it is hard to find a journalist on our press who is not a believer in and supporter of the Labor movement; but he has to earn his living, and, like many another under our cruel social system, he cannot be honest and gain a crust. The remedy is, after all, in the hands of the workers themselves. They have the power, if they had the will and the patience, to build up papers for the presentation of the truth.

There are papers which now pose as being in the interest of Labor, which, if every man stopped taking them, would soon amend their policy to suit. Public opinion is to a large extent made by the press, but public opinion could also, if it willed,

mould the press utterances. The present tendency
of the workers, however, is to have a Labor daily,
owned by themselves and run in their interests.
The ideal method would be to have it on the lines
of the present weekly " Workers," namely, owned
and controlled by the co-operating unions. There
would then be no shares to be sold, nor any chance
of capitalists getting possession. In Broken Hill,
N.S.W., the unionists have already realised. that
ideal, as on the 2nd November, 1908, appeared the
first issue of a union owned Labor daily—" The
Barrier Daily Truth."

The Australian Workers' Union is taking a
ballot of its members during this year to ascertain
whether they favor paying a couple of levies of £1
each for starting a Labor daily in Sydney. Money
is being subscribed in South Australia for starting
a Labor daily in Adelaide. When such papers start
they will require to arrange for a special cable
service, as the present combine will not allow them
to join.

The attitude of the existing newspaper proprietors was made apparent some time ago, when a
Labor daily was mooted in Sydney. The directors
of the " Daily Telegraph " immediately issued a
circular to all their newsagents warning them that
if they sold the Labor daily the sale of the " Telegraph " would be taken out of their hands. Yet
in its leading articles it advocates freedom of trade,
and denounces all forms of boycott. In regard to
the cable combine, it asserted that there was no
such thing—that there was full freedom for any
journal—whilst at the same time the chairman of its

board (Major Randal Carey) told the shareholders in his report that the arrangement had been renewed for another five years, and that it practically prohibited any other newspaper coming into the field.

In connection with the big Sydney dailies some highly interesting facts came out under examination by a Select Committee of the New South Wales Parliament, obtained by Labor members in 1902. The Sydney press is strongly capitalistic, and openly anti-Socialistic and anti-Labor. Capitalistic Governments depend upon the big dailies for their political existence. The influence of the big newspapers was sufficient to get a law passed granting free carriage of newspapers through the post. So far back as 1874 the two morning papers began sending their parcels direct to the railway station, and the Postal Department paid one-quarter parcel rates for them.

In May, 1887, Minister for Railways John Sutherland granted a special express goods train starting at 4.50 a.m., which, running from Sydney to Albury, delivered the parcels en route, the taxpayer paying the cost. In March, 1888, the railway people asked the Postal Department to pay £2000 for this work. They accepted £1500, but in 1890 asked for £2500, and it was agreed to pay that sum for three years. The department continued to pay that sum, however, until Federation came and knocked the whole scheme to pieces. The following two clauses from the report of the Select Committee clearly show what a profitable game these highly moral newspaper companies had on:—

Clause 7. " That for a number of years the
' Sydney Morning Herald ' and ' Daily Telegraph,' in plain contravention of clause 2 of
the Newspapers Postage Act, enclosed within
parcels of newspapers sent by post advertising
sheets known as contents bills, · specimen
pictures, etc., and that large quantities of this
matter were thus illegally transmitted free
when, according to law, they should have paid
postage.

" 8. That the contract entered into by the
New South Wales Railway Commissioners with
the proprietors of the Sydney newspapers to
carry their goods for a gross annual sum of
£3172, when according to their own legal adver-
tised rate (see Railway Time and Fare Table
Book, p. 157) they should be charged over
£10,000 (see appendix p. 15), is, in the opinion
of your Committee, both a breach of the Railway Act and an improper concession made to
a few newspaper proprietors at the expense of
the public revenue.''

This is another glaring ease of how capitalistic
Governments take the taxpayers' hard-earned cash
and transfer it into the pockets of a few persons
who control interests which may assist in keeping
capitalists in power. For many years Sydney
newspapers had £10,000 a year handed over to them
in this way, which of course went into dividends,
whilst country newspapers had to pay full freight
at goods rates on every pound of paper and other
material they used.

Prior to 1864 newspapers in New South Wales were sent free per post and by rail. Postage was charged from 1864 to 1874; from then up to Federation they were carried free. When the Commonwealth took over the Post Office in 1901 the Railway Commissioners made the arrangement with the newspapers referred to in the committee's report. Tasmania and West Australian Governments also carried newspapers free, the Postal Department of the Government paying in the former and the Government paying direct in the latter case. The total sums thus transferred into private pockets can only be guessed at, but they added considerably to taxation, and this is only one out of many items of a similar kind.

CHAPTER XVI.

UNION OUTRAGES.

THOSE who read of the so-called union outrages are not altogether to blame for taking the impression that it is a serious and very unlawful thing for a body of men to stop a mine, a factory, or other industry by ceasing work and preventing others from working in their places. It is only those who have taken part in such cases who can understand how quietly these things are often done. In everyday life disagreements between two individuals frequently lead to blows being struck, and one or other is punished for assault. Inevitably there is bitter feeling in most industrial battles. When works are stopped and picketed there is naturally a certain amount of risk. The pickets use moral suasion, and intend to use nothing else, but all the same there is always the risk of something occurring to provoke quarrels which lead further than strict moral suasion. Sometimes the " scab " interviewed is impudent, insulting, and a bully, and tries the patience of the interviewer too far, with the result of an assault being committed.

It is not easy to say where moral suasion ends and coercion begins. A strike is a fight. It is warfare, and must be judged by the ethics of war, if there be such. Killing is crime in ordinary times, but he who kills most in war time is honored and promoted. The great majority of strikes can be justified; very few wars can be. The state of mind of the unionist who is standing out against a reduction of his earnings is the same as that of a true patriot fighting against an invasion of his country and its hearths and homes. If our critics could but dimly realise this they would be more just in their judgment of men who have admittedly gone too far when a strike is on.

The moral influence of men who have right on their side is great. The effect of a demonstration by a large body of men is marvellous. I have taken part in scenes where, though we practically stopped mines from working, in reality we did nothing, as the managers themselves did all that was done. As illustrations, I will quote two instances—one where no harm was done, and the other where results were serious.

A mining company had got into conflict with the Miners' Association. A settlement was secured, and one clause of the agreement was that some men who had been discharged were to be put on again so soon as there was room for them. The association officers heard that the manager was about to put on men other than those promised. At a general meeting it was decided that members should muster at the mine at four o'clock next day, the time fixed for the starting of the new hands. The mine was situated in a small clearing surrounded by eucalyptus scrub. About half-past three we began to muster. I was the secretary of the association at the time. On the appearance of men coming out of the scrub from all directions, all converging on the mine, the manager did not wait till I had reached him, but rushed over to the shaft, and ordering the men up from below, stopped all work at the mine. On being interviewed, he said he would leave it to the directors; he would do nothing. The company's office was fourteen miles away. When the board met it appointed a new mining manager, who came to an entirely friendly settlement with us, and things worked smoothly.

I have taken part in several other similar cases, with somewhat similar results. In all such cases, however, the responsible officials of the union had charge. Here is a case of a different kind. In the shearers' fight with the pastoralists in 1894 all sorts of characters were raked up out of city slums to fill the places of unionists. A body of these were shipped on the "Rodney," a steamer trading on the Darling and Murray rivers. These boats carry goods on barges which trail behind whenever the river is navigable, and take wool-laden barges down stream in the wool season.

At Swan Hill, on the Murray, there was a camp of union men, and as the "Rodney" steamed past, the "scabs" jeered and hooted the men in the camp. They were very brave when out of danger. The 'Rodney" travelled on to the junction, and then made away up the River Darling. The captain's orders were that he should stop at Pooncarrie all night. He, however, pushed beyond Marara, and selected a spot where there is a small island in a big reedy swamp, tying up his craft to a gum tree. Though he felt sure no one could get on board, nevertheless he kept up his fires and placed a watchman on deck.

The boat and its attached barges had, however, been seen by the "enemy." No doubt word had been sent from Swan Hill. A number of men borrowed a boat from higher up the river, and quietly carried it on their shoulders along the river bank, out of sight of the watchman. With muffled oars they pulled across the river. Originally about twenty-five had agreed to join in the capture, but only about a dozen really did the work. Some of those who backed out wanted to batten down the "scabs" under the hatches and burn them, but the leaders refused to hear of any such terrible vengeance.

The men who formed the boarding party turned all their clothing inside out, and covered face, head, hair, and clothes with mud until recognition was impossible. About four o'clock in the morning they waded through the mud-swamp to the side of the tied-up boat. The watchman on his beat soon saw a muddy head appear over the side of the steamer. He gave the alarm to Captain Dickson, who cursed him because he had not tomahawked the head. The captain rushed aft and tackled the first man he met. This happened to be a good light-weight boxer, and science told, though he admitted that the captain was a tough snag. In a few minutes the steamer was captured. The crew tried to cut her adrift, but had no chance.

The forty "scabs," who had been so bold at Swan Hill, played a different tune now. Roused out of sleep, they evidently thought their end had come. They fell on their knees and begged for mercy. They were removed from the boat and taken ashore without harm. Two of those who had boarded the boat were below on a hunt for more "scabs." They had finished their search, when "the means to do ill deeds" in the shape of many tins of oil and other inflammable material caused one to remark suddenly to the other:

"What say if we burn the blanky boat?"

No sooner said than done. Quickly the reeds in the swamp glistened with the shimmer of flame; the water, the bank, and the big eucalyptus trees reflected the unwonted glare; whilst on the river bank, opposite the burning "Rodney," sat a young man with a concertina, playing "After the Ball is Over."

In spite of strict orders from the Union secretaries and executive that they were to do no violence, extreme actions, inexcusable and uncalled-for, were done. In the "Rodney" case there was but one idea in the minds of the men at the start, and that was to capture the non-unionists. The party had no hand in the burning, though the law would have held them responsible if it had caught them. One of the proprietors of the steamer admitted to me that, excepting for the loss of trade incurred before she could be replaced, the burning of the "Rodney" inflicted no injury, as she was covered by insurance. As it turned out, the insurance company refused to pay. The firm tried to induce the New South Wales Government to pay for the steamer. They did not succeed in that move, however.

Amongst the men arrested and tried for the burning of the "Rodney," but acquitted, was a

staunch unionist named Syd. Robertson. He was a
fine fellow, and the police could not find a pair of
handcuffs which would ·close on his wrists, so they
put. him in hobbles and chained him to other
prisoners. Apparently the police have not forgotten
him, as they '' ran him in '' again when they made
the recent attack on the peaceful citizens of Broken
Hill.

. At the time of the burning of the '' Rodney ''
feeling ran very high. The sheds had been mostly
filled by '' scabs,'' and good staunch men had no
chance whatever of work, and were therefore
penniless. They saw the work taken· from them by
the scum of society from the cities. There was a
pretty desperate body of unionists on·the Darling
then, and it only needed the removal of the leaders'
restraint for an outbreak· of a serious character to
eventuate. It was a marvel that the shooting of.
McLean and Murphy did not·lead to the shooting of
all the '' scabs.'' In most other countries it ·would·
have done so. It was not any fear· of· the·:police
which prevented it. It was simply union training
and discipline. What arms they had amongst 250
men were all sent on ahead in a buggy, and were
seized by·the police. Had they intended to .use the
weapons the unionists would not have· given· the
police a chance to get them.

Whilst the best and most ·tolerant friends of·
unionism must strongly condemn some things done
by, unionists during our many strikes, there is one
thing in their favor particularly noticeable, namely,
the proof that the Australian bushmen, with their
magnificent courage and resource, are the men to

depend on if Australia is ever invaded by a foreign foe. Trained to work and stand together, physically hardy, and with a high average intelligence, they will save Australia if such qualities make it possible.

As an example, in 1891 in Queensland a shed was completely surrounded by a cordon of watchful police. Two men on mere mischief bent crept in through the darkness and the police. They reached the shed and struck a match, when a bullet from a constable's rifle came " ping " between their heads. They did not move, but one laconically remarked to the other, " Aren't they mean blanky blanks," at the same time striking a second match. This is an instance of cool daring under circumstances which demanded great nerve.

Men do strange things in times of excitement. In Western Victoria a number of unionists went into a hut where a body of non-unionists were asleep. They roused them up and asked them to join the Union. The cook jumped up and fired a gun up the chimney—an agreed-upon signal with the boss. The latter came rushing down to the hut armed with a revolver, which he began to use, when one of the unionists pushed his thumb under the hammer just as the trigger was being pulled. It took a piece out of his thumb, but it probably saved lives. The weapon had to be forcibly abstracted from the mad squatter, who rolled on the ground and kicked in his resistance to those who only wanted to save him from himself. In the court afterwards Judge Kerferd found him such an erratic witness that he told him he would not hang a dog on his evidence.

N

After getting the boss quiet the unionists took the non-unionists away with them, but after travelling a few miles they began to ask one another what they were to do with them now they had them, and the only solution was to let them go. A number of the men were arrested, as was also an organizer of the Union who was eighteen miles away at the time—a fact which he clearly proved in the lower court. All were committed for trial. They all got off eventually, however. In this case there was no intention to do other than interview the men in the hut, and if the cook had kept quiet there would have been no disturbance. These few instances out of many hundreds which might be given show how difficult it is to avoid breaking the law if it is too strictly interpreted, and it is much more difficult when biased judges are on the Bench or capitalistic Governments are in power.

CHAPTER XVII.

CATCHING " SCABS."

THE first organized effort to introduce " scabs "
into the West of New South Wales was in 1891.
Mr. Nutting, of Fort Bourke Station, was in charge
of them. About seventy members of the Shearers'
Union met them. They formed two lines between
which the " scabs " were to pass, and it was agreed
that moral suasion was to be used as they passed
along to where they were to cross the river; but it
was understood that in any case they were not to
cross over to the station, which was about four miles
down the river on the opposite side.

At that time there were twelve cabs in Bourke,
and eleven owners out of the twelve had volunteered
to give a hand in carting away the swags of those who
consented to join the unionists. The unionist began
by carrying the swag of the man he was interviewing, but ere he had gone far he passed it into
the cab in anticipation of his success. Before the
crowd had got half way to the river bank the
unionists had been largely added to, and very soon
the " scabs " and unionists were all mixed up
together, and some lively work was put in, the
cabs being kept busy carting away swags and
" scabs " as well.

Finality was reached when the leader and his
remaining " scabs " reached the river crossing. At
the entrance to the punt, Mr. Nutting suddenly drew

a pick-handle from under his coat and raised it to strike a unionist. But it did not reach the head it was intended for, as a blow from someone's fist came straight on the point of Mr. Nutting's jaw, and he went down unconscious and was counted out. When he fell, a revolver fully loaded fell out of his pocket. The " scabs " were all marched into camp. There were six constables on the ground, but they had enough sense not to interfere, and perhaps saw no occasion to do so.

Mostly the alleged capture and forcible abduction of " free men," as the press usually put it, was in reality carried out in such a way that moral suasion was not exceeded. One case of a reported shooting is worth mentioning. The unionists wanted to get the " scabs " to leave a station called Ti-Tree, and had such a long ride to get there that their horses were knocked up or nearly so. Mr. Head, of Waterloo Station, showed his sympathy with them by lending them a full supply of horses, although he knew what game they were up to. They arrived at Ti-Tree, and whilst on their way to the hut to interview the " scabs " a shot was fired—no one knew by whom, but it is believed that it was by some constable. One of the unionists, who was previously noticed as being all of a tremble, fell down when the shot was fired out of sheer nervous fright. The man was reported in next day's press as having been shot.

It was often the way things were done that made for success without risk of being arrested for breaking the law. In 1889 there was a big camp of unionists at Walcha, N.S.W. One day it was known that a large number of " scabs " were to be brought through on coaches. There was a considerable body of police in the town under an inspector, and when the coaches were coming these were ranged up on each side of the road, the unionists crowding closely behind their backs.

A well-known character amongst the unionists— by name Ryan—squeezed his way inside the ranks of the police without being interfered with. Ryan was a big, powerful man, very strong in the arms, and so simple and good-natured that he was a general favorite. The coach containing the " scabs " was cunningly driven close behind the mail coach, with the view of deceiving the unionists. The squatters in charge of the " scabs " depended on the police for getting safely through, but the crowd became so great that the coaches had to stop in the centre of the two lines. No sooner had the coach stopped than Ryan calmly lifted the scabs out one by one, just as you would lift down a child, saying at the same time to the police: .

" We won't hurt 'em; but they must come out, you know."

No sooner had the surprised scab landed on the ground than he was hustled out amongst the unionists and lost. He was so bewildered at what had happened to him that he gave no trouble. In less time than it takes to tell it the coaches were empty. Before the coaches had arrived, a young constable, fresh from Sydney, drew his revolver and presented it at Ryan, saying " That is my weapon," and ordered Ryan to retire. The latter coolly put his clenched fist alongside the muzzle of the revolver

and said, "And that is my weapon." The inspector
at once ordered the constable to put away his weapon,
and threatened to send him back to the city
should he dare do such a thing again without orders.
This incident probably gave Ryan more freedom than
he might otherwise have had, as it made all hands
laugh at the constable. In all, about thirty " scabs "
were lifted out, and the man who had engaged them
lost his money and his men.

In that same camp there was a man who carefully picked his men, and numbered each, he being
" Number One." When wanted, they would
rendezvous in a quiet spot with covered faces, and
in the dark proceed under the leadership of "Number
One " to some hut in the neighborhood and rouse out
the ".' scabs." They had more than one narrow
escape. On opening the door on one occasion, the
constable stationed in the hut fired at random, but
fortunately missed. The police tried hard to capture
" Number One," but he was smuggled away by
one of the union organizers who had got wind of
the danger, and was never arrested. His use of
numbers was to avoid the men knowing the names
of those concerned in each little raid.

. Ryan's coolness with the constable reminds me
of the raid made in the Queensland bush in 1891.
A number of union men were peacefully sleeping in
the open, sheltered by some scrub, when just at
daybreak they were surrounded by a big body of
police, who, levelling their rifles at the sleeping
unionists, called upon them to surrender. One of
the sleepers, who was nearest to the muzzles of the
rifles, when awakened raised himself to his elbow

and calmly opened his shirt front at the breast, at
the same time telling the police to " Shoot away,
you blanky blanks."

In 1889 Mr. Wills-Allen, of Gunnible Station,
near Gunnedah, N.S.W., made a great pretence of
being anxious to effect a settlement between the
Shearers' Union and the Pastoralists. He agreed to
arrange for a conference between the pastoralists of
his district and the A.S.U. on a date fixed. The date
was for a Saturday, and accordingly the secretary
of the local branch (Mr. T. Williams) and myself
went to Gunnedah to meet Mr. Wills-Allen and his
friends. We held a meeting the night before in the
local hall. Gunnible was shearing with " scabs,"
and there was a union camp alongside of the Namoi
River, just across the bridge from the town.

With great parade of friendliness to the union,
Mr. Wills-Allen had allowed his " scabs " to come
on the Friday night to attend my meeting. About
one-half his hands came in. They did not, however,
turn up at bell-ring next morning. No special
notice was taken until after breakfast, when on
inquiry Mr. Wills-Allen found they had not come
home at all. He had met us, but did so alone, and
his real game was to get permission to " cut out "
that year without interference, on condition that
some agreement was arrived at for the future. He
was very suave and very polished in his interview
with us on the Friday, but it was a very different
man who came in next day to complain of his men
having been kept in the camp. I of course pointed
out they were there of their own free will, and
would not be detained if they wanted to go. He

had seen them already, and they had declined to leave camp. He threatened all sorts of things, and wired to the Chief Commissioner of Police.

Meantime, whilst he was fuming in Gunnedah and complaining to me about the unionists' action, a posse from the camp went to Gunnible—which, by the way, was nine miles out—and captured all the rest of his men. The same Ryan before referred to was one of the leaders in that raid. When the gentleman who was trying to run with the hare and hunt with the hounds got home that night, he found that he had no " scabs " at all. The night before, as a visitor to the homestead was crossing the bridge over the river, he was accosted by Ryan, who was on picket duty, and was asked if he were a shearer. Almost at once, Ryan saw that he was not a worker at all, so he was allowed to pass. Ryan was arrested for it, but got off when the case was tried.

The capture of the Gunnible " scabs " was so cleverly accomplished that, whilst I, as President of the Union, was giving orders that no man was to be kept in camp against his will, I could not help wishing that none would get away, even if some degree of pressure had to be used to retain them.

At Emu Creek, near Walcha, a strong log hut which was loop-holed for defence purposes, still stands. The owner was one of the many squatters who bitterly fought the Union, and in 1889 he armed his " scabs " and kept them in the hut ready for attack. He himself marched around on sentry all night, and caught such a cold that it led to his death.

Bicycle Corps, Strike Camp, Coonamble, 1902.

As I have elsewhere shown, the shearers' strikes were carried out very much in military style, except that arms were not used. In 1891 a message came to Bourke, N.S.W., from St. George, Queensland, asking for volunteers in the shape of some good unionists to give the " boys " in Queensland a hand. One of the first to volunteer was a young man who stands inches over six feet in height—by name Donald Macdonell—whose Highland strain in blood, as well as his staunch union principle, made him eager for the fray. About a dozen others joined him; and, mounting their steeds, they rode away over the border, three hundred miles to do ere they reached the St. George camp. On the way they picked up other volunteers, and arrived about twenty strong.

One of the first jobs allotted the new contingent was to interview the " scabs " at Noondoo Station. As the police were about and on the watch, they had to take a roundabout course, but finally, by riding straight across country—cutting the wire fences where they met them—they got close to the place they sought. After making their horses safe, they waited till midnight ere they approached the hut containing the " scabs." One or two of the unionists knew the place, and every detail of the interior of the hut. It was known that one of the " scabs " was a big, powerful man, and a great bully, who always slept with a revolver under his pillow, so our tall friend Donald, and another giant named Driscoll, who happened to know where the bully slept, were to be the first to rush the hut, so that they could safely disarm him. The raid was made at midnight, when they rushed the bully's bed, but it was empty!

Word had been sent to Noondoo, so that day the manager had sworn in seventeen special constables; and no sooner did he hear of the arrival of the unionists than he read the Riot Act. No notice was taken of his doing so, however, and a general argument followed, lasting until daylight, and resulting in the " scabs " being morally suaded to leave with the unionists. This made the party a very strong one, probably fifty or sixty at least. They rode away towards Doondi, another station belonging to the same owners. They were unaware that shearing was actually in progress, but as the first of the cavalcade was riding along the road, they came across two men who were passing just then, and on inquiry learned that shearing had begun. They at once made for the shed and invaded the hut, some of the " scabs " from Noondoo being the roughest in dealing with the Doondi " scabs."

One man was sitting on the table quietly cutting an apple with his pocket knife. As he had nothing to say, big Jack Driscoll, one of the unionist leaders, put his hand on his arm to urge him to say what he was going to do, when the man suddenly made a dash at Driscoll with the knife, and actually drew blood, in spite of his efforts to dodge it. In a few seconds the man was removed from the table and landed outside, considerably knocked about. One of the converts from Noondoo lifted a nail-can and bashed the apple-eater on the head with it, cutting him severely.

Amongst those in the hut was a constable in plain clothes. He was there in order to identify men afterwards. Having cleared these two stations of " scabs," the party returned to St. George. They were camped there when word came out that the police were going to make a raid on the camp on the Monday morning following. A number of the active spirits who knew; they were wanted left before daylight to go and look for their horses.

Our friend Macdonell did not, however, though he had been one of the most prominent in speech as well as in action. He lay in his tent asleep when the raid was made. On being awakened by the noise he sat up, and was just about to put on his trousers when the fly of the tent was thrown open, and the inspector, together with the constable who had been at Doondi in plain clothes, looked in. The constable was asked by the inspector if he recognised " this man." The constable, after looking at him, said he did not; so the fly was closed, and Donald Macdonell escaped at least three months' imprisonment. Had he been dressed and stood up, his height would have put him away, as he and Driscoll were the tallest men in the crowd. Donald Macdonell, who was later secretary of the Bourke Branch of the A.W.U., and is now General Secretary and a member of the State Parliament of New South Wales, claims ever since his escape that sleeping-in has its advantages sometimes.

CHAPTER XVIII.

POLITICAL ACTION.

THE effect of the maritime strike was to galvanise into life the hitherto latent idea that voting power carried with it not only choice of the Parliamentary representative, but also of the work he was expected to do when sent to the Legislature. Labor had, through its organizations, influenced legislation before, but it had always been content to allow its work to be done by those who were attached to old political parties, and who had but little influence as units in a party dominated by other aims than those of distinctly Labor interests. In many matters affecting trades interests something had been done, and unions had in that sense taken up political work; but the industrial war which saw the Governments siding with the capitalists, together with the enormous power displayed by organized capitalism, had at last brought home to the worker the fact that he had a weapon in his grasp stronger than Governments or capitalists.

The idea of self-government came to him in a new light, and he saw that he must not only vote, but must make the platform, and select his own political war-cry. Labor set about becoming a new force and a new party in political life. The awakening came in every colony, and in each, as opportunity offered, candidates from the new party were put into the field, and with a considerable measure of success. In each colony, for the first time, the truly democratic method of making laws was introduced. Reform was initiated by the people. Labor leagues were established, conferences were held, and a platform was drafted. These organizations then selected the men who were to carry the flag into action, and those not selected stood down so as to secure unanimity and avoid splitting the vote.

The first elections after this were held in 1891. In New South Wales thirty-six members were returned on the party's platform. Like all movements arising out of a time of excitement, much that was disappointing arose. The political organization was imperfect. The platform was too large, and a goodly number of those who as candidates adopted it only did so to catch votes. Too much was expected, and as a result there was partial failure. The most earnest and genuine of the party had no previous experience, and the wily old politicians soon found out the weak spots and saw how to produce division and that lack of cohesion so essential to their continuance in power.

The governing powers of every country depend upon ignorance and sectarianism to keep the masses in subjection. Thus fiscalism was the question upon which the party was split. Some, of course, had never really belonged to it, and stood aloof immediately after the election. Nevertheless, in spite of divisions and weakness, much good was done, and the voice of democracy was heard in a distinct and new form. Division and lack of cohesion were not confined to the party inside the House. It

characterised those outside also. The Central
Committee of the Labor Electoral League had big
ideas as to its functions, and at one time wanted
to dictate to those in Parliament as well as those
without.

It seems a universal tendency in all young
organizations to be imperialistic. They assume
autocratic powers at once, and the democratic idea
has to fight its way against obstacles, even amongst
those who set up as the mouthpiece and vanguard
of government by the people. With the exception
of one or two bodies, such as the A.W.U., the trades
unions had not then taken up political work as
organizations, hence there was always the opening
for mere adventurers to gather two or three
together in the name of Labor and get themselves
appointed as delegates to the Annual Conference.

Some of our enthusiastic workers, who, though
they do not realise it, are still in the imperialistic
stage of evolution, have a great idea that much is
accomplished by carrying a resolution. They are
strong on majority rule, and not over-sensitive as
to how the majority is secured. They forget that
passing a law before the people are educated up to
a desire for it, and consequently willing to observe
it, is only to add force to conservatism and to retard
progress. To carry a resolution by packing a
meeting beforehand is the worst kind of foolishness,
and can never have any other result than to create
division.

A large conference held in Sydney on November 9,
1893, did much harm to the Cause, owing first and
mainly to its constitution being opposed to the

democratic idea of fair representation. The members of the Central Committee were given seats on it, and also votes; though the Leagues of which they were the members were likewise represented by delegates. As the Central Committee was naturally composed of city men, the question of town versus country was raised. A form of pledge favored by the Central Committee was forced on the Conference, in spite of the fact that the men who had had experience in the House pointed out its impracticability. The result of this badly-organized Conference was to cause a split at the next election, and the loss of some good men to the party for some time. Subsequently, mainly by the intercession of the officers of the A.W.U., a modification of the pledge was agreed to, and several who had stood out came into the party again, and it has remained solid ever since.

The experience of the first party gave its warnings, and ever since then the party in the House has been guided by the trades union principle of acting as a solid body on all platform questions, with individual freedom on all other matters not considered essentials. The Labor Party got rid of sectarianism of every sort, and in addition was soon prepared to support or vote against a Government, no matter what their fiscal faith was. New South Wales elections had, prior to 1891, been run largely on sectarian grounds, and the advent of Labor purified politics by putting that into the background. The old political party, which had for years lived on such a cry, recently revived the silly appeal to ignorance, prejudice, and bigotry. It has

been helped by a considerable portion of the alleged
Protestant clergy, who have entered upon a crusade
against Labor which can only have the result of
doing injury to their own churches. This narrow
bigotry is not confined to New South Wales, but
has been extended to other States, and into Federal
politics also.

The Orange Institution has been used, not for
the purposes it claims to have been organized for,
but to-fight against Labor. No matter whether a
candidate was Catholic or Protestant, Liberal or
Conservative, so long as he was against the Labor
Party he was supported by them. This only shows
how desperate has become the position of the old
parties, who dare not oppose Labor on its political
proposals, but try to hold back the day of its
complete success by appeals to the lowest and most
unpatriotic of human frailties.

The worker has ever been foolish, and he is
only slowly awakening. He has never seen the
capitalists divided by any question of creed or
dogma. They are always alive to their own interests
as a class, but the workers allow themselves to be
deluded and divided by any silly bone of contention
thrown to them by wily schemers who live upon the
workers, and who hope to keep them in mental
slavery and ignorance. The whole spirit of Australian democratic feeling is in favor of the utmost
freedom of thought in regard to religious views.
They want everyone to be absolutely untrammelled
as to how he or she may choose to worship or
otherwise. There is no State Church, and a clause
in the Australian Constitution expressly forbids

religion being any bar to service under the Commonwealth. The Labor Party stands strongly for this attitude, hence it has the bigots against it.

Before giving some idea of the work aecomplished, I will briefly outline the method of organization. Taking New South Wales first, Political Labor Leagues, as they are now called, are formed in each electorate. With these are affiliated all trades unions willing to join. Subscriptions are paid in by members of the League, and the unions contribute so much per capita from their funds. Some time previous to an election, nominations of persons willing to contest the seat in the interests of Labor are called for. Such persons must have been members of some league or union for at least one year. If more than one nomination is received a ballot of the members of the league and unions is taken, and the highest on the poll, if approved by the Central Executive, is announced as the selected candidate. and he begins as soon as he likes to work up the electorate.

With the nomination a pledge is signed, and three copies are kept—one by the local league, one by the Central Executive, and the other by the Parliamentary Labor Party. The pledge has been found useful for two reasons. It is both a record and a test. Near election time men come forward and say that they quite believe in the Labor platform and are willing to support it in the House. They are asked to sign the pledge and stand for selection, when they at once find an excuse, and shy off. That sort of person is of no use to Labor, and cannot be depended on. He is of the old school of opportunists,

O

of whom too many are in political life to-day. In some cases, where no local organization is prepared to take up the work, or where they request the Executive to do so, the latter body makes the selection.

The method in other States is much the same, though the name may differ. In Victoria it is called the Political Labor Council. In South Australia it is the United Labor Party, which selects candidates by grouping a number of electorates, leaving to the central authority the final allotment of the men to the electorates. This allows for special knowledge being used to advantage, such, for instance, as sending a farmer for a farming constituency. In Queensland the name most used is that of the Workers' Political Association.

In each State annual conferences are held, the business for which has been sent in by the various sections, and then submitted in a printed agenda paper to all the branch leagues and unions, so that they may discuss it and instruct their delegates. Thus the voice of all who take enough interest in their country's well-being is heard through their representatives at the meeting of Labor's Parliament, as the press now terms it. The numbers present become greater each year. Dates when other people are enjoying a holiday are selected for the purpose by Labor, so as to save loss of wages or perhaps position by those attending as delegates. At the last conference in New South Wales, which met on Foundation Day (26th January), over 230 delegates were present. That held in Melbourne, opening on Good Friday, March 29, 1907, consisted

of 95 delegates; that of Queensland, held on March
11, 1907, consisted of 41; and South Australia's
conference, September 11, 1908, 112 delegates.

One has only to visit one of these conferences
to see that the movement is a live one, and is being
pushed on by able, earnest, and enthusiastic men
and women. The delegates are all practical, and
have had all their lives to face difficulties in their
struggle for a decent living. They call things by
their right names, and are strong and earnest in
their denunciation of injustice, because they have
felt and still feel it in their lives. Whilst each
strongly, and often positively, feels that his or her
own proposal may be the best, yet the discipline and
training of the unions and leagues prevent any
break in the loyalty to conference decisions. The
rules also check any sudden changes in the most
important matters, as for some proposals a two-
thirds majority is required. Labor members of
Parliament are present—some as delegates, others
as visitors—and their experience is found useful.

The splendid work put in, not only at these
gatherings but all the year round, and the unselfish
devotion to the Cause characteristic of most of the
members and officers of leagues and unions, are the
envy of other political parties. This is particularly
noticeable in the country districts. Union men have
walked thirty miles to record their votes. Men have
ridden over fifty miles, and have had to do the
same distance back again to get to their work. I
have known a man walk twenty-five miles to attend
a public meeting, and walk the same distance back
again next day. I am sorry to say that thousands

in our cities will hardly cross the street to attend
a meeting unless in times of great excitement.

Here are one or two instances of the loyalty of
bush unionists: Opalton, in the Mitchell electorate,
Queensland, had been refused a polling booth, though
there were eighty names on the roll. The electors
held a meeting, and decided to go to the nearest
polling place, which was eighty miles away. Horses
were mustered, and the whole of the voting strength
rode those eighty miles, recorded their votes for the
Labor candidate, and rode back. In another case
two men rode 200 miles to vote for George Kerr,
then straight Labor. When Donald Macdonell
contested the Barwon against the notorious W. N.
Willis, two men rode seventy miles and voted for
Donald, who was the Labor candidate.

Such men value the franchise, and from such
men Australia can hope for advancement and real
progress. Such men understand the need there is
for social reform, and when there is a majority of
men and women with similar intelligence and
earnestness, the social salvation of Australia will
have been accomplished.

' Since the advent of Labor into politics there has
been a noticeable change of thought in regard to
what may be termed Empire matters. Previously
there was a fairly widespread sentiment in favor of
republicanism. The Sydney " Bulletin " openly
advocated the latter form of government at one
time, and a good many public men, such as the late
Sir George Dibbs, Sir T. McIlwraith, and others, also
advocated the setting up of that form of government
for Australia. At the time of the Darling grant

trouble in Victoria there were loud threats of
" cutting the painter." In Queensland McIlwraith
ran an election practically on the separation idea,
and the local Tory press in at least one instance
supported him.' He was elected, which proves how
strong the feeling was.

The discussion of constitutional questions
evoked by the submission of the Australian Constitution brought us into closer acquaintance with the
defects in the American Constitution, and at the
same time increased our friendship towards that
great people. The practical independence of
government granted under the Australian Constitution, with the manifest advantages of being part
of a big Empire and under its protection if need
arose, together with the growth of the national
spirit of a " White Australia " and the broad
humanitarianism taught by the Labor Party, have
developed a feeling of loyalty to race rather than
to governments, but have abolished any talk of
either republicanism or of independence.

The desire for the unity of the white race is
strong. The recent visit of the " Great White
Fleet " of the American navy emphasised the feeling
of warm friendship previously existent, and the
very general desire that unity should be definitely
established between all self-governing parts of the
British Empire and the American nation. The
striking unity of the Labor Party nationally, and
the breadth of its teaching and aims, have made its
influence felt in Australian thought, and have
developed a higher and more intelligent loyalty than
previously existed.

CHAPTER XIX.

IN NEW SOUTH WALES.

THIS was the first of the colonies to return a
Labor Party. The seed idea was there years
before, but was not taken up seriously enough. The
trades unionists of Balmain sent Jacob Garrard into
Parliament in 1881, undertaking to pay him a
salary. There was no State payment of members
then. The attempt to pay their representative was
not a success, however, and he drifted away into
another party. Angus Cameron was sent in as a
direct Labor man for West Sydney in 1883, and
Frank Cotton ran for East Sydney in 1890, but was
defeated. The real fact was that the workers
generally were too apathetic to take up the idea
vigorously. It required the upheaval of an industrial war to awaken them.

The maritime strike of 1890 was more severe
in its effects in New South Wales than in any other
colony, and hence the political result was quickly
felt. No sooner had the industrial war ended than
a conference was arranged for by the Trades and
Labor Council. Previously a sub-committee of the
Council ·(Messrs. Boxall, Cotton, and Houghton) had
drafted rules and a platform for submission to the
conference. (See Appendix.)

Labor Electoral Leagues were organized as
rapidly and as widely as possible. · The late Sir

Henry Parkes was Premier at that time, and his Government being saved only by the casting vote of the Speaker, he sent the House to the country, and on June 17, 1891, Labor entered the field of politics for all time. There had not been time for anything like complete organization, hence it was natural that there should be some who, anxious only for seats, agreed to the Labor platform, but who, when trials came, deserted the flag. Out of forty-five candidates sent to the polls, thirty-six were returned, as follows:—Balmain—G. D. Clark, E. Darnley, J. Johnstone, W. A. Murphy; Balranald—J. Newton; Bogan—J. Morgan; Canterbury—T. Bavister, C. J. Danahey; Forbes—A. Gardiner and G. E. Hutchinson; Glebe—T. J. Houghton; Goulburn —L. T. Hollis; Gunnedah—J. Kirkpatrick; Grenfell —R. M. Vaughn; Hartley—J. Cook; Illawarra— J. B. Nicholson; Murrumbidgee—Arthur Rae; Namoi—J. L. Sheldon; Newcastle—J. L. Fegan, D. Scott; Newtown—F. Cotton, J. Hindle; Northumberland—A. Edden; Orange—H. W. Newman; Redfern—J. S. T. McGowen, W. H. Sharp; St. Leonards—E. M. Clark; Sturt—J. H. Cann; Upper Hunter—T. H. Williams; West Sydney—G. Black. T. M. Davis, J. D. Fitzgerald, A. J. Kelly; Young— J. G. Gough and J. A. Mackinnon. H. Langwell was also elected as a Laborite, but on a Labor platform framed locally by the Bourke League, and his entrance to the caucus was for a time regretfully refused.

Before the House met, the Party met in caucus and adopted the following:—

" (a) That in order to secure the solidarity of the Labor Party, only those will be allowed to assist at its private deliberations who are pledged to vote in the House as a majority of the party, sitting in caucus, has determined. (b) Therefore, we, the undersigned, in proof of our determination to vote as a majority of the Party may agree, on all occasions considered of such importance as to necessitate Party deliberation, have thereunto affixed our names."

This was a form of pledge which nearly all signed, but which at once brought out indications that the party was apt to split on the fiscal question, owing to the fact that Messrs. Edden, Gough, Mackinnon, Nicholson, Scott, Sheldon, Williams, and Vaughn had included Protection in their platform when seeking election. Mackinnon dropped out at once and left the party. No leader was chosen, and matters were left to a committee consisting of Messrs. Fitzgerald, Gough, McGowen, Sharp, and Houghton. The latter acted as secretary, and the late T. Davis was appointed " whip." It was probably a mistake not to have appointed a leader, as jealousy was created when George Black made a memorable speech, and declared what he conceived to be the policy of the party.

The party had decided to support Sir H. Parkes, because of the fact that he had placed no less than seven of the party's planks on his programme for the session. In spite of this, when a trap was set by the Protectionists by an amendment on the Address-in-Reply, six of the members of the party

J. S. T. McGOWEN, M.L.A.,
Leader of New South Wales Labor Party.

fell into it, namely, Messrs. Edden, Gough, Morgan, Scott, Sheldon, and Vaughn. Later the Parkes Government went down, not on a fiscal vote, but over the insertion of a clause limiting the hours of labor to eight per day in the Coal Mines Regulation Bill. Mr. G. R. Dibbs took office. He was a Protectionist, and proposed to raise the tariff. The fiscal question split the party hopelessly, and only about one-half remained at all solid. Mr. McGowen became leader of the section which acted together, and afterwards Mr. Joseph Cook was appointed leader.

In spite of the unhappy division of the party, it did good work in the 1891-4 Parliament, and after all, it fully represented the party outside the House, which was not at all united even apart from the fiscal question. The first party made a mistake in the form of a pledge it adopted, as a very short experience of Parliament proved the utter impossibility of voting according to caucus decision on all questions, simply because questions frequently arise so suddenly that it is impossible to hold a meeting of the party. There was also the fact that it was wrong in principle to bind members on any question outside the platform which they had submitted to the electors.

The Conference of the Leagues, which met on November 9, 1893, made matters worse. First of all, the conference was not representative, as the members of the Central Committee had seats, and the branches to which they belonged also had representatives on the committee. In other cases branches not properly constituted sent delegates who were simply adventurers. In spite of the members of the House showing how impracticable in working such a pledge was, as well as the strong opposition to signing it at all, the conference refused to listen.

The leader in urging the new form of pledge was Mr. Holman. The conference was very unruly, and was characterised by much abuse of the members who had been returned in 1891. The following form of pledge was carried, and was confirmed again in March, 1894:—

" (a) That a Parliamentary Labor Party, to be of any weight, must give a solid vote in the House upon all questions affecting the Labor Platform, the fate of the Ministry, or calculated to establish a monopoly, or concede further privileges on the already privileged classes, as they arise, and,

" (b) That accordingly every candidate who runs in the Labor interest should be required to pledge himself not only to the Fighting Platform and the Labor Platform, but also to vote on every occasion specified in Clause A as the majority of the Parliamentary Labor Party may in caucus decide."

The result was foreseen by every serious member of the leagues. The raising of the pledge as something of transcendent importance, and at the same time the introduction of much in the way of personalities, brought about a serious split. Leagues were divided, and two parties—both earnest Laborites—contested the election in 1894. Just prior to the

Parliament of 1891, payment of members had been passed. The House then numbered 141 members. The new Electoral Act reduced the membership to 125. The election took place on July 17, 1894. The organization had adopted a plan, followed ever since, of selecting certain planks upon which the public mind had been more or less educated as a fighting platform. Upon these the candidate is pledged, but is free to advocate other questions of local interest or even of national import if he so desires. The platform was as follows:—

" (1) Land Value Taxation; (2) Mining on Private Property; (3) Abolition of the Legislative Council and the substitution of the Initiative and Referendum; (4) Local Government; (5) the establishment of a National Bank; (6) Compulsory Eight Hours Legislation."

The Independent or Parliamentary Laborites ran 22 candidates, nearly all pledged in some way to the Leagues which had selected them. The elections resulted—Freetraders, 58; Protectionists, 40; Solidarities, 15; and Independent Laborites, 12. The following were the Solidarities:—Alma, J. Thomas; Balmain South, S. J. Law; Broken Hill, J. Cann; Coonamble, H. Macdonald; Granville, G. W. Smailes; Gunnedah, J. Kirkpatrick; Lang, W. M. Hughes; Pyrmont, T. M. Davis; Redfern, J. S. T. McGowen; Sturt, W. J. Ferguson; The Tweed, J. Willard; Wallsend, D. Watkins; Waratah, A. H. Griffith; Wilcannia, R. Sleath; Young, J. C. Watson. This number was reduced to fourteen by the unseating of Willard on the ground of insufficient residence, but restored to fifteen when Loughnarie, on a recount, unseated G. H. Greene for Grenfell. Mr. McGowen was chosen as leader, and Mr. Arthur Griffith as secretary. Mr. McGowen still holds office, but Mr. Griffith was succeeded by Mr. Niel Nielsen in 1903, when he ran for the Senate. Independent Labor—Ashfield, T. Bavister; Ashburnham, A. Gardiner; Condobolin, T. Brown; Darlington, W. F. Schey; Eden-Bombala, W. H. Wood; Gipps, G. Black; Goulburn, L. T. Hollis; Hartley, J. Cook; Kahibah, A. Edden; Illawarra, J. B Nicholson; Orange, H. W. Newman; Wickham, J. L. Fegan. Which is to say that there were 27 pledged and independent Labor members returned to a Parliament of 125 members, against a reputed 35 Laborites out of 141 members in 1891.

The Australian Workers' Union removed its head office from Victoria to Sydney in 1895, and one of its first efforts was to try to effect a reconciliation of the two sections of Labor. The writer, with four others, met representatives of those favoring the 1893-4 pledge, and secured a modification, the pledge of 1895 reading as follows:—

" I hereby pledge myself not to oppose the selected candidate of this or any other Branch of the Political Labor League. I also pledge myself, if returned to Parliament, on all occasions to do my utmost to ensure the carrying out of the principles embodied in the Labor Platform, and on all questions, and especially

on questions affecting the fate of a Government,
to vote as a majority of the Labor Party may
decide at a duly constituted caucus meeting.''

The result was a bringing together of the divided
forces, and Labor has been solid ever since.

Sir George Dibbs having been defeated at the
1894 elections, Mr. George Houston Reid got the
opportunity he had been so anxiously looking for as
leader of the Freetrade Party, previously led by
Sir Henry Parkes. Reid was cute enough to adopt
some of the planks of the Labor Party's platform,
and in addition, he promised to make good any loss
of revenue resulting from a lowering of the tariff
by the imposition of a land and income tax. Labor
held the balance of power, and hence an opportunist
like Reid was just the man for them.

Owing to the way the Legislative Council had
rejected measure after measure passed by the
Assembly, Reid obtained a dissolution in less than a
year, and in July, 1895, appealed to the electors on
the questions of direct taxation and Upper House
Reform. Reid's following and Labor ran together,
so as not to clash, and the result was:—Freetraders,
62; Protectionists, 45; and Laborites, 18 out of 45
seats contested. The Grenfell and Gunnedah seats
had been lost to Labor—the latter chiefly by the
tardy retirement of J. Kirkpatrick; but these losses
were balanced in the gain of the Botany and West
Newcastle seats by the return of J. R. Dacey and
J. Thomson. The party was also numerically
strengthened by the adhesion of Black, Brown, and
Edden, who had all, without pressure, gladly

accepted the new pledge. A few months later, the by-election at Narrabri, brought about by the death of Mr. Charles Collins, increased the party's number to 19. The Labor roll was then thus called:—Alma, J. Thomas; Balmain South, S. J. Law; Botany, J. R. Dacey; Broken Hill, J. H. Cann; Coonamble, H. Macdonald; Condobolin, T. Brown; Gipps, G. Black; Granville, G. W. Smailes; Kahibah, A. Edden; Lang, W. M. Hughes; Narrabri, H. Ross; Newcastle West, J. Thomson; Pyrmont, T. M. Davis; Redfern, J. S. T. McGowen; Sturt, W. J. Ferguson; Wallsend, D. Watkins; Waratah, A. H. Griffith; Wilcannia, R. Sleath; Young, J. C. Watson. Of the remaining nine members styled Independent Labor in the prior Parliament, all were again returned, save Albert Gardiner, defeated for Ashburnham through the splitting of the Labor vote. Of the remainder, J. B. Nicholson remained independent; Joseph Cook had become Postmaster-General; W. F. Schey and W. H. Wood joined the Protectionists; while T. Bavister, J. L. Fegan, Dr. L. T. Hollis, and W. H. Newman were absorbed by the Freetraders.

Mr. Reid carried out the promise of imposing land and income taxes, but left the work of reforming the Upper House untouched. The coming to power of a strong Labor Government is still awaited ere that Conservative stronghold can be successfully assaulted. It will then have to go altogether, as all institutions which have outgrown whatever useful purpose they may have served have to do. During that Parliament the method of carrying out public works by day labor was introduced, and proved a great success. The Parliament also took steps to shut out colored aliens. The Enabling Act was passed which dealt with the question of the adoption of the Australian Constitution, and fixed the limitation as to the majority required for its adoption by referendum.

The party's platform at the elections on July 27, 1898, was:—(a) Abolition of the Upper House; (b) the introduction of the Initiative and Referendum. 2. Establishment of a National Bank. 3. State Pensions for Aged and Infirm Persons. 4. Local Government. The elections resulted as follows:— Alma, J. Thomas; Balmain South, S. J. Law; Boorowa, N. Nielsen; Botany, J. R. Dacey; Broken Hill, J. H. Cann; Cobar, W. G. Spence; Coonamble, H. Macdonald; Condobolin, T. Brown; Grenfell, W. A. Holman; Kahibah, A. Edden; Lang, W. M. Hughes; Narrabri, H. Ross; Newcastle West, J. Thomson; Pyrmont, S. Smith; Redfern, J. S. T. McGowen; Sturt, W. J. Ferguson; Wallsend, D. Watkins; Waratah, A. H. Griffith; Wilcannia, R. Sleath; Young, J. C. Watson. T. M. Davis retired from the party's Parliamentary ranks through the illness which ended in his death. A by-election for Boorowa had added Mr. N. R. W. Nielsen to the party, thus making the number twenty.

After the election the state of parties in the House was—Freetrade 46, Protectionists 56, with 19 Labor members and 4 Independents. Edmund Barton had been defeated, but Frank Clarke resigned his seat for the Manning to give it to Barton. Wm. J. Lyne had tried to put Reid out and failed, so Barton was appointed leader of the Protectionists in his place. His trial, on a vote of censure, failed

worse than Lyne's. By this time, however, G. H.
Reid had begun to go too slowly. He was becoming
too conservative for the Labor Party, which had
kept him in power for five years simply because he
passed the measures they wanted.

When Reid would not move fast enough, Lyne
got his chance. The Protectionists had seen the
wisdom of re-instating him, and he soon found a peg
to hang a vote of censure on. Reid had a number of
measures on the stocks at this time, several of which
Labor wanted. The party was very evenly divided
as to whether it should put Reid out or no. He
would probably have had a few months more given
him but for the fact that Alf. Edden had discovered
that Reid had paid J. C. Neild (one of his supporters)
a sum of £300 on account of work done in collecting
data in connection with Old Age Pensions without
its having been passed by Parliament. The Opposition was cute enough to tack this on to the amendment, and so Edden and other members of the party
could not vote against it, owing to the stand they
had made when previously exposing the matter in
the House. Reid's action in connection with
Federation also caused votes to go against him, and
the various factors counted. It is certain, however,
that he would have been put out a month or two later
anyhow.

W. J. Lyne made very definite promises to some
of the party before the debate closed. He showed
the writer a list of democratic measures, which he
offered to give in writing and signed, to be used
against him if he failed to pass them through the
House. He kept his promise. Reid was passed out

after five years of office, and Lyne came in. He took office in September, 1899, and between that date and July, 1901, he passed ten highly important measures. He took up all Reid's measures of any value. The Upper House had rejected two very important measures—the Industrial Arbitration Bill and Workmen's Compensation Bill.

For the general elections of 1901 the party's Fighting Platform was as follows:—

1. Compulsory Arbitration.
2. (a) Abolition of the Legislative Council; (b) Introduction of the Initiative and Referendum.
3. Workmen's Compensation.
4. Adult Suffrage.
5. Free Education.
6. Local Government.

This election followed changes in the personnel of leaders. Barton, Lyne, Reid, and McMillan had all gone to the Commonwealth Parliament, as had also several of the leading Labor members. Labor lost five seats and gained nine. Labor was 24 strong, the Ministerialists 39, the Opposition 40. There were 18 Independents, and 4 unattached who called themselves Labor. After the passing of the Arbitration Act, Sam Smith was appointed judge for Labor Unions, and McNeill took his seat. A by-election for Inverell was won by Mr. G. A. Jones, which made the party twenty-five, as follows:—
Balmain South, S. J. Law; Balmain North, J. Storey; Boorowa, N. Nielsen; Botany, J. R. Dacey; Broken

Q

Hill, J. H. Cann; Cobar, Donald Macdonell; Coonamble, Hugh Macdonald; Condobolin, P. J. Clara; Darlington, P. H. Sullivan; Denison, A. J. Kelly; Erskine, R. Hollis; Gipps, W. M. Daley; Grenfell, W. A. Holman; Gunnedah, D. R. Hall; Inverell, G. A. Jones; Kahibah, A. Edden; Lang, J. J. Power; Monaro, G. T. C. Miller; Moree, W. Webster; Pyrmont, J. McNeill; Redfern, J. S. T. McGowen; Wallsend, J. Estell; Waratah, A. Griffith; Wentworth, J. Scobie; and Young, G. A. Burgess.

The Commonwealth elections of December, 1903, took away Mr. Webster, and his seat was lost owing to a bungle in not getting the nomination lodged in time. Mr. Syd. Law left the party during the Parliament. Mr. A. Griffith resigned, and ran for a seat in the Australian Senate, and Mr. Charlton was elected in his place. The party, therefore, at the close numbered twenty-three.

As a result of a ballot taken simultaneously with the Commonwealth elections in December, 1903, the number of members in the Legislative Assembly was reduced from 125 to 90. Sir John See, who had succeeded Sir William Lyne as Premier, resigned on June 13, 1904, and Mr. Waddell took his place. The elections on August 6, 1904, sent in twenty-five Labor men, as follows:—G. A. Burgess, Burrangong; J. H. Cann, Broken Hill; M. Charlton, Northumberberland; J. R. Dacey, Alexandria; W. M. Daley, Darling Harbor; A. Edden, Kahibah; J. Estell, Waratah; A. Gardiner, Orange; A. Griffith, Sturt; R. Hollis, Newtown; W. A. Holman, Cootamundra; G. A. Jones, The Gwydir; A. J. Kelly, The Lachlan; H. Macdonald, The Castlereagh; D. Macdonell, Cobar;

P. McGarry, The Murrumbidgee; J. S. T. McGowen,
Redfern; J. McNeill, Pyrmont; J. C. Meehan, The
Darling; G. T. C. Miller, Monaro; J. B. Nicholson,
Wollongong; N. R. W. Nielsen, Yass; R. Scobie, The
Murray; P. H. Sullivan, Phillip; T. H. Thrower, The
Macquarie.

The result of the elections frightened Mr.
Waddell, who did not attempt to carry on, but called
the House together on August 23, obtained supply,
and then resigned. Mr. Joseph Carruthers, who had
been leader of the Opposition, took office, and met
the House on September 20. Labor now became the
direct Opposition, with Mr. McGowen as leader. The
remnants of the Lyne-See party also sat with them,
but were an unreliable set of men when any fighting
had to be done. When McGowen moved votes of
censure in 1905 only one of them voted with Labor,
and in 1906 none at all.

The following two years cover the period of New
South Wales's greatest political disgrace—the
exposure of the land scandals, and the still worse
scandal of the Carruthers-Wade Government doing
its best to hide the corrupt practices and help the
guilty to escape. Mr. Carruthers had been Minister
for Lands for five years under Reid. He introduced
a system of Improvement Leases in the 1895 Land
Act. This was to enable the Department to let, at a
nominal rental, land covered with scrub, on condition
that the lessee made certain improvements. The
particular blocks had to be picked out and marked
on the map by the District Surveyor, but the letting
was practically in the control of the Minister. There
was a large area of land in New South Wales which

was of no use as it stood, but which would prove of high value if cleared and improved.

Such lands naturally suited someone in the immediate neighborhood better than any other person, and an excuse of this kind was given when the Minister was found granting leases to big squatters. Mr. Carruthers granted 502 leases, covering an area of 4,628,875 acres, at a rental of less than a halfpenny per acre. W. P. Crick, Lands Minister in the See Government, granted 628 improvement leases, embracing 3,807,601 acres, at a rental of nearly threepence per acre. In all, six Ministers had granted leases under this section covering 10,127,709 acres.

Owing to demands made by members of the Labor Party, but mainly because of certain disclosures in a law case of Sims versus Browne, the Government was forced to appoint a Royal Commission to hold an inquiry into the Sims case, the Myall Creek purchase (an estate sold to the Government for closer settlement), and also into the matter of land agents and their relations with the Department. Justice Owen was appointed. Evidence of a startling character soon came out. It was proved that one man in particular—W. N. Willis, for many years a member of the New South Wales Parliament, and a member whilst the smart practices were carried out—was the principal receiver of enormous sums, which were paid to him as land agent by big squatters, and intended as bribes to secure for them blocks of land. Three others had also been paid large sums. Evidence was given showing that fees aggregating £67,364 16s. 4d. had been paid in all to about twenty men. Willis had received £44,913, Peter Close £15,649, W. Bath £2575, and Senator E. D. Millen £1250.

As samples of the class of clients, I may mention Strahorn, who paid Willis £3951; McKay, £7675.; Edols and Co., £6000; Cornish, £3324. How this money was used after Mr. Willis got it remains a mystery. He was naturally the principal witness wanted. He pleaded ill-health as an excuse, and the judge agreed to take his evidence later. He at once cleared out to South Africa. Premier Carruthers was the principal in the firm of Carruthers and Wilson. He was, and had been for years, the legal adviser of Willis. He was the legal adviser when Minister for Lands in the Reid Ministry. As Premier, he did nothing to prevent the main and essential witness from leaving Australia. He knew that Willis was going, because his firm drew up the power of attorney for Willis to sign before leaving, which enabled those authorised to carry on Willis's business. No wonder Willis was a successful land agent, when he had first the Minister for Lands and next the Premier for legal adviser. Peter Close gave evidence that he had divided his fees with Minister for Lands Crick.

It was proved that not only had scrub lands, as originally intended, been let under improvement lease, but that good agricultural land had been granted, and hence the big sums paid. It should also be mentioned here that, under the Land Act, the Minister could arrange exchanges of blocks of land in one place for blocks in another. This was intended to permit of making up areas which were too small

by securing a portion of the adjoining land, and
giving a piece somewhere else in exchange. Some of
the money paid in fees was for this kind of work.
Sir Samuel McCaughey is probably the biggest land
holder in Australia. Likewise, he is one of the
richest men. Waddell, who was taken into the
Carruthers-Wade Ministry, is in partnership with
him. While Minister for Lands, Carruthers granted
half a million acres as improvement leases to Sir S.
McCaughey, after having refused five other applicants who offered more rent. Cunning lawyer that
he was, he so worked it that no enquiry at all was
made into his administration. Mr. Carruthers, when
leader of the Opposition, must have known of the
" dummying " carried on by Willis, as his firm paid
its own cheque for £770 3s. 6d. to prevent one of
the dummies being made bankrupt, and thus possibly
exposing the whole thing. This was during Willis's
absence.

A storm was raised when Willis was allowed to
leave the country, and no rest was given the
Carruthers Cabinet until steps were taken to bring
Willis back from South Africa. Eventually he was
brought back and tried, but got off. Crick was
tried also, but the Government made sure of his
getting off by not charging him on the indictment
suggested by Justice Owen. From beginning to end
of this disgraceful episode the Carruthers-Wade
Government did nothing they were not forced into
doing. Even the two big morning journals, by
whose support they were elected and kept in power,
spoke strongly, as the following quotations will
show:—

" ' Daily Telegraph,' July 24, 1906:—
Coming down to hard facts, how has the Government dealt with the land scandals, except by taking the course most likely to prevent anything at all being done? . . . It argued on both sides and deliberately played for defeat of its own move.

" ' Daily Telegraph,' August 2, 1906:—
From the first it (the ' Reform ' Government) showed an unwillingness to do any more than it was flogged into doing.

" ' Daily Telegraph,' July 14, 1906:—The Government always moved too late, and every time came shambling in at the heel of the hunt. The doing of the right thing was doggedly delayed until the arrival of the wrong time.

" Referring to Mr. Carruthers' previous dealings with Land Agent Willis—' A Citation of Plain Facts '—the ' Daily Telegraph ' says:—
The fact remains that he (Premier Carruthers) is supreme director of the proceedings in which both his land agent client (W. N. Willis) and the ex-Minister are mainly involved, and these proceedings have been bungled from the start in a way that has singularly suited the purposes of both.

" ' Daily Telegraph,' December 12, 1906:—
A lamer or more farcical conclusion to such a work as that of the Royal Commission has never been witnessed. . . . The Premier has preferred to use blank cartridge, and with this ineffective demonstration he expects the public to regard

the honor of Parliament 'as vindicated and the claims of justice satisfied.''

Though there was a clear admission that numbers of wealthy men had paid bribes, no action was taken against them. The persistent demands of the Labor Opposition, and the fright given Carruthers at the 1907 elections, secured legislation under which a Court is set up which has power to declare improvement leases. forfeited. Justice Owen presided, and recently he cancelled 95 leases to obtain which some of the thousands referred to. had been paid. How many others ought to be cancelled, if there had been an investigation, it is hard to even guess. Justice Owen sat as Commissioner 93 days, and examined 251 witnesses and 387 documents, but he did not get a chance to make the full inquiry required, as he was baulked by the Government. The Carruthers-Wade crowd were called a '' Reform '' Government, and yet they cloaked the most corrupt transactions which Australia has any cognisance of. In spite of that they are kept in power by men who call themselves decent, respectable, Christian citizens.

Such men will excuse anything—will condone any crime against the public—and stand the odium thereof rather than see Labor in office. They have no objection to Labor's political programme; they publicly admit that Labor members have improved the tone of the House; but just because they stand for the masses as against the classes, so they will swallow any dirt rather than permit clean, honest men to rule the affairs of the country. It is Conservatism become desperate, and fighting in its last ditch. It is Capitalism's last stand. They have been unable to corrupt the Labor movement. Money is powerless against the onward march of Australia's hosts, because they are not worshippers of the almighty dollar. Capitalism has failed to weaken any Labor Party in any Australian State from within or without. No man will take a bribe, and even if he did his influence would not count for enough to accomplish anything. Hence Capitalism must fight openly and in a way to which it is unaccustomed. Its day is doomed, and it is feeling desperate about it.

The party lost one of its most popular members and a good fighter in the Cause when Mr. Hugh Macdonald died, on October 23, 1906. Mr. J. L. Trefle, the Labor candidate, was elected to the vacancy.

The history of this period bristles with such glaring acts on the part of the capitalistic Government that they should bring home to the people the danger of keeping such a class in power. A case in point is provided by the Gloucester Estate and North Coast Railway jobs. This estate belonged to that octopus, the A. A. Company, and they offered it to the See Government at ten shillings per acre. It was not accepted, but almost immediately afterwards a syndicate of Sydney politicians, bank managers, company directors, and landlords purchased the estate at 12s. 6d. per acre. Ex-Premier See held 1000 shares, and Carruthers and several politicians of the same school had an interest. The next move was to send a proposal to the Public Works Committee to consider the matter of a railway along

the North Coast. The committee found that the
line would cost £2,700,000, and that there would be
a loss of £50,000 per annum in working it. They
were opposed to the line unless the land through
which it passed was loaded sufficiently to guard
against loss. The Government brought in a bill to
have the line constructed.

The Labor Party put up such a strong fight
against the measure that a few of the Government
supporters voted with them, and the bill was only
carried by two votes. Carruthers dropped it for the
time, but later brought up the measure again; and
cracking the whip by making the bill a party one,
and hinging the fate of the Government upon it, not
only succeeded in carrying the measure, but struck
out the loading provisions.

The line traverses the estate for forty-one miles,
and, needless to say, the railway will put thousands
of pounds into the pockets of the syndicate at the
expense of the taxpayer. From Maitland to the
estate is fifty-seven and a half miles, and thence
forty-one miles through the estate. This is to be
the first section done, and will cost £913,900. The
estate embraces 207,000 acres, and the holders will
get all the benefit. The whole object has been
gained so far as Carruthers and his clique are
concerned, and there is no justification for the line
on public grounds, as it would only be a few miles
from the sea all the way, and water carriage is much
cheaper. This is one of the cases which illustrate
their declared policy of helping private enterprise.

How little such a party cares for the poor is
proved by the fact that Carruthers tried to cut

down the sum allowed old age pensioners. But for Labor he would have succeeded. He made no attempt to cut down the £1820 per year pensions to judges on retirement. Though steadily increasing the indebtedness of the State by borrowing, he relieved the wealthy by removing the income tax of sixpence in the £ on all incomes over £4 per week. There had been no request for this to be done; but the doing of it, and the attempt to cut down the old age pensioners—whose maximum is ten shillings per week—exemplify the character of capitalistic Governments.

It was quite in keeping also that Carruthers and his gang had no patriotism. They are strongly anti-Australian. The work of the Federal Parliament had been too democratic to please them, and they lost no opportunity of trying to belittle Australia. It was in keeping with such small minds that the Premier of the mother State, as they were fond of calling it, forcibly seized sundry rolls of wire netting from His Majesty's Customs at Sydney Harbor. Poor little man, he thought to become a hero, but he only succeeded in becoming a bye-word and a disgrace. The Australian Government took no notice of him, and the High Court declared all State goods dutiable.

Joey Carruthers, as he was generally called, talked very big for a little man. He even threatened secession, and seemed to think that he owned New South Wales, but the results of the elections of September 10, 1907, gave him his quietus for ever. He put up a big fight, and called to his aid all the unscrupulous tactics of which he was a past master,

but lost ground. Labor came out of the battle with
32 members as follows:—G. ·S. 'Beeby, Blayney;
G. A. Burgess, Burrangong; J. H. Cann, Broken
Hill; A. C. Carmichael, Leichhardt; · M. Charlton,
Northumberland; · J. R. Dacey, Alexandria; · J.
Dooley, Hartley; Alf ·Edden, Kahibah; J. Estell;
Waratah; A. Griffith, Sturt; W. C. Grahame, Wick-
ham; R. Hollis, Newtown; ·H. ·E. Horne, Liverpool
Plains; ·W. A. Holman, Cootamundra; G. ·A. Jones,
The Gwydir; A. J. Kelly, The Lachlan; ·P. J. Lynch,
Ashburnham; D. Macdonell, ·Cobar; P. McGarry, The
Murrumbidgee; J. S. T. McGowen, Redfern; J.
McNeill, Pyrmont; J. C. Meehan, The Darling;
J. · B. ·Mercer, Rozelle; G. · T. C. Miller, Monaro;
J. B. Nicholson, Wollongong; N. R. W. Nielsen, Yass;
H. J. F. Peters, Deniliquin; J. Page, Botany; R. J.
Stuart-Robertson, Camperdown; R. Scobie, The
Murray; J. Storey, Balmain; J. L. Trefle, The Castle-
reagh.

    There · were · fifteen who called themselves
Independents, hence Carruthers was only left with
43 supporters. He saw that his day was done, and
was not prepared to face the risk of an enquiry into
his own administration, so on September 30, 1907,
he resigned, 'and: Wade ·became ·Premier, with
Waddell as Treasurer. Mr. Wade lives up to the
traditions of capitalism. He is a pliant tool in the
hands of the employing class, and hates trade
unionism like poison. The Arbitration Act expired
on June 30, 1908. Wade lost no time in preparing
another measure to take its place. It was a hybrid
kind of thing, called the Industrial Disputes Bill.
It was intended to crush unionism altogether. It

was designed to encourage the development of
"scab." He called Parliament together on March
10, 1908, specially to deal with this wonderful
measure. The storm raised by Labor frightened
him, however, and he altered it until, as now law,
it is a kind of cross between the Wages Board
system and the Arbitration Court method of settling
disputes.

As might be expected from the tyrant-minded,
he takes plenty of power to deal severely with
unionists who offend against his ideas of what the
worker ought to do, and when he got an opportunity
he did not fail to enforce the clauses. The Rock-
choppers went on strike, and Wade had their leaders
arrested and heavily fined. The Broken Hill
Proprietary Company at Broken Hill locked out
their workmen because they refused to accept a
lower rate of wages than all other mines had agreed
to pay. The miners had been working for two years
under an award of the Arbitration Court. It ter-
minated at the end of 1908, but prior to that date
the Combined Unions asked for a conference with
the mine-owners of the district. The conference was
held. Before its conclusion, however, the Proprietary Company withdrew its representatives. All
the other companies came to a friendly settlement
with the Combined Unions. The latter communicated with the Broken Hill Proprietary Company,
and tried to meet them in every way.

The other mines had accepted a renewal of the
agreement, but the modest request of the miners
was met by the richest company on the field with
a demand that their employees should accept a

reduction of 12½ per cent. on the rates which a
judge in a State tribunal had declared to be fair.
The reduction meant a shilling per day less for the
miner to live upon. The men had no option but to
refuse; they could not in fairness go back on their
mates or accept from the richest company less than
the poorer companies had willingly agreed to pay.
When they refused, the Company locked them out.

Section 42 of the Industrial Disputes Act of
New South Wales reads:—

> 42. If any person—
>   (a) does any act or thing in the nature
>   of a lock-out or strike, or takes
>   part in a lock-out or strike, or
>   suspends or discontinues employ-
>   ment or work in any industry; or
>   (b) instigates to or aids in any of the
>   abovementioned acts,
> he shall be liable to a penalty not exceeding
> one thousand pounds, or in default to imprison-
> ment not exceeding two months:
>   Provided that nothing in this section shall
> prohibit the suspension or discontinuance of any
> industry or the working of any persons therein
> for any cause not constituting a lock-out or
> strike.

The Broken Hill Proprietary Company has had
about £12,000,000 out of its mine, while many of the
others are collecting calls from their shareholders;
but Premier Wade, instead of taking action against
the rich law-breaking company, sent about 400 fully

armed police to browbeat the men into submission.
These police almost at once attacked the miners
whilst they were relieving pickets in the usual
orderly manner, and with rough handling arrested
twenty-eight men, including the leader, Tom Mann.
It was admitted that the leaders of the miners were
keeping the men under fine control, and that they
were well behaved. It was, of course, because of
this fact that the police were sent to provoke men
to riot. A change was made in the Bench by sending
up a special magistrate with a proper hatred of the
union worker, so that the law could be judicially
strained to punish those who upon any excuse or
no excuse had been brought before Wade's Police
Court.

The foolishness of thinking that workers can
be intimidated in this way! Australian unionists
may be starved into temporary submission; but they
have never allowed themselves to be intimidated.
It was because they were orderly that the men were
arrested. It was hoped that the sense of injustice
which brings indignation to any manly person would
excite men to a genuine breach of ordinary good
behaviour, and it speaks volumes for the discipline
of trade unionism that the men exercised such
marvellous self-control.

In this manner began the year 1909 at the
Barrier. Meantime, Justice Higgins offered to give
up his holidays and conciliate. The miners were
willing, and at once sent their officer to confer with
him, but the directors had the impudence to dictate
terms which very properly the judge reminded them
he had nothing to do with giving. Mr. Darling,

chairman of the directors, asked that the military should be sent to help enforce his starvation wage. He said that if the miners would give up gambling and drinking they could live on 7s. 6d. per shift!

Broken Hill is one of the most costly places in Australia to live in, and the rich robber-parasite Darling is not content with his share of the £12,000,000 taken out of the lead mines at the expense of the men's lives, but asks them not only to ruin their health for all their miserable existence, but that they should starve whilst doing it. And very properly, and quite in the natural order of things, Premier Wade does his best to help Darling to secure his outrageous ends. Most strange of all is the fact that there are working men who voted for Wade, and even for Darling. Truly Labor has an uphill fight in its efforts to secure social justice, and it is the worker who stands blocking the path of progress.

Of the twenty-eight arrested twenty-three were discharged by Mr. A. N. Barnett, S.M., and five were committed for trial. Of these the jury found no case against the leader, Tom Mann, and disagreed in the cases of W. Rosser and Joseph Lyons. W. Stokes and John May were sent up for three and two years respectively. H. Holland, a Socialist visitor from Sydney, was sentenced to two years' imprisonment with hard labor for alleged seditious remarks.

... Most excellent work was accomplished by the New South Wales Labor Party. It was due to one member of the Party (Mr. Sam Smith, for some years secretary of the Seamen's Union, but now, unfortunately for himself and the movement, laid aside by illness) that it has become safe to travel on some of the ferry boats of Sydney harbor. Prior to his taking the matter up in 1898-9, profit-making private enterprise was carrying thousands daily to Manly and other places in steamers the hulls of which were so rotten that if they had bumped a dead dog in the harbor they would have gone down. Rust and paint and marvellous luck carried them through. It was easy to poke holes through their sides with an umbrella, yet Government officers had passed such boats as fit for traffic. One steamer actually sank at her moorings.

When Sam Smith got at them, one of the worst was run into Mort's Dock to be replated. Sam had secured portions of the rotten plates as exhibits when moving on the matter in the House. One day a party of us went over to the Dock to have a look at the work. On arrival Sam discovered that the owners had removed the plates which had been taken off, and other old plates less worn out had been brought and laid alongside. This was done with a view of deceiving us and any inspector who might chance to call. Sam Smith knew all about it, and was able to tell them where the original plates had been planted, so they had to bring them back. They were eaten through with rust, and you could crumble them up in your fingers. Premier Reid put Sam on a Board after that, which stirred up things and gave some degree of safety to the lives of the public. Of the work done by the Party as a whole, I am indebted to an excellent pamphlet, " The Labor

P

Party in New South Wales," by Mr. Geo. Black, for the list of measures summarised below:—

"1. The Conciliation and Arbitration Act of 1891. This measure was voluntary. The Court could not compel the attendance of the parties to a dispute, nor make an award, nor enforce a decision.—Parkes.

"2. The Electoral Act of 1893, which made residence the voter's sole qualification—and thus abolished plural voting, and provided for single electorates, electoral rights, and an extension of the voting hours.—Dibbs.

"3. The Labor Settlements Act of 1893, which provided for the placing of the deserving unemployed in communal settlements on Crown land, where they were provided with huts, food, clothing, seeds, and implements of every description—these expenses to be a charge against the products of the ground and their labor.—Dibbs.

"4. The Land Tax Act of 1895—falling on unimproved values at the rate of 1d. per £ with an exemption up to £240.—Reid.

"5. The income Tax of 1895 of 6d. per £ with an exemption up to £200.—Reid.

"6. The Franchise Act—giving votes to the police.—Reid.

"7. Two Mining Acts Amendments Acts— which lowered the charge for miners' rights from 20s. per annum to 2s. 6d. for six months, dating from the issue of the right—with the right to mine for minerals other than gold;

reduced the cost of occupation leases from £17 10s. to £3 7s.; and imposed labor conditions on all special leases granted to landowners under the original Act.—Reid.

" 8. A Workshops and Factories Act which made registration imperative; provided for periodical inspection, sanitation, and ventilation; the fencing of dangerous machinery and belts; fixed meal hours; prevented the employ of children under 13, and permitted lads under 16 and females to work 48 hours only in factories and 52 hours in shops.—Reid.

" 9. Coal Mines Regulation Act, which makes managerial daily inspection and periodical Government inspection compulsory; insists on the appointment of certificated inspectors, arbitration in disputes, coroner's inquiries on accidents, notices of abandonment, the fencing of abandoned shafts, payment by weight, appointment of check weighers by men, impulsion to the working face of not less than 100 feet of air in each minute for each man, boy, and horse in each mine; prohibits the employment of women and boys under 14, and public-house payments, also single-shaft mines.—Reid.

" 10. The Selectors' Relief Act.—Reid.

" 11. Re-appraisement of Special Areas.— Reid.

" 12. The Perpetual Leasing Act.—Reid.

" 13. The Navigation Act Amendment Act —so mutilated by the Council that its main provision was one for the reduction of pilot fees.—Reid.

" 14. The Elections Act Amendment Acts of 1896, 1897, and 1898.—These reduced the period necessary to, qualify for a transfer from one electorate to another from three months to one month, and made voting under an original right valid until a transferred right is obtained—therefore the vote of the careful elector is practically continuous; revision courts sit monthly instead of half-yearly; the hours of polling were further lengthened; and the transmission of rights by post was permitted.—Reid.

" 15. The Exclusion of Inferior Races.—This had to be arrived at by means of an educational test.—Reid.

" 16. The Navigation Act Amendment Act of 1889, which abolished the Marine Board, constituted a Department of Navigation and Courts of Marine Enquiry; made inspection compulsory on the order of the Court; provided that all sea-going steamers shall carry holders of a first or second class engineer's certificate, and that other steam driven vessels shall carry a certificated engineer of the third class; also that all sea-going vessels shall carry a certificated captain and mate; also for the inspection of the load-line; also the provision of proper accommodation for seamen and others; of well-found boats, buoys, rafts, and life-belt; and so on.—Lyne.

"17. The Early Closing Act, which provides for the closing of all business premises at 6 p.m. on four nights of the week, at 1 p.m. on one day, and at 10 p.m. on another day.—Lyne.

" 18. The Act to Limit the Attachment of Wages—the exemption being up to £2 weekly. —Lyne.

" 20. The Truck Act.—This measure put a stop to payment in public houses or stores, compulsory residence in the dwellings of the employer, compulsory dealing at the employer's store, and so on.—Lyne.

" 21. Sam Smith Coal-Lumpers' Baskets Act.—This limited the capacity of the baskets carried by the coal-lumpers on their backs so that no fewer than eleven went to the ton of coal.—Lyne.

" 22. The Old Age Pensions Act of 1900, which provides for the payment of 10s. weekly to adults of 65 years, resident in the State for 25 years prior to application and not possessed of property exceeding the value of £300, or an income exceeding £52.—Lyne.

" 23. The Miners Accident Relief Act of 1900, which provides for allowances in cases of disablement; gives widows a funeral allowance of £12 and a weekly allowance of 8s., and 2s. 6d. for each child under 14 years of age.—Lyne

" 24. The City Council Amending Act, which abolishes plural voting and gives the lodger a vote.—Lyne.

" 25. The Wharves and Rocks Resumption Act.—This measure placed all the business wharves and waterside wharves of the city in the hands of the people, and also added to the common possessions a vast area of centrally situated land.—Lyne.

"26. An Act to Amend the Early Closing Act (1900), which made it applicable ·to all country shopping districts proclaimed by the Governor, where the hours of closing on four days shall be six o'clock, on one day 10 o'clock, and on another (Wednesday or Saturday) one o'clock. This Act also made 8 o'clock on five nights and 10 o'clock on the remaining ·night the hours for newsagents and booksellers; limited the hours of assistants employed in hotels, restaurants, and eating-houses, of minors, of all bread, meat, and milk carters, and fixed certain holidays for their use.—Lyne.

"27. The Shearers' Accommodation Act of 1901, which makes compulsory the erection, on all stations where shearers and shed hands are hired, of buildings for their use which shall give 240 cubic feet of air space to each sleeper, which shall provide separate cooking and dining apartments, with the provision of good water and proper cooking and washing vessels, also sufficient latrine accommodation at a safe distance from the huts, with separate sleeping and eating apartments for Asiatics.—See.

"28. The Miners' Accident Relief Amendment Act of 1901, which brings under the provisions of the Act all works in the neighborhood of mines where owners may treat ore, coal, or shale; which provides for the selection of the committee of inspection in the proportion of one Government inspector, two miners' representatives, and one mine-owners' representative; and which makes payable to the fund by every mine-owner a sum equal to one-half the aggregate of the sums deducted from the miners' wages for the support of the fund; and makes compulsory weekly payments to parents or unmarried sisters whose deceased brother supported them.—See.

" 29. The Industrial Arbitration Act of 1901, which provided for the registration and incorporation of industrial unions and the making and enforcing of industrial agreements; constituted a court of arbitration for the hearing and determination of industrial disputes, and matters referred to it; defined the jurisdiction, powers, and procedure of such Court; provided for the enforcement of its awards and orders; and had purposes consequent on or incidental to those objects. The Act made illegal either strikes or lock-outs on the part of either employees or employers who had entered into a collective agreement; gave preference to Union labor, all things being equal; made Unionism compulsory on claimants and respondents; fined up to £1000 those who did not obey the Court's awards; and so on.—See.

" 30. The Women's Franchise Act of 1902, which conferred on the women of New South Wales all the political rights enjoyed by men, save that of sitting in Parliament.—See.

" These are the legislative deeds of the Labor Party; their other doings are scarcely less important. They have not only educated Parliament and its successive leaders up to an understanding of what the people to-day demand, but have also exerted an important influence in the Governmental management of all departments of State, as the following list will testify:—(1) Establishment of a Minimum Wage; (2) The Substitution of Day for Contract Labor as far as possible on Governmental works; (3) An Eight Hours Day for Railway Men; (4) A Week's Holiday Annually to the State's manual laborers as well as to its clerical workers; (5) Trade Union wages to all Government employees; (6) Preference to Unionists on all Government jobs; (7) Preference to Unionists, all things being equal, under the Arbitration Act in all employments; (8) The Abolition of the Sub-letting of Government Contracts; (9) The Establishment of a Government Clothing Factory; and so on.

" The following list includes the total of democratic measures passed by the Parliament of New South Wales prior to the advent of the Labor Party:—

" 1. The Electoral Act of 1859—providing for manhood suffrage and vote by ballot.—Premier Cowper.

" 2. The Goldfields Act of 1860, which placed some restrictions on aliens.—Cowper.

" 3. The Robertson Crown Lands Alienation and Crown Lands Occupation Acts of 1861.—Cowper.

" 4. The Chinese Immigration and Restriction Act of 1861—permitting the entry of only one Chinaman to every ten tons burden, under a penalty of £10 per capita and a poll tax of

£10 on each Chinaman permitted to land, with an annual payment afterwards of £4.—Cowper.

" 5. The Public Instruction Act of 1880, which abolished State aid to denominational schools, and established a system of secular, compulsory, and partially free education.— Parkes.

" 6· The Chinese Restriction Act of 1880, which restricted the number entering the State by any vessel and imposed a poll tax of £10 on all entrants whether by sea or land.—Parkes.

" 7. The Chinese Restriction Act of 1888, which permitted vessels to carry only one Chinese passenger to every 300 tons, imposed a poll tax of £100 on all permitted to land, and refused them naturalisation and the right to mine without the permission of the Minister for Mines.—Parkes.

" 8. The O'Connor Allowances to Members Act of 1889.—Parkes."

From the above quotations from Mr. Black's pamphlet it will be seen that the interests of the masses had never been considered during the first 35 years of constitutional Government. Practically nothing was done until Labor took a hand. The thirty Acts listed by Mr. Black were passed by Governments kept in power by Labor. When Labor is put into Opposition by the coalition of the other two parties legislation of the kind ceases, and again the interests of capitalists dominate. The Income Tax is repealed, and renewal and amendment of the Arbitration Act are refused. Dominated by Labor,

Carruthers introduced and carried a system of perpetual leasing called homestead settlement. No sooner had he got a majority behind him sufficient to make him independent of Labor support than he declared himself in favor of altering the tenure of a homestead selection to conditional purchase. Under this system experience shows that land monopoly is built up. The tone of Parliament has changed again. Everything is now being done for the rich; nothing for the poor. A close study of the two periods—that prior to 1891, and that since 1904 —proves that nothing will ever be done for the welfare of the masses unless they place the Labor Party in a position to control legislation and administration.

Labor had no representation in the Legislative Council until April 11, 1899, when Messrs. N. J. Buzacott, J. Estell, J. Hepher, and James Wilson were called to that body. Messrs. Fred. Flowers and Hugh Langwell were added on June 12, 1900. On July 23, 1901, Mr. Estell resigned, and entered the Assembly; and on May 28, 1902, Mr. Langwell resigned owing to having been appointed a member of the Western Lands Commission, a position he still holds, and which he has filled with marked ability. In July, 1908, Mr. J. Travers was added to the Council, so that Labor now has five in the nominee House of New South Wales.

CHAPTER XX.

QUEENSLAND.

THE development of Labor-in-politics in this State had special features not found so manifest in any of the other States of the Commonwealth. When Labor took the field as an active political factor, it had to face what has become known as the "Continuous Government." One Premier after another retired to a good fat billet, his lieutenant took his place, and the Ministry filled vacancies from leading supporters; but it was the same crowd all the time. They were the most capitalistic, commercially governed party ever seen in any State, and none were more glaringly corrupt.

When examined closely, it will be found that they used the powers of Government, not in the interests of the people, but in order to further the welfare of their own friends and themselves. The strong language used by Mr. Buzzacott, M.L.C., in his paper will apply to other Governments than the particular one to which he directed his statement. He said: "There is irrefutable evidence that for more than a year past the Ministry has waded in political corruption. It may be safely said that the Nelson Government is the most corrupt administration that has ever ruled Queensland."

With a five years Parliament, a weak Opposition, and a typical second chamber of nominee capitalists and a capitalist-governed press, Labor had to tackle the most powerful of social forces. The Government took care to prevent the radical section of the workers having a vote at all. At the same time they made provision for plural voters to exercise their grossly unfair privilege by fixing polling places in Brisbane for every electorate. Thus a property owner could vote in every electorate in which he held property. Some held votes under this system in as many as thirty electorates.

In a new country like Queensland thousands of the most intelligent and energetic working men have to travel in connection with their several occupations, and these were denied votes. The census of 1891 showed that adult males in Queensland numbered 108;116. In 1892 the rolls only registered 98,065. The Government revised the rolls, and reduced the numbers to 83,005, a decrease of 15,060. Ten per cent. of the votes belonged to persons with more than one vote, which reduced the number to 75,005, leaving no less than 30,411 disfranchised. The law had been specially devised so that these could be legally disfranchised. The class of persons constituting the Legislative Assembly of the colony in 1891 is indicated by their occupations as follows: —Squatters, 17; merchants, 11; auctioneers and agents, 8; lawyers, 7; sawmillers and manufacturers, 6; mine-owners, 5; retired, 4; newspaper owners, 3; contractors, 3.

Practically the whole membership of the House consisted of men who lived by exploitation of the worker, and who had no strong desire to see the latter placed in a position to demand a greater share of the wealth produced than he had been

previously permitted to secure by his individual
effort. They were all decidedly anti-union in their
ideas, and strongly backed up the Government in
the great effort to crush out the trade union movement and introduce "freedom of contract." in 1891.
The Labor movement in Queensland differed from
that of the other colonies, in that it was decidedly
and definitely Socialistic from the jump. So soon
as it spoke in a collective way it declared for
Socialism, and thus we had the forces of the most
advanced thought clashing against the most conservative of capitalistic rule. The fight was bitter—
no quarter was given or taken; and hence the growth
of the movement is highly interesting.

One thing stands out clear as a powerful factor
in Queensland Labor politics, and that is the
influence of " The Worker " newspaper, the official
organ of the movement, and the pioneer of Australian Labor journalism. The originator of the idea
was William Lane, at the time one of the founders
and proprietors of the " Boomerang." To William
Lane, more than to any other man, we can attribute
the policy of the movement, and it was his magnificent writings in the early " Workers " which
touched the latent sentiment so strong in the
Australian bushmen, and which made the Shearers'
and Laborers' Unions in the country districts such
staunch adherents of the paper as well as loyal
supporters of Labor candidates in every subsequent
fight.

Mr. Lane was a journalist of great ability. He
did Parliamentary notes for one of the big dailies at
first, but got into more immediate touch with Labor

people as the writer of a column of " Labor. Notes "
which appeared in the '" Observer " in 1886, signed
" Sketcher." Socialist phrases were frequent in
these " Notes," and those who came, into contact
with " Billy " Lane, as he was called, soon, learned
to love and trust him. He was the father of the
very important idea of running a Labor paper on
the lines of union ownership and control, with a
regular subsidy contributed by the trade unions and
collected by them from their members as part of the
regular contributions. The paper is thus independent of advertisers, has a guaranteed circulation,
and puts all profit into improvement and development of the paper.

Lane discussed the idea with several of the
leaders in the unions in 1889, and on December 9 a
meeting was held in the old Maritime Hall, Eagle
Street, at which representatives of the Brisbane
District Council, A.L.F., the Building Trades
Council, Brisbane Shop Assistants' Association,
Boilermakers' Union, Charters Towers A.M.A., and
Gympie A.M.A., with Mr. Arthur Parnell (Secretary
of the Carriers and the General Laborers' Union)
representing the Bush Unions. The plan proposed
was approved, and on February 14, 1890, the first
formal meeting of the Board of Trustees was held.
There were present G. S. Casey (Central District
Council), Mat Reid (Building Trades Council),
Albert Hinchcliffe (Brisbane District Council,
A.L.F.), Chas. Seymour and W. Mabbott (Maritime
Council). There was some difference of opinion as
to choice of a name for the paper, but eventually
it was christened " The Worker.". William Lane

was appointed editor. The first issue was published on March 1, 1890—then Eight Hours Day. It started as a monthly, with a shilling per year subsidy from the unions. By November 1 of the same year it became an eight-page fortnightly; and in April, 1892, was made a weekly, with an increased subsidy.

The year 1889 also saw the launching of the Australian Labor Federation. It was instituted at a meeting held on June 11. A provisional committee was appointed, consisting of Messrs. M. Fanning, A. Hinchcliffe, C. McDonald, J. C. Stewart, T. Foley, and :R. Morrison, with Chas. Seymour general secretary, and G. S. Casey as organizer. In a year they had 15,000 members, as all the organizations readily joined. On August 1, 1890, it held its first annual meeting, at which Mr. Charles McDonald (now! Chairman of Committees in the Australian House of Representatives) was elected president, and Mr. Albert Hinchcliffe (now M.L.C. in Queensland and manager of " The Worker ") general secretary, a position Mr. Hinchcliffe has worthily and ably filled ever since. This gathering lasted several days, and much consideration was given to the question of political action. It was felt that the opposition of old parties would be just as strong against a moderate programme as one declaring for a " whole-hog " policy, and eventually the platform was adopted which appears in the Appendix.

Prior to this meeting, the A.L.F. had come into prominence in connection with what is known as the Jondaryan case, in which the Federation asked the shipowners not to load wool from Jondaryan Station, in the Darling Downs district. On 2nd

May, 1890, the A.L.F. decided to take action. On
the 5th they held a mass meeting of the 'maritime
men, who unanimously agreed to support the organization. On the same day the shipowners were asked
not to load the wool which had been shorn by non-
unionists. On the following day the B.I. and Q.A.
shipping companies asked the A.L.F. to confer with
the squatters, and the A.L.F. took steps to arrange
for a conference, which eventuated successfully on
May 17. Whilst the shipowners, the squatters,
and the A.L.F. were thus doing their part to avoid
a serious Labor trouble, it is worthy of note that the
then Premier (Mr. Morehead), at a meeting at
Rockhampton on May 8, roundly abused Labor
from the anti-union squatters' point of view. The
B.I. Shipping Co. had been put to some loss over the
blocking of the wool on the s.s. Jumna, and on
June 6 the A.L.F., unsolicited, paid £75 to the
company to cover the loss. On August 16 following,
the marine officers walked off their ships in Sydney
harbor, and the great battle known as the Maritime
Strike was precipitated. It was then that the shipowners declared that '' The shipowners would not
consult the public convenience if their cause was to
be weakened and their interests injured in the
matter.'' It is not often the supporters of private
enterprise set forth their attitude so honestly. The
public are slow to realise that private enterprise
works and schemes for gain and that only. It cares
not at any time for the effect of its action, except
from the point of view of profit-making.

The first attempt to secure direct representation of Labor in the Queensland Parliament was in

D. BOWMAN, M.L.A.,
Leader of Queensland Labor Party

1886, when W. M. Galloway stood for Fortitude Valley, and only secured 111 votes at a by-election. At the general election of 1888 four men ran as Labor candidates, but only got 1261 votes amongst them. At this election, Mr. T. Glassey ran as a supporter of the Griffith Ministry, and was elected for Bundamba. He afterwards left that party, and declared himself a straight-out Labor member. J. P. Hoolan joined him, and, in 1892, T. J. Ryan for the Barcoo and G. J. Hall for Bundaberg, were elected on the Labor platform, and these four formed the first distinct Labor Party in the House, Mr. Glassey acting as leader. The industrial troubles of 1890 were followed by the strike in the pastoral industry in 1891, and this fight, more than that of 1890, aroused the workers of Queensland into political activity. Ryan, a union secretary sent to jail and irons in 1891, was sent to Parliament in 1892.

The real character of the Government became clearer in 1891, and to understand it it is necessary to note a few facts. A colored census taken in 1898 showed that there were 24,366 colored aliens in Queensland—one for every five adult white males. Chinese predominated. In order to secure cheap labor for the sugar growers, the Government allowed what amounted practically to a slave trade to be carried on, and kanakas from the South Sea Islands were brought over, ostensibly under contract. Most readers will have heard of the "blackbirding" carried on about that time. The census of 1901 showed that the proportion of colored aliens was 47.59 per 1000. Owing to the action of

Q

the Labor Party in the Commonwealth Parliament, not only has the increase been stopped, but the kanakas have been sent back to their island homes.

To come back to 1891. The sugar growers succeeded in getting a supply of black men, and the squatters introduced Chinese labor. Griffith led in denunciation of kanaka importation in 1889, but recanted in 1892, and became a party to the importation of cheap Italian labor by the Government. The stand made by the shearers and shed employees in 1891 was not only against a reduction of wages and an attempt to introduce ". freedom of contract," but was principally against the introduction of Chinese labor. To understand what forces were arrayed against them, we have only to look at the return as to how land was held. In 1894, of unalienated land, eighteen banks held 81,174,880 acres, and twenty-seven finance institutions held 49,623,797 acres. Thus a total of 130,798,677 acres—or nearly one-half the total unalienated land of Queensland—was in the hands of 45 heartless, soulless finance companies. The rental paid was slightly over a farthing per acre. Of the banks, the Bank of New South Wales held over 17,000,000 acres, the Bank of Australasia over 16,000,000 acres, the Q.N. Bank over 10,000,000 acres.

Members of the Government and their supporters were all more or less directly interested in banks and stations, hence they used all the powers vested in the Government to crush the workers in general and organized labor in particular. The police and military were placed at the disposal of the Pastoralists' Union, of which the Cabinet was simply a committee to carry out instructions. Every branch of the public service was coerced into acting against the unionists so far as the Government could force them. A circular was issued calling upon all railway men to leave their union. On the slightest pretext they were discharged if suspected of being friendly towards the shearers. One man was asked if he were a Republican, and, deeming it a joke, replied that he was a red-hot Republican. He was dismissed. Another committed the sin of laughing at a constable of police who fell off a train. He had to go. It was admitted that thirty-one were discharged for trivial '' offences '' of this kind.

In Queensland, and likewise in New South Wales, the railways were at the disposal of pastoralists for carrying out the scum of the big cities which had been raked up to work in place of unionists. Professional criminals, well known to the police, were taken to fill the places of honest workmen. Blacklegs were armed, whilst unionists, many of whom made a living by shooting kangaroos, had their rifles taken from them. To the outside world the Government made a pretence of simply maintaining law and order, but the evidence of their actions in 1891 and again in 1894 proved them to have been, as already asserted, an agent for the owners of the stations in attempting to carry out their big scheme for the subjugation of the unionists and the procuring of cheap labor of any kind, color, or character.

Men were arrested and jailed on the slightest pretext. Union Organizer Gilbert Casey was locked up for a fortnight and then released without trial

This was done in order to break up a camp. In March, 1891, seventy-four men were travelling near Lorne when the grass caught fire; twenty-five were arrested and charged with rioting. There was no case, and they were discharged, but were at once re-arrested and charged with arson, and thirteen were committed for trial. Only one (J. Macnamara) was tried, and he was dragged about the country for 3000 miles before the trial. The jury found him not guilty of arson, but said he had aided and abetted, so the judge gave him three years. A man named C. F. Latrielle got a month, and some others two months, for calling another a "scab." A man named Jermyn was tried eleven times, but the police had no evidence, and he got clear every time. To be a unionist was enough. This incident in the court at St. George is full of meaning.

His Worship to the constable: "Did you search the prisoner?"

"I did, your Worship."

"What did you find on him?"

"I found a Union ticket, your Worship, which I produce in Court."

Men were sent to prison for various terms running from a fortnight to fifteen years. In another place I deal fully with many of the incidents of the 1891 and 1894 industrial wars, and simply remind the reader to keep in view the great influence they had on the minds of the masses in exposing the real character and aims of the Government with which the colony was cursed. The strike of 1891 was called off on June 11, 1891. Later in the year it extended into New South Wales, but was ended there by a conference with the Pastoralists' Union, at which an agreement was arrived at and which practically settled matters for all the colonies, but which the Pastoralists broke away from in 1894, thus bringing on the terrible struggle of that year.

The fight for " freedom of contract " cost the country over £170,000, and it was admitted in a report of the principal organizer of the P.U., given at one of their meetings, that it cost their union £42,000. At the same meeting it was agreed that it would be necessary to import " free labor " for years in order to crush the unions of the workers. There was rejoicing in the ranks of employers of labor when Griffith, in November, 1890, carried a vote for bringing Italian labor to the colony, and some of the employers wrote pointing out that they would be able to get the Italians to work in batches, as the women and children of such people would work together. The storm raised by Labor leaders, and the exposure in " The Worker " checked the scheme somewhat, and the Employers' Federation turned its attention to preventing at all hazards workers getting a vote.

No sooner had Labor issued its Platform than the employers got to work. In the report of their executive they said: " The question of the revision of voters' rolls has also engaged the attention of your executive, and circulars have been issued calling upon affiliated bodies to take the matter in hand. While our organization, from the nature of its constitution, cannot take a side in political questions, the executive feel that it is within their province to prevent if possible our political institutions being used as a lever to further the objects of trade unionists by the election of Labor delegates. They therefore urge upon every representative present the need of watchfulness in this direction, otherwise we may find ourselves outvoted.''

In this the view of all the organized employers of Australia is set forth. However they may be divided in opinion on other matters, they were—and are—solidly united against Labor, and would never have allowed either manhood or adult suffrage to come if they could have prevented it. The law and the Government helped them. Forms of application to be placed on the rolls had to be signed before a Justice of the Peace. Beside being often miles away, they were almost all unfriendly to Labor. Some who had given special facilities were struck off the roll of justices. Later on, the President of the P.U. sent a circular to Registrars practically instructing them to purify the rolls by striking names off. The law left ample loopholes for doing this, and full advantage was taken thereof.

The term of Parliaments was reduced in 1890 to three years, but they still retained the plan of running the elections in batches. What this means to the Government of the day was expressed by an experienced and cunning member of a New South Wales Government to the writer. He said it was equal to a gain of fifteen seats to the Government. To Labor is due the fact that all elections are now held on the same day. After the industrial battle of 1891 Labor prepared for the political contest, and the forces against them laid plans for defeating their object. They had a whole year in which to get ready. The great success attending the Labor Party in the New South Wales elections in 1891 gave courage to the workers, and put energy into the capitalistic organizations. The Government could see that their day was not to be a long one, and so they were going to help on a grand coup.

Two men loom large in the past of Queensland politics—the late Sir Thomas McIlwraith, and Sir Samuel Griffith, now Chief Justice in the High Court of Australia. McIlwraith first appeared in the McAlister Government in 1874 as Minister for Works, Mr. S. Griffith being Attorney-General. McIlwraith at once introduced the idea of railway construction on a land grant system. Premier McAlister dallied with the matter for a time, but finally, in an interview to the press, declared himself opposed to it. McIlwraith resigned and went into opposition. Later he became Premier, with Griffith leader of the opposition. In 1887 he was publicly charged with letting a contract for steel rails to his own relatives in London on such terms as unduly favored them at the expense of the taxpayers of the colony. A party vote just saved him. He also gave a shipping contract on terms of advantage to the shipowners, but against the interests of the people who had to pay. In all these his strong opponent and denouncer was Mr. Griffith. McIlwraith went out and Griffith came in in 1883; the latter was defeated in 1888, and McIlwraith once more returned to power. He gave up to Morehead, but in 1890 he formed a coalition with Griffith. McIlwraith was one of the promoters, and for some time a director

of the Queensland National Bank, and the balance
sheets of that institution for the ten years he was
Treasurer of the colony show how well he studied
the bank's interests at the expense of the taxpayer.
The following balances held by the Bank were due
to the colony on June 30 of each year named:—

1879 ..	£270,000	.. 1889 ..	£1,708,418
1880 ..	£685,366	.. 1890 ..	£1,902,306
1881 ..	£1,332,065	.. 1891 ..	£786,459
1882 ..	£1,824,332	.. 1892 ..	£1,403,793
1888 ..	£1,265,823	.. 1893 ..	£2,425,203

Sir T. McIlwraith went away travelling before
the great exposure of the bank, of which more anon.
Griffith, after first raising the salary by £1000 a
year, resigned and took the Supreme Court Bench
in March, 1893, so soon as Mr. Lilley resigned the
Chief Justiceship. Sir Hugh Nelson became Premier
in place of McIlwraith in October, 1893, and the
Continuous Government still misruled.

During 1892 a great scheme was introduced by
the Government. It was one of McIlwraith's best.
On paper, as put by the capitalistic press, it seemed
all right. When Labor's searchlight got on to it,
however, it was proved to be a clever attempt to
grab 200,000,000 acres of a colony whose total area
is an enormous one, namely, 668,497 square miles—
or 427,838,080 acres. When mountains and rough
country are taken out, and alienated land allowed
for, it will be seen that the boodlers originating the
grab wanted to secure all the good country that was
left. The Government, bad as it was, could make
2000 miles of railway for £14,000,000, but they were

going to force the people to pay £56,000,000 for it. The syndicate of land grabbers would thus have made £42,000,000. It was a great scheme, and would have got through but for Labor coming into the field. I give details in later pages.

(For the Labor Platform of 1893 see Appendix.)

The elections took place in May, 1893, and the following Labor members were returned:—W. H. Browne, Croydon; A. Dawson and J. Dunsford, Charters Towers; J. M. Cross, Clermont; H. Daniels, Cambooya; A. Fisher, Gympie; J. Fogarty, Drayton and Toowoomba; J. P. Hoolan, Burke; W. Lovejoy, Aubigny; R. King, Maranoa; M. Reid, Toowong; H. Turley, Brisbane South; G. Jackson, Kennedy; H. F. Hardacre, Leichhardt; C. McDonald, Flinders; and C. H. Rawlins, Woothakata. T. J. Ryan did not run again. He said: " The friends were too warm, the whisky too strong, and the cushions too soft for Tommy Ryan. His place is out amongst the shearers on the billabongs." He sums up the temptations of Parliament nicely. Mr. Glassey having been defeated, Mr. Hoolan resigned his seat for Burke and Mr. Glassey took his place. At a by-election for Townsville on July 17, 1894, Mr. A. Ogden was added to the party, and on the same date Mr. J. Wilkinson won in a by-election for Ipswich.

The results of the May contest, 1893, showed that Ministerialists got 29,144 votes, and non-Ministerialists 48,128—or a majority against the Government of 19,084 votes. Out of 62 contested seats the Government got 34, the others 28. The 34 Ministerialists represented 854 votes each, the 16 Labor members 1713 votes each. The result proved that the country was against the Government. They stuck to office, however. In the 1893 elections, Bowman was third for South Brisbane, Kidston and Larcombe were defeated for Rockhampton, and Stewart for Rockhampton North. Glassey lost Bundamba. Hinchcliffe also ran for a seat and lost.

The year 1893 was the period of the failure of private enterprise banks. The Queensland National Bank went under amongst the number. It held nearly two and a-half millions of Government money, and the Government came to its aid and saved it from liquidation. When it closed its doors, 7702 depositors' claims totalled £4,180,293. Over one-half of this sum was from the old country. Of 160,000 shares, 40,000 were on the London Register. It had paid in dividends £1,195,959 17s. 10d., returning original shareholders £10 15s. 4d. per share of £8 paid up. So bound up with the interests of the people was the institution that only six had the courage to vote against the Current Accounts Guarantee Bill when it was introduced in June, 1895 —namely, Messrs. Dawson, Turley, Dunsford, Kerr, McDonald, and Fitzgerald. The bill was rushed through in one night, and passed the Legislative Council in fifteen minutes. Eleven members of the Council and eight of the Assembly were shareholders.

Persistent demand·was made by Labor members for an investigation of the affairs of the bank, and week after week the little "Worker" newspaper raked up and exposed the facts apparent in the balance-sheets. In 1896 Nelson forced a measure through the House empowering him to make the best terms possible, and giving a thirty-five years' agreement. The gag was applied to the Labor members. They took so strong a stand, however, that the Ministry, after having refused it for three years, had to agree to appoint a commission of inquiry. The Commission reported in November, 1896. The Treasurer (Mr. Nelson) and a colleague (Mr. Barlow) had stated to the House in 1893 that they had made a minute and searching investigation of the bank's affairs and position, and found it quite sound and solvent. The Commission in 1896 found that though £747,872 had been written off as bad since 1893—the loss on long outstanding accounts, and showing on the books when Nelson examined them—the deficits, including overdrafts not paying interest, amounted to £3,000,000.

It was quite clear, therefore, that the bank was insolvent when Nelson declared it sound. The manager and two of the directors owed large sums. The Commission declared that profits were fictitious, and said: " We are decidedly of opinion that no dividends should have been paid since the reconstruction of the bank, but we are not in a position to state when and to what extent dividends prior to that period ceased to be justifiable." For the half-year ending June, 1894, the bank declared profits as £9797, out of which they made a dividend of £8400. In December, 1894, profits were alleged to be £11,374, and a dividend was declared of £9600. In June, 1895, a dividend of £10,800 was declared, and for December £12,000. This makes a total of £40,800 which the bank did not earn, but which the Government helped it wrongly to declare.

An additional report from the Commission states:—" We have the honor to report that in our opinion no dividend should have been . paid after 1889, or, at the latest, 1890." Another paragraph says: " Early in 1892 the board appears to have experienced great difficulty in meeting the wholesale withdrawals of British deposits at that time. The correspondence shows that the position occasioned much anxiety to the directors." This makes it clear that the directors knew that they had no funds out of which to declare the dividends of 1892 and 1893. It also makes one feel that there is likely to be truth in the report that some friends got the " tip," and that £60,000 was got out at the back door ere the bank closed its doors.

Had the Commission gone further back they would have found out more crooked work. In 22 years Queensland had paid £14,150,000 more in interest than she had received in principal, and her dealings with the Queensland National Bank cast some light on the reasons why the borrowing craze had such a hold upon the Treasurer of the day. It will also probably explain why all our capitalistic Governments of the past have been so anxious to run the country into debt. On one occasion Sir T. McIlwraith borrowed nine months before the loan was needed, and the country had to pay £32,000 in interest before it began to spend the loan money. This · was done to help along the disgracefully mismanaged Queensland National Bank.

The best example of how things are worked by private enterprise, aided by a Government of their own choosing, occurred in 1892. Though there was enough money in London to pay the interest due, nevertheless a draft was obtained from the Queensland National Bank for £300,000 and sent from Brisbane in December, but not entered in the bank's books until January 3, 1893. On December 23, £600,000 was borrowed by the Treasurer from the Bank of England. This enabled the bank to save on its balance and have £300,000 of public money. The bank declared a dividend of £40,000 in June, 1892, and another of £40,000 in June, 1893, and then closed its doors and reconstructed. Those two items were a clear £80,000 scooped out of depositors' funds, and clearly the balance-sheets were false. But few will believe that the Government were unaware of the real state of things, and hence their desire to hide the facts.

The " Investors' Review " of February, 1897, in an article headed " The Q.N. Bank Swindle," concludes by asking: " How can a community hope to prosper which allows swindles of this kind to flourish in its midst unpunished and unatoned for?" It took three years to secure inquiry, and it took considerable agitation ere the directors and manager were put on trial. Of course they got off. They belonged to the sacred circle of capitalists. Had they been trade unionists struggling for better conditions they would have got imprisonment for life. The help and succor given to shareholders in the bank by the Continuous Government naturally bound the shareholders to them politically, and made them fight Labor all the stronger. In 1897 a return obtained by the Labor Leader showed that twenty-two lawyers had received amongst them £36,439 9s. 5d. for work done for departments between June, 1890, and June, 1897. Three departments were not included. Attorney-General Byrne had scooped £6491 in addition to his salary of £1000 a year. No one but Government supporters shared in the spoil.

The following was the result of the elections held in March, 1896:—J. M. Cross, Clermont; T. Glassey, Bundaberg; H. Turley, Brisbane South; F. McDonnell, Fortitude Valley; T. D. Keogh, Rosewood; T. Dibley, Woollongabba; G. Kerr, Barcoo; W. Kidston, Rockhampton; J. C. Stewart, Rockhampton North; G. C. Sim, Carpentaria; J. Hoolan, Burke; H. Daniels, Cambooya; A. Dawson and J. Dunsford, Charters Towers; W. H. Browne, Croydon; C. McDonald, Flinders; G. Jackson, Kennedy; H. F. Hardacre, Leichhardt; C. B. Fitzgerald, Mitchell; R. King, Maranoa. This gave Labor 20 members, representing 30,392 votes, as against 34 Ministerialists, representing 40,113 votes, 10 Independents with 8745 votes, and eight Opposition members representing 7835 votes. Again it will be seen that the Ministry did not represent the will of the people as expressed at the ballot box, as the majority of votes was against them. Labor had several unexpected losses, such as Messrs. Fisher, Ogden, Rawlings, Reid, and Wilkinson.

In June, 1898, the Labor Convention adopted a new platform and the following form of pledge:—At nomination the candidate for selection to sign the following: " I, the undersigned candidate for selection by the ——— branch of the Labor Party's recognised Political Organization, hereby give my pledge that if not selected I will not in any way oppose the candidature of the duly selected nominee.'' Before nomination the selected candidate to sign as follows: '' I agree to advocate and support the principles contained in this platform.''

In August, 1898, an effort was made by the small party led by Mr. Drake to form an alliance with Labor, but the large majority of the party opposed it. Drake's party numbered five, but with one who had ratted from the Ministerialists and three who had been Labor men he thought it possible to end the career of the Continuous Government. Prior to the elections in 1899, an understanding was arrived at so that each would not fight the other, though each party maintained its independence. The work of the party had begun to tell on the minds of the people, and a splendid fight was put up.

The elections of March, 1899, returned 23 Labor members, as follows:—A. Fisher, Gympie; W. G. Higgs, Fortitude Valley; T. Glassey, Bundaberg; F. McDonnell, Fortitude Valley; T. Dibley, Woollongabba; G. Kerr, Barcoo; A. Dawson and J. Dunsford, Charters Towers; J. C. Stewart, Rockhampton North; C. B. Fitzgerald, Mitchell; W. Hamilton, Gregory; C. M. Jenkinson, Wide Bay; D. Bowman, Warrego; H. F. Hardacre, Leichhardt; T. Givens, Cairns; V. J. B. Lesina, Clermont; G. Ryland, Gympie; D. T. Keogh, Rosewood; W. H. Browne, Croydon; G. Jackson, Kennedy; C. McDonald, Flinders; W. Kidston, Rockhampton; W. Maxwell, Burke. Bowman's seat was contested and declared void in October, 1899, but he won it at the election

on December 16. In July Mr. Turley won South
Brisbane in a by-election, and Mat Reid won
Ennoggera in December of same year. This raised the
strength of the party to twenty-five members in a
House of 72.

In 1899 there were some important changes.
Tom Glassey was deposed from the leadership of the
Labor Party. For some time he had not given satisfaction. His egotism spoilt him, and he wanted to
run things himself. Andy Dawson was elected in his
place by eighteen to four. For some time there had
been an undercurrent of intrigue going on with the
view of putting the Government out and setting up
a coalition, of which the Labor Party was to be a
section. Some of Labor's bitterest opponents were
willing to take office if Labor would join them.
Quite a number of the Labor Party were willing to
end the Continuous Government on these conditions,
and it was a trying time for the Party.

Other sections of the House tried to force the
situation, and it came to a climax on November 22,
1899. A bill for the appointment of a Railways
Standing Committee was before the House, and had
passed the second reading. Mr. O'Connell moved to
make the bill extend to other public works, and his
amendment was accepted by the Government. On
division the motion was lost by 34 to 31. On the
motion that the Chairman leave the chair, Mr.
Dawson moved an amendment—'' That the House
proceed with the next order of the day,'' and 32
voted for and 33 against the amendment. On the
23rd the Government simply adjourned the House
until the following Tuesday, the 28th. On that date

the Government announced that they refused to carry on with only one of a majority, and had therefore resigned office, and Mr. Dawson had been sent for.

Those who expected a coalition were disappointed. The firm stand made by a number of the members of the party in caucus soon put the genuineness of the professions of members outside the party to the test, as it was decided to form a purely Labor Ministry and chance the results. Mr. Dawson met the House on Friday, December 1, and announced that he had formed a Government as follows:— Premier and Chief Secretary, Mr. A. Dawson; Attorney-General, Mr. C. B. Fitzgerald; Home Secretary, Mr. H. Turley; Treasurer and P.M.G., Mr. W. Kidston; Secretary for Mines and Public Instruction, Mr. W. H. Browne; Secretary for Lands and Agriculture, Mr. H. F. Hardacre; Secretary for Railways and Public Works, Mr. A. Fisher.

Mr. Dawson asked for an adjournment until the following Tuesday, in accordance with the usual custom, but it was refused by 36 to 26. Messrs. Drake, Curtis, Thorne, and Plunkett were the only members outside the Labor Party who voted with the Government. Thus the first of Labor Ministries in the Parliaments of the world was forced promptly to resign. That the Party took a wise step in forming a straight-out Labor Cabinet was made clear, and the schemers who wanted to make a tool of the Party were shown up in their true colors. The Dickson Ministry was reconstructed, and Philp came in as Premier. Later, Andy Dawson was induced to withdraw from the leadership of the Party, and Mr. W. H. Browne was elected in his stead.

R

In 1900 Tom Glassey went wrong. He had been taking up an unsatisfactory attitude for some time, and felt sore over the loss of the leadership. During the recess in June, 1900, he secretly made all arrangements for securing re-election, and suddenly resigned. The Party had no time to organize against him, and though they ran a good man against him the seat was lost to Labor, and Glassey was returned by the votes of the men he had fought for ten years, but who will take any traitor to their ranks so long as they can weaken the Labor cause.

The coming of Federation brought changes. Every State Parliament lost a number of its best men. After the election of the Commonwealth Parliament it was necessary to fill the places of those who had been sent there. The result of the 1901 elections was the return of the following Labor members:—P. Airey, Flinders; J. Dunsford and J. Burrows, Charters Towers; V. J. B. Lesina, Clermont; W. Maxwell, Burke; W. H. Browne, Croydon; T. Givens, Cairns; W. Hamilton, Gregory; G. Kerr, Barcoo; C. B. Fitzgerald, Mitchell; H. Turner, Rockhampton North; W. Kidston, Rockhampton; G. Ryland, Gympie; H. F. Hardacre, Leichhardt; H. Turley, Brisbane South; D. Bowman, Warrego; G. P. Barber, Bundaberg; T. Dibley, Woollongabba; D. Mulcahy, Gympie; F. McDonnell, Fortitude Valley; M. Reid, Ennoggera.

A change came in 1903. The utter incapacity of Philp became so apparent that even the prejudice against Labor could not prevent the inevitable. Philp's deficits for the three years totalled £1,100,000. He had spent £3500 on fireworks and £1147 on medals at Commonwealth time. He had paid £6744 on four Royal Commissions, £75,000 on the purchase of a block of land from a financial institution in Brisbane, £180,000 for worthless dredges, and £78,264 on tank engines which were a failure. £53,000 had been spent on immigration, and over £11,000 had gone to his friend Rutledge and others in legal expenses of various kinds. The House met for the second session on July 21, 1903.

Next day Mr. Browne, the leader of the Labor Party, moved a vote of want of confidence. This was defeated by 38 to 30. On August 5 following, Mr. Blair moved an amendment in Ways and Means. This was lost on August 25 by 34 to 30. On September 8 a series of amended resolutions on Ways and Means were only carried by 33 to 31. The Government resigned next day, and Mr. Browne was sent for. After careful consideration the party agreed to join in a coalition, and Mr. Morgan (then occupying the Chair as Speaker) was approached, and he agreed to resign the Speakership and form a Government. He took office on September 17, 1903, with Browne as Minister of Mines and Kidston as Treasurer. Thus the life of the Continuous Government ended—it was hoped for ever.

The Party lost a good man by the death of the Hon. W. H. Browne on April 12, 1904. His life as a miner had undermined his constitution. Peter Airey, who had taken his place as leader, was then taken into the Ministry, and Geo. Kerr was chosen as leader of the party. Very good work was done by the coalition. The Labor Treasurer soon made a change in the finances, and for the first time Queensland came out with a surplus instead of a deficit. W. S. Murphy took Mr. Browne's seat for Croydon.

A vote of want of confidence was moved by Mr. Cribb on June 7, 1904. The voting took place on the 22nd, and resulted 35 for and 36 against. The Government won by one vote. Six members had ratted, so with a view to securing a dissolution of Parliament, Morgan resigned. At a caucus of the Philp party that gentleman gave up the leadership to Sir Arthur Rutledge, who tried to form a Ministry. The House adjourned from day to day, and at last, on July 7, Rutledge returned his commission. On the 12th the Governor granted a dissolution, and the coalition appealed to the country against the Philp-Rutledge party. The result was a sweeping condemnation of the Philpites, and Labor came very nearly winning a majority of the seats without trying to oust any of its political allies.

The election of the fifteenth Parliament, on August 27, 1904, found the following 35 Labor members amongst the winners:—G. Jackson, Kennedy; P. Airey, Flinders; D. Bowman and F. McDonnell, Fortitude Valley; J. H. Dunsford and J. Burrows, Charters Towers; H. Cowan, Fitzroy; T. Dibley, Woollongabba; K. M. Grant, Rockhampton; W. Hamilton, Gregory; H. F. Hardacre, Leichhardt; A. J. Jones, Burnett; F. Kenna, Bowen; G. Kerr, Barcoo; W. Kidston, Rockhampton; E. M. Land, Balonne; V. B. J. Lesina, Clermont; J. Mann, Cairns; G. Martin, Burrum; W. J. R. Maughan, Ipswich; W. Maxwell, Burke; W. Mitchell, Maryborough; D. Mulcahy, Gympie; W. S. Murphy, Croydon; C. F. Neilson, Musgrove; J. Norman, Maryborough; J. O'Brien, Aubigny; C. H. W. Reinhold, Brisbane South; G. Ryland, Gympie; E. Smart, Drayton and Toowomba; H. Turner, Rockhampton North; M. J. R. Woods, Woothakata; T. M. Scott, Murilla; G. P. Barber, Bundaberg; A. J. W. Fudge, Mackay.

Mr. G. Martin died on May 14, 1905, and Mr. J. H. Dunsford on September 15, 1905. These two seats were lost to Labor.

Some very good work was done by the coalition. Important amendments were made in the Electoral Act by a special session held in January, 1905. On January 19, 1906, Premier Morgan resigned and took the position of President of the Legislative Council. Mr. Kidston became Premier. No man ever had such a chance as Kidston to do great work for the masses and the general good of his State. His handling of the finances had given him a name and a position. It was hoped that his old connection with and membership in trade unions would have kept him loyal; but, alas for human frailty, his lack of judgment soon appeared. He got swelled head, and thought he knew more than the combined intelligence of organized Labor. He chafed at the democratic methods of Labor, and desired to run things according to his own sweet will.

Kidston succeeded in splitting the Party. He made an excuse of the adoption of a new objective by the organizations to issue a statement which was signed by Kidston and about a dozen others. A convention was held in March, at which the whole position was discussed, and the independence of the Party asserted. Members had to choose between the straight Labor Party, nominated by duly recognised organizations and elected on the platform of the united bodies, and Mr. Kidston, who had deserted the party and was trying to run his party on the lines of the old politicians. Every chance was given to the "Statement" Party, as they were termed— all of whom were believers in coalition—to put their case, but the big majority was against them. The opinions of leagues and unions were obtained, and Bowman was chosen leader, and fourteen members of the Party stood by the Convention decision.

The elections were held in May, and the result to Labor was as follows:—J. Adamson, Maryborough; G. Barber, Warrego; G. P. Barber, Bundaberg; D. Bowman, Fortitude Valley; W. Hamilton, Gregory; H. F. Hardacre, Leichhardt; J. M. Hunter, Maranoa; A. J. Jones, Burnett; E. M. Land, Balonne; W. Lennon, Herbert; V. B. J. Lesina, Clermont; W. J. R. Maughan, Ipswich; J. May, Flinders; W. Mitchell, Maryborough; D. Mulcahy, Gympie; T. Nevitt, Carpentaria; J. Payne, Mitchell; G. Ryland, Gympie. This made eighteen, but Mr. G. Barber being unseated for the Warrego on petition, the number of the solid Party totalled seventeen. Twelve were members of the old party, only two having been defeated. Of the "Statement" Party twelve disappeared. Five did not run, and seven were rejected, viz., Messrs. Airey, Norman, Scott, Neilson, Murphy, Mann, and Dibley. The parties stood: Opposition 29, Ministerialists 24, Labor 18, Independent 1.

On July 3, 1907, Mr. P. Airey took a seat in the Council, at the same time holding a seat in the Ministry without portfolio. Mr. Geo. Kerr was taken into the Ministry. When the House met on July 23, 1907, there was trouble over the election of Speaker. Under the Electoral Act persons could vote by post, but this had been found so bad and dangerous a method that an attempt was made to amend the Act. The Upper House, true to its instincts, refused to pass such an amendment. Its attitude on this and other proposals caused Mr. Kidston to ask the Governor, Baron Chelmsford, to allow additions to be made to the Council by nominating sufficient members to carry out democratic legislation. His Excellency refused.

On November 12, 1907, Premier Kidston announced that he had resigned owing to the obstructive tactics of the Council. The Governor sent for Philp, who announced his list of Ministers on the 19th. Mr. Kidston moved—'' That the Chairman leave the chair and report no progress,'' and this was carried by 37 to 29, proving clearly that Mr. Philp had no majority and could not carry on, and had no grounds at first for assuring his Excellency that he could. Next day Philp informed the House that his Excellency had granted a dissolution. A motion for the adjournment of the House was rejected by 37 to 26, and supply was refused. On the 22nd, on the motion for supply, Mr. Kidston moved a lengthy amendment, setting out the position in a statement to the Governor. This assured him that Kidston could carry on the business of the country, and was carried by 37 to 27, showing a majority of 10.

In spite of this, the Governor refused to recognise the will of Parliament, and allowed Philp to remain in power, and sent the Parliament to the country. His Excellency not only stood by the conservative Council in its obstruction and ignored the majority in the Assembly, but actually aided Philp in spending the people's money without the authority of Parliament. Over half a million was paid away in this fashion by warrant of the King's representative. Other illegal and unconstitutional doings were condoned and winked at which were a disgrace to any Government.

In order to vote by post it was necessary to sign the ballot paper before a Justice of the Peace as witness. Philp appointed about 400 carefully selected men upon whom he could rely as justices just prior to the election. It was said that the position proved to be worth four guineas per day when the election came on. Labor had scarcely a friend among the justices, and hence was at tremendous disadvantage. The Philpite justice drove around, and hundreds of votes were influenced wrongly by pressure of various kinds. Mine-owners threatened to discharge men who voted against Philp, and thus miners' wives were terrorised into voting against their own political interests and desires. The threats were not idle, as was soon proved at Charters Towers and other places, where men were discharged because they voted for Labor or were active workers for a Labor candidate. This election was a severe trial of the unity of Labor.

When the dissolution came the fight was on a Constitutional point, and hence Labor had no choice but to help Kidston in his stand against the Council and the action of the Governor. It became a Kidston-Labor fight against Philp and the old gang of the boodle party. In order to make it hard for working men to get to the poll, Philp fixed the election day for Wednesday, February 5, 1908. The result, however, proved a victory for constitutional methods, and a direct slap in the face for the Governor. Labor secured twenty-two seats as follows:—E. M. Land, Balonne; J. Huxham, Brisbane South; G. P. Barber, Bundaberg; A. J. Jones, Burnett; W. Hamilton, Gregory; G. Ryland and D. Mulcahy, Gympie; W. Lennon, Herbert; T. Nevitt, Carpentaria; V. Winstanley and J. Mullan, Charters Towers; V. B. J. Lesina, Clermont; H. F. Hardacre, Leichhardt; D. Hunter, Woollongabba; W. Mitchell and J. Adamson, Maryborough; J. Payne, Mitchell; J. H. Coyne, Warrego; J. May, Flinders; D. Bowman and P. A. McLachlan, Fortitude Valley; W. J. R. Maughan, Ipswich. Labor did not lose any of the old members, and gained five new seats. Five of the party were unopposed. Kidston lost two and Philp ten.

On February 18 Philp resigned and Kidston again took office. The House met on March 3, when trouble arose for a second time over the election of Speaker, each of the three parties acting independently. Measures previously rejected by the Council, such as Abolition of the Postal Vote and a Wages Board Bill, were sent up and passed in a short session, after which Mr. Kidston took a trip

to England. Before he left he had paved the way
for joining the party he had so strongly denounced
a month or two previously. He had cunningly
screened Philp by working through hidden in the
Estimates the large sum wrongfully paid by Philp
and the Governor. He had stated that part of his
mission to England was to see the authorities and
have Baron Chelmsford recalled. Nothing further
was heard of it, and immediately upon his return in
October, 1908, he formed an alliance with Philp, and
his downward career as a self-seeking opportunist
has at last landed him amongst the old party which
disgraced political life in Queensland for years,
and against which democracy has had to fight its
way under every disadvantage.

With splendid opportunities for doing good
work for the people, Kidston has turned traitor to
all the principles he at one time so ably advocated.
He has become one with the boodle gang of land
grabbers and railway syndicators, and Labor has
become justified in its refusal to be dragged down
with him. It has a straight path before it, and no
longer can the electors be fooled by supporting the
" as-good-as-Labor " candidate. The outlook is
good, as is indicated by the capture of Bulloo by
Labor candidate B. S. F. Allen at the by-election of
March 27, 1909. The next fight will not be three-
cornered, but will be straight out between Labor
and anti-Labor—between democracy and conservatism—between those who consider the well-being of
the whole against those who act only in the interests
of capitalism. Democracy will win.

In the Queensland nominee Upper House, Labor has two representatives—Messrs. Albert Hinchcliffe and C. S. McGhie—who were called on May 5, 1904.

It is not easy to enumerate the work done by the Labor Party in Queensland. The good done has been rather in what they have prevented the capitalistic gang from doing. Prior to the 1907 elections " The Worker " published the following:—

" A CHAPTER OF BOODLEWRAITH.

" WHEN PHILP WAS KING.

" In 1900, when the Philp Government was in power, a number of syndicate railway proposals were brought before Parliament. The Labor Party at that time had reason to believe that certain agents of the syndicators were exercising corrupt influences on Parliament. It became known that more than one needy Parliamentarian suddenly became flush of funds, and the jest of the Assembly went round, ' Oh, a rich aunt died and left them money.'

" Acting in the belief that there was some cronk work going on in connection with the private syndicate lines, the Labor Party put up a stonewall in the Assembly against the proposals. Philp and his gang, to force the proposals through Parliament, introduced the notorious gag and guillotine rules of procedure.

" These, having been passed by a brutal majority, were at once acted upon, and a number of Labor members having been suspended from the sittings, the syndicators got every concession they required but one, the Normanton-Cloncurry Syndicate Railway.

" In connection with this latter, Harry Daniels supplied the Labor Party with startling evidence, and Kidston put forward a charge that a written offer of money and shares had been made to a certain person possessing influence, as a bribe to induce that person to use such influence in promoting the passing by the Assembly of a bill to authorise the construction and maintenance of the Normanton-Cloncurry Syndicate Railway. The matter was referred to the investigation of his Honor Judge Mansfield, and the following letter was tendered as evidence :—

" ' Beenleigh, Queensland,
" ' November 6, 1899.
" ' Dear Mr. Daniels,
" ' The syndicate I mentioned the other day has now been formed for taking up some copper lodes at Cloncurry in view of the passing of a bill for a railway to that place.

" ' I have arranged for a share for you. The payment is £125 each—that I pay, and should the bill become law, each share receives in ·cash £125, and 650 fully paid-up shares.

" ' I have no doubt that these shares will be worth over £2 each when the company is formed.·

" ' You can see some of the ore now at the Deposit Bank, in Adelaide-street. Any day you are in town I will show it to you.

" ' Yours very truly,

" ' HENRY WITHERS.'

" ' Queensland Club.'

" After fully going into the matter the concluding paragraph of the Judge's report reads:

" ' In my opinion this offer to Daniels was made as a bribe to induce him to abstain from stone-walling himself, and to use his influence to prevent others doing so—that is to say, to induce Daniels, from a hope of pecuniary gain, and not from conviction, to act in such a way as to make the passing of the Railway Bill more probable.

" E. MANSFIELD.

" ' Brisbane, December 11, 1890.'

" Both the Philp and Kidston parties are now in favor of syndicate railways. Electors who realise the corrupting influences of this unholy form of alliance between the State and Capitalism should vote straight for the endorsed Labor candidates on the 18th.' "

Labor got into Parliament just in time to prevent one of the biggest land steals ever attempted in any country. Early in 1893 a syndicate put forward a proposal of a very " taking " kind in more senses

than one. Eleven lines of railway were being
surveyed as follows:—

	Miles.
Charleville to Cunnamulla	125
Charleville to Thargominda	205
Charleville to Western Boundary ..	500
Longreach to Western Boundary ..	420
Longreach to Winton	110
Winton to Hughenden	140
Hughenden to Western Boundary ..	415
Normanton to Cloncurry	250
Granite Creek to Georgetown	185
Georgetown to Croydon	84
Gayndah to Degilbo	40
Total	2474

These were to be constructed under the Railway
Construction (Land Subsidy) Act of 1892. The
conditions briefly were : 1. The railways to remain
the property of the syndicate for fifty years, then to
become the property of the Government. 2. They
may become the property of the Government
immediately they are constructed without any
purchase except that which has already been made
by land grants. 3. They may remain the property
of the syndicate for any period up to ten years, when
in addition to grants of land, the colony must pay
for them. If constructed under number one the
amount of land may equal in value but not exceed
twice the cost of construction; if under condition
number two an amount equalling once the cost of

construction; if under number three once the cost of construction, and at the end of ten years or later, but not previously, a further payment at their value in solid cash.

To show what this meant let us take condition number one which is the most likely to have been agreed upon. The railways in existence had cost on an average £6917 per mile. Averaging these lines at £5000 per mile for 2500 miles, and valuing the land at the rate Mr. McIlwraith had put on it, the grab would have totalled 312,000 square miles, or 200,000,000 acres. Practically this meant securing possession in freehold of about one-half the unalienated lands of the colony, and as the proposed lines were all in good country, with very little waste of ranges, etc., to be taken out, it really meant securing possession of the whole.

The railways already constructed had cost over £16,000,000, and the projected lines were so designed as to take away the trade and divert it to the syndicate lines. The exposure by a gridiron map in " The Worker " and the active propaganda of the Labor members killed the scheme, but had they not been in Parliament there is not the slightest doubt that the scheme would have passed. The country through which the lines were to pass was all held by the squatters and banking companies, and it was intended of course to take this underhand method to secure a freehold title.

Other instances might be quoted if needed to prove how much the State owes to the Labor Party. They had also undoubted influence upon legislation.

But for their efforts the masses would still have been denied voting power.   Adult suffrage, factory acts, early closing, a weekly half-holiday, workers' compensation, shearers' hut accommodation, abolition of black labor, and many other reforms are due to their advocacy.   Though in a minority they became watch dogs of the administration, and put a stop to much of the favoritism constantly practised before.   Queensland will some day realise how much she owes to these pioneers of the path of honest government.

CHAPTER XXI.

VICTORIA.

In the very compact little colony of Victoria the separation of the people politically into two hostile camps took place very early. The first Labor member, Charles Jardine Don, was elected for Collingwood August 26th, 1859, and worked at his trade as a stonemason all day and attended Parliament at night. He was defeated by Graham Berry in August, 1861, by only 46 votes. At a later date Wilson Gray was also looked upon as a Labor man, and the diggers of Ballarat paid the expenses of Duncan Gillies, who afterwards turned out so conservative. In the days of Sir Henry Barkly—1856 to 1863—democratic advance was made, as State-aid to religion was abolished, property qualification for the Assembly was done away with, and manhood suffrage and vote by ballot were introduced. The most exciting time, however, began under Sir Charles Darling—1863 to 1866. The fiscal question had been raised into prominence, and mainly through the continuous and vigorous efforts of the late David Syme in the '' Age '' newspaper, the mass of the people had adopted Protection as the policy of the colony. Right on until the coming into power of the Coalition Government under James Service in March, 1883, we had exciting times and

S

active political thought.   The first Factories Act
was passed in that period.

The squatters had secured the freehold of their
huge estates by various methods of dummying, and
joined with the rich importers in fighting
democracy. The gold diggers had ever been
opposed to the land monopolist, and, as they had
now become wage-workers under mining companies,
they readily took up the cry for Protection to native
industries with the desire that an avenue of
employment should be found which would keep
their children out of the unhealthy and dangerous
mines. The wealthy class were revenue tariffists.
They called themselves "Freetraders," but as they
were, and are still, opposed to direct taxation they
were not prepared to accept free ports.

Entrenched in the Legislative Council the rich
minority resisted the masses in every step taken in
legislation. As employers they used the boycott at
every opportunity. In 1879 I was president of the
Creswick Branch of the National Reform and
Protection League, and Mr. W. Hogg was secretary.
Mr. Hogg made his living as a carrier of goods from
the railway to the mines. The chairman of the
leading mines in the Creswick district, together with
the legal manager, went to Ballarat and called upon
all the foundries and other business people with
whom they had dealings, and instructed them not to
consign any goods through Mr. Hogg. Thus they
intended to starve him out of the district because
he honestly differed in political opinion from the
class of men dominating the mines. Many similar

cases could be quoted. The ukase was only withdrawn when the A.M.A. took up the case and threatened strike.

Old residents of Victoria will remember " Black Wednesday," January 8, 1878. Graham Berry had included £18,000 for payment of members in the Appropriation Bill in order to force the Council to pass it. The Council rejected the Bill, and there were no funds to pay the " curled darlings," as the late Higinbotham termed the Civil Service officials of the day. The Government sacked the heads of departments, the judges, police magistrates, Crown prosecutors, etc., and there was much lamentation in the land. The poor wage-slaves may be discharged by the thousand, but not a word of sympathy is accorded them ; but a terrific storm arose over putting the well-paid out of office and employment.

The history of that period is highly interesting, but space forbids more than touching on it. Sir Charles Darling was recalled in 1866 over the fight with the Council. Berry came in in 1877, and after his struggle with the House of political fossils he and Pearson were sent to England to ask for an amendment of the Constitution. They were reminded that Victoria was a self-governing colony, and must work out its own salvation, politically and otherwise. The Upper House still sits as an incubus on democratic government.

The Liberal Party of the seventies was the Labor Party of that period insofar as class feeling and class interests dominated. Mr. Berry organized leagues all over Victoria prior to the election of 1877. The great and important difference between the Liberal Party and the Labor Party of to-day lies in the fact that the Liberal policy and platform were and are made by politicians, whilst those of the Labor Party are made by the organized unions and leagues at an annual conference. Reform is initiated by the people in the case of Labor, but is kept in the control of politicians in the case of the Liberal Party. The fact that there is practically no difference between the two old parties is proved by the way they have come together whenever there has been a domocratic awakening of the people. This coming together has always been against the welfare of the masses and in favor of the classes.

The idea of the workers selecting their own mates and sending them to Parliament was slow in evolving. In 1880 we selected the general secretary of the A.M.A. (Mr. Henry Taylor) to run for Creswick and Clunes, the workers undertaking his expenses. I put in a fortnight's work and a fortnight's wages to help, but we failed to secure his election. March, 1883, brought in the Coalition under James Service. It came because of sectarianism, one of the great curses with which the masses are still afflicted. The plea was that it was necessary to combine to prevent the Catholics getting a separate grant for their schools.

When politicians want to do a thing they always find an excuse. The cry of "The Education Act in danger" served as well or better in that case than any other. It diverted attention from the real issues

which were ripe for settlement, calmed down
political excitement, and incidentally, of course,
enabled leading politicians to secure a lengthy
tenure of office at good pay and under easy, peaceful
conditions. Service held office till February, 1886,
when the Gillies Coalition Government took charge,
and they hung on until 5th November, 1890.

Alfred Deakin was called for by the country
when Gillies took office, and effort was made to
revive the old Liberal Party, but he took the easy
way and joined the continuous Government, whose
motto was three P's—Peace, Progress, and
Prosperity. What irony lay under that motto was
soon to come to the people in the shock, misery, and
ruin of the financial disaster of 1893, which followed
the land boom. The three P's suited the gamblers
finely, as it gave the people confidence, lulled them
into security, and enabled the swindlers to work the
confidence game to the tune of millions. It was a
period of capitalism run mad without let or
hindrance. The Gillies-Deakin crew ran the show
during the maritime trouble. Being great lovers of
peace and comfort they got so scared because a
few trade unionists arranged for a public meeting
that they called nearly the whole military forces out,
as detailed elsewhere.

Victoria's practical start came in 1891. A
vacancy occurred in Collingwood owing to the death
of Mr. Langridge, and one of the leading unionists
in connection with the Trades Hall was asked to run
for the seat. A short Platform was drawn up by
the local committee, and on April 17, 1891, Mr. John

Hancock was elected by a big majority. It was then resolved that a Labor political organization should be formed, representing the whole colony. The following met on May 30:—Trades Hall Council, Messrs. Winter and Wylie; Ballarat Trades Council, Messrs. Hurdsfield and Wilson; Bendigo Trades Council, Messrs. Thomas and Egan; Geelong Trades Council, Messrs. Shepherd and Redmond; Shearers' Union, Messrs. Temple and Slattery; Amalgamated Miners' Association, Messrs. Lawn and Hunter; Social Democratic Federation, Mr. Flinn. The Knights of Labor asked for representation, but were refused on account of being a secret society. Mr. Joseph Winter acted as chairman, and Mr. D. Bennett as secretary. They sat for three days, and agreed upon the formation of an organization to be called the "Progressive Political League." The annual subscription was fixed at not less than one shilling, and seventeen rules were drafted for its government. The platform consisted of four planks.

This Platform was approved and adopted by the Trades Hall Council on June 1, 1891. On being submitted to the Executive Council of the Amalgamated Miners' Association, that body would not adopt it as drafted, but added a plank, "Maintenance of the Education Act," which, of course, put the A.M.A. outside the political Labor movement— where it remained till 1909, owing to the conservatism of its leaders. Such a plank was unnecessary in the first place, and would have led to disunion in the A.M.A. and other unions. But for the action of the narrow-minded bigots on the executive of the A.M.A.

at that time, Labor would have been in a much stronger position to-day in Victoria, and, incidentally, many lives of miners would have been saved, as better mining legislation would have been secured. It is only recently that the country electorates have returned Labor members, and that fact is due, not to the A.M.A., but to the A.W.U.

The Parliament of 1889 contained two members who could be classed as Labor men, Dr. Maloney and W. A. Trenwith. Mr. Beazley was also a member, and he joined in the new movement. Mr. Hancock (the first member elected on a straight-out Labor platform) was added in 1891, and in the elections of April 20, 1892, the following were elected under the new Platform:—W. D. Beazley, Collingwood; F. H. Bromley, Carlton; J. B. Burton, Stawell; W. T. Carter, Williamstown; W. Maloney, Melbourne West; J. Murray, Warrnambool; S. Samuel, Dundas; W. A. Trenwith, Richmond; J. Winter, Melbourne South; D. R. Wylie, Melbourne North. This made ten in a House of 90. Samuel died on July 28, and his seat was lost. Mr. Trenwith was appointed leader of the party, and Mr. Bromley secretary. The party and the movement lost a splendid man in D. R. Wylie, who died on May 10, 1893.

The elections turned largely on the subjects set out in the Labor Platform. Mr. Shiels practically jumped the Platform, and the country sent him back with a very large majority. He was like most of the politicians of the old school—great in talk, but very forgetful after the elections were over. Shiels took office in February, 1892, but did nothing to carry out his promises, and in January, 1893, the Patterson

Government came in. The result of the policy of
the three P's party was evidenced by a statement
made by Mr. Patterson that on January 23, 1893,
15,857 persons were registered as unemployed.

This was the time everything was booming,
according to the land gamblers. On a want of confidence motion moved by Mr. G. Turner being carried
against him, Patterson secured a dissolution, went
to the country, and lost. At this election, September
20, 1894, Labor secured sixteen seats, as follows:—
J. G. Barrett, Carlton South; W. D. Beazley, Colling-
wood; F. H. Bromley, Carlton; J. N. Hume Cook,
East Brunswick Boroughs; W. A. Hamilton,
Sandhurst; J. Hancock, Footscray; J. Murray,
Warrnambool; G. M. Prendergast, Melbourne North;
G. Sangster, Port Melbourne; T. Smith, Emerald
Hill; J. Styles, Williamstown; W. A. Trenwith,
Richmond; E. Wilkins, Collingwood; J. Winter,
Melbourne South; J. B. Burton, Stawell; W.
Maloney, Melbourne West.

The sixteenth Parliament opened on October 4,
1894, Mr. (now Sir) George Turner having taken
office on September 27. This was the great
retrenchment Government, and it started its policy
with fifteen Ministers—ten with portfolios, and five
without. The seven years of political peace had
brought on the land boom. The land boom had
produced the bank and other smashes and ruined
things generally, and now, to complete things, the
Turner Government cut salaries and stopped incre-
ments of the poorly paid, and started on the job
with fifteen Ministers for the Government of a

G. M. PRENDERGAST, M.L.A.,
Leader of Victorian Labor Party.

million people. They tried to cut members' allowances down to £200, but the House, on the casting vote of the Chair, made it £240. By sweating the public servants and letting public works stand still Turner made ends meet, and got the name of being a great Treasurer.

The right thing for Governments to do is to spend public money and carry out public works in times when private enterprise is in a bad way and unemployed are numerous, but all our Governments hitherto have reversed that method. When there are hard times, they make it worse by curtailing the purchasing power of the public service, and by discharging all the hands they can struggle along without. It is entirely a capitalistic method, and will go on until the people are wise enough to put in a Government whose training has been of the opposite kind.

The elections of October 14, 1897, returned the following direct Labor members:—W. D. Beazley and E. Wilkins, Collingwood; F. H. Bromley, Carlton; J. B. Burton, Stawell; J. Hancock, Footscray; W. Maloney, Melbourne West; J. Murray, Warrnambool; G. Sangster, Port Melbourne; T. Smith, Emerald Hill; J. Styles, Williamstown; W. A. Trenwith, Richmond; J. B. Tucker, Melbourne South; W. A. Hamilton, Sandhurst. Mr. Beazley was Chairman of Committees from 1897 until 1903, when he was elected Speaker, a position he held until June, 1904. One of the staunchest fighters and most popular of men died on November 22, 1899, in the person of Jack Hancock.

The eighteenth Parliament was elected on November 1, 1900, and Labor secured the following seats:—W. D. Beazley, Collingwood; J. B. Billson, Fitzroy; F. H. Bromley, Carlton; J. B. Burton, Stawell; E. Findley, Melbourne; Dr. W. Maloney, Melbourne West; G. M. Prendergast, Melbourne North; G. Sangster, Port Melbourne; T. Smith, Emerald Hill; W. A. Trenwith, Richmond; J. B. Tucker, Melbourne South; E. Warde, Essendon and Flemington; E. Wilkins, Collingwood. The temptations of office proved stronger than Labor principles in the case of two members, as Messrs. Trenwith and Burton both left the party and joined the Turner Ministry. They also helped to oust Mr. Findley on June 25, 1901—an act which shows how quickly men become degraded under an evil environment. Mr. Bromley was appointed leader and Mr. Billson secretary of the party.

Turner kept the Treasury benches for five years and seventy days. McLean then squeezed him out for eleven months, but he came back again on November 15, 1900. When Sir Geo. Turner went to the Federal Parliament, Peacock, who had been in both Turner's Ministries, took the Premiership in February, 1901. During the reign of Peacock an incident occurred worth more than passing notice.

One of the most noticeable characteristics of the wealthy classes in Australia is their snobbishness. They have the slave's instincts strongly developed. They would crawl in the dust if royalty, or aristocracy, would only condescend to look at them. Behind this snobbishness lies faith in force and coercion to curb the masses. The slightest criticism of anybody in authority or high position is utter blasphemy and disloyalty. Remarks about royalty which would be taken no notice of in England by anybody will render the person uttering them in Australia liable to severe penalty if the snobs can only move the authorities.

"The Irish People" had published an article adversely criticising royalty. The writer and proprietor was a member of the mother of Parliaments—the House of Commons. The attention of the authorities was called to the article, and they seized the unsold copies found in the office of the paper. The Government at the head of the Empire saw no occasion to go farther. Copies of "The Irish People" came to Australia. The article was reprinted in the "Southern Cross," of Adelaide. With a view of hitting at the manager (Mr. J. V. O'Loghlin, M.L.C.), a Liberal, some busybody sent a copy to the Governor, but he took no action, and nothing was done.

In Melbourne, a small Labor paper called the "Tocsin" had been struggling along under difficulties. It did not have a wide circle of readers, and was certainly not powerful enough to burst up the British Empire. It had various editors at this time. In its issue of June 20, 1901, appeared the article from "The Irish People," with comments severely condemning the article in question, and showing how wrong and foolish that sort of writing was. Late that evening a man from the conservative organ of Victoria, the "Argus," waited on the

Premier (Sir A. J. Peacock) and called his attention
to the fact that the article had been published, and
that the imprint on the paper showed that the name
of Mr. E. Findley, who had just before been elected
to the Assembly for Melbourne as a Labor man,
appeared as owner of the " Tocsin."

Sir Aleck said he would see his legal advisers
as to what could be done. Having been decorated
by a bit of ribbon and secured a handle to his name,
he was simply bursting with what he imagined was
loyalty, but which another term would more
correctly express. He urged the " Argus " to say
nothing until he moved. This did not suit the organ
of the classes, however, and next morning it called
attention to the article, and people who had never
heard of the little " Tocsin " rushed around to buy
a copy. Mr. Findley first knew of the article by
reading of it in the " Argus," and at once stopped
the further circulation of the " Tocsin." Newsagents
had sent in for copies. As much as a shilling had
been offered for a single copy, as people thought it
must be very wicked, and wanted to read it. Neither
the " Argus " nor anybody else outside a few of the
snobocracy were much troubled or affected by
anything the " Tocsin " might say, but they were
curious.

Poor Sir Aleck! He was not able to sleep. He
felt that something awful would happen to the King
if he did not do something. The Empire was in
danger, and he cabled at once to Joe Chamberlain.
Whether this was for advice or contained an assur-
ance that he would defend the King with his heart's
blood did not appear. Chamberlain was duly stirred,

and cabled his reply, which, though marked "secret and confidential," Sir Aleck was willing to let his friends see privately if they wished. He was willing to show everything privately, but would not give the House the benefit of it, which was a curious way to treat a thing marked "secret and confidential."

The House met on June 18, 1901. So soon as the preliminaries were over, Sir Aleck arose and made a statement about the matter. He had the resolution ready for the expulsion of Findley, but before it was moved someone hinted it might be as well to hear what the culprit had to say. Findley was allowed to make a statement, and he told them of the fact that he had nothing to do with the article. He did not know it was published until he saw it in the "Argus." He did not approve of it, and at once stopped the issue. He could do no more than that, and expressed his regret and apologised for its appearance. Less than that would have satisfied the House of Commons or the House of Lords, but the snobbish majority of the Victorian Parliament was lost to all sense of justice or common sense. Sir Aleck moved the following resolution:—

"That the honorable member for Melbourne, Mr. Edward Findley, being the printer and publisher of a newspaper known as the 'Tocsin,' in the issue of which on the 20th inst. there is published a seditious libel regarding His Majesty the King, is guilty of disloyalty to His Majesty, and committed an act discreditable to the honor of Parliament, and that he therefore be expelled this House."

It was all rigged up beforehand. It was a shocking thing for the heart of Melbourne City to be represented by a Labor man. It was made doubly bad when the Labor man was a Catholic in religion. If he could be got rid of there was no chance of his re-election, as at a by-election the property-owners, by their plural voting, could simply swamp the residential votes and put in the chosen of the " Argus." This was the plot, and Peacock was a pliant tool in the hands of the conservatives. It was appropriate that Sir Sam. Gillott, since exposed for another matter, seconded the motion, and in view of later developments it was not surprising that Mr. Irvine strongly supported. He spoke bitterly, and Mr. Prendergast interjected, " And you are a relative of John Mitchell."

Findley had been turned out of the House during the debates. Amendments less drastic were suggested, such as a week's suspension, but nothing less than capital punishment would suit the hypocritical snobs who, under pretence of extreme loyalty to the King, tried to hide the fact that their real desire was to get rid of a Labor member. An amendment suspending Findley for the session was lost, 17 voting for it and 64 against. Amongst those who perpetrated this gross injustice were the two Labor rats, Trenwith and Burton, who were members of the Peacock Ministry.

Findley was expelled, and a good conservative elected in his place. To the credit of the Victorian people, however, they elected Mr. Findley to the Commonwealth Senate at the first opportunity, a position he fills with credit and ability. Had Peacock not expelled Findley it is pretty certain that he would not have lost the Premiership when Iceberg Irvine moved his no confidence motion the following year, as the Labor Party voted with him. Mr. Boyd, who took Findley's seat for Melbourne, voted with the Tory Irvine, and the motion was only carried by three votes.

If Sir A. J. Peacock was sincere in his desire to uphold the honor of Parliament in the case of the " Tocsin " he has sadly degenerated since, as his recent connection with bribery and mining swindles proves. He has been exposed in the House and in the Courts; but he did not resign, nor did the Premier take any action to have him expelled. It all goes to show that there must not be even the semblance of evil on the part of a Labor member, but members of the other parties may do anything 'without its being considered a disgrace.

About this time the great agitation took place for reform of Parliament. All Peacock's Ministers, with one exception, had placed their resignations in his hands so that he could cut out some of the Ministers. It turned out, however, that they had post-dated their resignations five months ahead. W. H. Irvine, since known as " Iceberg Irvine," secured control of Victorian affairs on June 3, 1902. He became famous—and in some quarters infamous —for his Coercion Bill to put down the railway men who went on strike in his reign. The engine-drivers had in vain appealed to have their just grievances considered, and at last resorted to the good old industrial weapon of a strike. They decided to stop the wheels from going round, and to leave the people to walk if they desired to travel.

Irvine posed as the cool, strong man, able to put down insurrection. He was as cold as a Russian despot, and took the world-old method of the tyrant-minded—that of force. The Trades Hall Council of Melbourne is technically simply a committee to look after the affairs of the hall as a place of meeting with rooms to let. In practice it takes up industrial matters in an advisory way, but has no real power to make an organization do anything. In the railway service of the State there were a number of organizations, and these had been affiliated with the Trades Hall for about seventeen years. No complaint had been made or trouble caused by this connection. There had been unrest in the service owing to several causes. Heavy retrenchment by the Turner Government was one thing, and there were many grievances which ought to have been adjusted.

Instead of providing a remedy for the grievances, the Irvine-Bent Ministry issued a decree that every union of railway men affiliated with the Trades Hall Council must at once withdraw from same, under penalty of dismissal from the service. No reason was assigned, and the several executives declined to accede to the order. Mr. Irvine met them, but was unable to point out any justification for the order. He gave them a night to think it over. His Ministry gave them five days' grace, but the men not only refused to give up their freedom, but on May 8, 1903, the locomotive drivers came out on strike. Of course there was excitement. The public—who forget that their lives depend upon the character and ability of the man on the engine, and who howled for cutting his wages so as to save their pockets—then kicked because they were put to inconvenience by the act of a tyrannical Government.

Every effort was made to keep the trains going. Old drivers who had been discharged for drunkenness and incapacity were put on, with the promise of a permanent job. All sorts were raked up—in short, the usual scum which turns up when a few pounds can be got by doing any sort of mean and dirty work. The Government offered all sorts of bribes—even double pay and a £50 bonus—to influence men to go to work, but failed to get many. In a state of panic the " strong man " called Parliament together. His Attorney-General and himself had raked the laws of the world for ideas sufficiently drastic to satisfy the minds of those who hate a trade union worse than poison, and who would prefer to have all workers slaves without any liberty.

Victoria has become so degenerate since the days of the Eureka fight that it had elected a Parliament the majority of which voted for the most drastic and extreme Coercion Act which could possibly be drafted. The House met on May 13. The Iceberg spoke first. Sir A. Peacock, leader of the Opposition, also spoke, and with bitterness against the men. He moved an amendment that Parliament pledge itself to remedy their grievances if they would give in and go back to work. This did not suit the hungry wolves behind the Iceberg. The amendment was defeated by 58 to 30. The debate went on, and a splendid fight for freedom was put

T

up by Labor members. From a brilliant and impressive address delivered by Labor-member Frank Anstey, I quote the following:—

"I say beware before you let hatred and hostility carry you too far. Look well into the pages of history, and see how futile and trifling have been the results of the strong arm of authority. It has achieved nothing—realised nothing; it has left the sting of bitterness that years have not eradicated. The hand of fellowship and human love have done more than all the Coercion Acts that ever existed. You can achieve nothing by coercion. Spread throughout the country in every little hamlet there will be a man whose heart bears the sting, fearing to express himself, but feeling an intense hatred that nothing will ever be able to kill but years—long years. You do not govern your country well when you do these things!"

The debate continued until early on the morning of the 15th. It was then interrupted by the Premier making an announcement that he had received a communication from the executive of the union that they had called the strike off. There was apparently no longer any need for the Coercion Act, as the employees had given in to everything the Government had asked; but still Irvine went on with the measure, only changing it to meet future contingencies. The second reading was carried by 66 to 18. By 3 o'clock on the morning of May 19 the bill had passed. It was brought on again that afternoon, and another fight was put up by the Labor brigade, but the brutal majority passed it. It went to the Council, the members of which, true to their traditions where anything calculated to crush Labor is concerned, passed the measure through all its stages in an hour or two.

It is not worth while now discussing the wisdom or otherwise of the men coming out, nor of why they gave in so readily when they had gone on strike and were so well backed up outside. It is on occasions like these that we get a glimpse of the kind of men set up to govern us. They then come out in their true colors, and prove how tyrannically inclined they are towards organized Labor. In the past it has been quite common for employers to try to direct what their workmen shall do when off duty. A favorite plan is to try to control their political opinions. It is quite common for mining companies to use influence in this way, and in many cases they let it be known that only those who will vote as the board directs will get work. Sometimes a mine official will stand at the door of the pay office and collect cash from each man as he goes out to help the political campaign of the party supported by the capitalist. Every man knows that he will lose his job if he fails to drop in his shilling. Nothing is said, but men can read signs, and the foreman or someone allows it to leak out. They attempt also to control the workmen in other matters, such as how they spend their leisure, what shops they patronise, what lodge they belong to, and even their religion. In short, the tendency under the wage system is for employers to look upon the worker as being owned by them—as a slave who has no rights and no freedom. Governments have the same tendency.

They refuse citizen rights to their employees. In a
number of ways they control their actions when off
duty. This is manifestly wrong. The workman
enters into a contract with the State under certain
promises of advance and increased pay, etc., and in
return has specific duties to perform during specified hours and in specified places. His time off duty
should be his own, like that of any other private
citizen. If he wishes to join a union he should be at
liberty to do so. If his union wishes to take part in
any forward movement for the benefit of the masses
generally, why should it be prevented? The State
is only concerned in what requests it may make upon
the department in which the members are employed.

Not content with humiliating the men and with
forfeiting very large sums, due, some of them, as
retiring allowance, the Irvine Government carried
their bitterness so far as to place the whole public
service of the State on a different footing to
persons employed in any other capacity. They
disfranchised the whole service, and in order to
render them practically powerless allowed them
separate representation—the railway men to elect
two men to Parliament, the rest of the public service
one. It is satisfactory to know that this only lasted
for one Parliament. Irvine retired on February 16,
1904, and Mr. Thomas Bent took charge. Since then
Irvine disappeared from the State Parliament, his
Act regarding special representation has been
repealed, and the railway and public service employees put on the same footing as ordinary citizens.
His name will ever be associated with coercion, and

in the hearts of railway men and others the bitterness engendered by him will remain, as Anstey foretold, for " years—long years."

Public opinion was so strongly against the treatment meted out to the Victorian railway men that when a strike took place recently in New South Wales, where the whole State-owned tramway service went out, the capitalistic Government under Mr. Wade dared not go so far as to talk of a Coercion Act. The strike there was treated in the same way as if it had been under a private company.

The 1902 elections took place on October 1, and resulted as follows:—F. Anstey, East Bourke Boroughs; W. D. Beazley and E. Wilkins, Collingwood; J. W. Billson, Fitzroy; F. H. Bromley, Carlton; G. A. Elmslie, Albert Park; Dr. W. Maloney, Melbourne West; T. Smith, Emerald Hill; G. M. Prendergast, Melbourne North; J. B. Tucker, Melbourne South; E. C. Warde, Essendon and Flemington. Dr. Maloney retired and went to the Commonwealth Parliament on November 16, 1903, and Mr. T. Tunnecliffe took his place on December 21. Mr. G. E. Roberts was elected for Richmond on the same date.

The twentieth Parliament was elected on June 1st, 1904. Labor came out as follows:—F. Anstey, Brunswick; H. E. Beard, Jika Jika; W. D. Beazley, Abbotsford; H. S. Bennett, Ballarat; G. A. Elmslie, Albert Park; J. W. Billson, Fitzroy; F. H. Bromley, Carlton; W. H. Colechin, Geelong; J. Lemmon, Williamstown; D. C. McGrath, Grenville; A. R. Outtrim, Maryborough; G. M. Prendergast, North Melbourne; D. Smith, Bendigo West; E. Wilkins,

Collingwood; E. C. Warde, Flemington; M. Hannah and R. Solly, representing the railway men. D. Gaunson had been elected by the Public Service and had signed the platform, but failed to stick to his pledges. Mr. G. M. Prendergast was elected leader on June 7, 1904, and Mr. Elmslie secretary, positions still held by both. Prior to this election the number of members had been reduced from 95 to 68. Two seats were secured in the Legislative Council—Mr. W. J. Evans, representing the Public Service and Railways; and Mr. A. McLellan, who won a seat in the ordinary way.

For the twenty-first Parliament, elected March 15, 1907, fourteen seats were secured in the Assembly and two in the Council:—F. Anstey, Brunswick; W. D. Beazley, Abbotsford; J. W. Billson, Fitzroy; F. H. Bromley, Carlton; G. A. Elmslie, Albert Park; T. Glass, Bendigo East; J. Lemmon, Williamstown; D. C. McGrath, Grenville; A. R. Outtrim, Maryborough; G. M. Prendergast, North Melbourne; D. Smith, Bendigo West; G. Sangster, Port Melbourne; T. Tunnecliffe, Eaglehawk; E. C. Warde, Flemington. For the Council: W. J. Evans, Melbourne North; A. McLellan, Melbourne East. The striking out of the special representation clauses had reduced the numbers to 65 in the Assembly and 34 in the Council. The party was added to by Mr. Cotter winning Richmond on October 2, 1908. The party suffered a loss by the death of Mr. F. H. Bromley, but his seat was secured by Mr. R. Solly November 23, 1908.

When resigning the Premiership Mr. Irvine gave ill-health as the reason. The capitalistic section, known as the "Flinders Lane crowd," who are mainly importers, led by Mr. Butler, raised a subscription of £2000, which they presented to Mrs. Irvine. This was in recognition of Irvine's great achievements in coercion and in trying to prevent any more wages boards being appointed; also that he had cut a shilling a week off the poor old age pensioners! He also lowered the sum upon which income tax could be collected, so as to cut into the workers' wages. "The Bacchus Marsh Express" said: "Every chapter in the history of the Irvine Government is a disgrace to the whole of Victoria."

The six year period following the advent of Irvine will be found to correspond in many respects with that of the Continuous Government in Queensland. There is this difference, however. In Queensland the masses were denied votes, and were not a party to the corruption practised by Government. In Victoria the people have had votes for years, but have been apathetic, and so dominated by side issues that they have condoned anything. A State which could return a man like Bent with a majority has become degraded in its public life. Its standard of political morality has become so lowered as strongly to emphasise the need for as much watchfulness over the actions of Parliamentarians as over those of one's own children.

Tom Bent has been the laughing-stock of Victorians for some years. His erratic buffoonery and coarse vulgarity have been in evidence wherever he went, whilst his connection with various schemes of land speculation has been often exposed. When Minister for Railways in 1888 he declined to adopt

the recommendation of the engineer to purchase
outright the Kensington Hill. Earth was wanted for
filling in at North Melbourne Station. He could have
got the hill, a block of 160 acres, for £52,000, but
refused. A syndicate secured it for £48,000, and
Bent made the railway department pay £20,000 for
the earth which was removed in cutting down the
hill. The value of the land was increased to £74,250
by the removal of the hill. In a later case of
purchase of gravel from land held by Mrs. Bent, a
Select Committee was appointed to investigate.
It whitewashed him at that time. His connection
with other land purchases was not above suspicion.

The fact is that the capitalistic system has so
saturated people with its immoral teaching and
practices that to make money by using inside knowledge, and pulling the wires so as to produce
favorable results for one's own pockets are considered smart and really creditable things. When
reference is made to such conduct on the part of a
public man you too often get the reply: '' Oh, well,
why shouldn't he make money when he gets the
chance? They all do it if they get a show.'' If
Victoria does not wake up we shall soon have the
worst evils of American '' graft '' ruling political
life in the State. When Sir A. J. Peacock stood for
election he said on the public platform that when a
man came to speak of Bent he must put his hand to
his nose—indicating the smellful nature of much of
Bent's work—yet before the end of that Parliament
he had turned round on his promises and joined
Bent's Ministry. He had got so used to smellful jobs

that he failed to notice any longer the disagreeable odor around his leader.

The history of Bentism, if ever written, will be interesting. I have space for a few points only. His was the continuous Government which began with Irvine and came out of the Kyabram alleged reform movement. Careless and ignorant as the people are, Bent could only cling to office by placating critics—by giving them billets. He fooled electors with promises which were never kept, and retained support by a distribution of favors. Of the eleven in his Ministry in 1904, only three beside himself remained at the end of 1908. The found-outs had been got rid of, and new men put in to keep them quiet.

Owing to a charge being made against the Minister for Lands on January 27, 1903, a Select Committee was appointed to inquire into Mr. McKenzie's conduct of that important department. They condemned his action, and he resigned his seat. McKenzie had taken office in June, 1902, and lost no time in looking after himself. He held some 14,000 acres of land, and wanted 7300 acres adjoining. He secured it, and immediately sublet 25,000 acres, including both areas, to a Mr. Hugh Ross for £1000 a year. McKenzie paid about £25 to the Crown. The sub-letting was contrary to the practice of the department, and in contravention of minutes issued by McKenzie himself. The Department always forfeited a lease if it was sublet. He also took up a lease of 10,200 acres under grazing license, and, as Minister, refused another applicant for the block. A colleague became aware of it and warned him against this, and so he gave up the block, but at once got a friend who was a law student to apply for the same block in his behalf. The Minister ordered it to be granted to his dummy.

Another block of 13,400 acres was refused to a man named Findley, though he was the only applicant so far as the officers of the Department knew. The Minister directed refusal, and said Findley's was not the highest offer. When the officer pointed out that he was the only applicant, the Minister said he had another application in his bag. This was from his own son. The block was let to a man who was only acting as agent for his son.

The Select Committee dealt very gently with McKenzie, although they could do no other than condemn him. In one clause they say, " Your committee finds that he has failed to realise his position as a trustee of the public lands for the people of the State." Before the Committee, as also in his letter sending in his resignation, McKenzie claims to have been unconscious of wrong-doing, and asserts that he had no evil intent. His case is an example of the blunted moral perceptions resultant from our social environment. Trained to think it right to grab all he could get by slipping in before a competitor, he saw no wrong in using his position as Minister to feather his own nest at the expense of injustice to another man. Contrast the conduct of the Irvine-Bent-Peacock gang in Labor-member Findley's case with their action about one of their own Ministers. They refused even to censure the latter, but they expelled Findley for no offence at all.

The Hon. Robert Reid, M.L.C., was one of the first Ministers who had to go because of his firm having been bowled out as the perpetrators of extensive frauds on the Commonwealth Customs. On December 4, 1906, Sir S. Gillott resigned his position in the Ministry. He had been Chief Secretary, and it was his business to see that all evil places such as brothels were put down. Instead, it was disclosed that he was lending money to a notorious madame who was head of a house of ill-fame. His idea of morality was that he had nothing to do with the character of those he lent money to so long as the security was all right. That is, of course, strictly correct according to commercial ethics.

Other Ministers were mixed up in things at least suspicious. The Government policy was supposed to be that of preference to Australian-made articles of all kinds. In the face of this we find the Minister of Education (Mr. Sachse, M.L.C.) giving a contract for German pianos when he could have obtained Australian at nearly the same cost. Swinburne, Minister for Water Supply, imported machinery when a better and more suitable plant could have been got in the State for £3000 less cost. It evidently suited the Minister to break away from the declared policy of the country, and the true reason of why it did may never come out. No sane person accepts the alleged explanations in either case. Bentism is commercialism. Self first—the people only as a means to an end.

Without giving the Closer Settlement Board a chance to look into it, Bent purchased the Werribee Estate for £301,781—23,214 acres at £13 per acre.

It will probably cost £20 per acre to get it ready for irrigation. That was two years ago, and no new settlers have been put on it yet. He paid £8000 for 30 acres at Thornby, and £31,450 for Maribyrnong estate—in both cases more than what the Closer Settlement Board considered their value. He proposed to spend three or four millions in the purchase of a million acres in the western district. No wonder land values have gone up 30 per cent., and it is probably true, as asserted, that Bentism has put £20,000,000 into the pockets of the already rich big landowners of Victoria.

At last on 3rd December, 1908, a vote of want of confidence was carried by a majority of twelve, but that did not shift Bent. He asked the Governor for a dissolution, and, strange to say, he got it. The Parliament was young, and the House had not been tried. What sort of tale he narrated to the Governor it would be interesting to know. No supply had been granted, and so we had a repetition of Lord Chelmsford's action in Queensland when he sent to the country a Parliament in which there was a majority in favor of carrying on. Bent paid over £120,000 without authority.

The revelations which finally led to Bent's downfall should not have surprised those who had hitherto kept him in power. He had always been dabbling in land, buying under suspicious circumstances. He had taken over the Mont Park estate at £40 per acre, when land as good could be got for £25. The Chirnside estate was taken at £17 per acre, when it was valued for Land Tax purposes at £1. The thing they could not stand was when the truth came out about the construction of the electric tramline, St. Kilda to Brighton. In 1903 Bent tried to get Irvine to agree to the construction of the line, but without avail. He and a few friends had purchased 25 acres eight months previously, and knew how a line would raise prices. When Bent became Premier he brought in a Bill on 15th November, 1904, for the construction of a portion of the line.

All works costing over £20,000 have by law to go before the Standing Committee on Public Works. Bent got over this by doing the line in three jobs of £19,500, £8000, and £6500 respectively. Thus the law was actually broken, as the total cost was £34,000. While the bill was before the House the course of the line was changed, so that it eventually passed right through Bent's 25 acres. Bent paid £6562 for the land, and after the tramline came he asked £4 per foot for it, which, allowing for cutting up, gave him a profit of 200 per cent., or £13,670. When the bill was before the House he volunteered the statement that he had not a foot of land at the Red Bluff or near it. He thus deliberately misled the House as well as dodged the Act requiring all works over £20,000 to go before the Committee, and all this for personal gain.

How far other transactions brought gain or otherwise is hard to say, and may or may not be discovered, but it is clear that a State which could return such a man time after time has but a low state of public opinion. Its politics may be measured by the reply given by Labor rat Wilkins in Collingwood when asked why he voted for Bent. It was

because he had given a railway to Collingwood, and
removed the guarantee required against loss. Also
he had given the money for the covering of a drain
and granted land for a park.   Thus is shameless
bribery condoned, and gutter politics glorified.
Meantime land monopoly increases and the unemployed multiply, but Ministers are too busy scheming
to get into and hold on to office to do anything for
the good of the people as a whole.

The only party with a programme or thought-out
policy is that of Labor, but there is much educational
work to be done ere the people realise that there are
higher ideals than getting money out of the taxpayers' pocket to cover the dirty drains of their own
neglected neighborhood.   Property owners have
hitherto ruled in city, town, and shire, and their
policy is to tax the other fellow and improve their
own property and its rent-producing powers by
public funds or any other scheme which keeps their
own incomes untouched. Governments like Bent's,
which divide up the surplus revenue of good years
as bribes to constituencies, are exactly the kind of
Government they like. They look upon the Labor
agitator as a public nuisance and a danger to the
existing order of things. The Liberal who comes
round with promises of largesse is the man for them.

The wage slave who is not an active member of a
Labor League or affiliated Union is so mentally lazy
that he either takes his cue from his boss or the
press. He never attends a meeting of any kind, and
sometimes does not know the difference between a
State and Federal election. He can talk sport, but
never reads a book on any intelligent subject, and

never does any thinking. There are thousands in the big cities whom this description will fit, and it is not easy to reach them. They are conservative by instinct. Some of them are in Trade Unions, but do little beyond grumbling if the officers fail to secure advantages for them. About the only thing to wake them up a bit is to be out of employment. It gets into their thick skulls then that the existing order of things is not exactly going right. It takes a long time to educate such men to understand that the wage system is itself wrong, and must be abolished.

The elections took place on December 29th, 1908, and Labor came out with twenty-one members. All retiring members were re-elected and six additional: —F. Anstey, Brunswick; W. D. Beazley, Abbotsford; J. W. Billson, Fitzroy; E. J. Cotter, Richmond; G. A. Elmslie, Albert Park; T. Glass, Bendigo East; M. Hannah, Collingwood; J. Lemmon, Williamstown; D. C. McGrath, Grenville; A. N. McKissock, Ballarat West; J. W. McLachlan, Gippsland North; A. R. Outtrim, Maryborough; W. Plain, Geelong; G. M. Prendergast, North Melbourne; A. Rogers, Melbourne; G. Sangster, Port Melbourne; D. Smith, Bendigo West; R. H. Solly, Carlton; T. Tunnecliffe, Eaglehawk; J. Wall, Port Fairy; E. C. Warde, Flemington.

During the election but few would own up to being followers of Bent, and nominally there were three parties. In reality they are one outside of the Labor Party. Even the Press, though strongly antagonistic to Labor, admitted that the Labor Party was the only clean party and the only party with a programme. In their desperate efforts to keep

Labor out of power the conservatives will swallow anything or anybody.

Bent resigned, and Murray was sent for. Meetings and negotiations followed, with the result that a strong conservative Government was formed. It is the same gang. It is Bentism without Bent as the boss leader, but there all the same. Laborites sit in direct Opposition, and keen watchdogs they are. Their time will soon come now, because the Victorian electors are just awakening to the fact that the gang calling themselves Liberals are in reality the rankest of Tories, and are but the agents of landlordism and boodle. They call themselves a coalition, but in all coalitions conservatism controls, and, as the Melbourne "Argus" said, "No one can breathe the atmosphere which surrounds Mr. Bent without being corrupted by it." "Boodlewraith" in Queensland, "Carruthersism" in New South Wales, and "Bentism" in Victoria have become terms expressive of a kind of political immorality in which land grabs, land scandals, and the making use of political influence and power for private ends are only some of the sins.

It is not easy to present in a concrete form the work accomplished by the Labor Party in the House. What they have prevented is only known to those who closely follow "Hansard," and by no means all of it then. There are things that Governments would dare smuggle through if the watchdogs were absent or asleep, but which never crystallise under present circumstances. The average elector has no conception of the many proposals made by the party or some of its members which are defeated.

Taking one session at random I found twenty-two such. Their influence has secured much, and modified many measures, making them less severe against the masses. Here is a list of that kind:— Improved Tenancy Rights, Servants' Registry Office Regulation, Legitimation Laws, Opium Smoking Prohibition, Boilers Inspection, Lifts Regulation, Limitation of Garnishee of Wages, Reduction of Borrowing, Company Legislation, Water Conservation, Factory Legislation, Credit Foncier, Improved Small Holdings, Closer Settlement, Improvement of Franchise, Early Shop Closing, Minimum Wage, Pure Food Legislation, Dairy Supervision, Old-Age Pensions, Improved Mining Legislation.

U

CHAPTER XXII.

SOUTH AUSTRALIA.

THERE the idea was slow in development. Like a seed, it required heat to make it spring forth, and that heat was supplied by the maritime trouble. In 1874 the United Tradesmen Society was formed. In 1875 it had 16 branches, and changed its name to the Labor League of South Australia. It aimed at uniting all classes of Labor on a common platform. By 1881, however, there were only four societies left in it—the Carpenters, Tailors, Ironworkers, and the Typographical Society. The latter had about 200 members, the others about 80.; so the old society died. In 1882 the Typos started a new body called the National Liberal Reform League, and it held the field for a year or two.

On January 31, 1884, the United Trades and Labor Council was formed. It took considerable interest in politics. Indeed, many of the old trade unionists thought it took too much part in it. At the election of 1887, seven out of nine candidates approved by the Council were returned to the Legislative Assembly. In 1888 G. W. Cotton was returned to the Legislative Council as a Labor member. In 1890 fourteen out of twenty favored by the Council were returned, though none could be classed as straight-out Labor men.

It took the suffering of 1890 to wake up all hands, and so, in December of that year, the Council issued a circular to all unions and workers' clubs, asking their Executives to meet. The meeting was held in the Selborne Hotel on January 7, 1891. It was then resolved to run men for Parliament as direct representatives of Labor. A platform was drawn up, a form of pledge adopted, and later sixpence per member of affiliated societies was collected to pay expenses of candidates. In February Messrs. R. S. Guthrie, A. A. Kirkpatrick, and D. M. Charleston were selected to run for the Legislative Council. On May 9, 1891, Guthrie and Charleston were elected, and Mr. Kirkpatrick on the 16th.

This success gave encouragement, and on July 2 the Council decided to call for nominations for group selection, recommending that fifteen names be chosen from the highest on the poll. It was also decided to ask for one shilling per member from affiliated bodies per year. The voting was to be by members of the organizations affiliated. The method then adopted still obtains in South Australia. Sixty-two nominations were received. Just then Sir John Bray resigned to go to England as Agent-General, and the late Mr. J. A. McPherson was selected to run for the vacancy in the Assembly. The election took place on January 23, 1892, and the Labor nominee won by 174 votes.

The plebiscite for the fifteen took place on February 17, and it is worthy of note that the late Premier of South Australia (Mr. Tom Price) was sixteenth on the poll. By consent, his name was added, thus leaving sixteen to choose from when the elections came on. A vacancy occurred in the Council, owing to the death of Mr. G. W. Cotton, and Mr. W. A. Robinson was sent for it, winning by a large majority on April 15, 1892. On the same day the elections for the Assembly took place, and resulted in the return of the following Labor members:—R. Wood, J. A. McPherson, E. L. Batchelor, I. McGillivray, W. O. Archibald, F. W. Coneybeer, F. J. Hourigan, T. Price. The platform of the United Labor Party at this time will be found in the Appendix. Adams only lost by 24 votes, and in May, 1894, he was elected to the Legislative Council. Mr. McGregor won a seat for the same a few days later.

At the elections held April 25, 1896, the following Laborites were returned for the Assembly: —J. A. McPherson, East Adelaide (leader); E. L. Batchelor, West Adelaide; W. O. Archibald and I. McGillivray, Port Adelaide; F. J. Hourigan, West Torrens; F. W. Coneybeer, East Torrens; T. Price, Sturt; R. Hooper, Wallaroo; A. Poynton, Flinders; E. A. Roberts, Gladstone; W. H. Carpenter, Encounter Bay. The Party suffered a great loss by the death of the leader, Mr. McPherson, and Mr. J. Hutchison took his seat January 21, 1898. Mr. R. S. Guthrie had been elected to the Council on May 22, 1897, so that at this time the party numbered fifteen in the two Houses D. M. Charleston left the Party in 1897, and R. Wood was expelled in the same year for disloyalty.

The next Assembly elections took place on April 29, 1899, and the following Labor members were returned:—J. Hutchison, East Adelaide; E. L. Batchelor, West Adelaide; I. McGillivray and W. C. Archibald, Port Adelaide; F. J. Hourigan, West Torrens; F. W. Coneybeer, East Torens; T. Price, Sturt; W. H. Carpenter, Encounter Bay; R. Hooper, Wallaroo; E. A. Roberts, Gladstone; A. Poynton, Flinders. In 1900 Mr. W. A. Robinson lost his seat in the Council, but Mr. A. A. Kirkpatrick won in the same contest and for the same district. He had been defeated in 1897 when seeking re-election.

The Government, led by the late Right Honorable C. C. Kingston, and which had held office for over five years, resigned on November 29, 1899. Mr. Solomon formed a Ministry, in which Mr. A. Poynton accepted office without the consent of his party. This Government only lasted a week, and resigned on December 7. The party lost Messrs. Poynton and Roberts over this change. Roberts voted first to put Kingston out and Solomon in, and a few days afterwards voted to put Solomon out. Hooper drifted away from the Party also during this Parliament, leaving them three less than at first.

Mr. Holder then formed a Ministry, and by consent of the Party Mr. E. L. Batchelor, who had taken Mr. McPherson's place as leader, took office as Minister of Education and Agriculture. Mr. Tom Price was elected leader in place of Mr. Batchelor. On the coming of Federation, changes took place. Mr. Holder resigned May 1, 1901, and Mr. Jenkins took office on the 15th. The Constitution was amended in 1901, and the State divided into four districts for the Legislative Council returning 18

members, and twelve electorates for the Assembly
returning 40 members, and two for the Northern
Territory—making 42. Mr. McGregor resigned his
seat in the Council and went to the Commonwealth
Senate.

The elections under the new Act took place
on May 3, 1902, and Labor did rather badly.
Messrs. Kirkpatrick and Guthrie were returned
for the Council, and five were elected for the
Assembly:—I. McGillivray and W. O. Archibald for Port Adelaide; F. W. Coneybeer
and T. Price, Torrens; J. Verran, for Wallaroo. In
December, 1903, Mr. R. S. Guthrie was elected to
the Commonwealth Senate, leaving only one Labor
member in the Council.

The turn of the tide came in 1905. The Jenkins
Government had reconstructed twice, and on
March 1, 1905, the Butler Government came in. The
elections were held on May 27, and Labor scored a
signal victory, returning fifteen to the Assembly as
follows:—Adelaide, Messrs. W. D. Ponder, E. A.
Roberts, and J. Z. Sellar; Port Adelaide, W. O.
Archibald, I. McGillivray, and H. Chesson; Victoria
and Albert, W. Senior; Wallaroo, J. Verran. A. E.
Winter; Stanley, C. Goode; Torrens, F. W. Coneybeer, T. Price, C. Vaughan, T. H. Smeaton,
G. C. A. M. P. Dankel. The Labor strength, united
with that of the old Liberal party under Mr. Peake,
formed a good working majority.

The House met on Thursday, July 20, 1905.
After the election of Speaker and other formalities
had been completed, Mr. Price moved—'' That the

House do now adjourn." This was carried by 24 to 17. When the House met on the following Tuesday, Mr. Price wanted to know what the Government intended doing. Mr. Butler declined to do anything unless on a direct challenge, so Mr. Price again took the business out of their hands by moving the adjournment, which was also carried by 24 to 17. The Ministry resigned, and Mr. Price announced his team on the 26th as follows:—Premier, Minister for Public Works and Education, Mr. T. Price; Chief Secretary and Minister for Industry, Mr. A. A. Kirkpatrick, M.L.C.; Treasurer and Attorney-General, Mr. A. H. Peake; Commissioner of Lands, Immigration, Agriculture, and Northern Territory, Mr. L. O'Loghlin.

Like every other Australian State, South Australia is cursed with a Second Chamber, which takes every opportunity to thwart the will of the people. The Legislative Council was elected by a property vote, and it steadily held to the conviction that its business was not to study the welfare of the people generally, but that its particular mission was to see that every advantage was secured to the few whom it was elected by. Every attempt to broaden the franchise had been resisted. Mr. Kirkpatrick had brought in a Bill in 1894. Later, Mr. Grainger had a try. The Government of the day brought in a measure in 1895, and again in 1896. In 1897 two bills had been brought in. In 1898 Holder brought in a Household Suffrage Bill. He re-introduced the same measure in 1899. Solomon made an effort the same year.

A Franchise Extension Bill was brought in in 1900. , In 1904 the subject was revived, and the elections of 1905 had been fought on the same matter. The Labor Party favored adult suffrage, but their allies, the Liberals, would not go so far, and favored a £15 franchise. The elections proved that 119.204 electors favored adult suffrage, and 31,612 a £15 franchise, while 14,126 voted for candidates favoring £20 as a basis. But as one Labor man (Coneybeer) had received 12,543 votes, it was clear that the people wanted reform. There were 187,645 on the Assembly rolls, but only 52,000 on those of the Council. The State was therefore not governed by its people, even though they have adult suffrage, but was really governed by a clique of capitalistic property owners.

In spite of being hampered by the timid Liberals, Premier Price entered into the fight for reform of the Council with vigor. Fourteen bills had been dealt with in twelve years, and not one step had been gained. The Tory Council cared for nothing but the interest of the rich, and were like adamant to every appeal. Mr. Price sent up a bill in 1905. It was rejected. He sent up another in 1906, only to meet with the same fate. He then appealed to the country, and the country was with him, as the returns of the election which was held on November 3, 1906, show. In the metropolitan group Labor swept the poll. The result was:—Adelaide, W. J. Denny, W. D. Ponder, E. A. Roberts, J. Z. Sellar; Port Adelaide, W. O. Archibald, I. McGillivray, H. Chesson; Torrens, F. W. Coneybeer, T. Price, C.

J. VERRAN, M.L.A.,

Leader of South Australian Labor Party.

Vaughan, T. H. Smeaton, G. C. A. M. P. Dankel; Victoria and Albert, W. Senior, D. Campbell; Wallaroo, J. Verran, A. E. Winter; Stanley, C. Goode, H. Jackson; Burra Burra, J. Newland. This gave nineteen in the Assembly.

On October 20, 1906, Mr. D. Jelley had won a seat in the Council, and Mr. J. P. Wilson secured one at the general elections, which raised the party's strength to four in that hotbed of Conservatism. Mr. Sellar died, and Mr. R. P. Blundell took his place on January 26, 1907. Owing to the death of Mr. Jelley, Mr. F. S. Wallis was elected to the Council on March 2 of the same year. Mr. Roberts resigned and was elected to the Commonwealth Parliament for Adelaide in place of the late Mr. Kingston. Mr. E. A. Anstey secured his seat in the Assembly on June 20, 1908. In December, Mr. Crush was elected for the Northern Territory, thus raising the strength of the party in the Assembly to 20 in a House of 42.

Mr. Price lost no time in trying the temper of the Upper House again, but found them just as stubborn as ever. His colleagues, the Liberals, would not go to the country again, and so, after all the struggle and fighting, a compromise was accepted fixing the right to a Legislative Council vote on a £17 franchise. The experience of South Australia is that of all the States, and only proves that no party outside that of Labor has the courage to tackle the reform of the obstructive Upper Houses with any degree of sincerity. The crusted Tories in those Chambers are quite aware of this fact, hence they hold on to power. When Labor secures a majority it will go for the only true reform, namely, sweep them out of existence as an unnecessary and harmful excrescence.

How coalition hampers a party is illustrated by a recent incident. In November, 1908, Mr. Verran, leader of the Labor Party, brought forward a motion in favor of adult suffrage for the Legislative Council. The division showed the Premier in favor and his colleagues of the Liberals against. On a motion against selling any more land, O'Loghlin, the Minister for Lands, voted against the motion, the Premier and Treasurer for it. It was a ridiculous position for nine men to control a Government. Labor had twenty and Peake nine, and the Labor twenty had to give way to the nine.

Unfortunately, Tom Price has been lost to the Labor Movement and to Australia. He died on June 1, 1909—another victim to the perils of industrial life and to the strenuous career of an earnest Labor Leader. His death at the comparatively early age of 57 was due to lung injury resulting from his trade as a stone-cutter. He helped to build the Parliament House in which he figured so ably as Labor Leader and Premier. His last message was:

"Tell the boys to take courage. You will have your ups and downs, but the Labor cause is the cause of humanity—is the just cause, and must eventually win."

During Mr. Price's prolonged illness Mr. Kirkpatrick was Acting-Premier, but when the latter became Agent-General in London Mr. Peake took the position. Kirkpatrick's seat in the Legislative Council was lost at the by-election. On the death of Price Mr. Peake was sent for, but, instead of keeping to the understanding and allowing Labor the Premiership, he jumped the position, formed a Ministry of his own, and coalesced with the Conservative Opposition. On being challenged when the House met, he won by one vote.

Mr. T. Ryan secured the late Premier's seat for Torrens, and thus kept up the Labor strength. It will prove a good thing for Labor that the weak-kneed Liberals went over, as it will make the fight in future a straight-out one.

Tom Price had put up a big fight at the election which brought in his Government, and, needing rest, he accepted the offer of a friend who owned a cottage on Mount Lofty, which is the fashionable summer residence of the rich. George Reid's terrible bogey of Socialism had been the topic in the elections. Mr. Price took possession of the cottage quietly, and in the evening went to the local store for household supplies. The storekeeper knew him and nodded, but was too busy to attend to him for a few minutes. Whilst making up the order, he remarked:

"I have been much puzzled by the fact that there has been such a run on locks and bolts that I sold out, and had to send for a supply. I could not make it out, but I can see now how it is. It's because the leader of the Socialists has come up here to live."

As a brief outline of what the Party has accomplished in South Australia I quote the following from a leaflet issued in 1905:—

GENERAL.

1. Adult Suffrage, 1894.
2. Affiliation Law, 1898.
3. Children's Protection, 1898-9, 1904.
4. Colored Alien Immigration Restriction, 1891, 1896 (latter was reserved for assent, and shelved by British Government).
5. Consolidated Stock and Sinking Fund, 1896.
6. Constitution Amendment, 1901.
7. Electoral Code, 1896.
8. Free Education, 1891.
9. Health Act, 1898.
10. Land Values Assessment (Part XIX.), 1893-4, 1900.
11. Married Women's Protection and Property Acts, 1896 and 1898.
12. Money Lenders Act, 1903.
13. Probate and Succession Duties, 1891-3.
14. Progressive Land Values and Absentee Taxes, 1894.
15. Village Settlements, 1893, 1895, 1901.

INDUSTRIAL.

1. Conciliation, 1894 (largely inoperative owing to absence of compulsory clauses).
2. Early Closing, 1900, 1901, 1903.
3. Factories Acts, 1894, 1900, 1904.

—4. Liens Acts, 1893, 1896.

5. Railway Appeal Board, 1903.

6. Wages Attachment, 1898.

7. Workmen's Compensation, 1900, 1904.

MINING, PASTORAL, AGRICULTURAL.

1. Agricultural Holdings, 1891 (compensation to tenant farmers for improvements).

2. Closer Settlement (land repurchase), 1897, 1901, 1902.

3. Crown Lands (known as Reduction of Rents Act), 1898.

4. Butter Bonus, 1893.

5. Exchange of Lands and Reduction of Rents, 1894.

6. Fertilisers, 1894, 1898, 1900, 1903.

7. Pastoral Lands, 1898.

8. Seed Wheat Acts (6).

9. State Bank, 1895-6-7, 1901.

— 10. State Export Department, 1893.

11. Taxation Act Amendment, 1900 (reassessment of taxable values following reduction in rent or purchase-money).

— 12. Various amendments of Mining Acts, all tending to greater liberality and assisting legitimate mining on private and public lands.

13. Vermin and Vermin-Proof Fencing Acts (7).

14. Working Men's Blocks and Loans to Blockers (under different Homestead, Blockers, Loans to Blockers, Crown Lands, and Closer Settlement Acts).

Thus, instead of the country being ruined by the
Labor Party under a Labor Premier it has pros-
pered, and no Premier has ever been more popular.
He was a tiger for work. He passed twenty-nine
bills into law in the 1907 session, and twenty-four
others were put partly through. Tom Price had also
successfully dealt with some big things. The
contractors for the outer harbor were in a muddled
state with their work, and had not complied with
the terms of their contract, hence the Government
decided upon taking it over. The lawyers thought
they saw a chance of big fees, but Price sent for the
contractors, made an offer conditional upon there
being no litigation, and in a few minutes fixed
matters up in a highly satisfactory manner. He did
the same in the purchase of the tramways, where, by
promptitude and quick decision, he secured everything wanted for £20,000 less than had been claimed.
The question of disputed territory between Victoria
and South Australia, which has hung up for years,
was quickly settled by him. He proved to be
the most energetic Premier the State has had, and
the rich Anti-Socialists soon discovered that the
Socialist Premier was not only a safe neighbor, but
could be trusted with big business affairs.

CHAPTER XXIII.

WEST AUSTRALIA.

WEST AUSTRALIA has been kept back by the bad management of Downing-street. Huge areas were given away to those who had influence enough in the early days. Alleged "gentlemen" came to the colony, and hoped to live a life of ease by utilising the "free labor" of the poor convicts. The best lands were secured, and any bona fide settler had to go far afield. As if this were not enough to crush out any hope of settlement, the local Government (the Legislative Council) gave away millions of acres in connection with land grant railways. The line from Beverley to Albany was built in this way—40 miles each side the line kept out of settlement, and 12,000 acres given to the syndicate for every mile of road made. The line was opened on July 1, 1889, and sold to the Government in January, 1897, for £1,100,000.

Western Australia was a Crown colony until 1890. It was governed by a small Legislative Council working under the Colonial Office in London. Practically, the colony was ruled by what became known as the "six families." These were the families of Messrs. Forrest (3), Burt, Stone, and Hamersley. These six and their relatives by marriage really ran the affairs of Western Australia. Mr. (now Sir John) Forrest was the leader, and may be termed the Autocrat of Western Australia from its early history until he went to the Federal Parliament in 1901. Self-government was established in 1890, with a Legislative Assembly of 44 members, and a Legislative Council of 24 members. Parliament had a tenure of four years.

The discovery of gold over an extensive field brought a big rush of miners from the eastern colonies, and as miners take a keen interest in politics an agitation quickly set in for representation. The " Outlanders " demanded a vote, and did not rest until they secured a change. The gross inequalities which the Government of the day permitted are seen by a glance at the electoral roll: Ashburton, 42 electors; East Kimberley, 90; De Grey, 70; Irwin, 106; Rocburn, 128; Kimberley West, 145; Gascoyne, 180; Murchison, 163; Moore, 356. This makes a total of 1280 electors, who returned nine representatives. Needless to say, these were squatters' districts.

The rolls for the principal goldfields were Coolgardie East, 5674; North-east Coolgardie, 3370; Coolgardie, 3364; Coolgardie North, 1710—a total for four seats of 14,118 electors. The four city electorates had 8328 electors, and the Port's four seats had 6209. The agricultural districts had thirteen representatives for 7615 electors. The total number on the roll for the colony was 43,185. The whole of the goldfields had only eleven representatives for 17,711 electors.

Summed up, the pastoral and agricultural districts had 22 representatives for 8895 electors, whilst the 34,290 electors of other districts had only

T. H. BATH, M.L.A.,
Leader of West Australian Labor Party.

a similar number amongst them. The agitation
resulted in a change being made in the Constitution
in 1899, when the Assembly membership was
increased to 50 and the Council. to 30. The new
electorates were also put on a fairer basis. The
tenure of Parliament was reduced to three years.

One of the early moves in thé Labor cause was
in 1888, when the late R. H. Hornby, secretary of
Typographical Society, called a meeting in Perth
to establish a Trades and Labor Council. Mr. Pearce,
now a Labor Senator, occupied the chair. An Early
Closing Association was formed in Fremantle in
1889, and it succeeded in getting the closing hour
firstly at seven, and latterly at six o'clock. In 1892
Perth joined in, and one association was formed for
West Australia. The year 1890 saw the first Eight
Hour Demonstration.

A meeting to establish a Trades and Labor
Council for West Australia was held in Fremantle on
December 9, 1892. Nine delegates were present, and
a platform was adopted as follows:—Electoral
Reform, Manhood Suffrage, Eight Hour Day,
Conciliation and Arbitration, Prohibition of Chinese
and Kanakas, Amendment of Master and Servants'
Act, Lien Bill, Bill to legalise Trade Unions,
Employers' Liability, Shops and Factories Act,
Encouragement to Local Industry, The Making of all
Railway Rolling Stock· in the Colony, Equitable
Taxation, Taxation óf Land·held for speculative
purposes, Revision of the Tariff. About that time
they ran a Labor man, but he was defeated. In May,
1897, C. H. Oldham was elected as Labor representa-

V

tive for North Fremantle.   This was prior to
payment of members.

West Australia was the first of the colonies to
copy New Zealand by setting up Conciliation and
Arbitration.   It came about through the alertness
and activity of the Labor organizations.   The Act
came in in December, 1900, and was secured in this
way: The Emperor of the West (Sir John Forrest)
was still in power, and the leader of the Opposition
(Mr. Illingworth) had moved a motion of want of
confidence.   Labor saw its opportunity, and on
August 29 waited upon Sir John as a deputation
from the various organizations, urging him to
introduce a bill on the lines of the New Zealand Act.
Sir John agreed to do so if the deputation would
secure the defeat of the motion of want of confidence.   This they succeeded in doing, and Sir John
kept his promise.

The idea of unionism was carried to the goldfields of the West by miners from the eastern
colonies, and several branches of the A.M.A. were
established in the eighties whilst I was general
secretary.   The discovery of the rich fields of
Coolgardie, Kalgoorlie, and Boulder gave an impetus
to organization, and a new body (the Australian
Workers' Association) was established on I.W.W.
lines.   It aimed at having one union for all classes
of workers.   This plan worked all right so long as
the members were nearly all connected with the
mines, but when the building trades came in it was
soon found unworkable, and " craft unionism," as
it is termed, was substituted.

Early in 1899 Mr. Hugh De Largie (now a Senator), who was president of the A.W.A. and one of the most active organizers, suggested the idea of a Trade Union and Labor Congress, so as to bring all into line for common action. As the outcome, the first Congress was held in Coolgardie, opening on April 11, 1899, and lasting till the 15th. Twenty-one delegates attended. Political action was decided upon, and the following three planks agreed upon as a fighting platform:—1, Payment of Members; 2, Redistribution of seats on a population basis; 3, Compulsory Conciliation and Arbitration on lines similar to New Zealand.

Resolutions were carried for abolition of plural voting; for adult suffrage, six months' residence to qualify; election day to be a public holiday, with all hotels closed; Parliament to sit five days per week; no deposits for candidates; referendum; in Government works and contracts union wages to be paid and an eight hour day; a tax on land values, and stoppage of all land selling, with introduction of a system of perpetual leasing; State bank, with sole right of note issue; State purchase of large estates; settlers to be assisted by giving them employment locally on road-making, etc.; State or municipalities to control the drink traffic; old age pensions; exclusion of undesirable aliens; abolition of Legislative Council.

Resolutions were also carried in favor of the bill for federating the Australian colonies. It was decided to form a Council of the Australian Labor Federation. The following resolution was carried with enthusiasm:—"That this Congress advocates the national ownership of all means of production and distribution for the equal benefit of all." A form of pledge was adopted, and the various organizations in the different districts commenced preparations for securing the return of a united political party on the Labor platform adopted by Congress.

The elections took place in April, 1901, and the following direct representatives of Labor were returned:—H. Daglish, Subiaco; R. Hastie, Kanowna; W. D. Johnson, Kalgoorlie; F. Reid, Mount Burgess; J. Reside, Hannans; Geo. Taylor, Mount Margaret. Mr. J. B. Holman was added in December of same year. This was the first Labor Party in the West. Mr. R. Hastie was chosen as leader.

The Party did very good work, and the organizations outside became active, with the result that in June, 1904, under the new franchise, twenty-one members were returned, as follows:— W. C. Angwin, Fremantle East; T. H. Bath, Brown Hill; H. E. Bolton, Perth; H. Daglish, Subiaco; H. A. Ellis, Coolgardie; F. Gill, Balkatta; R. Hastie, Kanowna; E. C. Heitman, Cue; E. P. Henshaw, Collie; J. B. Holman, Murchison; A. A. Horan, Yilgarn; W. D. Johnson, Kalgoorlie; C. C. Keyser, Albany; P. J. Lynch, Mount Leonora; E. Needham, Fremantle; J. Scadden, Ivanhoe; G. Taylor, Mount Margaret; M. F. Troy, Mount Magnet; A. J. H. Watts, Northam; A. J. Wilson, Forrest; F. F. Wilson, North Perth.

Mr. Hastie retired from the leadership, and Mr. Daglish was elected in his place.. The result of the elections was to put the James Government in a minority, as there were five Independents in addition to the solid Labor Party. The House met on July 28, 1904, and the leader of the Labor Party at once moved a vote of no-confidence in the Government. This was debated until one o'clock on the morning of August '10' when the James Government was defeated by 27 to 19. Labor rejoiced at the knowledge that it had a Labor Government in power, and much was expected from the change. The Cabinet was made up as follows:—Treasurer and Minister of Education, Mr. H. Daglish; Mines and Justice, Mr. R. Hastie; Lands, Mr. J. M. Drew, M.L.C.; Works, Mr. W. D. Johnson; Colonial Secretary, Mr. G. Taylor; Railways and Labor, Mr. J. B. Holman; Mr. W. C. Angwin without portfolio.

Alas for the hopes and faith of those who had worked so hard to put a Labor Government in power. Ministers and members of the party lacked political experience. The leader was a weak man, though able on the platform. Very soon complaints were made by supporters as to poor administration, and Mr. Daglish decided to reconstruct his Ministry. He called upon them all to resign. One was away in his electorate when he was called, upon without warning to send in his resignation. When Mr. Daglish had finished, it was found that he had taken in Messrs. T. H. Bath and P. J. Lynch in place of Messrs. G. Taylor and J. B. Holman.

It was soon found that more than one who had a good conceit of himself felt that he ought to have been taken into the Ministry, and they did not add to the comfort of the Premier. Had the latter been a strong man, or one with tested Labor convictions, he could have continued in office and done good work. The party was loyal enough, and would have backed him up in pushing forward democratic measures, but he chose to resign on August 25, 1905. When informing the House on the 22nd that he had decided to resign, he said:—

" I have realised of late that it is impossible for the Government to carry on the affairs of the country with advantage to the State or with credit to its members owing to the fact that we cannot expect a united support from our own party."

As applied to the immediate cause of his action at that moment it was true, but it was not true generally. He had brought forward a motion— " That in the interests of the State the acquisition of the railways and lands of the Midland Railway Company of Western Australia, Limited, is desirable." It came out in debate that he had agreed practically to purchase from the company for £1,500,000, subject to the approval of the House. If the resolution had been carried that sum would have been paid. He had arranged to pay that sum in spite of the fact that he had been warned against doing so, and had been told by his Agent-General in London that the whole thing could be got for £1,100,000.

A brief history of this company is worth recording. A member of the House said of it that "it has never, so far as I can understand, done one straight thing or kept one solitary promise." This was absolutely true. The contract with the Government was made first in 1884. The syndicate was to construct about 300 miles of railway, purchase 3,000,000 acres of land, and introduce 5000 immigrants in seven years. They were to start at both ends of the proposed line, complete the first 100 miles within four years, and 50 miles per year afterwards. They were to get 12,000 acres of land for every mile of railway made. They had to put up £10,000 deposit by July 1, 1886. They put up the deposit, signed the contract in 1886, and then gave a big advertising banquet, at which Sir John Forrest told the people that they were "dealing with people of large means and great enterprise, who were prepared to carry out the contract."

The sequel soon proved how he was deceived. The syndicate only had £5000 left after the banquet. They could only raise £7000 for the contractor, who had spent £88,000 on the line. In June, 1887, the works stopped, and in November they were transferred to Sir B. Brown. The Legislative Council of the day passed a resolution calling for forfeiture and taking over of the works. This was not carried out, but six months' time was given the syndicate. Two of the latter then registered a company of 200,000 shares of £6 each, with £1 paid up. The National Bank, by arrangement, honored Mr. Keane's cheque for £88,000, and Mr. Bond's for £112,000. Simultaneously they floated debentures on the market to the tune of one million, and sold £670,000 worth. The first £200,000 of this they paid into the bank, so as to square up for the £1 per share paid up in the company when registered. It will thus be seen that not one penny of money was put into the concern except by the public.

The company was in financial difficulties all the time, as was inevitable when they had no money of their own and depended on scheming to get it. In 1891 they secured an advance from Sir John Forrest's Government of £60,000, and four months later asked for half a million. In spite of the warning and advice of the Government's financial advisers in London, who exposed the lack of bona fides of the company, interest on the loan was guaranteed, and it was floated, though £30,000 short—a sum which the National Bank made up. The company had no shareholders and no capital. Only £140,000 out of the half million went towards the object for which it was borrowed. What became of the rest seems to remain somewhat of a mystery. It is also astonishing to find a Government helping on what amounted to a fraud upon the public in the face of the warnings of the Agent-General and others. But with that help the company managed to live somehow, and then saw the advantage of trying to unload when a Labor Government was in power, knowing that it is the policy of Labor to have State-owned and controlled railways.

What influenced Premier **Daglish** to agree to such a large sum in the face of the information he possessed is best known to himself. The State was to get the railway and 2,350,000 acres of land, the company retaining 345,000 acres of the best land. Possibly the purchase at a million and a half may have eventually been found a good thing, but Daglish did not attempt to justify it, and though put into a corner by one of his own party he said nothing. It was creditable to the Labor Party that they preferred to see a Labor Ministry go out of office rather than help to benefit a rotten private enterprise at the expense of the taxpayers. When the motion of the Premier was put it was defeated on the voices, and Mr. Daglish at once resigned. He left the Party afterwards, and ran at next election as an Independent. He was never one who could be called a straight Labor man, and the movement is well rid of such men.

As might be expected, the action of Daglish and a few others had a bad effect on the party in the elections of October, 1905. The following were returned:—T. H. Bath, Brown Hill; H. E. Bolton, Fremantle North; P. Collier, Boulder; E. E. Heitman, Cue; J. B. Holman, Murchison; A. A. Horan, Yilgarn; J. Scadden, Ivanhoe; G. Taylor, Mount Margaret; M. F. Troy, Mount Magnet; T. Walker, Kanowna; F. J. Ware, Hannans; A. J. Wilson, Forrest. By-elections added C. A. Hudson, Dundas, in November, 1905; W. D. Johnson, Guildford, in July, 1906; R. H. Underwood, Pilbarra, in August, 1906; J. A. S. Stuart, Mount Leonora, November,

1906; and W. C. Angwin, Fremantle East, November, 1906. For disloyalty to the party A. J. Wilson was later on expelled from their ranks.

From the results at by-elections it will be seen that the Party was gaining ground, and it was not surprising to find that it reached high water mark at the elections of September 11, 1908, at which twenty-two Labor members were returned. These were:—W. C. Angwin, East Fremantle; T. H. Bath, Brown Hill; H. E. Bolton, North Fremantle; P. Collier, Boulder; C. McDougall, Coolgardie; A. A. Wilson, Collie; R. Buzacott, Menzies; E. E. Heitman, Cue; J. B. Holman, Murchison; A. A. Horan, Yilgarn; C. A. Hudson, Dundas; W. D. Johnson, Guildford; J. Scadden, Ivanhoe; — Gourlay, Leonora; G. Taylor, Mount Margaret; M. F. Troy, Mount Magnet; R. H. Underwood, Pilbarra; F. Gill, Balkatta; T. Walker, Kanowna; F. J. Ware, Hannans; P. T. O'Loghlen, Forrest; H. G. Swan, North Perth.

Unfortunately Mr. Buzacott was unseated on appeal; and on a fresh election taking place he failed to win the seat. Labor holds a splendid position in the West, and the next step will be to the Treasury Benches. Every seat gained renders it easier to capture those adjoining. The party which trusts the people and is of the people must win, and once in charge of the Government of the country it will be its own fault if it does not remain permanently in charge of affairs. The party that places the whole community's welfare as of the first consideration cannot fail to retain the confidence of the people.

CHAPTER XXIV.

TASMANIA.

NATURE was kind to the snug little island of Tasmania. It gave her a beautiful climate, splendid streams, grand mountain scenery, and lovely lakes. Only man, as represented by the English Government, was cruel. The awful cruelties of "The System," set forth with so much realism by the late Marcus Clarke, seem more out of harmony with Nature in Tasmania than they do in a less congenial clime. It takes long for evil influences to die out, and the experience of the curse of England's dreadful transportation scheme hung as a dark cloud, dropping evil on each of our early settled colonies.

Jingo writers and speakers assume that we are immensely indebted to the mother country. They say that England is a wonderful coloniser, and the greatest of all nations in managing her colonies. I admit that the people who leave the United Kingdom are great and successful colonisers, but the British Governments have done more to damage and retard than ever they did to help. They made our beautiful country a dumping ground for all those disturbers of the peace whom they wanted out of the way, whether they were Labor agitators, poachers or murderers; and if the real colonisers—

the pioneers—had not kicked, and, as in Victoria, refused to permit the shipload of convicts to land, there is no knowing how long the evil would have gone on. Tasmania kicked too, but not so successfully.

Under English rule, huge areas of our best lands were given away to individuals, and hence she started us with land monopoly before people had a chance to say what should be done. We have had a century of growth, and sixty years of self-government. We have grown into a young nation, and the British people know practically nothing about us, and their great British Government very little more. For years Downing-street was a by-word in Australia, owing to its ignorance and carelessness of the interests of the Australian people. England did little to help Australia, but the Australian States have been a fair godsend to the British moneylender. In no other country has he found such a safe market for his surplus riches.

Tasmania has been termed the land of " sleep-a-lot;" but it has got a move on, and will soon take its right place as one of the most go-ahead of the Australian States. It has two fine cities—Launceston, which is one of the most advanced in Australia in municipal Socialism; and Hobart, on the other side of the island, which is probably the worst managed city in Australasia. Hobart is the home of the great Australian gamble—Tattersall's. The Tasmanian is the only Parliament in Australia which gave the private enterprise gamble a resting place.

Members of the Government that gave the concession share in the huge lottery, and to keep electors quiet a percentage goes to the State Treasury. It has become a vested interest and a political issue. Tasmania has been governed by the vested interests of Tattersall's racing lottery, Henry Jones's jam factory, the Union Steamship Co., the Cascade Brewery, and the Commercial Banking Co.

Tasmania provides scores of illustrations, if any are needed, to show how incapable are capitalists and alleged business men to manage the affairs of even a small State like Tasmania. One of the roads along which the tourist is driven up to the side of Mount Wellington runs for a few miles through privately owned land, yet the Government made that road at the taxpayers' expense, and put thousands into the land-owners' pockets thereby. Their whole scheme of government runs on similar lines, and then they are surprised that they cannot carry on without borrowing and running hopelessly into debt. They oppose doing away with " Tatt's " on the grounds that they cannot do without the revenue. They threatened to fight the Commonwealth when it put a stop to the delivery of letters addressed to Geo. Adams, or " Tattersall." One of those who share in the spoil is sent into the Federal Parliament by a Tasmanian constituency, and he does not seem a bit ashamed.

Like other States, Tasmania provides many examples of how members of capitalistic Governments divert public money into their own pockets and those of their friends. To quote one 'case briefly:—The Government led by Sir E. Braddon appointed Captain Miles and Messrs. Hales, Hall, and Driffield to the position of Wardens on the Marine Board of Strachan. Six others were elected. The story of how Miles schemed to secure the position of Master Warden, and how he induced the Premier by wire to use his influence on two of the Government nominees to vote for him—how he tried to induce his opponent to retire—is highly interesting, but I have not space for it. Suffice it to say, he secured the position. Tenders were called for the West Breakwater contract, and twelve were sent in. The deposit money on all but the four lowest was returned. These were N. C. Langton, £45,382; S. Derbridge and Co., £43,963; B. Stocks and Co., £39,790; Hungerford and Sons, £33,731. Captain Miles's son, Leslie, aged 23, wrote out the tender of Derbridge and Co., and Miss Miles, aged 19, that of Stocks and Co., and the Captain put up the deposit money.

Leslie Miles was in the board room when tenders. were opened, and at once wired his brother in Hobart, who sent a telegram in the name of Stocks and Co., withdrawing their tender. Of course there was no such company, neither was there any Derbridge and Co., an alleged New Zealand firm. This left Hungerford to be got rid of. He was written to by Leslie, who offered him £250 to give up. He came to Tasmania, and was met by Leslie Miles, who ostensibly represented the New Zealand firm. Leslie offered £1000 or over, but Hungerford would not sell out. The Master Warden then took a hand. New regulations and new conditions hitherto unheard of were presented, and Hungerford was humbugged out of his contract under a promise that fresh tenders would be called for. Captain Miles about this stage became Minister for Lands and Works. His influence secured the contract for the bogus Derbridge and Co., and thus practically the Master Warden secured the work himself at £10,232 over what an experienced, genuine contractor was prepared to do it for. Agitation secured a Select Committee, and it said:— "Our opinion is that Captain Miles, while occupying the position of Master Warden of the Strachan Marine Board, was improperly and secretly interested in two of the tenders for the west breakwater, and used unworthy means to secure the acceptance by the board of the higher of them." On being found out, Captain Miles resigned from Parliament.

However, Tasmania is being stirred up, and will awake soon. There is much of Labor agitation and propaganda, and the Australian Workers' Union has opened a branch in the centre of the Island, which, in co-operation with the mining fields and the cities, will soon shift things. Labor made a move first in 1893, and quite a fillip was given when Launceston returned the late Allen McDonald in the following year. He was an able man and a staunch democrat. An organization was started, called the Liberal Progressive League. Like our friends in Victoria, it was timid about using the term "Labor." Later it added the word, however. It succeeded in returning Ronald Smith. In Hobart they had formed an organization called the "Labor

Liberal League "; and in April, 1896, a meeting was held in the old " Clipper " rooms of representatives of this league and Hobart Trades and Labor Council with a view of forming one political body.

This was accomplished, and the new organization was called " The Democratic Club." A platform was drawn up, and public meetings were held and public debates carried out with some success. In July, 1896, a conference was held with the Labor Liberal League of Launceston, presided over by that able writer on economic and land questions, Mr. A. J. Ogilvy. The name adopted for the new organization was " The Democratic League of Tasmania." The Platform adopted appears in the Appendix. The first meeting addressed by a pledged Labor man was held at North Hobart on December 22, 1896, when Mr. James Paton contested Hobart. The election was held under the Hare system of voting, and owing to several other men running who claimed that they were also Labor, Mr. Paton lost by a few votes on election day, January 20, 1897.

In February of same year it was resolved to run a ticket of ten men for the Federal Convention, and the League adopted the platform of the New South Wales Labor organization. Tasmania's Labor ten met with the same fate as Labor candidates for the Convention in other colonies, namely, defeat. In February, 1899, Mr. James Paton ran as a Labor candidate in the Propsting v. Patterson fight. He scored 510 against the winner's 810. It was said that Propsting's votes cost him £1 each, and his

J. EARLE, M.H.A.,
Leader of Tasmanian Labor Party.

opponent Patterson's cost over that. The Labor man spent £15.

It is worthy of note that Labor has enormously reduced the cost of elections. Capitalists are finding out that money will not buy a seat. A Labor seat has been won at a cost of £5; and one Labor candidate for a huge country Federal electorate in New South Wales started his campaign with only thirty shillings, and he won on that. Of course loyal friends lent him horses, etc., and his meetings were nearly all in the open air. The Australian working man may be misled—he may be fooled by having political dust thrown in his eyes—but he cannot be bought with money. Paton's 510 votes showed how Labor was improving. His first effort gave him 140. As one of the ten he secured 324 in Hobart, so that Labor was gaining ground. Federation gave a great lift to the Labor movement. The popularity of the work done by the Federal Parliament, and the admitted fact of Labor's influence in moulding the legislation helpèd the party in every State.

In the elections of 1903 Labor ran three successfully—J. J. Long, G. Burns, and W. Lamerton. Mr. L. Jensen, who was elected as an Independent, joined the Party, which made four in a House of 35 members. Lamerton afterwards ratted on the movement, and was got rid of. The elections of 1906 returned seven—Messrs. J. Earle (who had only lost in 1903 by three votes), J. J. Long, L. Jensen, J. E. Ogden, W. A. Woods, C. R. Howroyd, and Ben Watkins, who was the youngest member of Parliament in Australia, as he had just turned twenty-one before election. Mr. J. Earle is leader.

W

With a view of deterring Labor men and keeping the power in the hands of the capitalist class, only £100 per annum is allowed to members of each House in Tasmania. In spite of this small pay, splendid work has been put in by the Party inside and outside the House. Until Labor members took a hand such a thing as a Mining Bill had never been discussed in the Tasmanian Parliament. A Royal Commission was secured by the party's efforts to enquire into the question of sweating in shops and factories, and their investigations and report were an education for the Tasmanian people.

During last Parliament the Constitution was altered, reducing the membership of the Legislative Council to eighteen and that of the Legislative Assembly to thirty. The elections took place on April 30, 1909, and were carried out under the Hare-Clark system of voting. Electors were compelled to vote in order of preference, placing a number opposite the name of each candidate. They were compelled to vote for not less than three, but could vote for all in their order of preference. The State was divided into five electorates, taking the boundaries of the Federal electorates as those for the State. Labor scored a signal victory, as they secured twelve seats out of thirty, as against seven in a House of thirty-five in the previous Parliament. They ran twenty candidates. The following form the new party:—Darwin—Messrs. J. E. Ogden, J. J. Long, J. Belton, B. Watkins. Denison—W. A. Woods, W. Sheridan. Bass—J. Guy, C. H. Howroyd. Franklin—J. Earle (leader), D. E. Dicker. Wilmot —J. H. Jensen, J. A. Lyons. Mr. Earle, though

running in a new electorate, beat the Premier. The
Treasurer lost his seat. Tasmania has awakened,
and will soon be under Labor Government.

The situation in Tasmania is well set forth in
the manifesto of the Labor Party, from which I
quote the following:—

" Now what has the anti-Labor politician,
who has ruled this State for fifty years, done
to assist Nature to make the people happy and
prosperous? Nothing. On the contrary, he has
burdened you with the heaviest unproductive
debt per head of any people in the world. The
national debt of Tasmania stands at £10,380,122,
on which our small population has to pay over
£1000 per day in interest, and for which we can
only show £4,250,000 worth of public railways
and telegraphs. He has sold or given away
5,000,000 acres of the best land of the State,
more than half of which is held by some 290
persons. The land is mostly lying idle, affording
no work, and consequently producing nothing
for the common good of the people.

" Your anti-Laborite has encouraged the
monopoly and abuse of land by practically
exempting the large estates from taxation, and
has discouraged the industrious small farmer
and orchardist by taking to the last penny the
value of the improvements. Succeeding anti-
Labor Treasurers have received and expended
the State's profit on £28,000,000 worth of
minerals which have been extracted from the

country and cannot be replaced. And what have we to show for it? A few public works, largely unproductive, and 463½ miles of railway, mainly running through large estates carrying only a few bales of wool, and upon which you are losing between £70,000 and £80,000 each year; a loss which is being made up by Ability Tax and other imposts upon the people's industry.

"The lands are alienated and locked up. The minerals are being extracted. The national debt is rapidly increasing. Ten millions borrowed, ten millions paid in interest, ten millions owing. Tasmania, with all its gifts from Nature, is the only State in Australasia where year after year the people are leaving faster than they arrive. Since 1901 the departures exceeded the arrivals by about 13,000. In 1861 the total taxation per head was 32s.; in 1907 it was 68s.

"If these things are to be allowed to continue for the next ten or twelve years, what can be the inevitable result but bankruptcy for the State and crushing taxation for the individual, families broken up and scattered over the face of the earth; ruined homesteads, cold hearths, and sad hearts?"

The above is a true statement of the position of the snug little island. Not only have its people been driven out, but the education of the young has been so neglected that the State has by far the largest proportionate number of illiterate persons in the Commonwealth. The Party summarises its work in the following statement:—

" For the first time in the Tasmanian legislature, important political and economic principles have been raised and seriously discussed, and the anti-Labor members have been forced to seek more cogent excuse for the stagnation and retrogression of the State than the palsied plea that the ancient methods were ' good enough for grandfather.' The Party was able to force useful discussions and to have important divisions recorded in the journals of the House on such questions as—1. The right of every worker to a living wage. 2. The duty of the State in regard to the health of factory and shop employees. 3. The duty of the State in the matter of the education of children. 4. The stupid wrong and crying injustice of permitting one monopolist to own more land than he can use, while many of our own young men are being forced to seek homes abroad. 6. The injustice of taxing a settler's improvements—the result of his expenditure of capital and labor—instead of taxing the land-loafer's increment. 7. Fair reimbursement of members' expenses. 8. The dishonesty of increasing a huge unproductive public debt and passing it on to posterity. 9. The ruinous policy of selling the land, minerals, and other assets of the State and crediting the proceeds to revenue. 10. The needlessness of supporting two State Houses to do the work of one House. 11. The right of all citizens to an equal voice in the making of laws which all have to obey. 12. The need for a better method of recording members' speeches than a scrap-book compiled from the faked columns of a violently partisan and notoriously anti-Labor newspaper. These have all been made live questions during our term of Parliament; if they were ever discussed in Parliament before the advent of the Labor Party, it was in a purely academic and perfunctory way. Nobody cared, or even pretended to care. To-day the direct Parliamentary delegates of the working class care, and compel other members to at least pretend to care."

CHAPTER XXV.

LABOR IN THE COMMONWEALTH.

WHILST it must be admitted that there have been for many years a number of Australians who were genuinely in favor of a federation of all the colonies, it was found impossible to consummate their desire until after it became clear that Labor was going to try to capture the several Parliaments. A Convention held in 1891 drafted a Constitution and left it with the people. The press all over the colonies tried hard to galvanise the thing into life, but it fell flat. Later a move was again made, and with success. A Convention met in 1897, the delegates to which were elected by the people. Capitalists rejoiced in the hope that now they would have a Parliament to which Labor could never attain. Not a single Labor delegate secured a seat on the Convention, and it was therefore natural to expect that the Constitution was not so democratic as desired. It was submitted to the people, and after some slight alterations made by a Conference of Premiers was adopted, and the latest of all the world's federations started on its career.

On January 1, 1901, the Governor-General (Lord Hopetoun) landed in Sydney, and was publicly sworn in under a specially erected pagoda in the Centennial Park amidst the plaudits of many thousands of spectators. Sydney was en fete for a week, and money was lavishly spent in all sorts of entertainments in order to celebrate fully the important event of Australia having become a united people. The march of events since has more than confirmed the wisdom of the step then consummated. There have been a few miserable parochialists who have now and again raised their croak against Federation, but they secure no following, and Australians generally rejoice in the steady growth of the new nation in the Southern Seas. As a matter of fact, there is a strong desire for unification and abolition of the six State Parliaments. This feeling is quite a spontaneous one, and has not been fostered by politicians.

It is almost certain that, as time goes on, extended powers and functions will be vested in the Commonwealth Parliament, and those of the States decreased. The work done by the Commonwealth Parliament has popularised that body. This is easily understood when we remember that both Houses are elected by full adult suffrage. It cannot be denied that the influence of the Labor Party has forced humanitarian questions to the front, and such legislation appeals to the masses. The demand for a " White Australia," set forth in the Labor Party's platform and also supported by members of other parties, could only be met by legislation from a Federal authority. The abolition of the kanaka contract labor in the sugar industry of Queensland was another kindred matter which was early dealt with. The exclusion of alien and colored races gives a chance for the development on the Australian Island continent of a great nation of the white race,

HON. ANDREW FISHER, M.H.R.,
Leader of Australian Labor Party.

and that ideal has come to stay and dominates Australian sentiment very largely. The elections for the first Parliament took place on the 29th and 30th March, 1901, with the following Labor results:—

For the House of Representatives New South Wales returned six—J. C. Watson, Bland; J. Thomas, Barrier; W. M. Hughes, West Sydney; W. G. Spence, Darling; T. Brown, Canoblas; D. Watkins, Newcastle. Queensland returned four—F. W. Bamford, Herbert; A. Fisher, Wide Bay; C. McDonald, Kennedy; J. Page, Maranoa. South Australia one— Mr. E. L. Batchelor. Western Australia two—H. Mahon, Coolgardie; J. M. Fowler, Perth. Victoria two—F. G. Tudor, Yarra; J. B. Ronald, South Melbourne. Mr. King O'Malley, who ran as an Independent in Tasmania, joined the party as soon as the House met. This made sixteen.

For the Senate the result was: Queensland, three —Messrs. A. Dawson, W. G. Higgs, and J. C. Stewart. West Australia, two—Messrs. G. F. Pearce and H. de Largie. Victoria—J. G. Barrett. South Australia— G. McGregor. Tasmania—D. J. O'Keefe. This made eight—or a Party of twenty-four for the whole Parliament.

After the elections the first Ministry was formed. Sir W. Lyne, as Premier of the oldest State, had the call, but gave up to Mr. (now Sir) Edmund Barton. Messrs. Lyne, Deakin, Turner, Kingston, Forrest, Drake, O'Connor, and Fysh formed the Ministry under him. The Parliament was opened by His Royal Highness the Duke of Cornwall and York in the Exhibition Building, Melbourne, on May 9, 1901,

at noon. The function was a great and impressive
one. In connection with the visit of Royalty
Melbourne had a week of festivities equal to Commonwealth time in Sydney.

The House met at 2.30 p.m. on the 9th to elect
the Speaker in the Representatives, and the Senate
met at the same time to choose their President. The
members of the Labor Party were informally called
together to authorise some one to offer congratulations to the Speaker. It was thought that it was
well to assert themselves as a distinct party at once,
and Mr. J. C. Watson was asked to speak for the
party. Later, at a properly constituted caucus
meeting he was chosen as chairman and leader of the
party. The choice was a wise one, as he filled the
position with distinguished ability, tact, and judgment. His retirement at a recent date was a great
loss, as not only had he secured the confidence of
those within the Labor ranks, but also of those
unconnected with the Labor movement. His alertness and close acquaintance with the undercurrents
of political movements enabled him to checkmate
many attempts to undermine the Party's influence
which political enemies put forth.

Mr. Barton had included some of the Labor
Party's planks in his programme, hence the Party
naturally gave an independent support to the
Government. The elections had been fought on
fiscal lines so far as New South Wales was concerned, and the main body of the Opposition came
from Representatives of that State, led by Mr. G. H.
Reid. Mr. Reid had done some good work in the

New South Wales Parliament whilst kept in power and pushed on by Labor, but when he entered Federal politics he joined with the Conservatives and reactionaries of Victoria and other States, who, though calling themselves Freetraders, were simply Revenue Tariffists.

Of the three parties in the Commonwealth, Labor was the only one in favor of direct taxation for revenue purposes. The Government favored Protection of a revenue-raising kind, the Opposition a revenue tariff only. Labor members had each a free hand on the fiscal question, though the majority were Protectionists. Thus on the first Tariff some of the party voted with Mr. Reid, whilst the majority voted with Mr. Barton. The party was united and solid against purely revenue duties, and took steps in caucus to select a list of such items upon which to vote as a party. In all sixteen items were agreed to, including tea and kerosene, cotton goods, etc.—all items which could not be produced in Australia as yet, and duties upon which pressed heavily upon the workers. These items involved over £1,000,000 of taxation, which the party succeeded in having struck out of the tariff. It was found afterwards that there was ample revenue without that million.

The House met for business on May 21, 1901, and the debates on the Address-in-Reply lasted until June 5. The first division was on a motion by Mr. Joseph Cook, since Leader of the Opposition, who thought to trap Labor members by an addition to the Address expressing the opinion that the clause dealing with kanakas did not go far enough. The voting was 7 for and 39 against. Only one Labor member voted with him. This in no way indicated the strength of parties. The majority of the House favored democratic legislation, but were divided into three parties, Labor holding the balance of power. No time was lost in tackling the big measures such as Immigration Restriction, Adult Suffrage, Pacific Islanders, Public Service, etc. The foundations of the Commonwealth had to be laid and built upon. There were many machinery measures of a non-party character but of great importance, and for which there were practically no precedents. In all these Labor took an active part, and materially helped the Government to make the measures as near perfection as earnest men could make them.

The party meets every Wednesday morning. On measures affecting the platform the party votes solidly together. On all other questions each member is absolutely free to vote as he likes. All important bills, whether affecting the platform or not, are discussed and in most cases remitted to a committee of the party, who go through the measure and recommend amendments. The Leader would then take these amendments, if approved by caucus of the party, to the Minister in charge of the bill. Many would be accepted, others would be left to the House to decide. This method helped to improve legislation, and justified the claim that the party wielded an influence far greater than its mere numbers warranted. No other party worked so hard or so efficiently; hence the good done. The relations with the Government were open and above-board, nevertheless the Cabinet readily considered any suggestion made by the party. If not prepared to accept or to go so far, then the party tested the House on the question.

The policy of a " White Australia " was given effect to by the passing of the Immigration Restriction Act. The bill passed the second reading on August 2, 1901. Out of consideration for English fears and prejudices the Government provided for keeping out undesirable aliens by an education test. If the person desirous of entering Australia is considered undesirable the department finds out some language which it knows he does not understand, and then dictates fifty words to him. Of course he fails, and is then deported back to where he came from.

This is a round-about and mean sort of way to accomplish the end sought, and Labor believed in saying straight out that we did not want any other than the white race here. On reaching the clause on September 25, Mr. Watson moved to insert—" Any person who is an aboriginal native of Asia, Africa, or of the Islands thereof." On division this was lost by 31 to 36, only one Government supporter (Mr. Higgins) voting with the party. Mr. Watson, in another clause, secured the exclusion of manual laborers under contract. The measure as finally passed can only be made effective by careful and active administration, and depends too much on Customs officials, who may not in all cases be in sympathy with the spirit of the Act itself.

The kindred measure—the Pacific Island Laborers' Act—was passed, in which provision was made for deporting back to their old homes all kanakas who had been brought to Queensland. The work was to be done gradually, but has long since been completed. Associated with this measure was the adoption of a Sugar Bounty Act, under which a liberal bounty was paid to growers of sugar cane or sugar beet if produced by white labor, with an excise charged those who employed black labor. This has proved a great success. There has been not only the removal of the colored employees, and conse-- quent increase of employment for white men, but the industry has grown to such an extent that the supply of Australian-grown sugar is sufficient for the requirements of the people of the Commonwealth.

Another big measure was the Public Service Act. In this the abolition of political patronage is provided for, and the whole Service is placed under a Commissioner, while at the same time Ministerial responsibility is retained. The Labor Party took an active interest in this measure, and secured the provision for a minimum wage. All employees who reach the age of twenty-one years and have had three years' service must receive not less than £110 per annum. When the Postal Departments of the States were taken over it was found that in the two States of New South Wales and Victoria alone there were over 1100 above the age, and with from three to as high as twenty-three years' service, who were receiving under £110. Over 400 were being paid under £90 per annum. They all secured a rise after the Act became law.

Another principle secured by the party was that of equal pay for equal work for men and women. The sexes were placed on an equality in status and in pay. Apart from Supply Bills, twenty-four Acts of importance were passed in the first session, besides passing a tariff, which in itself was a very tedious and difficult matter owing to the differences in the several States.

The first test as to how parties stood came when we reached the tariff. On October 15, 1901, Mr. Reid tried to oust the Government on the tariff issue. The division resulted 39 for the Government and 25 for Mr. Reid. Five Labor members voted with Reid. The session lasted till October 10, 1902.

The second session opened on May 26, 1903. It lasted until October 22 of same year. The most important of the Acts passed during that session were the two measures setting up a High Court for Australia. We are now enabled to decide appeals within our own borders, and secure an interpretation of our constitutional powers whenever conflicts arise between Commonwealth and States. A Defence Act was also passed, in which the Party secured recognition of its plank of a Citizen Force. The next step will be to arrange for compulsory training somewhat on the lines obtaining in Switzerland.

Sir Edmund Barton and Senator O'Connor having been appointed to the High Court, Mr. Deakin became Premier on September 24, 1903.

In order to save the cost of having separate elections for the Senate and Representatives the House was dissolved, and the elections were held on December 16, 1903. The party was very successful. The retiring Victorian Senator, Mr. J. G. Barrett, declined to stand for selection by the leagues for the Senate, and therefore left the party and was defeated at the polls. Mr. E. Findley took his place, and every member of the previous party was returned in both Houses, with the following additions:—New South Wales—W. Webster, Gwydir. Queensland— Dr. M. Culpin, Brisbane; D. A. Thomson, Carpentaria; J. Wilkinson, Moreton. South Australia—J. Hutchison, Hindmarsh; A. Poynton, Grey (the latter had been in the previous Parliament as a Freetrader). West Australia added W. H. Carpenter, Fremantle; C. E. Frazer, Kalgoorlie. Victoria—Dr. W. Maloney won Melbourne after the election of Sir M. McEachern had been declared void on petition. For the Senate J. W. Croft and G. Henderson were added for West Australia; T. Givens and H. Turley for Queensland; and R. S. Guthrie and W. H. Storey for South Australia. This made twenty-five in the Representatives in a House of 75, and fourteen in the Senate in a House of 36—a party of 39 altogether.

The second Parliament opened on March 2, 1904. There were still three parties, and the relationship between Labor and the Government continued to be cordial and friendly. On March 17 Mr. Watson raised a rather important principle when he moved— " That the House records its grave objection to the entry of Chinese labor into the Transvaal until a referendum of the white population of the colony has been taken on the subject or responsible Government is granted.'' Objection was taken that this was an interference with matters outside our jurisdiction, and that we had nothing to do with what the Home Government had control of. The majority of the House claimed, however, that as a part of the British Empire we had a right to express an opinion upon any act calculated to injure our own kindred. An amendment was rejected by 45 to 13, and the motion was carried by 54 to 5.

It was during this session that the Labor Government came in. The change arose over the Conciliation and Arbitration Bill. That measure had been framed originally by Mr. Kingston, but, owing to his ill-health, was taken charge of by Mr. Deakin. It had been introduced in the first Parliament, the second reading passing without opposition on July 30, 1903. On September 8 a division took place on the Labor Party's proposal to make the measure apply to the Public Service of Commonwealth or State. This was lost by 28 to 21. An amendment by Labor member McDonald to make the Act apply to the railway servants of any State was carried by 26 to 21. The Premier, Sir Edmund Barton, at once said that the Government must consider its position, and next day announced that they had dropped the bill.

This naturally caused the question to arise at the election. Labor favored no limitations, and would have the measure apply to all that the

X

Constitution allowed. Mr. Deakin declared himself strongly opposed to inclusion of any of the Public Service. Thus both parties were pledged to opposite courses. The Bill was re-introduced and passed the second reading on March 22, 1904. On April 19 Mr. Fisher, on behalf of the party, moved to include the Public Service under the bill. On the 21st this was carried by 38 to 29. The Deakin Ministry resigned, and on April 27 a Labor Ministry took charge of the affairs of the Commonwealth, constituted as follows:

The Hon. J. C. Watson, Prime Minister and Treasurer.

The Hon. H. B. Higgins, Attorney-General.

The Hon. Andrew Fisher, Minister for Trade and Customs.

The Hon. W. M. Hughes, Minister for External Affairs.

The Hon. Hugh Mahon, Postmaster-General.

Senator The Hon. A. Dawson, Minister for Defence.

The Hon. E. L. Batchelor, Minister for Home Affairs.

Senator McGregor, Vice-President of Executive Council.

Mr. F. G. Tudor acted as Whip in the Representatives, and Senator O'Keefe in the Senate.

In selecting his Ministers, Mr. Watson followed precedent and tried to have every State represented. The Attorney-General, Mr. Higgins, was not a member of the party, but his views and votes had always been with Labor, and as Mr. Hughes had only recently passed as a barrister he refused to take the responsibility. Mr. Higgins—since raised to the High Court—was a great acquisition to the strength of the Cabinet. When the Labor Ministry met the House the scene was one to be remembered. Twenty-six sat on the Government side of the House, and the rest of the seventy-five crowded on to the other side or in the corner. The twenty-six were prepared to stand or fall on their measures, just as they had always supported measures and not men. They expected to get fair play. For a time they did so, but soon the restless schemers after office found an opportunity to cause the downfall of the Government.

Mr. Watson went on with the Conciliation and Arbitration Bill, and at four o'clock on Friday, 24th June, 1904—just at the close of the sitting, as members were leaving to catch their trains—Mr. McCay moved, on the question of preference to unionists, that " no preference be given unless the application is approved by a majority of those affected by the award who have interests in common with the applicants." There was no debate, and, to the surprise of the Government, the motion was carried by 27 to 22.

Mr. Watson announced that he would have the clause recommitted later on, and on August 10 he moved the recommittal of ten clauses, the schedule, and two new clauses. The schemers had ripened their plans by this time, and so Mr. McCay moved to strike out clause 48, which contained his own amendment. Debate followed, but it failed to prevent the anti-Labor section of the House from striking a blow

at Unionism and at a Government whose work in
the House and in the departments had been without
fault. They took the business out of the hands of
the Government by 36 to 34. Mr. Watson asked for
a dissolution, but was refused, and at once resigned.

Meantime some extraordinary proceedings had
taken place. Secret conferences and negotiations
were being carried out between Messrs. Reid, Turner,
and Deakin. A section of the Deakin party, led by
Mr. Isaacs, stood by Mr. Watson; hence it was
doubtful whether Mr. Reid could secure a working
majority. However, on August 18 a Government
with two heads equal in all things took charge. It
was the Reid-McLean or McLean-Reid Government.
It contained also Sir Josiah Symon, Sir G. Turner,
Mr. D. Thomson, Sydney Smith, McCay, and Drake.

On September 20, 1904, Mr. Watson moved a
vote of want of confidence. This was debated until
October 13, and resulted in 37 for and 35 against the
Government. The matter had been kept in doubt all
the time, because Mr. D. N. Cameron, of Tasmania,
could not make up his mind. Eventually he stood at
the centre of the table opposite Mr. Speaker, and
after " slating " and abusing both sides equally, he
announced his intention to vote for the Government
solely to avoid a dissolution. It was a disgraceful
exhibition, and no decent Government would have
held office under such circumstances, but the double-
headed Ministry had schemed too hard to secure
office to allow a thing like that to force them to give
up. The action of the anti-Labor party stood out

in marked contrast to the admittedly highly honorable conduct of the Labor Government.

The session ended on December 15, and Reid-McLean had passed one little Act called the Sea Carriage of Goods Act. The twin Government then took the longest recess any of the Cabinets has taken. They did not meet the House until June 28, 1905. Reid then made one of the many blunders he has made in Federal politics. Had he brought down a good programme of business he could have carried on, but instead, to the surprise of his own following —who were not consulted—he had a blank sheet as the Governor-General's speech. He proposed to pass a measure fixing new boundaries for electorates, and that was all. Deakin, in his anxiety to see only two parties in the House, had helped Reid, but had found out his mistake by this time; and so, after a lengthy speech he wound up by moving an addition to the address in reply as follows:—"But are of opinion that practical measures should be proceeded with." This was carried by 42 to 25. The twins thought they could get a dissolution, hence the brief programme; but when Mr. Reid applied for it he was refused, and so Deakin came back to power on July 5, 1905. He took in Isaacs, Lyne, Forrest, Chapman, Groom, Ewing, Playford, and Keating.

The Reid-McLean coalition period was an interesting one, as it showed the foolishness of trying to force a situation. The House had been doing good work with three parties. The work was too good to suit the Conservatives and anti-Laborites, hence the scheming to dish both Labor and Liberal forces.

Deakin's action only split his own party, and led to
there being four parties instead of three. For his
return to power he had to thank the alliance formed
between Labor and the section of the Liberal party
who remained true to their principles. The alliance
was in writing, and was agreed to at a joint meeting
of the two parties held on September 7, 1904. It ran
as follows:—

" CONDITIONS OF ALLIANCE.

" 1. Each party to retain its separate
identity.

" 2. Alliance to be for the life of this and
the next Parliament.

" 3. Each party to use its influence individually and collectively with its organizations
and supporters to secure support for and
immunity from opposition to members of the
other party during the currency of the alliance.

" 4. A joint election committee to consider
contested seats and make recommendations to
both parties.

" 5. Any member of Parliament who agrees
to these articles may, subject to the approval of
both parties, be admitted to this alliance.

" JOINT PLATFORM.

" 1. Conciliation and Arbitration Bill as
nearly as possible in accordance with the original
bill as introduced by the Deakin Government,
but any member is at liberty to adhere to his
votes already given.

" " 2. White Australia legislation.—Maintain Acts in their integrity, and effectively support their intentions by faithful administration.

✓ " 3. Navigation Bill.—Report of Royal Commission to be expedited, and, subject to this, bill to provide for (a) the protection of Australian shipping from unfair competition; (b) registration of all coastal vessels engaged in the coastal trade; (c) efficient manning of vessels; (d) proper accommodation for passengers and seamen; (e) proper loading gear and inspection of same.

✓ " 4. Trades Marks Bill.

✓ " 5. Fraudulent Marks Bill.

✓ " 6. High Commissioner Bill. The selection of the Commissioner to be subject to prior consent of Parliament; full utilisation of Federal staff for the benefit of all the States.

✓ " 7. Electoral Bill (amendment).

✓ " 8. Papua Bill.

✓ " 9. Anti-trust legislation.

" 10. Tobacco monopoly; appointment of the present Select Committee as a royal commission, with addition of members from both Houses of Parliament.

✓ " 11. Iron Bonus Bill.—Every member to have freedom of action as to method of control.

✓ " 12. Standing Committee on Trade, Commerce, and Agriculture.

✓ " 13. Preferential trade to be discussed by both parties at an early date.

✔ " 14. Legislation (including tariff legislation) shown to be necessary—(1) To develop Australian resources; (2) to preserve, encourage, and benefit Australian industries, primary and secondary; (3) to secure fair conditions of labor for all engaged in every form of industrial enterprise, and to advance their interests and well-being without distinction of class or social status; (4) as to any regulation arising under this paragraph only, any member of either party may as to any specific proposal—(a) Agree with the members of his own party to be bound by their joint determination or (b) decide for himself how far the particular circumstances prove necessity or the extent to which the proposal should be carried; (5) Royal Commission to be at once appointed to inquire as to the necessary tariff legislation—personnel to be approved by Parliament—Commission to report in sufficient time to enable any desired legislation to be introduced next session.

✓ " 15. Old Age Pensions on a basis fair and equitable to the several States and to individuals.

✓ " 16. Quarantine legislation.

" 17. Either party may at any time submit to the other any other subjects for consideration with a view to joint action."

Those who joined the Labor party in this were Messrs. Bonython, Chanter, Hume Cook, Crouch, Groom, Higgins, Isaacs, Kingston, Lyne, Mauger, and Storrer. These eleven, with twenty-five Laborites, made a party of thirty-six in the Representatives; and Messrs. Styles, Trenwith, and Playford, with fourteen Labor members, made seventeen in the Senate. There is no doubt that but for this alliance the Deakin party would not have got back to power. It prevented some of the eleven being nobbled by the Reid-McLean coalition, and secured the return of Deakin to his old party—shattered though it was by his own foolish junction with Reid.

The contrast between the Alliance of the Isaacs party and Labor, and that of Reid and Deakin, is most marked. In the latter case there was much of secret caucus and a little letter writing, but the object all through was not to do business in the interests of the country, but simply to crush the Labor Party. They were quarrelling about leadership and as to who were to be Ministers, but there was not a word about the kind of legislation to be carried out. On the other hand, with the Labor Alliance the whole question was how best to secure the passage of democratic legislation. Whatever was done was done in the light of day and given to the press immediately it was arrived at. When the country got the chance it expressed its disapproval of the Reid-Deakin tactics and negotiations by increasing the strength of the Labor Party at the expense of both the others.

The party nominally led by Reid, but really by Mr. Joseph Cook—years ago a rabid Labor man—shortly after the period under notice called themselves "Anti-Socialists." They came out in their true colors when the Government introduced the Commerce Bill and the Trade Marks Bill. They deliberately stonewalled these measures for weeks. The Government had to suspend business and force through amended Standing Orders giving power to apply the closure ere they could get the two important bills passed. The fight nearly killed the Opposition Whip, Mr. Wilks, who had to take to his bed seriously ill owing to the strain of the stonewall. One can understand the strong objection of capitalists to any interference with their profit-making, however dishonest it may be; but it is seldom they come into the open and fight. They generally use hired tools. They invariably exert secret influence in order to retain any advantage they may possess.

The Commerce Act of the Commonwealth was the forerunner of the Pure Foods Acts since passed in several of the States and promised in all. It simply demanded that the goods imported should contain an honest statement on their labels as to contents, weight, etc. Medicines, drugs, apparel (including boots and shoes), seeds and plants, etc., should state what they were and be true to name. No honest trader could object to such a measure. Those who have been making fortunes by selling the public colored water as patent medicines, or shoes made of paper and sold at leather prices, naturally objected, and moved heaven and earth to stop the bill from passing. They had strong champions in the Anti-Socialists.

The other measure—the Trade Marks Bill—was fought still harder. It contained a clause, put in at

the instance of the Labor Party, giving the same
protection to a trade mark registered by an organization of workers as was provided for any ordinary
business firm. The object was to protect Union
Labels, though the term was not used in the Act.
Days and nights the Anti-Socialist Opposition, led
by the renegade Labor man, fought this by a stonewall. They had no objection to others than a body
of working men having the protection of law for
their trade mark. In fact, they desired it. It was
to be made a crime to pirate such a trade mark, but
it was not to be a crime—in fact, it would be a
creditable thing—to pirate a workers' trade mark.
This open declaration of one law for the classes and
another for the masses characterises the Anti-
Socialists all through. Anything that would secure
improved conditions for the workers of the world
must be prevented from happening, as it might take
something from the unearned income of the
employing and exploiting class.

The measure was passed, however, and though
the best lawyers in the House—including two since
made High Court Judges—declared the Act to be
within the Constitution, the Anti-Socialists took a
case to the High Court, which by a majority vote
declared the clause ultra vires; so we now have the
immoral doctrine laid down that what is a sin for
one person is not a sin in another.

To return to the change of Government. When
Mr. Deakin took office after Mr. Reid he was interviewed by Mr. Watson, who wanted to know what

he proposed to do. Next day Mr. Watson received the following reply:—

" July 5, 1905.

" Dear Mr. Watson,—I am now able to inform you that the programme of business to be submitted to the present Parliament will include, in addition to the Budget and other ordinary requirements of that kind, any necessary legislation upon the matters and lines embraced in the Ballarat platform, 1903, or since arising out of the action of the House. I may mention among the subjects that we hope to deal with—some of them being already advanced more than one stage—are the following:—(1) White Australia; (2) Iron Bounty; (3) Preferential Trade; (4) Rural Development; (5) Navigation; (6) High Commissioner; (7) Tariff Commission Report; (8) Trade Marks; (9) Fraudulent Marks; (10) Papua; (11) Quarantine; (12) Electoral Requirements; (13) Population; (14) Old Age Pensions; (15) West Australian Railway Surveys; (16) Anti-trust Bill; (17) Defence; (18) State Debts. We cannot hope to dispose of all these great problems, but may be enabled to secure further consideration for those upon which legislative action is not yet desirable.

" Yours very truly,

" ALFRED DEAKIN."

This letter was submitted to the party, and the following resolution carried—" That this party, having been informed through Mr. Watson of the measures proposed to be submitted by Mr. Deakin, agrees to give his Ministry a general support during this Parliament in the transaction of public business.'' There was a clear understanding that each party maintained its independence. It was this understanding that enabled the Government to carry on, and to win through the stormy times of the stonewall already referred to. There is no doubt of the fact that Labor had an influence upon the business of Parliament, as can be seen from the programme agreed to in alliance with Mr. Isaacs, and later that just quoted from Mr. Deakin's letter, which itself was the outcome of Mr. Watson's interview with him.

It is not my purpose to give anything like a history of Federal legislation. Over 100 Acts have been passed, leaving out Appropriation Acts. Until quite recently Labor has held the balance of power, and has therefore more or less directly controlled legislation. Elsewhere I summarise this view. At present I am only touching on some of the more important incidents. No sooner had Mr. Reid been turned out of office than he began a systematic propaganda. He travelled over a large portion of all the States, warning the people against a Socialistic '' tiger,'' and denouncing a fearful and wonderful creation of his own which he called Socialism. The '' tiger '' was the Labor Party. Intelligent people laughed at him, and those who were ignorant of what Socialism meant began to read the subject up; hence Mr. Reid did a wonderful amount of good for Socialism.

Since he went round on the warpath it is quite safe to announce oneself as a Socialist. He told the people it meant that every one was to get a billet under Government—in fact, all were to have bosses' billets. This idea did not strike the poor out-of-work as being at all a bad thing, and, if that was Socialism, he was a Socialist straight away. Mr. Reid did not enlighten his audiences as to where the money was coming from which paid for his propaganda. It was well known that he had thousands of pounds behind him, and as he is known to be a comparatively poor man it was clear somebody put up the cash. In one place in Queensland he struck the town on the same night as a travelling theatrical company, which had the only hall. He paid them £40 to give up their entertainment so that he could run his " circus " instead.

When the elections came, on December 12, 1906, cash was so plentiful that some candidates in the Anti-Socialistic interest not only had their expenses paid, but were allowed in one case £10 per week and in another £4 per week besides, so that fighting Labor became quite a paying job. When one remembers the fight put up in opposition to all the measures which were calculated to strike a blow at capitalists' profit-grabbing methods, such as light weight, food adulteration, sweating, etc., we can easily guess whose business it was to make it worth while for an able barrister to go round with a bogey trying to throw dust in the eyes of the people, hoping for a re-action which might give the Conservatives power once more. " New Protection " proposals carried in connection with the harvesters and the anti-trust legislation all struck at the huge profits hitherto obtained, and made it worth spending some money if by so doing they could undo the work of the Labor Party.

The Women's National League, a body of women who probably never earned a meal in their lives, and who knew nothing of the social problem except in so far as it gave them a chance to be insultingly patronising to the poor, got out leaflets which for barefaced lies outdid Munchausen. They even misrepresented the dead, and misquoted writers to bolster up a cry that the Labor Party wanted to destroy the home and the marriage tie. The leader, who claimed to be a titled lady, knew it was untrue, but said " it would be a good move " to spread such an idea, as it would damage Labor men's chances at the election. They also went from house to house spreading the lie that Labor was in favor of the abolition of religion, and also wanted to have the State take all children away from their parents. These women held conferences and meetings, and also seemed to have plenty of money to spend in the " good cause " of Anti-Socialism. It was a big advantage to them that they knew nothing of Socialism, because they were thus enabled to wax enthusiastic over the terrible monster which George Reid had conjured up from a nightmare.

Reid had calculated upon securing a dissolution, and had started early with his bogey, but as it was refused and the elections did not come off until Parliament had run its full term, the people had

time to examine the features of his "tiger," and
found it was quite a harmless creature—in fact, they
discovered that Reid did not know a tiger when he
saw it. In spite of all his propaganda and the
spending of thousands of pounds, the result of his
work left him with a shattered party smaller than
ever, whilst Labor gained considerably. A little
knot of utter Tories got in as Protectionist Anti-
Socialists in Victoria, but they would not join Reid,
neither did they vote for Protection. Reid wanted
only two parties, but he forced members into four
sections, none united except Labor.

The elections came on December 12, 1906, and
Labor came out as follows:—Representatives:—New
South Wales—J. C. Watson, South Sydney; D.
Watkins, Newcastle; W. G. Spence, Darling; W. M.
Hughes, West Sydney; T. Brown, Calare; J. Thomas,
Barrier; W. Webster, Gwydir; E. S. Carr, Macquarie;
J. H. Catts, Cook; F. J. Foster, New England; D. R.
Hall, Werriwa. Queensland—F. W. Bamford,
Herbert; A. Fisher, Wide Bay; C. McDonald,
Kennedy; J. Page, Maranoa. South Australia—E. L.
Batchelor, Boothby; J. Hutchison, Hindmarsh; A.
Poynton, Grey. Victoria—W. Maloney, Melbourne;
J. Mathews, Melbourne Ports; J. K. McDougall,
Wannon; F. G. Tudor, Yarra. West Australia—
J. M. Fowler, Perth; C. E. Frazer, Kalgoorlie; II.
Mahon, Coolgardie. Tasmania—King O'Malley,
Darwin. The death of the Right Hon. C. C. Kingston
on May 12, 1908, left a vacancy for Adelaide, which
was filled by Mr. E. A. Roberts. This gave the
party twenty-seven in the Representatives.

After the elections the party's position in the Senate stood as follows:—Western Australia—G. F. Pearce, J. W. Croft, H. De Largie, G. Henderson, P. J. Lynch, E. Needham. South Australia—G. McGregor, R. S. Guthrie, W. Russell, W. H. Storey. Victoria—E. Findley, E. J. Russell. Queensland— T. Givens, J. C. Stewart, H. Turley. In South Australia Mr. Crosby, the Labor candidate, was actually elected, but died ere he could take his seat. Complications arose, and after a lengthy inquiry the election was declared void. On May 31 the State Parliament elected Mr. J. V. O'Loghlin to fill the vacancy. He belonged to the Liberal Party of the State, but joined Labor in the Federal Senate, thus making sixteen in that. House. The question as to whether the election by the State Parliament was valid under the circumstances was referred to the High Court by the Senate, and the Court decided against it. An appeal to the people lost the seat to Labor. This left the party with fifteen in the Senate, making forty-two in the two Houses.

It will be seen that the greatest gains were in Reid's own State, and the losses in Queensland. The latter were due to the disunited condition of the organizations, and it is confidently expected are only temporary. The party lost an able man there in Senator Higgs, who, had he been elected, was named for the position of President of the Senate.

The other parties in the new House were— Government, fifteen; direct Opposition, twenty-one; with a nondescript lot. in the Opposition corner

Y

numbering eleven. Sir John Forrest had left the
Deakin Government in the previous Parliament,
expecting to make a crisis, but no one troubled about
him, hence he joined the corner eleven. Irvine, of
Coercion Act fame, also belonged to the corner party.
They were alleged Protectionists of the Anti-Socialist
school. Labor had the biggest party, and the country
had expressed more approval of it than of any other,
yet it had no choice but to continue the arrangement
of 1905, and therefore supported the Deakin Government. Not only had the Government fewer supporters, but the personnel of the Cabinet had
weakened considerably. In 1906 Messrs. Higgins
and Isaacs had been placed on the bench of the High
Court, and with their acknowledged ability, their
removal was a loss to the Government and the House
generally.

The party and the movement suffered a great
loss in October, 1907, owing to the resignation of the
leadership by Mr. J. C. Watson. Not only had he
displayed distinguished ability, but his fine personal
qualities had endeared him to every member of the
party. His reasons were entirely private and
personal. During the period in which he held office
as Prime Minister the strain had told upon his
health, and shortly after, to relieve him somewhat,
Mr. Andrew Fisher had been appointed deputy
chairman, and was subsequently chosen as successor.
There is every confidence that Mr. Fisher will do
well. He is in the prime of life, and has been in the
movement from boyhood. He has already had many
years of Parliamentary life, first in the Queensland

Parliament, and, since Federation, in the House of Representatives.

The year 1908 saw changes in the relationship of parties. Something of a crisis took place in April. Complaints as to the management of the Postal Department had been rife for a year or more. The Government had appointed a committee from the Cabinet to examine into the matter, but it was seen by members that it was unlikely that they would condemn a colleague. Mr. Webster had a motion for the appointment of a Royal Commission, and being afraid that he would not get another chance ere the session ended he wanted to press the matter to a division. The Government wanted the matter adjourned until they were satisfied that a Commission was absolutely necessary. A motion for the adjournment of the debate was defeated by 31 to 28, several Labor members voting with the Opposition, who saw a chance to get at the Government.

Mr. Deakin adjourned the House, and said he would have to consider his position. Considerable excitement ensued. Deakin announced that he would resign. Members of his Ministry pressed him very hard to continue in office. Negotiations were opened up with the Labor Party, and tempting offers of coalition were made. Mr. Deakin expressed himself as willing to personally support a Labor Government, but could not answer for his followers. Strong pressure was brought to bear from many outside sources, and eventually Mr. Deakin agreed to go on with business and to appoint a Royal Commission.

Out of the crisis we secured the passage of an Invalid and Old Age Pension Act. It is the most advanced of its kind in the world. Labor had been urging the matter for eight years, and only secured it then by first pointing out to the Government how the necessary funds could be raised. On 24th June, 1903, Mr. King O'Malley asked Mr. Barton "Whether in view of the large surplus of the Commonwealth revenue, as shown by him yesterday, he will immediately bring it a bill to establish a system of national old age pensions." Barton replied to the effect that the surplus went to the States, and to keep it would lead to the financial embarrassment of the States; and that there was not sufficient anyhow. At various times Labor members have made other suggestions. Senator Pearce suggested taking over the tobacco monopoly and letting the profits provide for old age pensions, and his motion embodying that idea was carried. At last Mr. Fisher revived the idea of setting apart and saving up the surplus revenue, and the Government agreed to it and introduced a bill accordingly, which went through the Parliament quickly. The Bill for Invalid and Old Age Pensions followed it and went through the House of Representatives on 3rd June, 1908, in one sitting, and passed the Senate next day without amendment.

Labor members generally are good fighters. They are also keen critics. Most of them are more comfortable in opposition than supporting a Government with much of whose work they are dissatisfied. The Deakin Ministers had not been as alert in enforcing the White Australia policy as was desired. The Postal Department had been starved for want of funds, whilst surplus moneys had been paid over to the States enabling them to have huge surpluses. There had been a great demand for telephone extension, but no funds in the department to meet it. These facts had been largely hidden until the Commission began its inquiry, though they were evidently known to every Postmaster-General and Treasurer.

It was a tired and weak Government which attempted to struggle along with the responsibilities of a great Commonwealth, and it became evident that a change was inevitable. It was only a question of when and how. The leader of the Anti-Socialists (Mr. Reid) noticed the unrest. He had been trying hard in a blundering sort of way to unite the direct Opposition and the corner nondescripts. Negotiations were still going on when he thought to force the matter to an issue and at the same time test the feeling of Labor. On 20th October, 1908, he moved, " That the financial proposals of the Government are unsatisfactory to this House."

The Labor Party decided in caucus that they would all sit silent, but would vote for the Government. They could not defend the Government, but would choose their own time for putting it out. The Government was weak, but was better than the Anti-Socialists. Mr. Reid tried hard to draw Laborites, but failed.

Sir John Forrest, with whom Mr. Reid had been carrying on negotiations, but whom he had not consulted with regard to the censure motion,

moved to amend it by striking out the
words " are unsatisfactory to this House."
This was carried by 43 to 21. He then
moved to insert the words " be considered in
Committee on the Budget." This was negatived
by 60 votes to 7. Reid's henchman, Johnson, then
moved to insert " ought to make better provision
for the payment of old age pensions," and 18 voted
for this and 42 against, so the censure ended in a
farce. The incident emphasised the fact that the
Opposition was still divided, and Mr. Reid, realising
that he could not secure a united party of
Anti-Socialists, announced his retirement from the
leadership, and the direct Opposition elected Mr.
Joseph Cook in his place. Meantime, Labor was
thinking over the situation.

Early in November the feeling of dissatisfaction
came to a climax. It was felt that the policy of
financial drift could no longer be tolerated. The
party could not afford to keep a Government in
power which made no provision for the large sums
certain to be required in the near future for Old
Age Pensions, for development of the Northern
Territory, for Defence purposes, and for putting
the Postal Department in a state of efficiency. It
was clear that a difference must arise between the
party and the Government next session over the
proposals for amendment of the Constitution
submitted by the Government, as they did not go
far enough, and the party could not support them.
This was in relation to carrying out " New
Protection."

The only real difference of opinion in the party was as to whether they should take action at once or await the session of 1909. It was resolved to act at once, and the leader was authorised to convey the intimation to Mr. Deakin that the party could no longer support him. It was desired to avoid any recriminative debate, and it was thought that after the long and loyal support accorded the small party on the Treasury benches it was only reasonable to expect that they would give a Labor Government a fair chance. Mr. Deakin did not take kindly to the idea, and, when reminded of his previous statement that he would support a Labor Ministry, he said that he had since changed his mind.

On 6th November, 1908, Mr. Fisher made a statement in the House, simply and briefly that the Labor Party could no longer support the Government. Mr. Deakin seemed to expect that the statement would be followed by a motion. Within a day or two, however, the Government was willing to retire, and on the 10th, after making a statement to the House, Mr. Deakin moved formally an alteration in the hour of meeting next day. Mr. Reid objected to this, which meant that notice must be given and a day's delay would be secured; but to his surprise Mr. Deakin at once moved that the House at its rising adjourn until next day at three o'clock. Mr. Fisher quickly rose and moved to amend the motion by leaving out all the words after "that." The division was taken immediately, and resulted in 13 for the Government and 49 against.

The Opposition leader seemed to be taken back and missed his opportunity. He could easily have prevented the Labor Party getting into office by voting against them and taking his chance of after developments. He complained of the Speaker not calling him in preference to Mr. Fisher, but the Speaker called the man who rose first. As it turned out, Labor had the unique distinction of being put into power by its opponents. In these peculiar circumstances the second Labor Ministry came into office. Mr. Fisher left the choice of his Ministers to the caucus, and the following members were selected by that body but appointed to their respective offices by Mr. Fisher:—

The Honorable Andrew Fisher to be Prime Minister and Treasurer;

The Honorable William Morris Hughes to be Attorney-General;

The Honorable Egerton Lee Batchelor to be Minister of State for External Affairs;

The Honorable Hugh Mahon to be Minister of State for Home Affairs;

The Honorable Josiah Thomas to be Postmaster-General;

The Honorable George Foster Pearce to be Minister of State for Defence;

The Honorable Frank Gwynne Tudor to be Minister of State for Trade and Customs;

The Honorable Gregor McGregor to be Vice-President of the Federal Executive Council;

James Hutchison, Esquire, to be an Executive Councillor and Honorary Minister.

The Honorable D. Watkins was elected Whip and Secretary in the Representatives, and Mr. H. De Largie Whip in the Senate.

The new Ministry met the House on the 17th November, 1908, put through the Estimates and one or two minor matters, and then went into recess. Immediately upon doing so, the Labor Ministry began a vigorous policy of administration. The defence of Australia by Australians was provided for in accord with that self-reliant spirit taught in Labor's Objective. The building of the first ships for an Australian Navy was commenced; arrangements were made for the establishment of a factory for the manufacture of arms, etc., as well as for the starting of a Commonwealth Clothing Factory. Better administration of the White Australia policy was set up, and more undesirable aliens were sent back to their own country in a few months than previous Governments had discovered in years.

On March 30 the Prime Minister delivered his policy speech in Gympie. It was the first time a Labor Government had had a chance to frame a business policy for submission to Parliament, and it was admitted to be the boldest and most National Australian policy ever enunciated. Anti-Labor was struck dumb, and failed to find a flaw in it. Though they dare not openly attack the policy, the Conservatives secretly determined to defeat it, and so commenced an intrigue which finally brought together all the parties opposing Labor. Men who had for a lifetime advocated Freetrade as a great and sacred principle agreed to accept and support Protection. Members who had fought for Protection for years agreed to become one with the party which had for years fought against it, and who outnumbered them in both Houses. Thus the last of the Liberals sold themselves to the Conservatives in order to prevent Labor carrying into effect a programme to which they had no declared objection.

We have now reached the stage in Federal and in State political life when two parties face each other. On the one side there are the land monopolists, syndicators, money-grabbers, rings, trusts, combines, and the whole body of exploiters of society. They are led industrially and politically by the Federated Employers' Union. On the other side stands the people's party—those who work for the uplifting of the masses and the setting up of social justice. They are organised in Trades Unions and Labor Leagues. Conservatism has but a temporary victory, as Labor looks forward with confidence to the coming elections.

The House met on 26th May, 1909, for the fourth session of the third Parliament of the Commonwealth. A splendid programme of business was set forth in the Speech of the Governor-General. The first step towards striking a blow at land monopoly was taken by the introduction of a Bill for a graduated Land Tax. On the 27th the Address-in-Reply was moved and seconded. The new leader of the Opposition (Mr. Deakin) saw that the proposals of the Government as set out in the Speech were popular, and took steps at once to gag Parliament and prevent discussion. He put up Willie Kelly to do the dirty work. The latter moved the adjournment of the debate, and on division the combined Opposition won by 39 to 30, thus taking the business out of the hands of the

Government. Sir Wm. Lyne, and Messrs. Chanter, Wise, and Storrer voted with the Labor Party, and declined to sell their principles by following 'their late leader, Deakin. In a full House the parties stand 43 against 31. On the motion for adjournment of the House some vigorous speeches were delivered in exposure of Deakin's tactics. Mr. Fisher asked for a dissolution, but was refused, and on 2nd June Mr. Deakin and his crew of remnants of discredited parties took office and Labor went into Opposition.

What is known as "New Protection" is a proposal which entirely originated with the Labor Party. Hitherto protective duties benefited only the manufacturer. New Protection on the lines attempted by Commonwealth legislation means that the people, through the power of Parliament, undertake to guarantee to Australian manufacturers the Australian market on the understanding that they pay fair and reasonable wages to their employees, and do not enter into combines or trusts, or overcharge consumers for their goods. Several Acts control this policy directly and indirectly, all more or less contributing to enforce the principle. These are the Australian Industries Preservation Act, Bounties Act, Customs Act, Customs Tariff Act, Excise Tariff Act (Agricultural Machinery), Secret Commissions Act, Commerce Act, and Trade Marks Act.

Power is taken to stop the dumping of foreign-made goods at prices under which they can be honestly manufactured. Local makers are prohibited from selling under cost, and if any

manufacturer feels that a competitor is doing so he
can hale him to Court and make him prove that he
can produce the article at the price and pay fair and
reasonable wages. In such a case the complainant
cannot succeed if in his own case he has an
out-of-date plant. Rebates and secret commissions
are prohibited, and all goods imported must be of
the correct weight and state the contents of the
manufacture; and most of the States having passed
similar laws applying locally, fair competition all
round is assured so far as lawmaking can do it.

Under the Excise Act power was taken to
compel the makers of agricultural machinery to pay
excise as per the schedule of the Act. Taking
harvesters as example, they had to pay £6 each as
excise unless they secured exemption, which was at
once granted so soon as they satisfied the proper
authority that they paid fair and reasonable wages.
Under the tariff they had a protective duty of £12
per machine, which enabled them to pay Australian
wages. In that connection a limitation was placed
on the selling price, but the intention is to provide
for a Commission or Board of Trade which shall have
power to ascertain the cost of manufacture of all
kinds of locally-made articles and report to
Parliament. If it is found that prices asked for the
goods are over and above a fair profit, Parliament
will reduce the tariff.   If, on the other hand, it
appears that foreign competition is preventing the
industry from carrying on successfully under
efficient management, Parliament will be expected
to raise the duty on that particular line.   Further,
it is intended to have all articles made under fair

wage conditions stamped with the Commonwealth stamp, so that purchasers can become aware of whether they are patronising a sweater or a fair employer.

The experience already gained of this entirely new and experimental legislation is highly interesting from more than one point of view. One of the grievances against the Deakin Government was their laxity and slowness in enforcing the Act. When they at last began to enforce it the attitude of the capitalist toward legislation giving fair conditions to working men soon became notably apparent. The firm which had made more noise than any other about the unfair competition of a foreign trust fought bitterly against fair play being conceded the workers employed by them. This was the firm of McKay Brothers, makers of the Sunshine Harvesters. To get outside the jurisdiction of the Wages Boards of Victoria they had removed from Ballarat to Braybrook Junction, just outside the metropolitan area. Though taking full advantage of the high tariff and the anti-trust legislation which stopped the dumping of foreign-made harvesters, they refused to comply with the Excise Act or pay fair wages. Other firms followed their example. At last action was taken and the firms were cited to the Commonwealth Court of Conciliation and Arbitration. The case was heard by Justice Higgins, and his award marks an era of advance in this kind of legislative interference with private enterprise. Not only did he order a rise in wages running from a shilling up to three shillings per day increase on

rates previously paid, but, most important of all, he
laid down a principle as a guide in fixing wages.
On this point the learned Judge says in his award :—

"The provision for fair and reasonable
remuneration is obviously designed for the
benefit of the employees in the industry; and it
must be meant to secure to them something
which they cannot get by the ordinary system
of individual bargaining with employers. If
Parliament meant that the conditions shall be
such as they can get by individual bargaining
—if it meant that those conditions are to be
fair and reasonable which employees will accept
and employers will give in contracts of service
—there would have been no need for this
provision. The remuneration could safely have
been left to the usual, but unequal, contest, the
' higgling of the market ' for labor, with the
pressure for bread on one side and the pressure
for profits on the other. The standard of ' fair
and reasonable ' must therefore be something
else; and I cannot think of any other standard
appropriate than the normal needs of the
average employee, regarded as a human
being living in a civilised community. I have
invited counsel and all concerned to suggest
any other standard; and they have been unable
to do so. If, instead of individual bargaining,
one can conceive of a collective agreement—an
agreement between all the employers in a given
trade on the one side, and all the employees,
on the other—it seems to me that the framers

of the agreement would have to take, as the first and dominant factor, the cost of living as a civilised being. If A lets B have the use of his horses, on the terms that he give them fair and reasonable treatment, I have no doubt that it is B's duty to give them proper food and water, and such shelter and rest as they need; and, as wages are the means of obtaining commodities, surely the State, in stipulating for fair and reasonable remuneration for the employees, means that the wages shall be sufficient to provide these things, and clothing and a condition of frugal comfort estimated by current human standards. This, then, is the primary test, the test which I shall apply in ascertaining the minimum wage that can be treated as 'fair and reasonable' in the case of unskilled laborers."

McKay Brothers' employees, with the exception of a few, were not organized, hence the conditions indicate what happens in such cases, and are a very complete exposition of " freedom of contract." The Judge says:—

" It is absurd to pretend that any foreman, however discriminating, can assess values of work with such nicety as these wages indicate— one penny a day sometimes, or sixpence a week. Mr. McKay, who fixes the wages for the factory, says that he pays the men—nearly 500 in number, and of many different trades— according to their values. Of course, he means according to his opinion of their values. Yet when I asked what was the difference between an improver at 7s. 10d. a day and a journeyman at 8s. a day in the department of sheet-iron workers, Mr. McKay admitted that there was no appreciable recognisable difference between the men corresponding to the 1s. a week difference between their wages. One of the applicant's witnesses, Mr. Rigby, of the Austral Otis Company, complacently assured me, on the strength of a brief inspection of the factory, and of the list submitted by the applicant, and without knowing the qualifications of the individual men, that the wages paid are, in his opinion, fair and reasonable. He did not consider the quality of the men at all, but the class of work. I can only say that I am not going to accept as final the employer's unchecked opinion as to an employee's worth in wages, any more than I should accept the value of a horse on the word of an intending vendor. The one-sided nature of an employer's valuation of an employee is indicated clearly by the frank statements of Mr. Geo. McKay:—' I pay the men what I consider them to be honestly worth. In fixing the wages I have endeavored to get labor at the cheapest price that I honestly could.' "

When dealing with the class termed " unskilled labor " and those termed " improvers " or partially trained, Justice Higgins remarks:—

" The existence of this class is a standing menace to industrial order and industrial peace, as well as a hindrance to industrial efficiency. As one witness has said:—' Employers will take on the slightly inferior tradesmen if they ask for a little less than the standard wage, and the result is that the efficient tradesman has often to walk about. . . . Unless the efficient tradesman cuts his rates, the imperfectly-trained men are taken on. . . . We journeymen have to go without work months and months, because we cannot get a journeyman's wage.' It is this body of half-trained men, hanging on to the skirts of a trade, that is used for the purpose of pulling down the wages of men fully trained. On this irregular force of industrial inefficients an employer can always rely for temporary assistance in industrial crises.'"

After a visit to McKay Brothers' factory he says:—

" The factory bears every sign of business-like management, of devices for economy in labor, of devices for keeping employees at high pressure. The work is minutely subdivided; the pace of the men is increased by ' repetition ' work; and all the latest labor-saving appliances are adopted. All these economies are, of course, legitimate, so far as the Excise Tariff is concerned. The employer can displace men by introducing machinery as he chooses. He can make the work as monotonous and as mind-stupifying as he thinks to be for his advantage. He has an absolute power of choice of men and of dismissal. He is allowed—if my view of the Act is correct—to make any profits that he can,

z

and they are not subject to investigation. But
when he comes, in the course of his economies,
to economise at the expense of human life, when
his economy involves the withholding from his
employees of reasonable remuneration, or
reasonable conditions of human existence, then,
as I understand the Act, Parliament insists on
the payment of Excise duty. The applicant
seems to me to have fallen, most naturally, into
the practice of not spending more in the payment
of his employees than is sufficient to induce
them to work for him. Most naturally, as he
buys his raw material, his iron, and his wood
in the cheapest market, he in many cases pays
no more to the workmen than the price at which
they can be got. There is no evidence that he
is a bad or an unfeeling employer. His mode of
dealing with his employees is reasonable from
an employer's point of view, as a purchaser of
labor as a commodity.''

In the New South Wales Arbitration Court,
Judge Heydon laid down the principle that no
industry should be permitted to exist if it could not
pay a '' living wage '' to its employees. Justice
Higgins, under the more explicit terms of the
Federal law, fixes a better standard—'' the normal
needs of the average employee, regarded as a human
being living in a civilised community.'' This
declaration will live, and it is only a matter of a
short time ere the Constitution of the Commonwealth
will be altered so that the Court can enforce the
Judge's decision.

After exhaustive evidence, Justice Higgins hesitated between 7s. 6d. per day and 7s., eventually fixing the latter as the lowest rate to be paid to the most unskilled laborer, and in his opinion the lowest rate of wage upon which a workman could live decently in Victoria. In connection with the anti-trust legislation and kindred laws, the Labor Party does not expect it to prove entirely successful. They are opposed to the continuance of the competitive system, and look forward to the setting up of a co-operative commonwealth; but as practical politicians, they are forced to recognise existing political thought. The great mass of the electors favor legislative restriction, and hence it has to be tried and found wanting ere the next step can be taken.

The Party strongly favors taking over a number of monopolies, but the Constitution is against it, and the public are hardly yet educated up to an amendment taking such wide powers — more especially as existing State Governments in almost every case fight against any extension of Federal powers. Mr. Thomas, the Labor Postmaster-General, secured the appointment of a Royal Commission, of which he was Chairman, which reported in favor of the Commonwealth running its own mail steamships between Australia and Great Britain. The people are beginning to realise the tremendous taxing power now used by the shipping ring which controls shipping on the Australian coast; hence on all these matters there is the pressure of evil conditions and unjust burdens on one side and the active propaganda of Labor men on the other, both of which are tending in the direction of securing Labor's ideal.

As to the composition of the Commonwealth Labor Party, it contains more than one member possessed of independent means, as well as a doctor, journalists, lawyers, artists, engineers, metallurgists, miners, and many tradesmen. They have all had a varied experience, and it is interesting to know that few if any of them have not at some time in their lives engaged in manual labor. All are more or less well acquainted with economic questions, and several are close students of science and philosophy. In the first two Parliaments the party also included a clergyman, but he deserted at last election. For varied knowledge of life, for intensity of purpose and whole-souled devotion to that purpose, no other party stands equal to Labor.

CHAPTER XXVI.

THE SUFFRAGE AND SELF-GOVERNMENT.

AUSTRALIA has given to the world many object lessons in the shape of advanced legislation, as well as some experiences to be avoided. Real progress can only be made where the people as a whole rule their own destinies. Except in the Commonwealth, the masses have not yet secured control of their own law-making. In the mother colony of New South Wales, when they were drafting a new Constitution for responsible government, they referred the matter to a committee, which deliberately declared that in its opinion a conservative element was necessary in the Constitution, hence they proposed that a hereditary nobility should be created for the second Chamber. The Crown was to decide whether the first holders of titles should have a life tenure, but afterwards the Council was to be elected by the aristocracy from members of their own class.

This would have been adopted but for the storm the project raised. Numerous public meetings were held, and the late Henry Parkes and others fought the matter so strongly that the Legislative Council of the day had to give way, and the nominee system was adopted. The new Constitution giving responsible government was adopted on 21st December, 1853. A property qualification was required for electors for the Assembly, and in the Victorian

Constitution, proclaimed November 23, 1855, the same provision was made.

Manhood suffrage and vote by ballot were first instituted in Australia in the Constitution adopted by South Australia when it secured responsible government on December 26, 1855. Victoria followed by adopting vote by ballot on March 19, 1856. The property qualification for Assembly electors was abolished August 27, 1857, and manhood suffrage adopted on November 24, 1857. New South Wales adopted manhood suffrage and vote by ballot on November 24, 1858. Queensland secured manhood suffrage on January 22, 1872. Tasmania did not get it until January 28, 1901.

It was the advent of Labor in politics which brought womanhood suffrage, and in that, as in many other matters, South Australia led the way. The measure conferring votes on women was reserved for royal assent on December 21, 1894. It had a narrow escape, as it only just secured the necessary two-thirds majority on the second reading in the Assembly, and would not have passed but for an accidental circumstance. The Government Whip had secured the number required, viz., twenty-eight, but one of these was wobbly. This was Jimmy Howe, who had not the courage to vote against the measure, but openly said he was not going to stay at the House after eleven o'clock for anybody. On the night of December 11, 1894, the House was ready for the vote on the second reading. Solomon had the floor before 11 o'clock, and was making a stonewalling speech against the bill. The Opposition Whip had his eye on Jimmy Howe, and at last saw the latter leave for home—true to his assertion that he would not stay after eleven. The Whip handed a slip of paper to his leader, and on it was pencilled:

" It's alright, Sol.; there are only twenty-seven present now."

" Sol " stopped; the division bells rang; but, to the utter consternation of the Opposition, Jimmy Howe turned up in division. It transpired that as Jimmy was going down the steps of Parliament House on his way home, he was met by Sir Langdon Bonython, who was on his way to see how things were going, and detained Jimmy in conversation until the bells rang, when of course the wobbler had to go in and vote as he had promised, and thus adult suffrage was originated in Australia.

West Australia adopted it next, on December 16, 1899. It came mainly because of Federation. Sir John Forrest's Government had an opinion that women would vote against the adoption of the Federal Bill, and therefore arranged for the women to exercise the privilege on the Referendum. It turned out that they voted for Federation. The next to adopt adult suffrage was the Commonwealth Parliament. Their measure was assented to on October 10, 1902. New South Wales followed on January 6, 1903. Tasmania was next, their Act being assented to on February 29, 1904. The Queensland Act is dated January 25, 1905. Victoria only secured the passage of the measure in November, 1908. The Assembly of that State passed the measure about sixteen times, but the Council had always rejected the measure hitherto. Australia

has now gained full adult suffrage in the Commonwealth and for the Assemblies in all the States.

The next great struggle will be for the abolition
of the second chamber in all the States. These
branches of the Legislature have remained
wonderfully loyal to the principle laid down by the
committee which drafted the New South Wales
Constitution. They are indeed a "conservative
element." Their idea of conservatism is to keep
all powers, privileges, and advantages enjoyed by
the rich safe in their hands, and to oppose any
forward movement calculated to make brighter the
lives of the masses. Every measure of social justice
is either rejected or so emasculated as to be
valueless. In word they claim to be the House of
Revision and a check upon hasty and ill-considered
legislation, but in deed they are the bulwarks of
legalised exploitation and robbery of the people.

In State matters the people have not yet secured
full self-government. So long as they permit the
Upper House to exist, real advance is held back,
and social justice is denied. Spasmodic effort has
been made in almost every State to reform the
Council, but every Government hitherto has given
up the struggle just when the people were waking
up. Electors have yet to be educated to realise that
it is the extreme of foolishness to run a bicameral
system in which one House spends its energies in
framing and passing such laws as the people are
suffering for the want of, while at the same time
the other House deems it its bounden duty to put
the result in the waste-paper basket. There are
years of effort before the Labor Party ere they

educate the people out of the superstition that we must have two Houses of Parliament. No other party has the courage or the interest to fight the Council; no other party has the machinery outside the House to keep up the struggle until the result shall be assured.

The Legislative Council in every State is a part —and the most important part—of the vested interests of the capitalist class. The land question and the ownership and control of machinery lie at the root of the social problem, and the Upper Houses are almost entirely composed of landowners and capitalists. The passing of a law giving manhood suffrage does not imply that the people really were able to enjoy the privilege. In almost all the States the electoral machinery was against the masses, and it took a long struggle on the part of Labor to secure the measure of self-government now enjoyed.

CHAPTER XXVII.

EIGHTEEN YEARS OF SOCIAL EVOLUTION.

THE influence of the Labor Movement on the political thought of the Australian people is not to be measured by the number of members returned to Parliament. A solid, united, compact body acting together, even though numerically few, can exert a wonderful influence upon other parties less united. For about five years in each case the party held the balance of power and supported a Government. This was the situation in South Australia with Kingston as Premier; in New South Wales with Reid, and after that with Lyne; and in Victoria with Turner and Peacock. The most democratic measures hitherto passed were put through under those circumstances. It also accounts for the fact that until Federation came the Party did not grow in numbers as one would have expected. When the party entered into the active political life of each colony it was sneered at and looked upon as but a passing phase arising out of a temporary excitement. The intense earnestness of members of the party, their close attendance to duty, their habit of asking ugly questions and probing into matters which needed to have daylight let in on them, soon caused Governments and their followers to look upon Labor as a factor to be reckoned with.

Labor members took politics as a serious business, and forced the House to look upon law-making as something of serious importance to the people. By persistent pressure they forced questions of a humanitarian character to the front, until of late years the most prominent political question is that of the social problem, and no political platform is without a proposal dealing with some phase of it. Taking the membership of the Labor Party from its inception as found in the Legislative Assembly of each State and for both Houses of the Commonwealth Parliament, the numbers present the following barometer:—

Year.	Total Members.	Year.	Total Members.
1891	36	1901	98
1892	57	1902	94
1893	69	1903	111
1894	69	1904	147
1895	61	1905	147
1896	66	1906	158
1897	64	1907	148
1898	65	1908	165
1899	70	1909	171
1900	67		

I have included the Senate with the above because both Houses are elected by the same franchise, whereas in four States the Legislative Council is elected on a property qualification, and in the other two it is a nominee Chamber.

Australia is lacking in statistics connected with the problems in which Labor is interested, and it would take immense research to get at the results of the voting at each election, but taking the

number of members elected it will be seen that the
greatest advance has been made since Federation.
The gain is greater than it appears, as there has
been an increase of 62 Labor members in the several
States, whilst at the same time there has been a
decrease of 81 in the total membership of the
Assemblies. In 1900 we totalled 67 out of 428; in
1909 we have 129 out of 347. Labor has also 13
members in the Legislative Councils, which gives a
total of 184 Labor members for Commonwealth and
State Parliaments. Gauged by membership, the
first ten years showed a struggle, Labor just holding
its own apparently; whilst it has had a continuous
increase during the last eight years. Tested by the
work done, however, we find that in the States
Labor secured more beneficial legislation during
that ten-year period. In the Commonwealth Parliament it has held the balance of power and secured
legislation, while steadily gaining in numbers.

The evolution has been from (1) supporting a
Government which would pass Labor measures; to
(2) becoming the direct Opposition; (3) becoming
the Government. Coming in as a third party they
naturally supported those who would take up any
of the Labor Platform, and when those whom they
supported joined the Conservatives—as they
invariably have done in every State—Labor became
the Opposition. When clear of other parties they
steadily increase at every election, and cannot fail
to capture the position of Government very soon in
all the States. Labor has been much criticised
because it refuses to enter into a coalition with the
so-called Liberal parties. Labor men are students

of political and social science, and know that in a coalition conservatism invariably wins. The mere superficial observer imagines that, because he finds a similarity between the political proposals of other parties and those of Labor, it would therefore be wise for Labor to unite with them. As a matter of fact, there is nothing in common between Labor and any other party. They can and do work together when forced to do so, as we have seen, but they are wide as the poles when we come to consider them as political parties outside the House.

The Labor Party does not control or govern the movement. The platform is not framed by the party inside, but emanates from the people. A Labor member cannot fool the people, even if he wanted to. Members of other political parties can and do fool the people. Their constituencies are selected for them by other politicians, and, at the best, electors have but little say as to who shall represent them. In the case of Labor, the electors frame the policy, and select the man they want to carry their banner to the polls. Every Labor member has to submit himself to the leagues and unions in his electorate for selection prior to every contest; no other politician similarly submits himself. It is a people's movement, controlled by the people; and so long as it remains true to that principle, so long will continue to grow. Coalitions of any kind are an invasion of that principle and antagonistic to it. Coalitions necessarily involve the question of immunity at election time, and this is an interference with the rights of the electors of each constituency concerned. It would be simply going back to the old parties' methods of the politicians running things instead of the people concerned doing so. The Labor Movement is based upon a recognition of the right of the people to govern themselves in their own way and according to their own ideas.

Critics who think that a discussion is settled by the mere use of catchwords have charged Labor members with being subject to the control of a " machine." By this they infer that the leagues and unions directing the Labor Movement are akin to the " machine " run by American Bosses. He must be a stupid man indeed who can see any analogy between the two. Bossism is simply the Boss and his friends controlling a limited organization for their own ends. The Labor Movement has no Bosses, and no personal ends to gain. In the past a few men have come into it to try to make it a stepping stone by which to attain political position, but one has only to look at its rules to see that there is but little if any chance for that sort of person to do so now. The Australian Trades Union and Political Labor Movement has been absolutely without a suspicion of anything of the kind known as " graft " in America. Such an evil as bribery is unknown. Members of the organizations are a suspicious and alert body of men, and selfish schemers are soon seen through and get short shrift.

The greatest difference of all between Labor and other parties lies in the fact that Labor has an ideal. It realises that there never can be social justice under a capitalistic system of production, distribution, and exchange. It aims at a gradual but nevertheless complete and permanent change. Capitalism, commercialism, competition and its concomitant, wage slavery, must go. Co-operation and production for use must come. Every other political party in Australia is opposed to those ideas. Every one of them wants to retain the present awful, wicked system, wasting time and trying to hide glaring evils by putting patches on them to cover them up until after next election. They are all parties of expediency. It is come-day-go-day and hold on to office by dodging everything which demands a firm stand and involves risk to their political skins.

Labor's opponents admit that it has high ideals. They admit that Labor has done good work and has a clean record. They admit that its members are as able as other politicians, and yet they have resorted to every artifice in order to prevent Labor getting into power. This is only what must be expected of them. The social problem is the line of demarcation between other parties and Labor. There are but two parties—those who want to abolish injustice and wage slavery, with all that comes of poverty and unemployment; and those who think that the present system is right enough with just a little touching up here and there. The Conservatives have no policy, and adopted an honest label when they declared themselves Anti-Socialists. They are anti-social. They care not for the masses, except in so far as they are useful to maintain the rich in unearned luxury. Economically ignorant, they cannot conceive it possible that the present social system can be improved. Their hopelessness is

declared by their leader, Mr. G. H. Reid.   In his
"Essays on Freetrade," page 66, published in 1875,
he said:

> "Will it not be time enough to manufac-
> ture everything for ourselves when we can save,
> instead of now when we would lose, by the
> operation? Will it not be well to reap the advan-
> tage of the pauper labor of other countries until
> we are so great a nation that we have pauper
> labor of our own?"

On October 31, 1901, in the Commonwealth
Parliament, he said:

> "How are we going to compete with these
> underpaid, sweated countries until our own
> labor is underpaid and sweated too? . . . It
> seems to me that the prospect of growing these
> noxious weeds of sweated industries on this
> bright continent should cause a man associated
> with the interests of Labor to shudder.   In the
> plenitude of time, when our millions become
> tens of millions, we shall have a crop of misery
> which will solve the difficulty in regard to
> cheap manufactures."

Apparently Reid has no hope that we can escape
from the misery of old lands. Labor not only hopes,
but can see the way to bring about highly improved
conditions of life long before there are tens of
millions in Australia. Labor has confidence in the
Australian people. It has patience to work for and
await results. Labor looks ahead, lays its plans, and
works along well-thought-out lines. No other party

First Commonwealth Labor Ministry, 1904.

Fisher. H. Mahon. W. M. Hughes.

ever showed that it trusted the people. With very few exceptions Governments always arranged the elections in such a way that thousands of electors have been disfranchised. In every State, though nominally the suffrage demanded had been granted, a certain class of electors was always disfranchised by various devices. It was invariably the workers. The Labor Party in every State has been fighting for electoral reform and administration so that this evil could be abolished. In order to defeat Labor men the Governments select the most unsuitable day for elections, so that electors cannot get to vote. Plural voting is still permitted to the rich.

The people are at last awaking to the fact that men professing democracy will not trust the democracy, and are the worst kind of conservatives. In choosing between the two old parties it was only a question of degree. Labor has forced them into one camp, and the country can now see that they were really one crowd all the time. Some of my friends of other parties will feel annoyed at this, and will claim that their motives are just as pure as Labor's, and that they are equally sympathetic. I do not deny that some of them are unconscious of evil motive. Their intentions may be alright, but the road to a certain warm place is said to be paved with good intentions. However, I am writing of the effects of the actions and teachings of politicians, not of what they may conceive their motives to be.

Political questions are now economic questions, and require that those who understand economics shall handle them. The days of slipshod expediency

AA

have gone by. The pressure of life is keener and the influence of law greater and more distinctly felt. Labor members have been termed professional politicians, and they do not object to the term. They are proud to be called professional law makers. The country has been governed by quacks long enough. Labor members have long since diagnosed social diseases, and know what remedy to apply when the country calls them in.

It has been distinctly good for Australia that Labor took a hand in law making and in the management of public affairs. Compared with previous experience, employers have enjoyed a period of industrial peace. This was not because the workers were more justly treated, but because they had set up courts to deal with such disputes on the one hand, and because, on the other, they had their energies and funds directed towards securing political control, and were willing to put up with a good deal until the more lasting changes came by constitutional methods.

Employers have themselves also turned their attention to the political field. They have spent much money and put up a very united effort to try to prevent the Labor advance. Their efforts have of course delayed the inevitable, but have only caused delay. The more clearly they appear in the fight the better for Labor, as it opens the eyes of the sleepy worker who has been falsely taught that the interests of capital and Labor are one, and, while rubbing his eyes, he begins to think. The farmer's son, now grown up and wanting land, as well as the man who wants to start farming, is finding out that to the bad government of old parties is due the land monopoly which exists to-day, and which shuts them off from a chance of making a home. They begin to see that the Labor Party is the only one fighting the monopolist, whether of land or anything else. They realise that Labor members want to get the workers out of the wage market; hence they want him to get a chance to go on the land, where he need call no man master.

The Labor Party does far more platform propaganda than the other party, and every new member is an additional propagandist. The Conservatives depend on the half-heartedness of hired brains in the press, but the press itself is carrying less weight than it did eighteen years ago. People realise that it is but a commercial concern, which stands by those who pay it best. Time was when no man could win a Liberal seat in Victoria if the Melbourne " Age " was against him; now it is quite common for men to win in spite of it. At the last election, Labor secured 21 seats in that State in spite of the press. The Labor Party is the only Australian Party. The organizations are all united throughout the continent. A Labor member visiting any State or the Federal House walks right into the Labor Party's room, and is welcomed as a comrade and brother. He takes part as opportunity offers in elections for any State. All have one common aim— one grand ideal.

This unity of thought and purpose must tell with increasing force and power as time rolls on. The safety and the success of the party depend on recognition of the organization. There is the same human tendency amongst Labor politicians as amongst all others to want to " run the show." In Queensland, Kidston kicked against the democratic method, and has gone " scab " on the movement; and, like all such, has become a worse man than his conservative opponents. Non-interference by the organizations with the Party in the House between elections, but full control of the movement outside as hitherto, is the only successful method. Each must do its own work.

Whilst it is admitted that the Labor Party was not alone in its advocacy of a White Australia, there is one phase of that question in which it specially led the way. A few years ago it was a common cry that the tropical portion of Australia was not a white man's country. It was held that women and children could not live in North Queensland, for instance, or in the Northern Territory. Outside of the ranks of the Labor Party this idea was generally accepted. It was asserted that sugar could not be grown if the growers had to depend upon white labor. It was not merely a question of wages; it was claimed that he could not stand the work in that climate. Labor was the only political party in the States which held an opposite view. Federally, it had the help of the Barton-Deakin party, but time has proved that the Labor Party's foresight and knowledge were correct. Sugar is successfully produced by white labor, and the figures of Mr. Knibbs, the Commonwealth Statistician, prove Queensland to be the healthiest place in the world for women and children, as the increase of population by excess of births over deaths is 1720 per 100,000, whereas the average for the Commonwealth is 1694.

The Anti-Socialist is invariably the most unpatriotic person to be found. He belongs to the " stinking fish " party. If he cannot get his own stupid way he denounces the country in which he has done so well. The bedrock of the cry for a color line across the continent, so that Anti-Socialists could boss niggers and yellow men, is found in the Anti-Socialist's nature. He is a born tyrant, and as the white Australian will not stand his tyranny he must have a nigger to order about. There is no patriotism in the Anti-Socialist press, hence it barracks for anything the capitalist crowd asks for.

Whilst giving due credit to many public men of other political parties who individually spoke up for a White Australia, I have no hesitation in asserting that but for Labor there would have been a compromise, and Australia would not have been a white man's country to-day. Labor admittedly forced the drawing of the color line on the mail-boats running to England. The Anti-Socialists would alter that to-morrow if they had the power. The public have been educated, and now see that Labor was right. Success tells. The policy of the party as applied to sugar growing has resulted as follows:—In 1902 12,254 tons were grown by white labor, and 65,581 by black; in 1907 157,000 tons were produced by white labor, and only 16,870 by black. The total production increased from 77,000 tons in 1902 to 173,000 tons in 1907, and the area under sugar from 95,697 acres in 1902 to 133,148 acres in 1907.

But for the Labor Party the Commonwealth would have started its life in debt. The borrowing policy has had such a grip of Australian Governments that it amounts to a craze, and is enough to make one wonder whether they are not really agents for the British money-lender. I deal with this elsewhere, but it is important to record here that the first Treasurer actually proposed that the Commonwealth should borrow half a million for public works. The Labor Party stopped it, and thus laid the foundation for the system of constructing all public works from revenue. Since the setting up of the Commonwealth, over £2,000,000 have been expended on public works out of revenue, and not only has this been done, but over six millions more have been paid to the States than they had any claim to under the Constitution. The Barton Government might be called the pick of past Governments, yet no stronger evidence could be adduced of the incapacity of such men to manage public financial affairs than this attempt to perpetuate the mad borrowing craze, and Labor had to show a better way.

One of the most noticeable effects of Labor's advent and increased strength in all the States is that it has demonstrated to the people the fact that there was no real difference between the two old parties of so-called Liberals and Conservatives. There are no " Conservatives " now. They have all become " Liberals " since Labor took a hand. In their desperate efforts to retain power and office they are forced to take the Labor Party's planks one after another, and to pass laws supposed to carry the ideas of Labor into effect. These laws, however, contain little more than the name, as the Second Chamber still fulfils its mission of retarding every effort calculated to abolish privilege. They cannot fool the people all the time; and as Labor is now the direct Opposition, and as all other Governments are more or less disappointing, it will not be long ere the people will give the party its chance in every State.

The party has had a modifying influence upon the Conservative party in every Parliament. Acts passed with many imperfections would have been much worse but for the work put in when the measures were in committee. The Labor members' point of view has always been so different that when it was put it made an impression. Even the Houses of Privilege are not quite so extreme as they were, though they still stand in the way of real progress in every State. The grumbler who sneeringly asks: " What has the Labor Party done?'' has no conception of the hundred and one times in which the party has prevented worse things happening to the people than have come about from imperfect legislation. The party's mere presence counts. Their solidarity has made them a power to be reckoned with, and Ministers, when drafting a measure, take that disturbing fact into consideration.

The tone of Parliament has changed. The presence of the party and its constant note of humanitarianism have forced the social problem to the front. Parliamentarians have been obliged to

state definitely their attitude towards the great
problems involved. They have been forced to go
either into one camp or the other. The welfare of
the masses is now the dominant idea, much as
politicians may differ in detail as to how that
welfare may best be secured. Since the advent of
Labor-in-politics it has been admitted by their
political opponents that the character of the several
Parliaments has been raised. The men who looked
upon the House as a sort of club, to be dropped into
at their leisure, where they might casually take a
hand by occasionally delivering an ill-prepared
speech, are finding that they are out of place, and
that the people demand serious and active work
from them.

Then there is the highly important, though
unrecorded and unseen influence upon administration—the cheek upon the scheming of private enterprise to get advantages at the expense of the general
community, and the enforcement of a more sympa·
thetic examination of grievances or cases of
injustice in connection with the public service. The
members of the Labor Party devote their whole
time to the work of the country, and hence they
have stirred up departmental officials in a way very
much needed, and the public are steadily finding out
that the " professional politicians," as some have
termed members of the Labor Party, are the best
kind to have. Law-making and administration are
daily becoming of more importance to the people,
and they are not going to be satisfied as of yore
with those who gave their best energy to their own
personal interests and the fag end of their tired

brains to the work which the country paid them to perform.

Turning to the industrial side, the change has been almost a revolution. From "freedom of contract" to compulsory collective bargaining is "a far cry, yet it has been realised. The Employers' Union in its blindness set out in 1890 to crush trade unionism. It was going to manage its several businesses as seemed best to the employer. The latter was to dictate his terms, and the seeker for work had the freedom to take the job at the boss's rate or to go elsewhere. The employer was to be free to carry on his undertaking as he liked. He was an individualist. He objected to the State, a trade union, or any other collective power interfering with him. When the Employers' Union won the fight of 1890—which, as I have elsewhere shown, should be known as a lock-out—they held banquets and congratulated themselves on their success. They followed it up with the attack on the Queensland bushmen in 1891 and the Broken Hill miners in 1892, winning, as they thought, in each case. They fell on each other's necks with joy.

They were as ignorant as mere children of history and of human nature. They overlooked the fact that the best workmen are in the unions, though they are invariably selected by them for employment. The unionists are the most intelligent of the workers. The employers prefer the workman who is vigorous. The vigorous person has energy, is broad in the head, and is combative. The silly fellows who had charge in the Employers' Union never dreamt of these facts when they took on the job planned in

1890. They touched the combative brain centre, and aroused the latent energy of the worker. The latter listened to the advice of his own leaders, and was also impressed with the advice of the capitalist press, which as usual counselled peaceful, constitutional methods of doing everything.

The unionists read the old gag in a new light, and began to reach out on new lines. With evolution of thought given expression in action, the unionist applied trade union methods to politics, and we can now look back on the result. The employer thought that he had secured "freedom of contract," but now he realises that he has lost most of the freedom he then enjoyed. Unionism has not been crushed, but has grown stronger than ever. Not only is this so, but it has extended into new fields. Even the clerks, who used to think themselves superior to the average trade unionist, have become organised, and actually fraternise with "ordinary tradesmen" and "common laborers."

The domestic servant has her Domestic Workers' Union, which in its office keeps a register of the mistresses and how they behave towards those who now condescend to work for them. Their union secretary keeps a black list, and on it are found the names of all those who are "bad pays," those who starve girls—and they are many—those who lock up the food, those who give way to temper and throw things at the maid—in short, all the shortcomings of the superior persons who form so-called Society, with a big "S." Many others, such as undertakers' assistants, cabmen, white workers, etc., have organized into unions. Then, think of what these common working people are doing in their behavior towards the employers, "don't-you-know." Why, instead of the employer dictating terms he will soon have no say in the matter at all.

There are Wages Boards by the score in Victoria, and a similar system in Queensland and South Australia; whilst we have had the Arbitration Court method in New South Wales and West Australia. There is also the Commonwealth Court, before which the great wool kings and others have had to appear. Thus, instead of freedom of contract, there are courts and boards before which the employer can be haled, and in which the workers whom he employs stand on the same footing as himself, and he has to justify before a judge or a chairman any wage rate he asks should be accepted. He is no longer allowed to dictate terms; no longer can he sweat his workers or pay this man one rate and that another. He is practically forced to recognise unionism and enter into a collective bargain. Further, he finds that he cannot break his word just as he likes, as in the good old days. If he does not carry out the order of the court or board he is treated as an ordinary common law breaker and is fined. Recently one was fined £50 and another £25 for paying less than award rates of wages.

As a matter of fact, we have quite a new class of crimes now. In the police court cases reported in the morning newspaper the longest list of offences is for breaches of the latest Acts protecting the community against those incipient murderers, the food adulterers. The most frequent is the case of the Christian brother who brings around the milk. His freedom to sell much water with a little milk has been done away with. He is no longer permitted to dispense water at fourpence per quart, as in the days of freedom of contract. All sellers of food become criminals if they do not act with moderate honesty.

There is also some attention paid to health and sanitation. Until Labor takes more control in municipal government we shall not get the full benefit, as the old style of councillor does not like these innovations, and it takes a deal of prodding to make him enforce the law.

Then we have the Early Closing Act. Just think of having to close the shop at six o'clock, and, worse still, to give half a day a week as a holiday. In connection with this I remember one scene with pleasure. I was a member of the New South Wales Parliament when Labor and Sir William Lyne passed the Act. On the night of the first half-holiday under it I chanced to visit the Theatre Royal, and found on getting inside that the family circle had been almost entirely filled by an early-door crowd. That in itself was nothing, but I soon observed that they all seemed to know one another, and were remarkably jolly and happy. Upon inquiry I found that they were all employees of one of the big firms which had always fought against early closing, and which previously used to work its shop-hands up till nine o'clock at night. This was the first opportunity they ever had enjoyed of attending a theatre, hence their excitement and pleasure.

Not only is the employer compelled to close at a reasonable hour, but he must provide seats for his shop girls. In the factory he is kept up to certain regulations in regard to hours, safety of machinery, sanitation, etc., all of which he neglected under the freedom-of-contract days of 1890.

There has naturally been an upward evolution in social status. The worker is becoming quite a respectable member of society. Since he asserted himself he has gained in self-respect, and also has raised himself in the estimation of his fellow man. The employer, being forced to meet him on an equality in the eye of the law, can no longer treat him as an inferior being. He kicked at first, but now, when unionists have him prosecuted for ignoring an award, or for not doing what inspectors have ordered to be done, he discovers that even his old friends the magistrates treat him as an ordinary law-breaker. He quickly finds his level, and is beginning to look upon the worker as a human being and a man, who has as much say in the management of public affairs as he has—in fact, is having more and more say.

Freedom of contract, indeed! Few of them like to hear about it now at all, and not many of them whine for the right to manage their business in their own way without interference. They are glad to go hat in hand to a Labor Premier, it may be, to ask for modification of certain enactments. They never speak of repeal, and neither do conservative politicians. The fact is, the more intelligent of the employing class are finding out that the legislation has been beneficial rather than harmful, and the honest trader frankly admits it.

There are other restrictions also under the anti-trust law and " New Protection " which touch the profit-making side of manufacturing—two important principles that have been well established by Labor influence in politics. There is no longer any question of the right, as well as of the power, of the State to interfere in affairs previously held to be private. To take over private enterprise concerns is but another step, and already the public mind is prepared for compulsory land resumption on the lines laid down in an early Federal Act. It has also been established that the State or Federal authority, as the case may be, can successfully carry on business enterprises—can run them much more economically and efficiently than private enterprise.

As already remarked, the work of the Anti-Socialist in the political field has caused people to be less alarmed about Socialism, and when they learn that the successful enterprises, such as Newport Workshops, are really Socialism in our own time they ask for more of it; hence we are nearly ready for the next big step—that of taking over every monopoly. Socialism is here. The measure we already have, so far from destroying the marriage tie, has improved the marriage rate and made the tie more secure, because it has provided more wages with which to make home more agreeable, and consequently more happy. The originator of that silly story—the Women's National League—has begun to read up Socialism and to try its hand at constructive politics, so it will soon lose its enthusiasm; and, instead of cursing Labor, may turn to bless its work.

Eighteen years ago we had no Australian literature, and no Labor press. Now we have Labor organs in every big city, a union-owned daily newspaper in Broken Hill, and many friends and open supporters amongst country newspapers. It is so long since some societies had a strike that they have nearly forgotten what a terrible thing it is. Good unionists never sought strikes and never will, but they will never cease working for better conditions, and the forward movement will never stop until social justice is done and every child born has equal opportunity.

CHAPTER XXVIII.

SOCIALISTIC ENTERPRISES.

FORTUNATELY for Australia, Governments realised at an early stage that it was wise to have the ownership and control of such business undertakings as railways and posts and telegraphs vested in the people. The cost of the first railway lines was enormous, owing to having them done under contract. One line in Victoria cost £47,790 per mile, and one in New South Wales £29,420 per mile. In both States they are now being constructed for less than £2000 per mile on the average in country not too rough. Several lines averaged about £1200 per mile. In the Commonwealth there are 14,189 miles of State-owned railways open. The cost totals £137,196,168. This covers all equipment. They employ 47,325 persons. In spite of the high rate of interest on the older loans, and the outrageous profits of contractors on their construction, they return a net percentage of 4.35.

Owing to the absence of water carriage inland, railways are a necessity in order to open up the country. When a Socialist Government takes office they will be run practically free. Hitherto they have been run in the interest mainly of big cities. In Victoria and in New South Wales every effort is made to draw everything to the capitals. Nearly half the population of the State in each case is found in the metropolitan area. They are there because of the people who pioneer, open up, and work the out-back country. If the country interests flourish the metropolitan cannot help going ahead. Up to date this fact has not dawned upon any political party outside Labor. The man in the country has to pay freights on what he sells and what he buys, interest on cost of construction, and the whole cost of running the lines, whilst the city dweller goes scot free. The country worker also has to pay part of the rents going to city landlords and the travelling expenses of the commercial traveller who goes round as agent for big warehouses, trying to induce him to buy what he does not want.

What is needed is a commencement by way of an advance of a certain amount from the general revenue, and a corresponding reduction in freights and fares; increase the sum steadily year after year, and make it good by a tax on unimproved land values; continue this until the railways have the same relationship to the people as the lifts to a big hotel or warehouse, viz., a part of the running cost. The effect would be to reduce rents, to stop the growth of land monopoly, to equalise land values, and to place the producer who lives far back in a position of almost equal advantage with the man nearer the market. As it is, the railways have to come to the help of the farmer and grazier in times of drought by carrying his starving stock at a loss, and they have often carried water over 100 miles and supplied a large community at very much below cost.

BB

With more efficient management in the direction of the supply of material the cost of running could be lessened. With a State-owned coalmine the railways of New South Wales could save over £30,000 per annum which they now pay to a coal combine. Coalmines could be got on every main line in that State. The Labor Premier of South Australia was alive to this advantage, and took steps to secure a coalmine in New South Wales, and if the shipping ring ˜overcharges for carriage of the coal no doubt State-owned ships will be put on.

The advantages of State-owned and controlled business undertakings have never been fairly stated by old-school politicians. They are so strongly in favor of everything being left to private enterprise that they try carefully to hide the facts regarding Australian experience in things publicly owned. Under capitalistic Governments it was inevitable that the administration should be unsympathetic, and that consequently the results have not been equal to what they would be under more interested and efficient control. Profits have not been shown as plainly as they ought to have been. For one thing, the Treasurer of the day did not want to encourage any further extension of the Socialistic movement; and, for another, he desired to quietly grab all sources of revenue in order to make out a good case for his financing.

The Auditor-General of New South Wales, in his report for the year ending June, 1908, points out the necessity for separating the records of business undertakings from those of administration. Taking four of the large undertakings run by the State, namely, railways and tramways, Sydney Harbor Trust, Metropolitan Water and Sewerage, and Hunter District Water Supply and Sewerage, he shows that the net profits for the past seven years total £1,690,044. Instead of giving this back in improved services or lowered rates, the Government quietly put it into the revenue account. The Auditor-General (Mr. Vernon) very properly says:

" The fact cannot be too often emphasised that these services were not established to yield profits above working expenses and charges for interest on loan capital and depreciation, hence the large excess credit of £1,690,044 should not be treated as a pure and final credit to the revenue—that is to say, these moneys should not be regarded as applicable year in and year out to expenditure on ordinary administrative functions. . . . . To take the business establishment in the first instance, here we have a series of flourishing enterprises which, in the hands of any private company working on true business lines and for profit, would return a sum largely in excess of the present revenue, which is rated very largely from the point of view of the State's or public benefit; and such being the case, the business undertakings may be taken as more than providing for themselves or their financial requirements, with a wide margin of safety as regards rating power. The business

undertakings are thus of no burden whatever
to the State, and £67,000,000 of the State's
public debt is wiped out by the value of the
works upon which the money was spent. Not
only so, but upon proper adjustments being
made—that is, the removal of charges for
interest now paid on account of States, etc.—
it is found that over and above their own
liabilities the business undertakings returned a
sum of £75,874 in excess of the annual interest
charge on the remaining loan liabilities of the
State, viz., £13,476,096, upon which the interest
at the average rate now paid (3.64 per cent.)
would amount to £490,530. It is thus plainly
to be seen that during the year 1906-7 the
business undertakings not only squared their
own liabilities, but also relieved the State of
any burden on account of loan liabilities.''

There are only 1068 miles of privately owned
railways in Australia, only 615 miles being open for
traffic by the public. Their charges are in most
cases double, and in many places treble, those of
the State-owned, both in fares and freights. They
give no concessions in time of drought. In
tramways there are 585 miles, of which 174 miles
are owned by Government, 222 by municipalities, and
188 privately. The net earnings on the Government
trams for 1907 were 4.92 per cent. The charges
on the privately owned are much higher than on
those controlled by the State, and with one exception
the service under private enterprise is very much
inferior.

The city of Adelaide had the first trams in Australia. They were horse tràction, and owned by private enterprise. As is usual with those having a monopoly, the service got worse as the vehicles became worn and shaky and the poor horses got older and slower. Labor Premier Tom Price was not long in office before with quick business acumen he secured the ownership of the whole concern for the public, and an up-to-date electric tram service has been the result.

New South Wales, Victoria, Queensland, South Australia, and West Australia have each magnificent workshops for the manufacture and repair of rolling stock. The buildings cover a very large area, and the machinery is the very best in every department. The works at Newport, Victoria, turn out all sorts of castings in iron, steel, and brass. During 1907 they were turning out castings at the rate of 250 tons per month. The huge forge turned out 2538 axles during 1907. For a number of years the railway engines had been made by the Phoenix Foundry Company at Ballarat. Extra prices were deliberately given at first to enable the company to put in the necessary plant.

The Phoenix Foundry Company started in 1870. Prior to the introduction of the engines known as the D.D. class they had made 344 locomotives for the Victorian railways at a cost of £1,263,568; including seven D.D. engines, 351 for £1,293,834. From March, 1873, to December, 1893, the average cost per ton was £84 1s., from July, 1899, to October, 1903, £76 10s. 10d.; and for the new engines of D.D. class, £67 2s. per ton.   Owing to the pressure of the Socialistic agitation of Labor, the manager of Newport Workshops was asked to tender against all others for thirty-nine engines of the D.D. class. When the tenders were received the prices put in were as follows:—Australian Otis Co., £5036 per engine, or £76 13s. per ton; Phoenix Foundry Co., £5020 per engine, or £76 8s. per ton; Newport Workshops, £3792, or £58 per ton.

Private enterprise took alarm at this, and moved heaven and earth to try to prove that the manager of the Government Workshops did not know his business, and had not allowed for everything.   Parliament   appointed   a   Royal Commission to investigate. The Commission made an exhaustive examination, heard all that private enterprise had to say, and finally reported that the cost could be reduced still more by the Newport shops.   In the meantime, the Phoenix Foundry Co. cut its price down by £8 per ton, and eventually the Government gave it a few engines to make— more for the sake of the workmen than for anything else.   The Commission estimated that the Newport shops would construct the thirty-nine engines for £1186 per engine under the Australian Otis firm, and £1173 per engine under the Phoenix Co.—a total saving of £46,254 in the first case, and £45,747 in the other, as against private enterprise.

Taking the actual experience since, the cost has proved to be much less. The average of the last series of thirteen came out at £2119 per engine less than the best tender of private enterprise for the thirty-nine. The cost for the thirty-nine at the present rate is £82,641 less than under private enterprise. This saving the Railway Commissioner has given to the people who use the railways, and yet the majority of the farmers oppose Socialism which gives them this advantage. Fifty - six locomotives have been made in the workshops since 1903. Careful records of the cost have been kept, and after allowing for everything the result has been as follows:—

	Average Cost per Engine.	Average Cost per Ton.
First series of 10....	£3364	£52 4 0
Second series of 10..	£3048	£47 11 0
Third series of 10...	£2857	£43 15 0
Fourth series of 13..	£2901	£44 7 10

An increase in the price of metals accounts for the increased cost of the last series. These were all engines of the D.D. type. They have also built very large engines for the express passenger trains. The great advantage to the patrons of the railway by the saving in the cost of rolling stock is seen by the fact of the Commissioner having reduced fares and freights by £114,000 per annum. Recently a magnificent dining-room for the use of the workmen has been erected, where first class meals are well served at a very low rate. The dining rooms are under the control of the men themselves.

New South Wales has every facility for turning out the whole of the rolling stock required at much lower cost than private firms can do it, but has not been allowed to do so. It is paying over £80 per ton for the same engine that Newport turns out at £44. The Government follows the old idea of putting as much as it can in the way of its friends at the expense of the taxpayer, hence only a portion of the work has been done at the workshops. Long ago it was proved that six Pullman cars could be made locally for a sum no greater than would be paid for four imported cars. The sleeping cars now designed and constructed in the Eveleigh workshops, N.S.W., and Newport, Vic., are much superior to the Pullman from every point of view.

South Australia, in addition to its railway workshops, has a Government pipe foundry at Granville. It employs 429 men and 93 boys. It has proved very successful. It carried out one contract for £11,332 less than the lowest tender in opposition. Private enterprise has already discovered that it has no chance of successfully competing, as it is conducted for profit only, whilst the other is serving the public at cost. Twenty-five municipalities own their gasworks in New South Wales, and six, including the city of Sydney, have their own electric light. Melbourne and Metropolitan Board of Works controls the water supply and sewerage of twenty cities, towns, and boroughs, and four shires. These serve a population of 513,000. The board is a State department. It made a profit on sheep at the Werribee sewerage farm of £11,948 last year. Adelaide sewerage farm netted £989 16s. 10d., or 4.002 per cent.

All the States do much for the farmer. South Australia was the first to start. In 1879 it set up a school of agriculture.   It has an agricultural college and three State farms.   Lectures are given in country districts.   Victoria has two agricultural colleges and five farms.   Experts travel and lecture also.   Queensland has a central college at Gatton and six experimental farms.   A dairy expert travels. New South Wales has a fine agricultural college and farm at Hawkesbury, and twelve experimental farms in different parts of the State.   West Australia has three State experimental farms, and does much in other respects to help men to qualify as agricultural workers.

South Australia is the most advanced in regard to export arrangements, and has an export department which handles perishable produce and frozen foods.   It arranges for space on the steamships, takes delivery of fruit, etc., at any railway station, and sends it to the world's market. This is done at bare cost—really for one-half the sum paid by Tasmanians to a private firm for similar work.   Fruit, eggs, poultry, and lambs, are all handled in this way.   The new killing yards and freezing works at Port Adelaide can treat 8000 lambs per day, and have cold storage for 200,000 carcases.   Under the poultry expert and export department, an inter-State trade of £120,210 was done in 1907, in addition to £2000 worth sent to England.   An order for 5000 eggs had even been filled for New Zealand, and no less than 36,487 dozen placed in cool storage.   Poultry was exported to the value of £20,000.   Recently the department has taken over the handling of the farmers' grain in the same way. It takes delivery at the railway station, and sends direct to the market in the old world, saving all middlemen's charges.

An illustration of how the producers are at the mercy of the middlemen occurred in Sydney in March, 1904. The Sydney Wool Buyers' Association and the wool-selling brokers have a rule of their organization which reads as follows:—"Cataloguing wool more than twice, penalty £50. No lot or portion thereof shall be offered at auction more than twice. Once a lot of wool has been shown and catalogued by one broker and unsold, such unsold wool or any portion thereof shall not go to another broker for public or private sale. To guard against any lot of wool being offered more than twice, when wool is received into the store the brand must not be altered or tampered with. The full brand must be always given on catalogues, also on invoices and specifications." The firm of John Bridge and Co. had dared to infringe this rule, and was not only fined £50 but suffered a boycott by the buyers until it fell into line with the others. These are the people who denounce Labor for objecting to work with non-unionists.

In South Australia private enterprise was robbing the dairy farmer of the value of much of his cream, and so in September, 1906, the Government started a butter factory, which is now turning out four tons per week, and is proving so successful that another £75,000 is being expended in extensions. The export department takes the butter direct from the factory and ships it to England for sale. Not only are the middleman's charges saved and put into the producer's pockets, but there is a guarantee that the quality is first-class, and higher prices are thus secured, while a constantly widening market is obtained owing to the confidence there is in the State brand.

Contrast these Socialist methods with the Government-aided private-enterprise methods of Victoria, where in 1889-90 £230,000 was set aside in bonuses for agriculture, dairying, fruit, and wine industries. For want of a Government export department a couple of private firms swindled the dairy farmers and butter-makers out of nearly one-half their share of this. Two firms and one company, by means of secret rebates from shipping companies, did all the handling, and got hold of £52,447 of the bonus. These firms stuck at nothing which would bring profit. They got hold of the Government stamp and put it on inferior butter. They swindled the poor Tommies who were in the field at the Boer war by supplying tins containing only fourteen ounces when they were being paid for sixteen. South Australian methods leave no chance for this kind of thing, and it is no wonder that with what is, on the whole, inferior country the South Australian farmer is doing better than the Victorian. He does not allow the term Socialism to frighten him, but looks at any proposal from a common-sense point of view, and merely asks if it will prove advantageous.

Since the starting of the South Australian export department thirteen years ago, land within the Goyder line of rainfall has increased in value by £1 per acre, owing to the facilities provided by the Government for the export of lamb and mutton. The State abattoirs utilise all by-products in a scientific way. The various works under the department, when additions now being made are finished, will have cost £170,000. The loss since starting totals £6016. Last year's profit, after allowing for everything, came to £1753 13s. 9d.— £1626 11s. 3d. on the freezing works, and £127 2s. 6d. on the butter factory. About £20,000 was paid for cream to the 775 suppliers, and £500 was distributed in bonus. The average price—local, inter-State, and English—secured for all grades of butter was 11¾d. per pound, and producers received this. No canvassers or middlemen come into the transaction, as the bonus draws trade and is paid on the percentage of cream supplied. The whole business is run on co-operative lines. The Export Department sold last year the following:— Lamb and mutton, 276,119 carcases; wine, 55,618 gallons; fruit, 153,904 cases; eggs, 51,943 dozen; honey, 95,468 pound; oranges, 1645 cases; and lemons, 400 cases; in addition to poultry as before stated. Altogether the total value exported came to £282,817 4s. 3d.

Most of the States have Commercial Agents abroad looking up markets for Australian products. All the States, except Tasmania, have some system of assisting the man on the land financially. South Australia has a State Bank, which made a profit last year of £3797 14s. 9d. West Australia has an Agricultural Bank, and Victoria a Credit Foncier. The sum of £1,601,637 was advanced last year to help men on the land. Altogether, a total of £5,377,307 has been advanced, and the balance due at the end of 1907 was £2,702,816. The profits, exclusive of New South Wales, amounted to £14,772. In many other ways much is done. The New South Wales Government recently imported £40,339 worth of wire netting, which is supplied to farmers on deferred payments. When private enterprise was going to rob the South Australian farmers by exorbitant prices for wire netting, the Government came to their aid and secured the article at a very much reduced rate. Some millions of money have been spent on water conservation and in boring for artesian supplies.

Only two of the States—West Australia and Queensland—give facilities for new men to take up land. The States of New South Wales and Victoria have so far done more to build up big estates and help the growth of land monopoly than to settle upon the land men who will stay there and work it to advantage. New South Wales has immense unpeopled areas of good land, but fails to make it available. For every block thrown open there are hundreds of applicants. Some are no doubt speculators, but there are more bona-fide applicants than can get a chance to make a home for themselves and help to develop the country.

During the period from 1889 to 1903 inclusive, New South Wales Government supplied seed wheat to farmers at a cost of £126,726. There is a balance owing of £31,670. It was a very badly managed affair, as in many cases auctioneers and agents instead of the poor farmer got hold of the wheat and sold it at a big profit. For educational purposes, in addition to the lectures by experts, the Government departments in several of the States issue a monthly magazine of high value to the man on the land.

Considerable amounts have been spent in mining development, though much money has been wasted. In New South Wales £388,702 has been spent in prospecting. Only £1610 has been repaid. In Victoria £13,124 has been spent on diamond-drill boring for leads; £271,022 has been spent out of loan money on mining enterprise, which included £27,839 advances to miners for prospecting, and £125,669 to mining companies to help in development. We cannot class this as Socialistic enterprise. It is rather too much in keeping with the policy which has proved so ruinous to Australia, viz., using the taxpayers' money to help private individuals.

Take, for instance, the fact that the Victorian Government paid £11,302 to the Railway Department to carry the coal of a private company at a cheap rate, thus enabling the company to put dividends in its shareholders' pockets to that amount. In the same way £25,000 was paid to the department to make good the carriage of farm produce at losing rates. This was for last year only. If we take the last five years we find that £31,623 has gone to coalmining companies in that way, and £167,588 to Victorian farmers. It would take pages to detail the many amounts of this kind which have been taken out of the pockets of the taxpayer and diverted into those of a class. They have various names, such as loans, advances, and bonus.

In every other State capitalistic Governments have similarly abused their power and bolstered up private enterprise at the expense of the taxpayers. One of the most glaring cases occurred in West Australia under Sir John Forrest. The Collie coal field, the only coal field on the west coast of Australia, was discovered by prospectors in the employ of the Forrest Government. This mine was opened out, and the value of the coal proved by the Government, which paid the miners for the coal produced. A tunnel was driven, and everything put in working order. A railway was also built by the Government, and altogether about £50,000 was laid out, after which the whole concern was quietly handed over to a private company of capitalistic sharks. The Government purchased coal from this company, paying as high as 13s. 6d. per ton, loaded into trucks at the mine, whereas better coal in New South Wales cost less than five shillings at the mine.

Thus the Government first used public money to find and open up a coal field—which the State sadly needed—and then not only gave the result of that expenditure to a private syndicate, but placed it in a position to levy blackmail permanently upon the people who use the railways. Whatever were the inducements offered the Government, they were kept secret; but it is a striking example of the methods of Government adopted by Anti-Socialists. Labor would have retained that mine for the good of the whole community and supplied the railways at cost of production, and the people would have had a continuous dividend in the shape of reduced freights and fares.

Another glaring case in West Australia was the sale of the Government smelting plant at Ravensthorpe. The plant was erected by the Government at a cost of £18,000 for the use of the miners. To make it a success it needed a railway, but in spite of petitions from the miners this was refused. The Government then sold the whole plant to a Mr. Kauffman for £5000, and that gentleman obtained £5000 worth of metal from the slag which was on the ground. He applied for a railway from Hopetoun, and the present Government at once agreed to build it for him. Thus he has a free gift of the smelters, which cost the taxpayers £18,000, and a railway to enable him to make still more profit by exploiting the fool public.

West Australia has successfully managed Government ironworks in Fremantle. They turn out work at considerably less than private enterprise. From July to December, 1907, pipes to the value of £21,763 were turned out by the Government works, whilst private firms made £30,817 worth. A deputation recently asked the Premier to close up the works and leave all to private enterprise, but he refused, and said that the Government intended to keep the departmental works going as a check on private enterprise. Experience had shown that without this check they would have to pay exorbitant prices for their requirements.

The influence of Labor was sufficiently strong in Commonwealth affairs to ensure that our first national effort in shipbuilding was carried out in State dockyards. The Commonwealth decided to conduct a series of experiments in deep-sea fishing off the Australian coast, and for this purpose needed a steam trawler constructed on the most up-to-date lines and with all the latest improvements. The management of the State-owned Fitzroy Dock, Cockatoo Island, N.S.W., took on the contract for £14,445. This covered everything except the winches, which cost £750 extra. The keel was laid on June 1st, and the boat was launched on 27th August, 1908. She is 135 feet long, and 23ft. 6in. beam, with 12ft. depth. She has 450-horse-power triple expansion engines, and can travel over 10 knots per hour. She can steam 4000 miles without coaling. The trawler section weighs ten tons, and is one of the biggest in the world. The boat has been named the "Endeavor."

From time to time the cry for village settlements has been raised, and a good deal has been done in that way, the most successful being in South Australia. Many a working man has been enabled to secure a home in the suburbs under this provision. In Victoria land has been purchased by the State and cut up into residential blocks, and persons settled thereon. The Closer Settlement Board in Victoria is limited to an expenditure of £500,000 per annum for five years. It can purchase land and cut it up into farms not to exceed £1500 in value, agricultural laborers' blocks not to exceed £200, and workmen's allotments not to be over £100 in value.

CC

By the end of 1907 it had purchased 40 estates,
totalling 207,788 acres and costing £1,458,645—an
average of £7 1s. per acre. It has made available
1216 holdings, upon which there is a residential
population of 3772. These represent holdings
totalling 164,561 acres of a capital value of
£1,240,135. This gives an average of £1020 per
holding. The work of the board can hardly be
called a success, as owing to the absence of a land
tax the price of the land is too high. Many of the
lessees have been unable to pay up their instalments,
and have asked for payment of their second, third,
and fourth instalments to be deferred, and have
paid the fine imposed in such cases. A land tax
and compulsory purchase are required.

The experience in New South Wales is similar,
although it has more land. Under a better
Government — and consequently superior management—the principle will prove a success, but so far
the State invariably gets the worst of the deal in
purchasing land for any purpose, and it must do
so until a good progressive land-value tax knocks
out the gambler's speculative value, and brings the
price down to real use value.

Of other works the Sydney Water Supply gives
a return of £3 17s. per cent. on a capital value of
£9,062,000. The Harbor Trust, Sydney, has a return
of £4 12s. per cent. on a capital value of £5,145,000.
The capital cost of Socialistic enterprises under the
State in New South Wales was £63,480,000, and the
net return £4 16s. 7d. per cent. A big and successful
enterprise was carried out in West Australia by the
Government in the shape of a goldfields water

supply scheme costing nearly £3,000,000, which carries water 351 miles and raises it 1200 feet on the way by pumping. Melbourne Harbor Trust made a profit last year of £60,412 on an expenditure of £99,252.

The Geelong Harbor Trust carries out a State farm upon which are successfully settled a large number of people. In their report for the year ended December, 1907, the Commissioners say:—

"The lands controlled by the Commissioners, which for the most part were waste areas, merely bringing in nominal rentals, or being used by various local authorities as commons, and yielding little or no surplus above maintenance charges, have been put to more profitable purposes, and will eventually prove a source of assured income, sufficient, it is confidently hoped, to meet all future financial obligations of the Trust and make a substantial contribution towards harbor developments, whilst demonstrating in no unmistakable way the possibilities of scientific agriculture along right lines."

The Commissioners only began this work three years ago. They have reclaimed 2000 acres of land which was level with the sea at high tide. They have also reclaimed and drained 1750 acres of Reedy Lake, which was all under water after heavy rain. Land originally used for a racecourse has been turned into an irrigation farm with up-to-date appointments. It has an area of 727 acres. They have 413 head of cattle, 20 horses, and 151 pigs. Produce from the dairy, etc., is sold in Melbourne and locally. It is reckoned that taxation on shipping is reduced by the profits on the scientific use of the land, and there is also the value of the object lesson to be considered.

The State Clothing Factory in New South Wales was established as the result of a deputation from the Labor Party, led by Mr. McGowen, which waited on the then Premier (the late Sir John See) on 13th September, 1901. It was urged that the clothing for the military, railway, and post-office officials should be made by the State in a factory of its own. Previously 34,523 garments had been made in the jails, and 31,500 by private enterprise firms. The cost was high, and the quality of work and material alike inferior. The Government agreed to make the experiment, and a factory was started. But little chance was given the manager, and he was limited to 21 hands. The result of the first year was a loss of £179 10s. 5d. Wages averaged 18s. 6d. per week as against 15s. 2d. (the highest) and 10s. 0½d. (the lowest) rate in representative private firms. The Public Service Board held an inquiry and recommended going on, estimating that if all the State work was given to the factory the loss would only be £693, but this would be more than made up in quality. Since then the factory has carried on successfully, and had a total output for 1908 of £31,449 15s. 11d. This included fire brigade uniforms to the value of £2552 18s. 9d., and railway and tramway £13,360 9s. 3d. Under the able management of Mr. W. J. Fallon the factory is now working up to the limit of its capacity. It is overloaded with work, and cannot put on another hand. There are 177 employed, and generally they are getting rather over the Arbitration Court Award rates, which apply to all private firms as well as the State factory. The Government has been forced to start the erection of new premises.

The attitude of capitalistic Governments toward State enterprise is exemplified in connection with this factory. In order to provide constant work and thus reduce expenses the management wanted to tender for outside work, but the Carruthers Government prohibited them from doing so. The Cabinet minute gives as a reason that it would interfere with private enterprise. They admit that the State factory does better work and pays better wages, yet can do work at a lower cost than private firms, but they refuse to allow the public to reap the advantages. True to their nature, they help the few to take advantage of the many.

The Sydney City Council runs a big electric plant, supplying light and power, and returning thousands of pounds per annum in profit. Melbourne City Council does the same, and clears close upon £10,000 per annum. Many of the municipalities now own baths, sale-yards, abattoirs, etc. Launceston, Tasmania, is the most advanced. It owns practically all public utilities. It has a splendid electric power and light supply produced by water power obtained by putting a tunnel through a hill and tapping a river. From the profits of their water supply they built a large hall. They have large workshops, and possess hot, cold, and swimming baths, a fine museum and art gallery, a zoo, and public gardens. They have a pension system for their employees, and altogether they are up-to-date. Contrast the work of Launceston aldermen with that of the boosters-up of private enterprise dominating the City Council of Hobart. These latter geniuses actually granted a private company the right to run trams in the streets in perpetuity—a monopoly for ever! Other matters are mismanaged on similar lines.

These notes would be incomplete without some reference to the " New Australia " movement. Its founder was William Lane, and the idea grew out of the village settlement proposals. The latter subject was taken up by the Trades and Labor Council of Brisbane in 1886. A public meeting was held on 13th January, 1887, at which a definite scheme was adopted. Lane later conceived the idea of a co-operative settlement on communal lines. He was then running a paper called " The Boomerang," in conducting which he was assisted by Alf. Walker and the late Frank Barnes. Lane first tried to secure land for such a settlement in Australia. He failed to do so, as not one of the Governments would attempt to make provision. He wrote to West Australia and to South America, and received a favorable reply from the latter country with offers of land before he had an acknowledgment from West Australia of his communication. I myself tried the New South Wales Government, but all they had to say was that they had no power under the Land Act to grant the area required.

New Australia took a large number of our best men and women, as well as a considerable sum of money, out of Australia, but we have to blame the Governments of the various colonies for it.   In April, 1891, Alf. Walker went to South America, and, after arrangements had been made and land chosen in Paraguay, emigration of members of the association commenced. They purchased a sailing ship called the " Royal Tar," which was to sail from Sydney, and those who were to go came there to await the day.   The Government was suddenly awakened. Premier Dibbs, who had never troubled his head to find land for them in unpeopled New South Wales when asked for it, did everything he could to put obstacles in the way of the " Royal Tar " getting away.

The steamers carrying thousands of passengers daily past the " Royal Tar " to Manly were rotten and dangerous, but not a word was said.   The " Royal Tar " was a good ship, well found, and in good order, but it was marvellous how much red tape had to be surmounted ere she was permitted to sail.   After a long search an Act regulating emigration was discovered. It was the only copy in the colony, and was over fifty years old.   It suited Dibbs, as he was openly trying to block the party from going. It was such a reflection on the Governments of the colonies for a batch of nearly three hundred to be leaving, so he put his weight in to stop them. Fittings had to be put in the ship, and all sorts of more or less silly requirements had to be complied with. Billy Lane put up with it all patiently, though in a tight position financially. At

last, when all was ready, one family was ordered
ashore because the medical officer sent by the
Premier considered one child had a touch of measles.
The "Royal Tar" sailed for New Australia on the
16th July, 1893.

I do not propose to follow the fortunes and
misfortunes of those on board, but will expose still
further the action of the Government which refused
them land and then tried to stop them from getting
away.   The Australian Workers' Union had a
project on foot for forming a co-operative
settlement, if it could get land and could put itself
on a legal footing. I waited upon the late Henry
Copeland, who was then Minister for Lands in New
South Wales. He professed sympathy, but pointed
out difficulties. He had "no power to do it under
the Act," etc. I urged that he should alter the
Act, and pointed out that bad laws drove away the
New Australians, and said we were prepared to use
Union funds for the development of New South
Wales; but he only discovered difficulties and was
not disposed to do anything that would enable us
to carry out our idea, though he had a scheme for
co-operative settlements under consideration.

Just about that time a syndicate had two private
bills before the New South Wales Parliament. On
the surface one had nothing to do with the other.
Different names were given as those of the parties
interested. One measure was introduced into the
Legislative Council, the other in the Assembly. The
Council was asked to pass a bill to permit a
syndicate to construct a line of railway—or
tramway, as they termed it—from Broken Hill to

the Menindie Lakes, on the Darling River. The bill brought into the Assembly was to grant the use and control of these lakes and about 22,000 acres of land as freehold on condition that the syndicate would establish an irrigation settlement. There was a market of over 40,000 people at Broken Hill, so the idea seemed alright.

The gentleman who had charge of the scheme on behalf of the syndicate, and who had done the lobbying, sent for me when he heard of my request to the Government and submitted a proposal. Shortly stated, he was prepared to grant to our Union a large area—he had drawn a line across the plan, and when scaled we found it contained 7300 acres—upon condition that we would find the men and settle them upon it, the syndicate on its part undertaking to employ our men three days a week on its works. I said to him:

" But you will never get this measure through the House. The Government is bound to oppose it, as Lyne has an Irrigation Bill to pass."

The engineer smiled, and quietly replied:

" It will pass alright. Why, every member of both Houses outside the Labor Party has an interest in it."

The Labor Party had been fighting against the measure, hence his offer to me was intended to induce me to influence the Party to withdraw its opposition and enable the A.W.U. to carry out its land settlement scheme. I gave our party the information, and they amended the bill so as to stop alienation, confining the syndicate to leasing.

Nothing ever came of the scheme, but just observe the action of the Government.   Neither Lane nor I could get any concession.   They would not alter the law to enable us to develop unused country and help workers to settle on it.   In our schemes there were no profit-makers.   At the same time a syndicate which was openly out for gain could get 22,000 acres of land and a splendid supply of water without any trouble.   We were to be forced to go to the syndicate to get a piece of land at the time held by the Crown.   All this is in keeping with capitalistic methods, and comes quite natural to them.   It is helping their friends and giving " encouragement " to private enterprise, and therefore in their opinion quite right.   Labor's plan is to get rid of the middleman and all parasites, and to secure for those who work the full result of their industry.

CHAPTER XXIX.

CONCILIATION AND ARBITRATION.

EVERY time a more than usually severe industrial struggle took place the question was discussed of how to provide a means whereby these troubles should not only be settled, but absolutely prevented. The ignorant partisan of the employers would simply settle it to his satisfaction by urging that workmen should not go on strike—that such a thing was wrong and injurious to society. The self-evident and sensible plan of the parties meeting and coming to terms, or in the event of disagreement submitting it to arbitration, was seldom adopted. The workers' side was always prepared to come to terms in that way, but the employers in most cases objected. Many of the unions provide for such a course in their rules, and in connection with gold mining in Victoria the plan has been successfully carried out for many years. In other industries, however, and especially in the larger undertakings which are in the hands of companies, it was seldom that the employers would agree even to meet the workmen; and after they became organized and adopted the freedom-of-contract craze they declined on principle. No doubt it is natural for both parties, where they feel that they have a good case or are confident of winning the fight, to prefer to hold out rather than allow any outsider to come in and decide for them.

The extensive area and large interests involved in the big maritime struggle brought the question up in a new light. Every effort at conciliation had failed, and it was seen that it was necessary, if a way could be found, that some tribunal should be set up which would prevent such troubles coming upon the community. As a result of the report of the Royal Commission which investigated the causes of the maritime strike in New South Wales, legislation was passed providing for the appointment of a Board of Conciliation for the settlement of industrial disputes. The Board was appointed and remained in existence for four years, but proved a failure. It was clear that if parties who always had the option of meeting, and who could, if they desired, appoint arbitrators of their own choosing, failed to adopt that method, it was not likely that they would voluntarily call in the board set up for such cases. In South Australia a somewhat similar board has done a little, but it has not had much call upon it.

The weak point under any system of the kind lay in the fact that whilst there was a law legalising and enforcing any contract or bargain made between individuals or companies, there was none to enforce any decision or agreement arrived at between a trade union and employers. The idea of compulsory conciliation was the first step in advance that was to compel the parties to meet—or, at any rate, to make the refusing side meet the other in cases where they objected to doing so willingly. How to make the awards compulsory and binding was the difficulty, and yet it was seen that unless they were so it was but little use enforcing conciliation, as the side which thought it had the best of the fight would stand firm.

The father of the present system of Compulsory Arbitration was the late Hon. Charles Cameron Kingston, for some years Premier of South Australia, and afterwards a member of the Commonwealth Parliament. He introduced a bill in the South Australian Parliament on 12th December, 1890, the preamble of which read: "An Act to encourage the Formation of Industrial Unions and Associations, and to Facilitate the Settlement of Industrial Disputes." The bill contained 85 clauses. It provided for the granting of a block of land by the Government for the purpose of erecting a hall to be called Conciliation Hall. This was to be in or near the city of Adelaide. The erection could be either partly or wholly paid for by the Government. Unions could register, and would then become subject to the Board of Conciliation and be bound by their own rules and by industrial agreements and awards, and for default were liable to a penalty not exceeding £20. Agreements were binding on all concerned under a penalty, in case of an organization, of £500, and in case of an individual of £50. Provision was made for the appointment of Boards. Private Boards could be appointed, and there were two systems of Public Boards—one local, the other a central or State Board. In all cases the agreements arrived at, whether by the private or the public board, were to be registered and would then have the force of law and could be enforced. Fines not exceeding £20, with a term not exceeding three months' imprisonment in default, was a provision; and, most important of all, lockout or strike was declared illegal, with penalties of £500 in the case of an organization, and £20 in case of an individual being guilty of either. This brief outline indicates the general lines of the proposed measure.

Public opinion was not yet ripe, however, and so it failed to become law until 1894, but it bore fruit in New Zealand, where, in 1892, the Hon. W. Pember Reeves, taking Mr. Kingston's measure as his guide, framed and passed a bill which was assented to on 31st August, 1894, and came into force on January 1st, 1895, and which has had the effect of making Maoriland noted as the country without strikes. The measure had been thrice rejected by the Legislative Council, but was sent up a third time and passed. The preamble to Mr. Reeves' Act reads, " An Act to encourage the formation of Industrial Unions and Associations, and to Facilitate the Settlement, of Industrial Disputes by Conciliation and Arbitration." This has since been shortened, and the title now reads, " An Act to Facilitate. the Settlement of Industrial Disputes by Conciliation and Arbitration." The Act provides for two Courts—one for Conciliation, the other for Arbitration. If the award of the Conciliation Board, as it is termed, is not accepted, the parties go to the Arbitration Court, whose award must be accepted, as it is enforceable by law. The Act was amended in October, 1895, and again in October, 1896; November, 1898; in 1901, and 1908. New Zealand, having a democratic

Government, lost no time in remedying defects in the Act brought out in working or making alterations required to meet changing conditions.

There has been no thought in New Zealand of reverting to the old and barbarous method of strikes. It has been asserted by opponents of the measure, who are in all cases employers, that the Act has not yet had a trial. That is because the decisions have been mostly in favor of Labor. "Wait," they say, "till New Zealand meets depression and wages have to come down, and the Act will fail." What these croakers overlook is the fact that the colony has taken such steps as will prevent depression, and is finding out how to keep things on the up grade by wise legislation. When Labor secures full control in Australia, enforced poverty will assuredly disappear.

West Australia followed the example of New Zealand in 1900, but amended the Act in 1902 by dropping Conciliation Boards. In 1900 the Hon. B. R. Wise introduced a measure into the Parliament of New South Wales. Mr. Wise, however, made a distinct departure, as he provided at once for Compulsory Arbitration only. He was of opinion that the history of the working of the Act in New Zealand showed that the Conciliation Boards seldom effected a settlement, and that they caused delay and added unnecessarily to cost. He failed to pass the measure through the Upper House in 1900, but he was nominated afterwards to that Chamber, and the measure was eventually passed in 1901. During the interval Judge Backhouse had been sent to New Zealand as Commissioner to make inquiries, and his report helped to put the measure through. Mr. Wise, instead of closely following the New Zealand Act, drafted his bill in a more condensed form, and it has broken down in a number of points under test cases, where it obviously does not carry out the intention of the Legislature. He foolishly allowed lawyers to appear in the Arbitration Court, and this provision at once made it technical in administration. The Labor Party in Parliament and the trade unions worked hard to get the measure passed, but in the meantime decisions adverse to unionism had been given by the courts of the old world, and these stimulated opposition to the bill.

Owing to the fact that the first decision given under the Act was favorable to Labor a dead set was made against it by employers, and on every point where its jurisdiction could be tested cases were taken to other Courts, and the Act has had no chance to carry out what it was intended for. The Act, in spite of these drawbacks, did much good. It raised wages and shortened hours in many industries. The Court had so much work to do that it was unable to overtake it, which of itself was evidence of there being a mass of felt injustice to be remedied. The admission of the legal gentlemen, whilst it was really a godsend to some of them, has proved costly to the unions, and has in some cases left them short of funds.

The judges in the other courts seemed eager to get opportunities to declare the Act ultra vires on any pretext, and some of them did not hesitate to extend their functions by making speeches from the bench condemning such legislation. Their purely technical and biased legal minds have no sympathy with the spirit which should underlie the administration of such an Act as Arbitration. It was never intended that there should be any appeal, but the lawyers soon found a way to get to the other courts, and then we had the spectacle of the clear intentions of the Parliament being upset and reversed by judge-made law. For how much of this we can blame the draftsman no one can say, but we can see clearly enough that had there been a Government in power which had the slightest sympathy with Labor the defects in the Act would have been remedied long ere this. The Government and the employers rejoiced to see the Labor organizations tied up. They could not strike under the Act, and they could not get their grievances remedied except in some minor degree and in special cases. The Acting-Judge of the Court put the position very clearly when he made the following remarks:—

"The court," said his Honor, "had provided that when contracts were within its jurisdiction contract prices should be fixed, so as to give an average competent workman at least the minimum wage prescribed for a day's work. It seemed probable, looking at the recent decision in the Haberfield case, that none of the mine contracts were within the court's jurisdiction, but that they must be decided on the facts. The real protection of men against contracts being used to reduce

DD

their earnings was that it would not suit either the employers to attempt it, or the men to submit to it. It was just the sort of thing about which strikes occurred. Strikes were usually considered to be industrial disputes, and accordingly when the Act on the one hand forbade strikes, and on the other created a tribunal to settle ' industrial disputes,' it was thought at first that one was a substitute for the other, and that the domains of each were the same. When the Legislature said ' Don't strike, but go to the court,' it was thought that the court was to settle what a strike would have settled. That view was now shown to be superficial. A critical analysis of the wording of the Act had revealed that the incautious use of the words employer and employee in the definition of industrial matters had upset everything. The raising of a dispute was now like self decapitation. In consequence of recent discoveries of the true meaning of the Act access to the court was blocked. The area of its operations was narrowed almost to a vanishing point; its freedom of movement checked with bonds, and all its actions paralysed. When this was the condition of the tribunal which was to end strikes, could anyone wonder that strikes were not ended? The principle of settling industrial troubles by tribunal might be very mischievous and quite impracticable. As to that, his Honor said nothing whatever, but if it were necessary to try it before condemning it, then he thought it was not condemned by anything that had happened since he had been on the court, for it had not been tried; it had not been possible to try it."

By an amendment put in by the Legislative Council the Act only remained in force until 1908, hence the more it was made a failure the more the friends of the capitalists rejoiced, as it gave them alleged arguments against re-enactment and amendment. That is one of the reasons why there was such active opposition. The capitalistic Wade Government introduced a new measure to take the place of the old one, and based it upon a Wages Board system. The strong opposition of the Labor Party made them depart from this to some extent, and the measure passed in a mixed form. The strong anti-union feeling of the Government and their following led them to pass a measure which favors the non-unionist more than the unionist, so instead of bringing peace it has led to war, as many unions refused to recognise the Act at all, and it is quite clear it will have to be reconstructed before it will work and prevent the evils of strikes or lock-outs.

Victoria was the first colony to pass a Factory Act. That was in 1873. In 1891 an Act providing for Councils of Conciliation was passed, and it came into force in 1892. It was of no use, however. The Factory Act was amended in 1885, again in 1893, and in 1896 the new principle of provision for wages boards was introduced. The main Act dealt with hours, sanitation, condition of workshops, etc., and fixed a minimum wage for beginners of 2s. 6d. per week. The wages boards were to fix wages and regulate the number of apprentices, etc. The boards are constituted of an equal number of employers and employees, the full board to appoint its chairman. The number may be from four to ten on each side. The Act limited its term, but was re-enacted with some amendments in 1900 and continued until 1902, when it lapsed on the dissolution of Parliament. At that time there were thirty-eight special boards under the Act, and they had done some very good work. They had raised wages in the furniture trade by 66 per cent., and in seventeen other trades the average increase was 21 per cent. in the seven years. The Act was again passed in 1903, but with important changes. A board could not be appointed unless a resolution had passed both Houses of Parliament. Under the previous Act a resolution of either House would do. The boards had to be constituted of actual employers and employees engaged in the industry, and there was an appeal allowed to a court in the person of a Supreme Court Judge. The wages board system was adopted in South Australia, but it could not be set in force until the regulations had been laid on the table of both Houses and approved. The Legislative Council refused to approve, so the Act was a dead letter.

We have thus in Australia the two systems side by side, and it must be readily admitted that each has been an improvement on old conditions. Employers who realise that something in the way

of means to avoid strikes is forced on them favor
the special board system, as it leaves more power in
their hands. As the workers' delegates are in their
employ they have the power to discharge, and
have not scrupled to use it on several occasions.
In more than one case the whole of the members of
the board lost their positions shortly after an award
was made. This is the main drawback, and the
principal reason the workers are more in favor of
the Compulsory Arbitration Court system.

Of the two I think the latter much the better,
provided of course that the Act is so framed that
it carries out the work it is intended to perform.
The court is composed of one representative from
each side elected by delegates of the whole of the
unions registered, and the president is a Supreme
Court Judge. With a good Act the whole question
of its success rests upon the judge. He must be a
man with special qualifications for such a position.
He must be well acquainted with economic questions
and the ideas and aspirations of Labor, as well as
have a knowledge of business methods and a wide,
general knowledge of the technicalities of the
various occupations and enterprises.

With such a president the great advantage
over the other system lies in the fact that the
court takes cognisance of the relationship of one
trade to another. If the cost of production is raised
in one industry it often affects the cost in another.
One industry makes an article required for
production in a second industry, and hence in all
awards the court has to allow for that fact. It may
be that an award in a new case will necessitate the

revision of an award given in some other industry. This position cannot be taken up under the wages board system, as each trade deals only with its own troubles. Again, there is the power of the court to make a common rule, thus securing fair competition amongst employers, and putting the workman into the position that he cannot get a job by undercutting his fellow in wages, but must get it by his superior skill. With preference to unionists the Act is safeguarded by the members of the union doing the policing themselves and securing due enforcement, and preventing the unscrupulous employer dodging the law to his own advantage and to the disadvantage alike of his competitor and his employees.

The maker of anything to sell would secure the market by the high quality of his goods rather than by the lowness of the selling price. The sweater disappears under the system, Labor becomes more fully organized, and, at the same time, strikes do not occur to upset industry. The investor knows exactly what labor will cost him, and, further, he is assured of settled conditions both as to the labor he may engage, and also as to the fact that there will be no falling off in the purchasing power of the masses, which is inevitable under the old regime of non-interference with strikes and lock-outs. The condition of industry to-day is constantly changing owing to the extension of machinery and applied science, hence some power which possesses continuity must be always ready to revise awards and adjust them to the new and altered circumstances. Here again, the court is superior to the wages boards.

We have gone beyond the period when the objection to interference with the management and control of any person's business is worth discussion. In a score of ways it has been found wise to interfere with private enterprise, because failure to do so brought other evils of a far worse kind. The more or less powerful organization of each side renders the risk of industrial war too great, and the people see that there is no justification for permitting two parties to upset the whole well-being of society and cause suffering to the innocent when there is a better way out. That there are difficulties is inevitable. The competitive system is in itself bad, and it cannot be expected that any system dovetailed into it will work smoothly or with satisfaction. It is a question of the lesser of two evils, and the better way is certainly that of industrial peace, with the guarantee that, whilst the court does nothing to secure to the worker his full share of production, it at any rate stops the sweater and provides a living wage, leaving the future in the hands of the masses themselves to bring about such alterations as will abolish the foolish system under which they now live and toil.

The trade unionist did not advocate Compulsory Arbitration without realising that he, too, was surrendering a very large and important portion of long-fought-for liberty. The strike had proved to be a powerful weapon, and it was long ere he was prepared to hand over his destinies to a Supreme Court Judge who, he knew, had come from a different stock, and who had never shown any sympathy with him or his class. In the person of the late Chief Justice Higinbotham and one or two others we have had examples of men in whom the masses would willingly place their welfare, but such men are rare in any country. West Australia had experience of a wrong choice being made in appointing the president of the Arbitration Court. It speaks volumes for the loyalty and long-suffering patience of the Australian unionists that they have waited so long for an amendment and administration of the law on the lines found to have been so beneficial in New Zealand.

The capitalists are slow to learn that they can no longer rule everything. The future will have more of the collective bargaining, and they will be forced to obey the law in a way they have never yet done. Industries which cannot pay a decent wage must close up, as the president of the New South Wales Court (Judge Cohen) frankly declared in a case where employees were worked from 90 to 100 hours per week for a wage of ten shillings and poor food. The employer had pleaded that if he paid more he would have to close up and go out of business. The fight against the Act was mainly to render it ineffective and so dishearten the unions that they may weaken in strength. The Act led to a very large increase in the membership of existing unions as well as the formation of new ones.

In twenty out of twenty-two cases in New South Wales preference to unionists had been conceded voluntarily by employers. The Employers' Union then took a hand and opposed the granting of preference, not because it is any disadvantage to employers—indeed it is often a good thing for them —but because they are afraid of the political power of the unions. This came out when the Arbitration Bill was before the Commonwealth Parliament. They even succeeded in getting a clause inserted in that bill limiting the power of the court to grant preference—in fact, prohibiting it if the union had political objects. The Federal Act is limited by the Constitution to disputes extending beyond the boundary of any one State. The Act is based on similar lines to that of New South Wales, but provides power for the president to try conciliation first and seek a settlement that way before letting the case go to the Court. The president is a Judge of the High Court of Australia. Each party can appoint an assessor to sit with the judge, but they are not in the position of the members of the late Court in New South Wales. The Court has done good work already. Constitutional limitations in a legal sense leave us uncertain as to what are its full powers.

The arbitration method has come to stay in Australia, and it is only a matter of a short time when Labor will become politically strong enough to make the Act what it was intended to be, and thus provide a peaceful means of avoiding strife, leaving the Labor unions free to devote their time, their money, and their energies to securing permanent and lasting reform by means of political action. Employees in the great pastoral industry have been working for the past two years under an award of the court, and the relations between employers and employees are excellent. I have elsewhere called attention to the principle laid down regarding wages, and here will add another illustration.

In the Broken Hill case decided in 1909 by the Federal Arbitration Court, Justice Higgins, in granting the demands made by the miners, made the following observations:—

" Now, the first condition in the settlement of this industrial dispute as to wages is that at the very least a living wage should be secured to the employees. I cannot conceive of any such industrial dispute as this being settled effectively which fails to secure to the laborer enough wherewith to renew his strength, and to maintain his home from day to day. He will dispute—he must dispute—until he gets this minimum even as a man immersed can never rest until he gets his head above water. Nor do I see any reason yet for modifying my view of a living wage as expressed in the harvester case. In finding a living wage I look, therefore, to find what money is necessary to satisfy the moral needs of the average employee regarded as a human being in a civilised community. In the present case it is reassuring to find that counsel for the company, the general manager, and even the chairman of directors, notwithstanding his strong prepossessions in favor of the inexorable laws of demand and supply, all assented to the doctrine that no man ought to be asked to work for less than a living wage. The result of this admission is that I may proceed to consider the prices of necessary commodities at Broken Hill and at Port Pirie, in order to ascertain what is the least sum that will enable an unskilled laborer to live in the sense to which I have referred. For Broken Hill the company offered 7s. 6d. per day, and the union asked 8s. 7½d. per day, the wages paid by the company and other companies in 1907-8 and still paid by the nine companies. For Port Pirie the company offered 7s. 2d. per day, while the union asked for 8s. 3d. per day, the wages of 1907-8. . . . . The main struggle of the case has been with regard to a living wage, and with regard to the financial position of the company. No evidence has been adduced to show that any of the men who have been receiving more than unskilled laborers' wage are overpaid.

"There is no evidence, for instance, that if 8s. 7½d. is a proper wage for a trucker, the wage of 9s. 1d. is too great for a tool man, nor the wage of 10s. too great for a miner (on wages). In this case, during the time an unskilled laborer got 7s. 6d. the miner (on wages) got 9s. When the unskilled laborer got 8s. 7½d. the miner (on wages) got 10s. I think that, having fixed the wage for the unskilled laborer at 8s. 7½d., I may reasonably leave the minimum wage of the miner (on wages) at 10s., and similarly, with the other skilled employees. . . . . The proprietors, in an inquiry such as this is, would seem to ascertain first the wage to be paid to the unskilled laborer, then the proper wages to be paid to those who have extra skill, on the assumption that the employers can pay whatever wages are proper, and then to hear any evidence and consider any arguments adduced, to show that the employer ought not to be asked to pay such wages. First of all, is an employer who is poor to be ordered to pay as high wages as an employer who is rich? Now, without laying down a rule absolute and unconditional, under all the circumstances I strongly hold the view that, unless the circumstances are very exceptional, the needy employer should, under an award, pay at the same rate as his richer rival. It would not otherwise be possible to prevent sweating of employees, the growth of parasitic enterprises, and the spirit of industrial unrest—unrest which it is the function of this Court to allay. If a man cannot maintain his enterprise without cutting down wages which are proper to be paid to his employees —at all events the wages which are essential to their living—it would be better he should abandon the enterprise. This is the view independently adopted by Mr. Justice Gordon in Adelaide, and by Mr. Justice Burnside in West Australia. It is not the function of this Court to foster slackness in any industry, and if ' A,' by his alertness and enterprise, and by his use of the best and most recent appliances, can make his undertaking pay on the basis of giving proper wages to his workmen, it would be most unjust to allow ' B,' his lazy and thriftless rival, to pay his workmen lower wages. In short, the remuneration of employees cannot be allowed to depend on the profits actually made by his individual employer. This proposition does not mean that the possible profits or returns of an industry as a whole are never to be taken into account in settling wages. For instance, the fact that an industry is novel and that those who

undertake it have at first to move very warily and
economically, might be favorably considered so long
as every employee gets a living wage. I can well
understand that workmen of skill might consent
to work in such a case for less than their proper
wages, not only to get present employment, but in
order to assist an enterprise which will afford them,
and their comrades, more opportunities for
employment hereafter. For this purpose it is
advisable to make the demarcation as clear and as
definite as possible between that part of the wages
which is for mere living, and that of the wages
which is due to skill, or to monopoly, or to other
considerations. Unless great multitudes of people
are to be irretrievably injured in themselves and in
their families, unless society is to be perpetually
in industrial unrest, it is necessary to keep this
living wage as a thing sacrosanct beyond the reach
of bargaining; but when a skilled worker has once
secured a living wage he has attained nearly to a
fair contractual level with the employer, and, with
caution, bargaining may be allowed to operate.''

CHAPTER XXX.

LABOR FEDERATION.

It is not my purpose to attempt a record of the many strikes and lock-outs Labor in Australia has had to face. The coal-miners have ever been good fighters, and the conditions of coal seams, as well as the competition between mine proprietors in cutting for trade, render the calling one of uncertainty, and place it on a different footing from that of gold-mining, where the product has a fixed price. The coal-miners of Newcastle and Illawarra districts in New South Wales have paid many thousands of pounds in strike pay, and have lost much time by enforced idleness; nevertheless, when the output of coal is taken—as furnished in the Government returns—and the difference between what the coal-miners wanted to pay and that which they were forced to pay by the miners' unions is calculated, it clearly proves that the men have gained more than they lost—in short, it paid to strike.

In the wool industry the gain is also clear. One of our Union organizers was met one day by a squatter who knew him. He said:

"Well, Pat, I see you have a nice easy billet now, riding about the country. I suppose the Union pays you well; you seem to be doing alright out of it."

494

Pat replied: " You make a mistake. I am not being paid by the Union."

" No?" said the squatter. " Who pays you, then?"

" You and your friends are paying me," said Pat.

The employers are not so foolish as to spend time and money and worry themselves in fighting unless they are going to gain by it, and they know well that the millions diverted into the pockets of the workers would remain in their own—and, what is perhaps more valued by some of them, they could act the autocrat more completely—if the Union could be crushed out of existence. These facts account for the vigorous but ineffectual efforts made by the Pastoralists' Union to crush the A.W.U. Nearly all the unions have had their industrial battles, some of the most severe being between the years 1880 and 1890, which period saw great activity amongst the workers in a trade union sense.

As to the present strength of the trade unions in Australia there is no official record except in New South Wales, where those registered under the Arbitration Act numbered about 86,000. Making allowance for those who for various reasons cannot become organized, or do not need to, the majority of workers in that State are members of unions. Probably there are at least 300,000 trade unionists in actual membership in Australia. I venture the opinion that in union spirit the workers of Australia stand higher in proportion to population than workers in any other country. Unionism is also strongly Federal. Industrial battles have proved

that. The more severe the struggle the more closely
it united the different unions, and the ready
response for monetary aid drew organizations of
Labor nearer to a federation of Labor.

The first attempt was made in October, 1879,
when an Intercolonial Congress was called together
in Sydney, N.S.W. There were thirty-six delegates,
representing 11,087 members. These were practically
all from New South Wales, as only three outside
societies were represented. A second Congress was
held in Melbourne in April, 1884. This was attended
by fifty delegates from Victoria, fifteen from New
South Wales, and four from South Australia—
sixty-nine in all. No returns were given as to
numbers represented, but it is recorded that the
Trades Hall Council, Melbourne, represented 10,000,
the Trades and Labor Council of South Australia
3000, the Trades and Labor Council of New South
Wales 8000, the Coal-miners 2500, the Seamen's
Union 1000, and the Amalgamated Miners'
Association of Victoria 8000. Two lady delegates
were present. The third Congress met in Sydney
in October, 1885. There were 100 delegates present,
including two ladies. It was roughly estimated that
the Congress represented about 150,000 unionists.
New Zealand and all the colonies except West
Australia sent delegates. At the fourth Congress,
held in Adelaide, S.A., in September, 1886,
sixty-eight delegates were present. The fifth met
in Brisbane, Queensland, in March, 1888, sixty-six
delegates attending. The sixth met in Hobart,
Tasmania, in February, 1889, with fifty-seven
delegates present. The seventh Congress met in

Intercolonial Trades Union Congress, 1884.

April, 1891, in Ballarat, Victoria, 114 attending, one of whom was a lady.

If any evidence was needed to prove that the workers will never get their demands recognised in Parliament until they elect enough members of their own choice to form a majority it can be found on looking back over these several Congresses. The following subjects were submitted to the first Congress in 1879:—Eight Hours, Encouragement of Native Industries, Legalisation of Trades Unions, Laws Affecting Mercantile Marine, Question of holding an Annual Intercolonial Congress, Factory and Workshops Act, Co-operation, Education, Land Boilers Inspection, and Workmen's Compensation Act. Nearly all these questions were dealt with at each succeeding Congress.

The following additional items were debated at the second Congress:—Amendment of Master and Servants Act, Payment of Members, Direct Representation of Labor in Parliament, Local Government, Amendment of Mining Regulations, Employers' Liability, Mining on Private Property, Amalgamation and Federation of Unions, Recidivist Question.

At the third the Enfranchisement of Seamen came on.

At the fourth Arbitration and Conciliation and Land Value Taxation were discussed, in addition to the old questions.

At the fifth, in Brisbane, we find added to the previous list:—Organization of Labor, One Man One Vote, Marine and Sanitary Inspection, Apprentice Question, Land Nationalisation, Labor Lien and

EE

Wages Act, Technical Education, Inspection of Scaffolding, Wages on Government Contracts, and Competitive Examinations in Civil Service.

The sixth added Early Closing, and Limitation of Age in Government Offices.

The seventh brought up Political Organization, a General Defence Fund, Labor Department, Profit Sharing, Prohibition of Government Officers taking Outside Work, Abolition of Free Passes on the Railways, Abolition of Sweating, Extension of the Government as an Employer, and Best Means of Educating the Workers in Unionism. It is worthy of note that though this Congress followed the Maritime struggle of 1890, it was the largest ever held, there being 114 delegates present.

The eighth Congress was held in Adelaide in September, 1898, at which thirty-one attended. The following items were discussed in addition to old questions:—Weekly Half-Holiday, Old Age Pensions, Shearers' Hut Accommodation, Abolition of Contract under Government, Minimum Wage, Payment of Jurors, Trade Union Officer to be permitted to attend inquests.

The first Commonwealth Congress was held in November, 1902, in Sydney at which all the States were represented. In addition to many of those previously named, the following new items came up:—Nationalisation of Coal Mines, Uniform Factory Laws, Trade Union Label, Railway Carriages to be constructed in Government Workshops, Federal Arbitration Act, Full Citizen Rights, Labor Bureaux, Nationalisation of the Iron Industry, Amendment of Taff Vale Law,

Nationalisation of the Drink Traffic, Abolition of State Governors, Weights and Measures, State or Municipal Lodging Houses, Right of Access to Shearing Sheds, etc.

The Congress of 1907, which met in Melbourne in February, added the following to our list:— Immigration, Boys in Sugar-cane Fields to be Limited, Free Transfer in Unions, Protection against Dangerous Machinery, All work to be done in Australia, Uniform Fruit Cases, Monopoly of Machines in Boot-trade, Child Labor, Mine Ventilation, Light Work for Old Men, Prison Labor, Medical Examination of School Children, Feeding of School Children, and Abolition of Sunday Work.

Great interest has always been taken by the public in these Congresses, and prior to Labor taking a hand in politics Premiers and Cabinet Ministers frequently attended as visitors. The subjects were discussed each time with earnestness and enthusiasm. Delegates seemed filled with hope and confidence, based on the sweet reasonableness of their claims; but, alas, what has been the result of all these years of effort and talk? Trade unionists meeting time after time, voicing their grievances into apparently sympathetic ears, only to find failure and broken promises after twenty-eight years of united Australian work, to say nothing of the local demands. And yet some unions, so-called, stand aloof. Practically about seventy of these questions remain to be dealt with by law in spite of all the effort, time, and money spent in urging them on Cabinets and candidates. Surely in face of these facts members of trade unions should see that the

only way to secure needed legislation is to put their
own men into power.   One is also struck with the
fact that nearly all the questions are such as require
political action.

The Congresses were termed Trade Union
Congresses, yet the matters over which the trade
unions, as such, have control are very few indeed.
Out of over eighty questions, only seven can be dealt
with by the unions.   The earlier Congresses held
lengthy debates on the fiscal question, and in each
case went strongly for a protective tariff.   It was
only at the later Congresses that the importance of
the land question was seen.   At each gathering
delegates favored some form of Labor Federation.
In the Congress of 1884 the following resolution
moved by myself was, after discussion, carried
unanimously:—

> " That the Congress recommend the
> federation of the trade unions of each colony
> after the following manner:—Each trade to be
> recommended to amalgamate the several unions
> of the same trade under one head or governing
> body; each of the latter heads then to appoint
> representatives to a conference at which a
> Federal Council shall be elected who shall watch
> over the interests of the whole and deal with
> matters affecting the well-being of the working
> classes generally."

This proposal bore fruit, as many unions became
one where engaged in the same calling.   The second
part of the proposal has only been carried out in

Queensland, where they have a federation of all the unions under the title of the "Australian Labor Federation." At the Congress of 1891 the Queensland system was recommended and a comprehensive scheme adopted by Congress. New South Wales adopted the scheme for a time, but has since reverted to the old system of a Trades and Labor Council—in fact all the States except Queensland and Western Australia work on that system.

The introduction of Compulsory Arbitration and Wages Boards has rendered the complete Federation of Labor less a necessity than formerly. At the first Commonwealth Trades Union Congress, held in November, 1902, a scheme of federation was agreed to under which the organizations are now working. It meets the circumstances, and is found more practicable in its operations than the larger and more ambitious scheme of the Ballarat Congress of 1891. The first three rules of the new body will give its basis, and are as follows:—

Name and Constitution.

1. The central consultative and recommendatory authority shall be called the Federal Council of the Australian Labor Unions, and shall consist of six delegates elected by and from each State, the delegation to be apportioned in such manner as may secure the most complete representation of all Labor unions. Each State to bear the expenses of its delegation.

Objects.

2. The objects shall be (a) to strengthen and consolidate the Labor Unions throughout the Commonwealth; (b) to confer upon all matters of general concern to wage-earners; and (c) to promote and extend such legislative reforms as will secure justice to all.

Federal Council Sessions.

3. The Federal Council shall sit at such time and place as may be from time to time decided upon, and not less frequently than once in three years.

Provision is made for calling special sessions and for an executive, the duties of the latter being defined.

A special Intercolonial Congress was held in Brisbane in 1899, at which a comprehensive scheme of federation was adopted, to be brought into operation when three or more colonies adopted it, but it was never put into force. The scheme provided for proper control in case of strike or lock-out, and for providing funds. The rules were very complete, but the following will indicate the difference in the objects between the two schemes of 1899 and 1902, those of 1899 being:—

The following shall be the objects of the Federation:—(a) To improve, protect, and foster the best interests of all classes of labor throughout Australasia. (b) To secure direct Labor representation in the various Parliaments, and to promote and extend such legislative reforms as will ensure social justice to Australasian workers. (c) To prevent, as far as possible, any strike or dispute between the members of the Federation and their employers by conciliatory means, and by appeal to any recognised Board of Arbitration. (d) To uphold the rules of all federated bodies and ensure justice to all their members. (e) To provide funds for the assistance of any Federated Union involved in a dispute, such funds to be used only after all conciliatory measures have failed. (f) To secure a better advocacy of the principles and rights of Labor through the press, and, if deemed necessary, to establish journals for the promulgation and defence of all classes of Australasian workers. (g) To prevent the influx of colored races.

Interstate Congresses are now held triennially and have a smaller delegation, the delegates being mainly Labor Members of Parliament, as their possession of free railway passes enables them to attend at small cost. Labor unions have also come to realise that all big questions are political. As a consequence the Political Conferences in each State have grown in importance and the others have lessened. Interstate Political Conferences are held every three years for dealing with Federal matters and for framing the platform for the Commonwealth elections.

The Parliamentary Committee of the 1884 Congress, in its report presented to the Congress in 1885, introduced the question of direct representation of Labor in Parliament, and the subject was discussed at that and succeeding Congresses. Delegates could not, however, induce their societies to take up the matter, and it was not until 1898 that the unions in New South Wales affiliated with the political section of Labor. The unions in the other colonies were several years ahead of them in that respect. The Shearers' Union stood up all along in favor of political action, and not only passed a resolution at its 1891 Conference, but appointed a committee to draft a platform. Several unions still hold out and take no part in political work. The members are gradually awakening, however, and when they do take the matter in hand they will soon over-ride the narrow-minded persons who now fight against electing to Parliament their own men so that they may remedy the evils which have been brought under the notice of the legislature in vain for thirty years past.

During the sittings of the Intercolonial Congress in Brisbane in 1888, the then Premier (Sir S. W. Griffith), now Chief Justice of the High Court of Australia, issued a political manifesto in which the following passage appeared:—

" The relations between Labor and Capital constitute one of the great difficulties of the day. I look to the recognition of the principle that a share of the profits of productive labor belongs of right to the laborer as of the greatest importance in the future adjustment of these relations. The experiment of giving to workmen a personal interest in the success of the industrial undertakings in which they are engaged has already been tried in a few cases by the individual of the employers, and has resulted in conspicuous advantage to all parties. I entertain a strong hope that before long this principle will form a part of the positive law of Queensland.''

Like the other promises of old political parties nothing was done by Sir S. W. Griffith, though he had a splendid opportunity, and the pressure of an evil social system is daily becoming more severe in Queensland as elsewhere.

The trade union has not become less necessary because of political activity. It has become more than ever important. It has still plenty to do in watching over the bread-and-butter question which is with us all the time, and it is at the same time the backbone of the political Labor movement. The unions give stability, continuity, and solidarity to it. They form a training ground for future Parliaments. It is rare that a member trained and disciplined in a trade union goes back on his principles. The unionist is more loyal and reliable, and will stand the decisions of the party with less strain than others. The organization of unions must not, therefore, be neglected if the masses wish to work out their political and industrial salvation.

The Melbourne Trades Hall Council has a very fine set of buildings in Carlton. The old hall, which is still in use, was built in 1857. The foundation stone of the first portion of the new building was laid on 26th January, 1874, and that of the second part on October 21st, 1882. The approximate cost to date is £24,000.

The Trades and Labor Council of Sydney made a start to secure its Trades Hall in 1884. The committee appointed had £17 to start with. The foundation stone was laid by Baron Carrington (then Governor) on 28th January, 1888. The building and property are now valued at £26,000.

The Trades Hall in Adelaide, S.A., took eleven years' agitation to get. The foundation stone was laid on Eight-Hour Day, September 2, 1895, by Mrs. C. C. Kingston. It was opened on the 14th March, 1896, by Mr. T. Price, and cost £6490.

The Trades Hall, Brisbane, Q., was officially opened on May 5th, 1894, and cost £5200.

CHAPTER XXXI.

THE EIGHT-HOUR MOVEMENT.

> In the truly organized society labor must be pleasure, and nothing should be made by manual labor which is not worth making.

So WROTE the Socialist poet, William Morris. The statement is true, and yet how few grasp the fact that it can be made a reality. Work should be for the nutrition of the social organism. Work should be both a pleasure and a healthful exercise. To think of the needless slavery, long hours, and life-shortening drudgery forced on the mass, and enforced idleness and the misery of helpless begging for toil on the part of others, is enough to make one doubt the sanity of humankind.

Over-production and under-consumption side by side! Useless, wanton waste—and starving men, women, and children! Millionaires' wives spending fortunes on dog and pig parties, freak dinners, and the like—whilst those who provide the wealth are in dire want within a few yards of them! The waste of wars in seeking new markets for the commercial profit-making robber! The sending of missionaries to teach the nigger to wear clothes—when he does not need them and is happier without them! The efforts of agents to induce the millions of Japan and China to wear woollen goods, so that a market may be found for surplus stock—and all the time the very makers of the goods are short of necessaries of life! Surely we are far from being civilised yet, and our profession of Christianity is a sham, a humbug, and hypocrisy.

Up till about a hundred and fifty years ago the production of wealth was a problem which loomed large in human life. There was some excuse, perhaps, for long hours then, but in this age the production of wealth has ceased to be a problem. The control of nature's forces in applied science and machinery has left us but the problem of organization and distribution. Invention is ever simplifying processes. Machines are now more simple, cost less, and require less fuel. Electrical energy produced by water power uses no fuel at all, and costs hardly anything for wear and tear. Every branch of knowledge is being drawn upon to find cheaper, quicker, and simpler methods of producing things " to sell." As yet the idea of making them for use has not gripped the collective brain of man in any country.

As illustrating the rapidity of modern production, in Pennsylvania a number of sheep were shorn and the wool made into clothing in six hours four minutes. A steer was killed and its hide tanned and made into shoes in 24 hours. The steel frames of the huge sky-scraping buildings in the United States are put together by an electric riveter which does two rivets per minute. Wooden matches are made by a machine which splits 10,000,000 per day. A machine, attended by a boy, cuts out garments at the rate of 500 per day. A little girl looks after a machine which turns out fruit baskets at the rate of 12,000 per day, or 20 a minute. A pair of boots can be made in seventeen minutes, and a Baldwin railway engine in eight days. Weaving machinery is now so perfect that it runs all meal hours and for an hour and a-half after knock off time without any attendant.

Professor Hertzka, of Austria, in "The Laws of Social Evolution," states that 5,000,000 able-bodied men can produce in two hours and twelve minutes per day, working 300 days a year, everything imaginable of luxury and necessity required by 22,000,000 people. His estimate is supported by other mathematicians. This means that every person could have all that a millionaire now enjoys by so little work that it would not be other than a pleasure. When we think of the possibilities within reach of a civilised people sufficiently intelligent to take advantage of what man's brain and study have brought within their ken, it puts one out of patience with the timidity of the workers in not seeking at least a huge shortening of the hours of labor.

There was a long struggle in Australia to secure eight hours as a day's work, and the average worker seems content to let it stand at that. It is, however, not by any means universal even now. The history of the movement has been well set forth in an interesting volume by Mr. W. E. Murphy, of Melbourne, so that I shall only give a brief account of it. The movement is essentially Australian. It is interesting to note that when the "Otago Association" for settlement in New Zealand was being organized in Scotland by the Rev. Thomas Burns in 1847, they had originally a clause fixing an

eight-hour day.   As this could not be legally
enforced it was left out of the articles.   It was
tacitly understood, however, and the first strike
as a consequence took place in Dunedin, New
Zealand, in 1848 in support of the eight hours.

The oldest Union in Australia is the Operative
Stonemasons' Society, and at a meeting of the New
South Wales section of that body held in the
Parramatta Hotel, Sydney, on 22nd September, 1855,
the following resolution was moved by Hugh
Laundry, and seconded by Thomas Eaves: " That
in the opinion of this Society eight hours should
be the maximum of a day's labor."   This was
carried unanimously, and in less than a fortnight
eight hours became the accepted period of work,
the only opposition coming from Tooth Bros.
—just then building their brewery.   The Operative
Stonemasons of Melbourne moved in the matter
early in 1856, and, after securing the extension of
their own Society and the co-operation of some other
trades, successfully launched the eight hours at a
monster meeting held in the Queen's Theatre on
26th March, 1856, and it was agreed that it should
come into force on 21st April following.   Upon the
latter date is held the Eight-Hour Demonstration,
which is carried out annually.   The first Monday in
October is observed in the same way in Sydney.
Each   of   the   other   States   has   its   annual
demonstration—Queensland on 1st March; Tasmania,
26th February; South Australia, 1st September;
West Australia, 21st October, whilst New Zealand
celebrates it on 28th October.   The demonstrations
held in city and country centres give evidence of

the strength of the trade union movement, and the number of societies taking part indicates how far the eight hours have been conceded.   Probably there are a total of 250 bodies taking part, all enjoying the boon.

In Victoria the eight hours rapidly extended, and in the building trades especially it was almost universally adopted.   Taken generally, public opinion in Australia is in favor of an eight hours' limit.   When, however, unionists try to get it conceded to them the employer, who, perhaps, at dinners and banquets speaks in favor of it, is slow to grant it to his workmen.   It is only in a few cases that it has been made illegal to work more than eight hours per day or 48 per week.   Victoria was the first to pass Factory legislation, and in the Act of 1873 no woman or girl was permitted to work more than eight hours per day.   Later amendments limited the hours to forty-eight per week.   In 1873 the Regulation of Mines and Machinery Act came into force, and it provided that no girl or woman and no boy under fourteen should be employed underground, and no male under eighteen should work more than forty-eight hours per week.   This was amended in 1877 by fixing eight hours per day and forty-eight hours per week as the limit for all employed underground.

The effect of the legislation for factories and early closing passed in nearly all the States has been to shorten hours, but nevertheless proposals to make eight hours a legal limit of a day's work have failed to get through any of the legislatures.   Owing to attempts being made to work miners more than eight hours at Bethanga and Bendigo, in Victoria, the A.M.A. secured an amendment allowing half-an-hour for meals, to be deducted, so that the legal working hours are now limited in the gold-mines of that State to seven and a-half per day. Where the temperature is high, six hours are now the limit. Practically miners do not work forty-eight hours per week including meal time, as in most districts they stop work at ten o'clock on Saturday night, the night shift starting at one o'clock on Monday morning.

Several of the building trades have gained a forty-four hours week, notably the Stonemasons and Painters. The demand for a Saturday half-holiday was so strong that in the large cities practically the only workers not now enjoying it are the retail shop employees. In Brisbane, however, shops are closed at one o'clock on Saturday, and in 1909 the Victorian legislature passed an Act legalising a similar boon for the shop-assistants of Melbourne. In the shearing sheds throughout the Commonwealth members of the A.W.U. work only half a day on Saturday.

Whilst there has as yet been no organized effort to secure the recognition of less than eight hours, the concession has been made in metalliferous mines, as in many cases the shift is six hours. For some years the A.M.A. has had a six hour shift in wet shafts and other difficult places. As a very striking proof of the fact that short hours are an advantage rather than a loss to the employer the recent experience in the coal and lignite mines of

Austria may be quoted. By the Mining Act of 1884 the hours were fixed at twelve per day from bank to bank. By an amendment of the law which came into force in July, 1902, the hours were reduced to nine per day. This affected about seventy per cent. of the miners only. The Government obtained a return of the output of coal in all mines producing more than 1000 metric tons per year. The result showed that the output per man per shift for 1903 was over three per cent. greater than that for 1901, and for 1904 it was over six per cent. higher than that of 1901. In lignite mines the difference was over seven and nine per cent. respectively. This proves that the greedy employers have been losing money all these years by compelling the miners to work long hours.

Other tests of a similar kind have in most cases brought out a similar result, and prove that the employers and the workers are equally foolish in not agreeing on a very much shorter day than that now obtaining. In support of this a splendid illustration can be quoted from Victorian gold-mining experience. In the well-known Madame Berry Co.'s mine it was found necessary to sink the shaft deeper owing to the gutter having dipped away below the level of the drive from which the work had previously been carried on. There were over 200 men employed, and it meant that they would be out of employment until the shaft had been deepened. The mine was yielding a dividend of 2s. 6d. per share per month, and stoppage of the upper workings meant loss of that regular return. Hence the need for saving time.

FF

The directors wanted to let the job by contract, arguing that men would thus have an inducement to work harder. The mine manager (Mr. W. Maughan), who was not only a most capable manager, but a very fine man to work under, objected; and, as he always insisted on having his own way in the management, he was allowed to carry out his idea. It was the startling one of "two-hour shifts at top wages." He picked his men, taking of course those of experience in shaft work, and put them on two-hour shifts at the rate usually paid for the full eight hours. I am not sure now that they did not have a bonus as well. The work went on with a rush day and night, one set of men relieving the other, and all going as hard as they could without a stop of any kind for the two hours out of the twenty-four which they had to work. Men can stand a heavy strain for two hours when they have the other twenty-two to rest before again tackling the work. The consequence was that the shaft was sunk to the required depth in one month less time than under the contract or longer hour wage-system used in other mines in exactly the same ground. Thus the shareholders secured their dividends and two hundred miners their wages one month earlier.

What is needed is an agitation for shorter hours. Eight are too many, but might be made the maximum, with no limit to the minimum. Where men or women are placed in charge of a machine— or, as is often the case in factories, between machines whose speed regulates the pace of the employees' work—the strain is too great for other than a very few hours per day. The effect on mentality is ruinous, and we can quite realise the truthfulness of the statement made by Hobson in his " Psychology of Jingoism " that " in every nation which has proceeded far in modern industrialism the prevalence of neurotic diseases attests the general nervous strain to which the population is subjected." As machinery is made more perfect, so is its speed increased; and hence, though machines once driven by the foot of the person attending them, such as sewing machines, are now driven by electric or steam power, the work is not less hard, as the strain of constant watchfulness is severe. Also, where there was one needle before there are in some cases ten to-day. In drilling iron, one often can see sixteen drills driven by one machine, and all having to be watched by one pair of human eyes with loss of employment staring the operator in the face if anything goes wrong.

It is well known that physical toil, even though hard, will not kill so quickly as mental worry; but it seems to be forgotten that just as machines become more complex, more complete, and speedy, so is the strain on the person attending to them becoming at the same time a continuous mental worry. No one can last long at such work, and no one does. The old-fashioned employer or the old-style worker looking on for a few minutes contrasts it with the manual work of his young days, and speaks of it as not being work at all, but mere play. A little practical experience would change that. So far as the capitalist owners of the machines are concerned they care not, because they can fill the place of the killed or maimed without one moment's interference with the work. The masses are individually helpless and weak, so there is no hope except in collective action.

The greatest enemy of the worker is not the capitalist, but the ignorance and foolishness of the worker himself. Put him on piece-work, and, if not stopped by some power other than his own will, he will work longer hours than he would agree to do on wages. Even though he knows that where his earnings rise much above the recognised standard wage his piece-work rate will be reduced he takes the risk. Man has to be fenced in by coercion to do the right thing, hence, until the day of complete co-operation comes and production is only for use, we must look to legislation for the shortening of hours and other improvements essential to saving the Australian citizen from becoming a physical wreck under the pressure of his struggle for existence.

We should not aim at uniformity, but rather take each industry on its merits — or, speaking perhaps more correctly, its demerits. For instance, shearers work eight hours. They have several breaks for " smoke-oh," and work 48 hours per week, so arranging the hours that they finish by noon on Saturday. They are away from home, and the work is only available for a short time each year, therefore, all concerned are anxious to get it over, except of course the shed laborer, who is on weekly wages. The shearer does not seem to be anxious to shorten his day, even though the work is such that he could not keep up the pace if it had to be done all the year round. In harvest work, also, there is generally believed to be a difficulty in fixing a limit. It is an occupation which is only temporary, lasting but a few weeks.

In reality, I doubt if there is any practical difficulty in the way of carrying on any industry under a system of eight hours, or even less. One of the most experienced dairymen I have met is a believer in short hours. He had to get up at three o'clock in the morning when a boy, and declared that he would never work his children as he was made to work. He does all the work of a large dairy under an eight-hour system, and all in time for his children to enjoy their evenings, and they are not called out of bed before a reasonable hour in the morning. If a limit of even considerably less than eight hours were placed on the day's work the industries of the country would still carry on, and would make a bigger profit than now, because there is the economic aspect of the question to be considered. It would mean more employment, and a bigger demand for all production.

The time is ripe for raising the demand for a further shortening of hours in any case, and the worker as well as the employer should be taught that the eight-hour day is but one milestone on the road to still better things, and that the movement is not something in which eight hours is the goal, but that it really means a movement which aims at such continuous shortening of the work-day as will find room for all those now squeezed out of employment by machinery. Man—every man—has

the natural right to live. It is his duty to earn his
own living, and no man has any right to deny him
the opportunity to do so. If a machine is to do
a man's work the man must be there to attend
that machine, and so the question of hours is only
one of how short must they become to absorb all
those now idle.

The goal mankind is working towards is to
make machinery do all the work of the world, and
for Nature to supply human wants and luxuries by
man simply pressing a button. But that idea has
not yet been made to loom large in the minds of
men. The wage-slave dreams of nothing but having
to work for some other man; the capitalist dreams
only of how to make more profit and get rich.
When man gets time to think he will realise that
all Nature's forces—all material things, such as land
and machinery—should be the common property of
all; and that Nature has ample stores and is ever
ready to supply all human needs, leaving man to
the development of his wonderful mentality and
the enjoyment of all which high intellectuality
brings to his ken.

CHAPTER XXXII.

TRADE UNIONISM.

IF Altruism is the ideal of human brotherhood and high civilisation, the trade union is the first step towards it. Like most of the world's evolutionary developments, it starts on what may be termed the material plane. It begins mostly in connection with the bread-and-butter question, and too many " within " want to keep it there, whilst those " without " misjudge it as looking after nothing else. Unfortunately, the main struggle of life is in getting the bread and butter, hence if unionism did no more than secure butter where there was none before it would amply justify its existence. Unionism is a necessity under present conditions. Organization will always be a necessity under any highly civilised state of society, therefore unionism has come to stay as a principle, though its objects and methods may change to meet changing conditions.

All experience proves that wages are higher, hours of labor shorter, and conditions generally immensely better in an industry where the workers are organized than in the same industry and same country where the workers are without a union. Without it there is no standard wage. No one can tell what the wage rate is, because it is left to the greed of the man who wants someone to work for him, and the needs of the man who is looking for work impel him to accept it. As there are always more than one man looking for a boss, and scarcely ever two employers looking for a worker, it inevitably follows that the poor, needy work-seeker gets the worst of it. The law of supply and demand being unrestricted in such a case, wages fall below a bare subsistence level. On the other hand, when a union is established, the first thing it does is to set up a standard of wages and other conditions for the particular industry its members are engaged in. It may be that it does not in all cases secure a minimum rate at once; still, though some employers may pay less, there are others who pay more, so that the average will be the union minimum. The main point is that the rate is known and published abroad, so that any man seeking work expects to get that rate. Many will not accept less. Some employers decline to pay less, so as to avoid trouble.

Custom is the parent of law. The trade union is a law-maker, as it sets up a new custom, and the parties concerned are driven to an approximate observance of the new law. The law of custom always precedes Statute law. The union gives courage to its members. It opens a door for the ventilation of each member's grievance. It provides a court to which the individual can appeal. He is heard with sympathy, and, if he suffers injustice, his feelings of indignation spread to others who feel his cause to be theirs, and steps are taken to seek a remedy. The success attending the attempt gives encouragement to the timid, who, fearful of losing their position, suffered in silence until the union gave them courage to speak; and thus

Federal Labor Party, 1907.

members one after another realise what an advantage the union is to them. In the mind of the employer the union appears, not as a person working for him, but as a giant fighting for each one of his employees. The giant has, in fact, swallowed his employees, and he loses sight of their individual personality. The union speaks through its mouthpiece, and has completely changed the position. An employer can no longer send an employee away or refuse to listen to his request, assured of the helplessness of the worker to resist if the employer was unprepared to grant it.

The difference between the collective and the individualistic is so great that, when an individual worker asks for some concession which the employer knows the union is supporting, he has a dim, half-conscious idea that the poor worker is being coerced into making the request, and therefore he does not send him away without hearing him, nor does he readily refuse. Man generally has a respect for power, and anything big is treated with much more consideration than anything weak and unable to hit back. Man crushes an ant under his heel, but gets out of the way of a bull.

As an illustration of how the unit is swallowed up in the collective mass, I will quote a case which occurred some years ago in connection with the Miners' Association. As Secretary of the A.M.A. I became aware that a mining company was going to offer its bracemen on the next pay-day a rate of wages lower than the union rate. It expected the three men concerned to accept the reduction and say nothing. I wrote a letter to each of the men,

calling attention to the standard rate of the union,
which was paid in other mines, and pointing out to
them that no member of the union was allowed to
accept less.. I instructed each of the men to take
the letter with him on pay-day, and when he saw
the paysheet and found the rate to be below the
right amount he was to hand my letter to the
paymaster, who was manager.   The men acted
accordingly, and, on the first man handing over my
letter, the manager read it and without a word
raised the sum to the union rate and paid it over.
The men did not have to speak, and were not
discharged, nor was a word said to them by way
of complaint.   The A.M.A. was like the blue coat
of the police constable—the wrong doer is not afraid
of the man in the coat, but of the power behind the
uniform.   The company in the case referred to
recognised the power behind the three men, and
was not prepared for a trial of strength with it.

Another case will illustrate the law-making
effect of unionism.   A party of six men was put
to work in a paddock held by the Madame Berry Co.
They were engaged on boring, and were strangers
to the district, and not then members of the A.M.A.
They had received one pay when I learned that the
rate paid them and without demur accepted was
lower than the rate fixed by the A.M.A.   I waited
upon the manager and called his attention to the
fact, and he readily agreed to pay the higher and
correct amount next pay day.   He kept his word,
and to the surprise of the men concerned they
received an increase in their wages without having
to ask for it.   This is one of many instances which

could be given showing that the non-member benefits by unionism, and has no right to escape paying his quota to the funds necessary to carry on an organization.

One of the subjects often discussed is that of whether unions should use coercion in regard to non-members. It is too late in the day to object to the principle of coercion. Every municipality enforces payment of rates and taxes. The State does the same, and they justify so doing by the fact that the moneys thus collected are utilised for the common good. In a municipality you may be forced to pay rates from the expenditure of which you get no direct benefit in your immediate neighborhood, but any objection you may make on that score is not listened to. The man who will take the advantages which other men's efforts bring to him, and refuse to give in return either effort or cash payment for the maintenance of the organization which secures to him those advantages, is not only mean, but should receive no more consideration than is given to any one who tries to escape the payment of just taxes.

Those outside of unions are of different classes. There are many who are unionistic in principle, but who have not organized a union in their calling as yet. These are simply non-members, and there is no feeling against them except a complaint of their apathy. On the other extreme there is the anti-unionist—the creature who hires himself out to take the place of unionists when standing out for better conditions. They are the strike-breakers. Such persons are of a very low class. They belong to the criminal type—the person who cares for nothing but the gratification of his present wishes, regardless of what effect his actions may have on anyone else. Then there is the non-unionist—the man who is sometimes in the union, and sometimes out—who pays up if he cannot escape it. He is often induced to go in against his fellow in time of trouble. Strong unionists call him " scab " and " blackleg." Some of this rather bad breed are eventually made better men, but most of them require watching, and are ever a source of weakness.

In my thirty years' experience and association with many thousands of men I have never known an anti-unionist who was any good. If I was an employer I would not have him near my workshop. The non-unionist—the " scab "—is only a trifle better. He will take advantage of the employer if he gets a chance. By nature narrowly selfish, he uses any means to gratify his own desires; and, whilst he will cringe and crawl after the boss, he will act just as unfairly to him behind his back as he does to his fellow-worker when it suits him.

Unionism has a markedly beneficial effect on character. It inculcates brotherhood. It gives the right to one member of the union to speak to another if he thinks that he is doing or contemplating a wrong act. The effect of discipline is seen at its best, and its effect is to make men better citizens, better husbands, and better fathers. The principle of sacrifice of self for the good of others is seen in operation in unions as nowhere else. They readily help other bodies which are fighting against injustice, and the interest taken in such cases broadens the minds of members and enlarges their world. The extension of unionism over the world will do more to bring peace than all that can be accomplished by Hague Conferences.

Where those engaged in an industry are combined in a union, or where all unions are associated together as in a Labor Federation, they become a community within society doing good unseen all the time. In the Creswick mining district the Miners' Association has for nearly thirty years enforced the rule that every person working there in connection with the mines must become and remain a member, and there has been no complaint about it from the employers. Large benefits are paid. No widow is allowed to go short of the necessaries of life. Every case of hardship is looked into and a sum collected to help. All is done without parade, and is prompted by the feeling that all are one family and mutual help should be their guiding principle.

The real fact is that a unionist does not pay his contribution—it comes out of the industry, and the employers have to pay it. The workers are slow to grip this salient fact, but it is well known to the capitalists. Elsewhere I give illustrations of the same truth. I mention it here to support the position I take up in favor of the enforcement by law if necessary of the payment of dues to a union which the majority in any occupation may have established. I justify it on the grounds that unionism is a necessity, is a good thing in itself, is highly beneficial to society, and makes for the uplifting of the human race.

In organizing a new society or union it is well to watch for a favorable opportunity. There are waves of feeling which pass over men's minds, and it is best to take one of those occasions when something has arisen to arouse a feeling either of discontent or of desire to become part of a big movement. It is best for some experienced officer of a union already in existence in the same trade to get the new society under way. The most important of all, and a matter workers are most frequently careless about, is the selection of the persons who are to fill the offices.

All organizations of any size should have a paid secretary, who can give his whole time to the work of looking after members' interests. In such case they should select the ablest man they can find. It should never be a question of giving a friend a billet. One large branch of the A.M.A. in a district where there were 4000 miners put the most unsuitable man into the position of secretary out of sympathy, and because he had had the misfortune to lose an arm in a mining accident. It would have paid them better to give him a pension of an amount equal to his salary, and then put the most brainy man they could find into the position. Sympathy must be extended to the mass of the members, and they need the best man and the most intelligent amongst themselves, or even from outside if he is a tried man.

The secretary should remember that he is a manager, not a clerk. He is an elected officer, not a mere hired scribe. He is the recognised constitutional adviser, and is answerable to the members. He needs to have energy, enthusiasm, calmness, good judgment, and tact. He must have a knowledge of the Labor problem, and a knowledge of men—of human nature. The secretary of a big union has a more difficult task to perform than any other person in the community. He must be able to keep his own counsel, must be always sober and vigilant, and must never give the enemy a chance to take an advantage. He will find scores of things which he himself can do which it is unwise to allow anyone else to know, even his president or committee. If a secretary is vigilant he can nip in the bud incipient strikes—that is, he can stop a trouble from arising because he will find that it is over the little things that quarrels arise, which if dealt with in time are never heard of, but which, if they are allowed to grow, drag other matters in and a conflagration ensues which is hard to put out.

If a difficulty threatens, get it put off. Very often the excitement cools down and a way out is found which is impossible at first. "Avoid strikes as long as possible" is a good motto; at the same time do not give away anything. Work for delay, and things will often come right. Don't assume anything. Get at the facts. If possible, get inside the enemy's camp and learn how he looks at matters, and if he is in any way prepared to recede without appearing to back down, find a door to enable him to do so. Never let temper get into the question. Never try to humble or humiliate your opponent. It will leave a bad taste in his mouth, and he will watch a chance to seek revenge. There is some human nature left even in capitalists.

As to how the official is to get inside information no general rule can be laid down, except that he must be one who never betrays a confidence. My own method was to act promptly and quietly in any threatened trouble. The managers controlling affairs for companies do not want any quarrel to arise, as it often puts them in a false position. Many of them are good friends to unionism, but it does not suit to have the fact paraded. When a member of the A.M.A. came to me complaining that he had been wrongfully dismissed I did not wait for a meeting of the committee, but went at once to see the manager of the mine from which the man had been discharged. Frequently mutual explanations would result in the manager saying, "Tell him to come to work to-morrow;" and I would so inform the member interested. The latter would perhaps want to know what had been done or said, when I would remind him that as he had got his job back again it was all that concerned him. It went no further, and was not even reported to the other officers or the committee. This prevented directors hearing a possibly garbled account and making it unpleasant for the manager at next board meeting.

Tact is required in all these matters. You must study the kind of man you have to interview. I never bluntly introduced the subject I had called about when interviewing a man for the first time. Get into conversation first and find out his hobby. Put him in good humor, then mention your matter in quite a casual way as if it was only a trifle. I once drove some twelve miles to interview a stubborn old Scotch mine manager about the discharge of a workman, and after the interview was over and he walked to the fence where I had left my horse and buggy he said on saying " Good-bye " that he knew when he saw me coming what I was after, and had made up his mind not to tell me a word or even to discuss the case of dismissal, yet he said, " You have got it all out of me." It all depends on how you go about it!

A study of mental science questions and of how to read character is essential. This is especially the case where a conference is held between representatives of Labor and capital, or where delegates from a union meet employers. As a rule employers will only meet when they feel their position to be such that it pays better to compromise than to fight. The management of the conference is therefore all important. The side which carries out its share with most ability and in the ablest manner will get the best of the other. When you hire a lawyer to conduct a case you select the best and brainiest man you can afford. Delegates to a conference must be very carefully selected. Pick the most calm, level-headed men, not the noisy talkers. Choose the men who are far-seeing and tactful. You must have men who carefully choose their words.

You may have the worst case and yet get the best of the bargain if you run the conference on what I term scientific lines. See that the place of meeting is a quiet room undisturbed by external noises. Arrange to sit opposite each other at a narrow table. If men have to raise their voices it

GG

raises their tempers, and that must be avoided in conciliation, as men become stubborn when out of temper. Get to the meeting place early. The first arrival from the other side must be closely studied without the appearance of doing so. Read him by the language of movement, which I will assume you understand. You will mostly find that he enters with a serious expression on his countenance. He is full of the importance of his mission, and feels weighted with responsibility. His mind has been crammed with points which he must not forget, and you must quietly start to make him forget them. You will be introduced. Meet him genially; keep up conversation in a light vein. Any light topic will do, but avoid the matter about which you are meeting as far as you can. Tell a funny story and make him laugh. Treat each the same way, and before the preliminaries are over your opponents will have become genial and forgotten all the strong points they had so prominently in their minds, and will have been made insensibly to feel that there is nothing worth quarrelling about after all, as these Labor chaps seem to take things easy and have no worry.

After arranging about a chairman, etc., it is sometimes best to take the points of minor importance first. On these you can afford to give away a good deal, and in their discussion you have the chance of feeling each of your opponents and seeing how he is likely to go on the main issue, and can lay your plans accordingly. When it comes to the real point at issue the advantage is shown of a knowledge of men and their mentality. Jump into the lead at once. Put forward all your strongest arguments first. Keep these to the front all the time. Your opponent will reply, but if he makes a point that you have no effective rejoinder to, ignore it and again state your own. Whilst courteous all the time, take care that you keep the strong points of your own side prominent all the time, even for hours. Do not give a chance to the other side to do so with theirs. By this method you break down opposition. There is a law in mental science which causes an idea kept under attention in consciousness to gather strength by drawing to itself all contiguous ideas bearing on the same subject which may be floating about on the sea of memory, or which may be suggested by argument of those present.

As all thoughts involving action have a tendency to act themselves out, so by the method indicated you force your opponents to give way by wearing down their objections and tiring their powers of concentration. It is seldom that the employers send men who are much accustomed to sustained argument, and hence if Labor picks the right man it starts with an advantage. By the method indicated thus briefly you will, after it is all over, often hear remarks made by one employer's representative to another, such as, "Why didn't you bring forward such and such a point?" The other will reply, "Oh, I quite forgot; and those Labor chaps gave me no chance."

One point to be remembered in trying to win by argument or conciliation is that you must never contradict a combative man. He is easily read, and nearly always has a soft side. Differ with him in argument, but in a round-about way. If you contradict him direct he becomes fightable and stubborn. Appeal to him on behalf of the women and children. That will generally touch the softest side of him; if it does, keep using it. Many a strike has been brought about by sending one combative man to interview another. You might as well apply fire to powder and not expect an explosion.

As a case in point, I will mention that in 1887 a strike took place at the Kaitangata coal-mine, New Zealand. All efforts at settlement had failed. Several mediators had tried ineffectually, and it had cost the A.M.A. over £3000. I was on a visit to New Zealand, and had to report to the A.M.A. Executive. On arrival in Dunedin I went to see the company's general manager, Mr. Henderson. He was pointed out to me in the street whilst on my way to his office. I saw at a glance that he was decidedly combative in character, but genial and kindly in disposition if you took him the right way. In our interview I simply kept appealing on behalf of the women and children. When he expressed his soreness at the way the miners had treated him by burning his effigy, etc., when he had really gone out to the mine prepared to come to a settlement I took care not to say a word against his denunciation, but brought in the women and little ones again. Briefly, I got all I expected to get in the circumstances, and we parted with a letter of introduction in my pocket to the mine manager and a free pass on the company's railway. I did not use the latter, but walked the four and a-half miles from Stirling and

passed amongst the men who were idle without their
knowing I was there. I saw the mine manager and
with him went underground, so that I saw how many
and what sort of non-unionists he had at work, and
finally came to a understanding with him as to
putting on the unionists if the strike was declared
off. I then called on the union leaders, and found
in the president a splendid fellow, a man of ability,
and a sturdy stubborn fighter for the interests of
the unionists; but he was also combative, and to send
him to meet the general manager of the company was
not the right way to secure a settlement, as they were
bound to quarrel.

Another illustration occurs to me of a different
kind. A trouble arose in St. Arnaud, Victoria, and
the president of the A.M.A. (the late Mr. M.
Stapleton) and myself went there to effect a settlement if possible. We went up to the office of the
mine manager (Mr. Z. Lane). We knocked at the
door, and it was opened by a big dignified man of
very austere appearance. He invited us in, and
taking a chair slowly set it down in the corner of
the room so that each of its four legs struck the
floor quietly at the same moment of time. Without
a word he pointed to the chair as an indication for
me to sit down. Taking another, in the same
methodical manner he set it in the opposite corner
and indicated to Mr. Stapleton to take it. He next
closed the office door, which was on the side and
close to the other end of the room; and then, placing
a chair just inside the door, he sat himself squarely
down upon it, and with his hands thumb outwards
on his thighs he faced us. His movements spoke as

plainly as words, and said to us in the silent language of movement, "I have the best of this case. I have you two cornered. I am ready for both of you; so come on." We entered on a discussion of the difficulty, and soon found that he had taken up three points. He took the weakest one first. Very soon he began to wriggle on his chair, and presently he gave up that line of argument and took his second point. We beat him out of this, and he assumed the third position, which he felt was impregnable. To his surprise we gave way at once and admitted that, whilst he was technically right, the attitude was not one which a dignified person could uphold. This so upset him that we were able to arrive at a settlement. He expected us to support and uphold the attitude taken up by the local branch, whereas we did not do so, and this made him amenable to a satisfactory solution of the trouble. He was a man with whom sound reasoning counted, and he could not fight against it.

The settlement of the Jondaryan shearing difficulty in Queensland was a case illustrative of the value of keeping to the front the strong points of your case and tiring out your opponents. There were seven of us, and those who were to act for the pastoralists numbered three. There were, however, nearly forty present—all anxious to see how things went. They were capitalists, and sat round in horse shoe form, with our little band across between the toes. The chairman was a capitalist. For three hours or over we kept at those three men. They retired frequently to consider our proposals, only to return without giving way. Again we repeated our strongest arguments just as if they were new, and again they would retire. We were ready to keep on all day, as we were not prepared to take " no " for an answer, and we knew secretly that we had the shipping company with us that time. At last, when it got past dinner-hour, the fat men began to get hungry, and the chairman came to our aid and said our proposals seemed so reasonable that he really thought the representatives of the pastoralists might very well accept them and thus come to an amicable settlement and prevent trouble. That settled it, and they gave way; but what won the day was our patient persistence and the power of an idea kept prominently over the minds of those concerned.

Once in Ballarat, Victoria, five of us from the Shearers' Union met sixteen representatives of the pastoralists. We had held a couple of conferences previously, and they knew our strength in argument. On this occasion they had organized the work of the conference, so to say, and had placed the leadership of their side in the hands of an able man who was a good debater, and who took notes of our remarks so as to reply. The crucial question was, as usual, that of shearing rates; and when we came to a deadlock on that, with a shilling per hundred between us, one of the biggest employers suddenly got up in an apparent huff, saying that he could see that " it was no use wasting time, as it was evident the shearers' delegates were not prepared to come to an understanding no matter what they did." He bounced out of his chair and said he was going home. We learned afterwards that this move had been rehearsed beforehand, and was intended to bluff us into giving way, as they knew we were anxious for a settlement. He made one mistake, however, as instead of clearing out he went and sat down in a corner of the room. That told us that his action was only bluff, and so we took no notice of it.

Leaving these phases of the movement, I want to emphasise the need for unions being more careful than some have been in selecting representatives to act for them in any capacity. They should remember that a body is judged by its representatives. Some Labor Conferences have been spoiled in their results by neglect of this precaution. The apathetic do not attend the meetings of their union, and so the selfish seeker after a billet or prominence of any kind is sent to a gathering where he makes himself a nuisance and spoils the temper of everybody. Unions should pick the man who comes the nearest to an ideal man. He should be one who does them credit, and by whom they would not object to be judged. The work of unionism is becoming of more importance day by day, and its work is such that it demands the best intellect to be found within the ranks of Labor. The man who needs to be drawn out is generally a more reliable man than the noisy seeker after prominence. Members should seek out the brains within their ranks, and give opportunity for its influence to be felt in the larger field of annual conference and the like occasions. The level-headed trade unionist of experience is the most practical man or woman in the world, and God knows the world has need of them to push on the work of social and political reform.

CHAPTER XXXIII.

TRADE UNIONISM AS AN INVESTMENT.

ONE of the many foolish excuses given by men for not joining a Union is that they cannot afford to pay the contributions. The fact is that one of the first effects of unionism is to make the industry pay the cost of the workers' organizations. It is a very weak and badly managed union which fails to secure for its members more in return than the amount of contributions and levies paid. As illustrations I will quote a few cases. Whilst secretary of the Creswick Branch of the Amalgamated Miners' Association, I prepared a special report of the results of its first ten years' history. The union had sprung into existence to resist a reduction of wages of two shillings per week, and did so successfully. Four years later we secured a rise of three shillings per week per man. Without organization the earnings of miners would have been forced to even a lower wage than was first attempted, but without taking that into consideration, the gain in actual cash for the ten years totalled £129,480. Direct benefits from accident pay, funeral allowance, assistance to members, and strike pay, totalled £13,221. Added to wages, this makes a total of £142,701. The total amount paid in entrance fees, contributions, and levies was £19,773, or taking off the balance in hand,

£18,013. This leaves a clear gain in hard cash of £124,688, or about £100 per member clear of all cost for the ten years. The gain for the ten years following would be still greater. In addition to the above, the sums paid to help other unions, to assist members in difficulties, to support local hospital, etc., totalled £4505. It will thus be seen that a vigorous union not only made the industry bear the cost but return the handsome dividend of £10 per year to each member.

Take another case. The Australian Workers' Union is not only the largest, but the most vigorous and aggressive of Labor organizations. I have recently finished a summary of the total receipts and expenditure of the organization since its inception in 1886, including the Queensland section. All cross entries have been eliminated so far as I could trace them. The various items have been concentrated under as few heads as possible, so as to present the statement in a simple form. The following is the result of my investigation of the various balance-sheets :—

RECEIPTS.

	£	s.	d.
To Entrance Fees and Contributions..	273,327	5	8
Levies	19,700	12	6
Fines	1,826	19	10
Donations	16,735	14	6
Various other items, such as rent, sales of material, etc.	5,721	9	5
Total .. ..£	317,312	1	11

EXPENDITURE.

	£	s.	d.
By Salaries	61,320	1	2
Organizers' Wages and Expenses	39,913	11	1
Strike Expenses	54,533	1	9
Law Expenses and Legal Charges	12,823	18	11
Printing and Advertising	20,922	8	6
Postage, Telegrams, Etc.	13,946	17	9
Committee Expenses	4,703	12	5
Donations to other Unions and various objects	26,537	12	0
Co-operation, "Worker," Etc. ..	44,491	0	2
Political and Parliamentary	6,465	5	7
Refunds, Fines, Forfeited Wages, Etc.	5,543	13	7
Various Other Items, totalling ..	15,128	10	10

Total Expenditure £306,329	13	9
Leaving balance in hand of £10,982	8	2

Of the above the following may be classed as direct benefits returned to Unionists:—

	£	s.	d.
Strike Expenses	54,533	1	9
Legal Charges	12,823	18	11
Donations	21,537	12	0
"Worker," Etc.	44,491	0	2
Refunds	5,543	13	7
Political	6,465	5	7

Total £150,394	12	0

Practically one-half the moneys paid are returned in benefits, the other half paying for cost of running the Union. No allowance is made for the very large saving effected by having the two '' Workers '' as a means of communication between the office and the members. Thousands of pounds per annum are saved in advertisements alone. As a matter of fact the Union could not carry on its work at present cost without having its own organs. This is looking at it from a purely business point of view. From the educational standpoint the good done is simply incalculable. In our Universities teaching is carried on by means of lectures. Professors condense into a series of lectures the essence of thought and knowledge of the world, thus enabling the youthful listeners to start at the point of evolution now attained. '' The Worker '' and the travelling organizers are the educators of our members. They give extension lectures. They tell of progress made. They set forth the ideals of the great Labor movement. In that sense they do University work, and the cost is more than repaid in the enlightenment of our members, who are notoriously the best informed of Australian unionists.

To return to the economic. In order to present in a concrete form the monetary gain, I have taken the number of sheep in the four States in which the union has hitherto operated. Making a deduction for those slaughtered unshorn I find the average per year about 76,000,000. I have taken the last twenty-one years. Making allowance for actual increase in shearing rates, abolition of second price, saving in cost of rations, etc., and adding on the gain to shed hands in wages, together with the direct return in Union benefits beforementioned, the total gain for twenty-one years in round figures reaches about £4,000,000. For this shearers in Southern States have paid £12 17s. 6d., and shed hands £7 15s.; in the aggregate £306,329, including Queensland. The gain to the shearer would be about £1 per week on the average. The shed hands in Queensland organized about the same time as the shearers, but in the Southern States they did not unite till 1890. In Victoria-Riverina they did not rally into the union until 1900. Since that date their increase in wages can safely be stated as ten shillings per week per man. The gain in South Australia would be similar. The gain in other States is not quite so much on the average, but is not less than five shillings per week in any case. Taken all round the gain would be from five to ten shillings per week above what the employers wanted to cut it down to. We must also never forget the fact that the rate offered in the face of an existing organization is itself much higher than it would be under full "freedom of contract," as desired by employers.

In a comparison table of the wages paid in 1886 and in 1896, issued by the Statistician of Victoria, covering twenty-two rural industries and occupations, only one had secured an increase, namely, the shearers. All others had suffered reductions varying from twenty to forty-seven per cent. The shearers had not only not suffered a reduction, but had obtained an increase. Of the twenty-two sections of labor on the list they were the only section organized. Looked at as a commercial

investment, the cash contributed to a union secures
a return which, in its percentage of profit, would
make a Rockefeller's mouth water. Leaving out
Queensland, our A.S.U. and A.W.U. charged
entrance fees for shearers and cooks for three years
of two shillings and sixpence, two years ten shillings,
and seven years of five shillings. Contributions
were, one year at five shillings, twelve years ten
shillings, four years twelve shillings and sixpence,
half-a-crown of which went to "The Worker," and
four years at fifteen shillings, five of which go to
"The Worker" as subsidy for which members get
the paper weekly free of further cost. In addition,
a levy of £1 was paid. Shed hands, six years a ten
shillings contribution; two years two shillings and
sixpence entrance fee, and five shillings contribution; one year five shillings, with no entrance fee;
four years seven shillings and sixpence, two shillings
and sixpence of which went to "The Worker"; and
four years ten shillings, five of which go to "The
Worker." Totalled and averaged for the twenty-
one years, members in the three Southern States
have paid twelve shillings and threepence per annum
for shearers and cooks. Shed hands' payments to
the union have averaged eight shillings and sixpence
per member for seventeen years. Let shearers make
up their tallies at four shillings per hundred sheep
shorn, and shed hands their gain on the time worked,
and they will find the percentage higher as a result
of paying into a union than any investor can secure
in any enterprise other than monopolies. It must
also be noted that shearing only lasts about three
months each year.

We must not forget in this connection that unionism has been applied to politics. Unionism has sent its own men into Parliament, and as a result trade unions have now an opportunity in several States and in the Commonwealth of bringing injustice into the light of day in an open court such as Arbitration or Wages Boards. It was by means of arbitration that the members of the A.W.U. secured such a rise in rates as will restore their wage to what they originally forced it up to by means of strikes. Labor in Politics has secured the increase by peaceful methods, and enabled the work to be carried on under more harmonious conditions as between employer and employee.

Take another instance of Labor in Politics. From the report of the Inspector of Factories in Victoria I find there were 160 separate industries in which the Wages Boards gave an increase in wages. These employ 40,680 hands. I have taken out each case separately, and find that the increases total in the aggregate no less than £343,584 13s. 4d. per year. It means so much increased purchasing power, so much increased demand for the things which the workers require, and which they and other workers have to make. It means so much increased sales to people who are distributors. It means that large sum distributed amongst 40,680 persons instead of its going into the pockets of a mere few. The average is £8 8s. 9d. each, but actual amounts vary, of course. For a few pence per week contribution to the union and the trouble of walking to the polling booth once in three years and voting straight, the unionists secure an average of £8 8s. 9d., and no lost time or fighting. The bakers gained an increase of ten shillings and twopence per week. That means £26 8s. 8d. per man per year. The coopers got 11s. 10d. per week increase. That is £30 15s. 4d. per year. Is any stronger evidence needed in support of Unionism and Labor in Politics? You must not forget that it was the declared intention of at least one Premier in Victoria to abolish the Wages Boards, and it has only been by the continuous fighting of Labor-members that new Boards have been appointed.

Other cases as illustrations could be added by the score. In December, 1908, the Marine Cooks', Bakers', and Butchers' Association of Australasia haled the shipowners before the Federal Court of Conciliation and Arbitration, and secured an award which means £4000 a year increase in wages. The Engine Drivers on the goldfields in West Australia raised their wages for first-class from 13s. 4d. to 15s. per day by unionism. When Labor secured the Arbitration Act, they took the employers to Court and gained another 2s. per day; that means a gain through union effort of £57 4s. per year per man. It is admitted that the workers have not always won in these courts. In Western Australia on the average the results are about even. Without unionism wages would certainly have fallen. New South Wales experience shows that thousands of pounds have been gained by the workers in wages, and shorter hours and better conditions have also been secured. The strong opposition of the employers, and the action of the present Government —which is elected by the employing classes and their tools—are clear evidence of the value of such a means of settling industrial disputes. Previous to the setting up of Arbitration in Sydney the case of the bakers provides a fine example of the difference between workers who look after their own interests and those who do not; in short, between unionists and non-unionists. Union bakers were getting £2 12s. per week of eight hours in decent bakehouses, whilst non-union bakers were slaving ninety hours per week in insanitary bakehouses for thirty-six shillings per week. Illustrations like these could be multiplied if space permitted. A striking case showing the value of maintaining a strong union in the face of powerful opposition is that of the seamen on the Australian coast. Their union costs 24s. per member per year. They have forced up their wages by £3 per month. That means £36 per man per year. For 10,000 men it means £360,000 a year. It means that large sums circulated amongst commercial firms. It means more home comforts, with increased happiness and contentment; it means a higher standard of life, even though far short of what it should be, and what it will be when more of the workers realise their power and their duty.

The unions of the Commonwealth probably bring a gain to the workers of six and a half millions per year. Amongst many trades unionists there is a tendency to overlook the real object of an organization of this kind. A trade union is not a benefit society in the sense in which the law provides for Friendly Societies. Just as a live union makes the industry pay the upkeep of the organization, so should it make the industry pay for all contingencies,

HH

such as accident, sickness, etc. If all the unions took up the work we would soon have such Acts of Parliament as would force the profit-grabbing employer to make provision for all that concerns his employees, out of whose labor his profits come. Unions with Friendly Society benefits simply relieve the employer. If they could enforce higher wages to such an extent as to make up for what they now contribute to accident funds, etc., it might meet the case; but they are almost invariably so hampered by the necessity for keeping funds in hand to meet benefit claims on the one hand and by the objection of special levies on the other, that such unions are seldom found amongst aggressive forward unionism.

Again, a trade union is not a commercial, money-making concern. So soon as it goes in for the saving of money and piling up of funds it becomes conservative, and a block in the way of industrial progress. Money is power, but active unity is greater than money. It is wise to have something in hand for contingencies, but it is essential to remember that success comes not from hoarding funds but from spending them—wisely, of course, but keep on spending. When any group of persons, such as a union or any other organization, becomes proud of its funds or its benefits to members paid out of members' own pockets, it is becoming a danger, and the sooner it ceases to exist the better. The whole object of unionism is to find a common ground of agreement, so that all can act together. Unity and effort of a united kind are the sole aim of organization. Funds are only necessary for paying inevitable expenses. The best work of the world's workers has been and still is being done without money. A financially strong but numerically weak union is of much less value and influence than a penniless organization which contains within its ranks all having a common industrial interest. The conditions of industrial life have changed. Unions must adapt themselves to the altered conditions, or they cease to be properly classed as unions. Such an organization as the M.S.U. was clearly a union in the interests of the employers. In effect there are other unions whose bona fides no one doubts, which are nevertheless acting the part of a bogus union, and may be termed non-union unions so far as the movement is concerned.

When a strike takes place every union man is expected to cease working in the particular industry concerned. The large mass of unionists in Australia have declared a strike against electing any but Labor men to Parliament, realising that the battle ground is now on the floor of the law-making chamber; yet some unions stand aloof and decline to join in support, thus helping to defeat the main body. Neither rules nor benefits should stand in the way. Old laws made by the dead have hampered progress, and it is our duty to change them. It would be better to wind up all such unions as feel tied up by rules, and reorganize on up-to-date modern lines. Unions are good, and are profitable only whilst they live up to the ideals underlying the movement which gave them birth. Such a union is worth belonging to, and the return is great. Its

members gain in social status, in self-respect, and
in development of social instinct and interest in the
realisation of social and political power. Industrial
unionism is the first step toward securing a
Co-operative Commonwealth. The second step is
the application of union principles and machinery
to the exercise of political power. With all workers
organized and acting together complete control of
the country's Parliament is assured, and the
banishment of enforced poverty certain. Injustice
will disappear, a new and healthier environment
be created, and mankind raised to a higher plane
of existence. The workers who stand aloof from
unionism retard progress, and help to add to the
sum of human misery. Those who join become part
of the grand army working for better and saner
conditions of life.

CHAPTER XXXIV.

PROPAGANDA WORK.

VERY early in my work as a union organizer I realised how hopeless the struggle of the masses against the capitalists must prove unless the unions took up the more important question of taking control of the law-making machine. Not only were the laws bad, but their administration was worse. It was always against the masses, and in favor of a class minority. The organization of the shearers gave an opportunity denied to me by the miners, and hence I was able to do some effective work in co-operation with the many splendid officers and members of that large body. Active propaganda has been the special feature of the organization.

Very soon we had a paper of our own. At first a paper was run by a private firm solely in the interests of the union, and its policy was controlled by the officers of the A.S.U. Later a union-owned paper was started, which has since grown into a power. Many pounds were spent annually in the dissemination of literature. For instance, we purchased many hundred copies of Bellamy's "Looking Backward," as soon as it was published, and sent these out amongst the members. We did the same with "Merrie England." Leaflets, articles, etc., were sent out by the thousand. At the opening of each Annual Conference of the

A.S.U., as president, I delivered an address dealing with some phase of the social problem. This appeared in the official report, and thus reached thousands of readers. Secretaries of branches generally touched on the subject of social reform in their reports.

As a sample of the line of reasoning followed, and also of the method adopted, I quote a portion of one of my reports when general secretary of the General Laborers' Union prior to its amalgamation with the Amalgamated Shearers' Union. After dealing with the details of work done and attempted, the report runs as follows:—

" The unfortunates who form the mass from which non-unionists are drawn are the products of our present social system. Natural opportunities being in the possession of the few, who employ workers only for the purpose of making a profit out of their labor, together with the effect of competition and the steady displacement of men and women by machinery, it of necessity follows that there must be a large number of unemployed. Employers select the best workmen only, hence the inferior tradesman is driven out and becomes absorbed into the ranks of the class called unskilled —a mass embracing in its ranks not only the strong general laborer, but also the weak, the improvident, the helpless. To make an effort to change our social system so as to give full opportunity to every honest man to earn a livelihood for himself and those dependent upon him, to give hope to the despondent and help to the weak, and to secure the moral improvement of all, should be the aim of our organization. To accomplish this there must be unity of purpose and method on the part, not only of our particular union, but of Labor organizations generally.

" Already the platform of unionism has been extended, its aims broadened, and new methods adopted. We realise that to continue upon old lines would never bring about that change in our social system absolutely necessary to secure more just and happier conditions for mankind. Old trade unionism has done a wonderful work. It has been the only institution that has in a practical form done something to improve the lot of the workers of the world. It has paved the way for and given a start to co-operation. So long, however, as it confined its attention to the trade interests of its own members it could do nothing for the ever-increasing mass which our keenly competitive social system constantly forces out of the ranks of organized Labor. Workmen are in competition with each other for employment, which decreases in ratio of population, relatively fewer being required to supply the wants of the world. Old unionism has done much, but it has failed to shorten hours or increase wages in keeping with scientific, social, and economic changes.

" Fighting by the old method of strikes it can accomplish less now—in the days when production is in the hands of powerful syndicates—when the employing classes have their unions and world-wide federations—than it could when greater numbers rendered employers' unions more difficult of

establishment. In the past we have permitted
ourselves to be governed and ruled by the class
whose members form the minority—those who
enjoy class privileges, who hold a monopoly of those
natural opportunities which justly are the common
heritage of the whole human family. They make
and administer the laws, control the education of
our children, own and direct the policy and tone
of that great educator, the press. They can swamp
the Labor market with men, women, and children
needing bread whenever they think that trade
interests demand such a step. An insane competition
places commercial and trade interests—the profit-
making, money-getting of a few—above the
well-being, the happiness, and even the lives of the
many. Competition forces employers to act unjustly,
and under the conditions which regulate production
in society, as now constituted, they must continue
to crush their weaker or more unfortunate brother.

" We must look behind the employer and carry
that bitter feeling, which injustice naturally gives
rise to, beyond and away from the employer, and
let it burn in its fullest intensity against the system
which produces for profit instead of, as it ought
to, for use, for the satisfaction of human wants and
desires—the utilisation of Nature's unlimited bounty
for making mankind as happy as our control of
conditions can render the human family. No man
or set of men can change our social conditions. We
cannot even blame any man or set of men for the
continuance of an admittedly evil system. We cannot
expect the ruling classes to do other than go on
selfishly looking after and maintaining the interests

of their class. They do not govern because of any superior ability, but simply because they have secured control, and because the masses have been apathetic, easy going, and careless, and have allowed themselves to be split up into factions.

"If any body of persons in Australia is to blame for the evils of our social systm, it is the working classes. We have the intelligence and the power to change the conditions of life for the better, and have only to put forth our energy, and by unity of effort we can gain all that is required. We know what unionism has accomplished in trade matters. It has forced numerous reforms in connection with all industries—has even influenced legislatures, and the stamp of its moral force is seen in our laws. Apply the same method—the same principle—to effort in the direction of the larger reforms absolutely necessary to effect social reconstruction, and we are certain of success. The masses must not only take a deeper interest in political questions, but they must make the politics of the country. The welfare of the people must be raised to the first place—must be the uppermost and foremost consideration. How best to secure the good of all without injury to any should be the aim—not commercial supremacy, not cheap production regardless of the human misery following, but rather the broadest justice, the widest extension of human happiness, and the attainment of the highest intellectual and moral standard of civilised nations should be our aim.

"To accomplish this the social machinery must be put together, set in motion, and kept steadily going until we weave the web of that destiny which we as a people decide shall be that of the Australian nation. The first step, then, is that of ceasing to leave the matter to others, and of taking an interest in the management and direction of the affairs of the country. To provide the machinery necessary even to ascertain the views of the mass, organization is required. When once organized the power is in our own hands, and practical reforms would immediately follow. Experience has over and over again taught us the lesson that an unorganized and undisciplined mass has but little if any influence for good. Time and again thousands of unemployed have met, and, after publicly stating their difficulties, have sent deputations representing starving men, women, and children to the well-to-do member of the Government, from whom they reasonably expected sympathy and help, only to be snubbed or at best put off with paltry excuses. The spectacle of thousands of idle men in a rich country like Australia is a disgrace to Australian democracy. Not only have the Governments of the colonies proved their utter incapacity for dealing with the great social question of the age, but they have displayed a lack of sympathy with the masses, and have made their burden greater and their lot worse.

"As before indicated, those who suffer most under a social system which favors the strongest— and in many cases the most unscrupulous—are the great mass known as unskilled labor. It does not deserve the name, as it contains thousands of men superior in skill to many an artisan. There is an

ever-increasing mass of men who are forced out
of steady, settled employment, and who frequently
change both their place and occupation, and it
is this class in particular that this union was
established to assist, protect, and secure the
co-operation of, in the endeavor to bring about such
changes as will give every man the chance, as he
has the right, to earn his living. Thousands are now
denied the right to live. Although craving the
privilege, they are denied the opportunity of
working for the wherewithal to feed and clothe
themselves or their families. They offer to hand
over one-half or even seventy-five per cent. of what
they would earn to those who hold a monopoly of
the sources of production, but the employing classes
will not accept. The market is overstocked. We
have overproduced, and men and women can starve
and die in the midst of too much food. We have
an unpeopled continent where honest men are denied
work. No change will come until the masses awake
and elect their own Parliaments, make and
administer laws that give equality of justice and
opportunity to all—that does not make the success
of one depend, as now, upon the crushing down of
another. Already we rejoice to see Labor asserting
itself, and, undismayed by the howls of let-things-be
Conservatism, it has secured a place in our Legislatures, and has already done immensely good work
in several colonies.''

The statement of the problem in that report
is the same as I would write to-day, though the
report was for the year 1891—the year of the turning
point in the history of the Labor Movement in

Australia. In that year we returned thirty-six members to the Parliament of New South Wales, and I am proud of having addressed public meetings and organized leagues in all the largest towns of eight electorates, my expenses being paid by the A.S.U. and G.L.U. Later on, after amalgamation, as president of the Australian Workers' Union, for four years in succession I averaged about fifteen thousand miles of travel each year, addressing meetings and advocating the cause of Labor in politics. The A.W.U. paid the expenses. In addition to my work and that of the branch officers, we send out organizers every shearing season, who all do propaganda work according to their several abilities. Last year we had twenty-eight out for several months. The result of this combined work of addresses, literature, and "The Worker" newspapers is seen in the fact that in all the electorates under A.W.U. control the electors are represented by Labor members.

This is true of all the States. We try to arrange for an agent in every country town, and have several hundred already. At shearing time there is a man selected by the members themselves as their representative, who becomes an active organizer and preacher of the doctrines of the union. Probably there are between two and three thousand of such men at work each year—splendid fellows, whose work tells. During 1908 we had in addition an able man in each of the States of New South Wales, Victoria, and South Australia, and in conjunction with the A.L.F. also in Queensland, whose whole time and abilities were devoted to political and industrial organizing. They were paid £6 per week and expenses by the union. This work will be continued in every State during 1909, the A.W.U. bearing the cost. If other organizations only roused up and did as much, the capture of Parliament by the workers would be a reality in less than three years

CHAPTER XXXV.

AUSTRALIA IN . 1908.

THE Labor Party all over the continent is one. The same electors vote in Federal and State elections. The same organizations select the candidates and work for them. It is only in the Commonwealth, however, where there is a chance to democratise both Houses of Parliament. In all the States there is a second chamber, composed of the most crusted Tories and Conservatives, and they carefully block every measure of a radical or even moderately liberal kind. Thus we have the rule of a class, and are not yet a self-governing democracy. The particulars which follow will give a rough idea of our past and present situation, and indicate what has to be done before Australia can take a forward step.

The total value of wealth in Australasia is, according to Coghlan, £1,204,042,000. £152,000,000 worth of this is held outside. The value of land in private hands is £461,255,000. The people owe to the money-lender £407,290,000, or £85 per head, and the yearly tribute totals £18,102,500. Confining ourselves to the Commonwealth, we are in debt to the tune of £86 16s. 3d. per inhabitant, a total sum of £343,938,000 of State, local bodies, and private borrowings. For this we are levied to the tune of £15,508,000 per annum, including £400,000 income of absentees.

The primary producers and the industrial workers in the Commonwealth total (male and female) 959,339. As they have to produce the whole of the wealth which pays all burdens, it means that they have to produce over £16 each for the money-lender ere they get a loaf of bread for themselves or their dependents. This almost equals Coghlan's estimate of the average cost of food per inhabitant, £16 14s. They get absolutely no return for this. They have already paid to the British money-lender £116,000,000 in about 33 years, but not a penny of the principal yet. As we have more detail for New South Wales than other States, let us take it as illustrating what has been done all over the continent.

In 1903 there were 735,589 adults in New South Wales. Of these 190,617 possessed property, and 544,972 own no property. The total value of property in the State was £368,778,000. Of this, £130,521,000, or 35 per cent., was held by 987 persons, 2086 owned 45 per cent., and about 3000 persons owned one-half the total. Twenty per cent. was owned outside, ten per cent. in Britain, and six per cent. in Victoria.

Alienated land in New South Wales is held thusly:—

5¼ million acres in 57,342 holdings of 400 acres and under.

5½ million acres in 8488 holdings of from 401 to 1000 acres.

13 million acres in 4399 holdings of from 1001 to 10,000 acres.

21 million acres in 676 holdings of 10,000 acres and upward.

Total, 44¾ million acres.

A very small percentage is cultivated, the highest in any district being only 18 per cent.—of course, by the smaller holders. The larger holdings only run from a-quarter to one per cent. for whole districts. Out of the whole only 2,400,000 acres, or five per cent., are cultivated, and only one per cent. put under artificial grass.

The census of 1901 gave the total number of breadwinners, male and female, in New South Wales, as 564,799. Employers number 53,844, the commercial class 77,664, and wage-earners 362,205, with 24,403 unemployed. Though the wage-earners outnumber other classes combined, they have in the past allowed the capitalist class to govern the country.

Here are some additional figures, showing how, under the conditional purchase system, which was designed to allow the poor man to obtain land on easy terms, the number of large estates in New South Wales has increased. Since 1882, 44,352,613 acres of conditional purchase lands have been transferred, and only 18,481,880 acres have been applied for. At present, 22,830,261 acres in New South Wales are held by 722 persons, or companies, whose holdings average an area of 31,621 acres each, and the total area alienated comprises 48,081,314 acres. In South Australia, 304 persons, or companies, own 3,545,000 acres, whilst 1,269,704 acres are held by 30. The following table gives the names of the thirty largest land-owners in South Australia, together with their area and the unimproved value of their holdings:—

	Acres.	Value.
Angas Estate	81,502	£200,238
W. J. T. Clarke	76,000	159,556
Canowie	68,450	139,700
Robertson	67,709	151,400
Dutton	66,000	132,862
Maslin	53,791	85,436
S.A. Company	52,579	262,400
University	53,228	36,000
J. J. Duncan	50,230	107,622
Willowie	49,799	88,000
Mortlock .. ;. ..	49,536	56,642
McFarlane	43,996	76,862
T. R. Bowman	41,919	78,000
Smith (Hynam)	38,000	76,000
T. E. Barr Smith ..	36,000	62,000
Ellis (Benara)	35,000	81,000
Watson (Riddoch) ..	34,000	52,000
Queensland Land Coy.	33,000	31,000
Dutton and Melrose ..	33,000	75,000
A. S. Browne	33,000	83,000
Duffield Estate	32,000	56,000
James Melrose	31,000	27,000
Dickson	29,000	56,000
G. T. Melrose	28,000	47,000
K. D. Bowman	28,000	50,000
Lawson	26,000	42,000
C. H. Angas	25,345	47,498
L. G. Browne	23,731	74,178
A. G. Laidlaw	23,902	33,456
L. McBean	26,077	30,818

II

In many parts of South Australia one may travel
all day by train without seeing more than a few
individuals, the scanty population of many districts
being due to the fact that the land has been
alienated, and not put to proper use.

In the rich lands of the Western district of
Victoria 4000 square miles are held by 60 families.
Total dwellings thereon, including tents, 1285.
Total population, 7869. The Government built 362
miles of railway through about 40 owners' lands
at a cost of £3,753,000. In the shires of Hampden
and Mortlake, 20 families own over 800,000 acres.
They hold closed roads embracing 16,337 acres, for
which nothing is paid. Outside of towns there is
one human habitation for each seven square miles.
One-eighth of all privately-owned lands in Western
Victoria is held by 525 people. Over 1,000,000 acres
are held by 11 persons, and 1,240,000 acres by 18.
No wonder that Victoria lost by excess of emigration
over immigration 143,542, mostly adults, between
1891 and 1904.

There are three main sources from which the
few have become possessors of the riches held so
disproportionately. The commercial man by
exorbitant charges, adulteration, etc.; the contractor
by high prices and inferior work and material;
the owner of land by taking increased rents or
selling at values enhanced by the energy and efforts
of others. Some have made money in mining or
other speculation, but as a matter of fact, all place
their money in land ownership either directly or
indirectly—that is, the contractor and the commercial
man after acquiring money becomes a landowner.

We had no Labor members in Parliament till 1891; no solid party till 1894. Before that the capitalist class had matters in their own hands. They very early began to grab the land. Some secured large areas by grant prior to constitutional government. Having secured possession of the land, they proceeded to raise its value—not by doing anything to develop it themselves, but by inducing the Government to make roads, construct railways, bridge streams, and erect public buildings, many of which were never required, but all put money into the pockets of the ruling class. In more than one case roads were made through private estates with Government money. All these works were done by what the capitalists term private enterprise—that is, they were let by a friendly Government to their own class on contract, and paid for out of loans floated in London. Fortunes were made by contractors. One railway contract, one big bridge or large building was sufficient to enable a contractor to retire for life. Municipalities were established, governed by the same class, and carrying on in the same way, added to the openings for private gain at public loss. The waste of public funds was enormous and cannot be estimated. Huge buildings were erected, the elaborate furnishings of which rival those of the palace of an Eastern potentate. Carved book-cases, marble statuary in the offices of Cabinet Ministers, all speak eloquently of the largess thrown with lavish hand to the middleman. Every Ministry found billets for its needy friends, quite irrespective of whether there was any work for them to do, or whether they were fit to do it if there had been. In Victoria this was so much the case that departmental work practically came to a deadlock, as four separate offices were dealing with the same matters, and it took additional officers to enter upon a search to find what had become of your particular set of red-taped papers. New South Wales was just as bad.

·The commercial middleman shared in the Government distribution of loan· money. He had the advantage of coming in between the user and the producer, and had the supply of contractors and workmen. The press controlled public opinion, and was itself controlled by the advertiser, and the commercial man is the advertiser. All were in the swim together, whilst the fool public were gulled and the wage-earners were denied voting power.

In 1871, the public debt of New South Wales was £20 10s. per capita. In 1891, it was £45 10s. 8d. In Victoria, it was £16 0s. 11d. and £37 14s. 4d. respectively. During the eighties the boom was worked up. Banks grew up like mushrooms, until there was one for every 3000 of the population. From 1871 to 1892 private capital was introduced into New South Wales in excess of withdrawals to the total of £19,000,000, and over £23,000,000 was brought in by immigrants. The greatest bulk for investment came in the period 1886-90.

In New South Wales, from 1882 to 1892, land sales were enormous. The population increased 50 per cent., and £51,200,000 was introduced, yet agriculture only increased 28 per cent., or from 660,000 acres to 846,000 acres. In the years of the greatest introduction of capital—namely, 1885,

£11,470,000, and 1886, £10,028,000—the export of domestic produce was the lowest for any period since the gold discovery.

In 1886-7 the great strike against reduction of wages took place in the Southern collieries, followed by a similar strike in the Northern in 1888. In 1889, about 12,000 men were thrown out by the stoppage of various works, and about 40,000 were unemployed a couple of years later. All this proves that the workers did not get much of the loan money, and that the inrush of capital was not used for development.

In Victoria, for the five years 1886-90, £54,694,000 came in, and was spent in the same reckless way as obtained in the mother State. Queensland, in the same five years, had £9,581,000.

Holders of land, who had worked the thing up, cut up land around the big cities and grabbed the money sent for investment. Government lavished loan money in what they termed a "vigorous public works policy." Contractors, commercial men, bankers, the press, and lawyers, all shared, and millions out of State and municipal borrowings went into their pockets.

At a very low estimate New South Wales railways cost in construction and equipment £12,000,000 more than they would if they had been constructed under day labor, as is now the established method. The same would apply to all other public works. Out of our debt of over £80,000 000, probably £20,000,000 has been wasted in that way in order to boost private enterprise. The real object of the governing class of that period was not the development of the State. That idea was put forward to cloak their class designs. There was no need to have borrowed at all, and more genuine and healthy progress would have been made by doing public works out of taxation and by direct methods of construction under efficient management. If the sum we now pay in interest were available for public enterprises, we would soon become a prosperous people. As it is, the country producer has to pay interest on the £12,000,000 extra cost of railways which was diverted into the pockets of contractors.

Railways were built in Victoria at enormous cost, which have since been closed and the rails taken up. All this was done by the "business men" we hear so much of from the capitalists. Under their management in 1892, twenty-one companies in Victoria and twenty in Sydney went down for £25,000,000. Over £18,000,000 belonged to the public; £14,500,000 in the form of deposits and debentures. Nearly £4,000,000 was due to British depositors and debenture holders, and £7,000,000 was due to shareholders. There were a few cases of prosecution for fraud, and men were jailed; but the full exposures of all the various swindles never came out, because the "keen business men" we hear of had secured the passage of an Act of Parliament allowing them to wind up in a voluntary manner.

In addition to this, in 1893, as a result of capitalistic management, twelve banks of issue suspended—five of these were Victorian, two New South Wales, and two British. They reconstructed, and closed on £54,000,000 out of £86,000,000 of deposits lodged with them. In Victoria they seized on business men's current account. In New South Wales they were saved by the Government coming to their aid.

I need not dwell on the inevitable ruin and suffering of the thousands of poor and middle class who had trusted the capitalistic ring who controlled affairs, and who took care to save themselves. It was simply a huge gamble; the sharpers won, the flats lost. Millions changed hands, but tested by those things which are genuine signs of progress the result of class government and commercial control proved to be not only a failure, but to be in many ways demoralising.

Just as men are drawn from honest industry by the card table or the racecourse, where they try to live on the game, so in the gamble over land swarms of parasites grew up. The cry was, "Let posterity share the burden," and so every municipal council, every society of any kind whatsoever appealed to Government. Roads, now grass grown, were made; harbor works started but not finished; parks fenced and laid out, sometimes on land bought from private owners. Bonuses, subsidies to private companies, and money to private individuals were drawn from Government. In Victoria, capitalists obtained so many free passes on the railways that the list filled eleven columns of "The Age" in small type. The system followed has neither been private enterprise nor public enterprise, but a demoralising system of commercialism, which means to take advantage of anybody if you see a chance of profit. We have

now to undo the mischief and introduce the
collective and co-operative methods; to abolish all
needless and costly excrescences, such as State
Governors, State Second Chambers, all parasites and
middlemen, and see that each has opportunity to
utilise the energy and the good that is in him and
have the results conserved to him.

The exposures made by Labor members of
matters which the capitalistic press tried to hide
or condone have tended to make people doubt the
wisdom of trusting their affairs to so-called business
people. Railway syndicates, land scandals, and
Bentism are explaining why it is that Australia,
which is the finest country under the sun, should
be in the bad way it is. Capitalist Governments
have proved a dead failure. They have plunged the
country into debt, the burden of which is so great
that if we were attacked by an enemy we would be
in a helpless position financially, and could not put
up a fight even though we have the bravest
men on God's earth. Bad land laws and
maladministration have left no room for people
in at least two States which had the start.

Of alienated land in New South Wales, 728
persons or companies own 45 per cent., 100 own
one-fifth, 44,000 hold under 100 acres each, whilst
104 own over 50,000 acres each; 1,500,000 people
own no land at all. In Victoria there are thirty-
seven counties. In thirteen the population is
becoming less, and these are the best as regards
quality of land. In sixteen counties the population
has been stationary for some years; eight show less
than twenty years ago; six less than thirty years

ago; and five less than forty years ago. The male population has decreased, the female increased. Victoria has more old people than any other State. She has 66,000 over 65 years of age, whilst New South Wales, with a larger population, has only 47,000. The women have overtaken the men in numbers. The birth rate is low; the death rate high.

The Victorian " Settlers' Guide " says, on page 7:—" It is a fact that the maps of many of the early settled parishes of Victoria, subdivided as they originally were into numerous valuable farm sections, present the appearance of so many draught board squares from which the men are missing, the land of whole parishes having become in many instances merged in one large estate—the property of one person." No wonder that forty-five per cent. of the population live in Melbourne. Thirty per cent. of New South Wales people are in Sydney, and of South Australians forty-two per cent. are found in Adelaide. In New South Wales forty-nine million acres are alienated, in Victoria twenty-one million, Queensland fifteen, South Australia twelve, West Australia six, and Tasmania four million acres. The country is a sheep-walk, and if the owners sell at all it is only at prohibitive prices.

Nothing has been done to alter this condition of things, and nothing will be done by the men whom the people elect as Liberals or Reformers. Labor has at last educated the people up to a desire for a progressive land tax, but it is unlikely that any Government other than Labor will succeed in passing it into law. With their own people squeezed out of these two States, the "Liberals" spend the money of the workers in spreading lies in the old world for the purpose of attracting immigrants, so as to secure cheap labor and crush the worker here. Australia needs people badly. The Labor Party is ready to give a welcome to all desirable white people, but it wants that welcome to be genuine. It wants to provide a place and opportunity for the newcomer before he arrives, so that the welcome is to a mate and not to a competitor. It is positive cruelty, when there are already thousands of unemployed in every city of Australia, to bring out other persons to add to the list. The land must be thrown open first, and then bring the people.

Recently there has been much agitation about giving encouragement to immigration, yet the facts are that we are not making room for our own people. Statistics show that the departures exceeded arrivals by 4446 during the past four years. We have an immense unpeopled continent, and yet the sons of our own farmers cannot get land. The Commonwealth Government has communicated with every State Premier, and not one of them has any land to offer immigrants, however desirable they may be. A system has been introduced by the big land-owners called the shares system. It is the most cruel and complete system of sweating. It is being helped and encouraged by each anti-Labor Government. In every State except South Australia the Governemnts of to-day favor the big landlord, and oppose any proposal to stop land monopoly or to force land into use.

With second Chambers constituted as they are, the only hope for any immediate relief lies with the Federal Labor Party, which has recently appealed to the people on the question of a progressive land tax, expressly proposed to force the cutting up of the large estates. They propose exemption of all estates up to £5000 value exclusive of improvements. The following are the latest figures available in regard to the land values in Australia:—

	Land Alienated.	Value, exclusive of Improvements.	Per acre,		
	Acres.	£		s.	d.
New South Wales	48,851,524	136,417,000		15	10
Victoria	24,526,255	126,078,000		2	9
Queensland ..	16,901,127	41,800,000		8	8
South Australia	14,149,171	35,957,000		10	10
West Australia .	10,548,057	11,095,000	£	2	9
Tasmania	5,040,413	21,852,000	4	6	7
	120,106,547	373,679,000	3	2	3
New Zealand ..	23,857,633	87,576,000	3	13	5
Australasia ..	143,964,180	461,255,000	3	4	1

The figures just given have been made up to 1906, and show existing values; but if New Zealand methods of valuing were adopted, the amounts would be largely increased.

The land problem is the first and most important one to be dealt with, and the only political party even proposing to touch it is that of Labor. With a tax so heavy in its incidence as to make it unprofitable to hold a big estate, the gambling, speculative value would be at once struck at and land thrown into the market at such a price as would enable many who are anxious for farms to acquire them. This, together with a system of banking or of Credit Foncier by the States, will prove of immense and immediate value, and will greatly aid development.

New South Wales and Victoria have a system of Closer Settlement under Acts empowering the purchase of estates. In both cases the prices they have to pay are too high, and it is evident that the speculative value, to say nothing of that value given by the increase of population, must be struck at by a land tax. The Australian people are undoubtedly in favor of a tax on the unimproved value of land, and probably if a vote were taken it would favor the New Zealand system of a progressive tax, with power to resume at a price plus ten per cent. over owner's valuation. Land and Finance are the two big problems, and they press for a solution which cannot long be delayed.

Capitalistic Governments have always endeavored to hide facts which expose the rottenness of the present social system, hence they have prevented our statisticians from giving us any information of a clear kind as to the distribution of wealth. There will have to be quite a new line of inquiry centred upon when Labor acquires power. From a speech by Labor-member Hugh Mahon I give a few figures which he worked out from the basis of Coghlan's statistics. He estimates the private wealth of

Australia at £1,000,000,000. This is based on an extension of New South Wales figures, which are the most complete. Of this 8450 persons own £810,000,000; 1,283,540 own £190,000,000; and 2,635,000 own nothing. Taking the Victorian Income Tax returns, they show that 92 out of every 100 are under the sum taxable, namely, £151. Of taxable income 60 per cent. is divided amongst 12.4 per cent. of the taxpayers receiving over £500, and the remaining 87.6 per cent. of taxpayers divide the other 40 per cent. Those getting over £1000 per annum constitute 4.3 per cent., yet they receive 40 per cent. Of incomes from property 68 per cent. is received by those with over £500—less than 17 per cent. of the taxpayers—and 32 per cent. is divided between 83 per cent. of the taxpayers.

Thus in relation to taxation and defence Mr. Mahon says that a fraction of the people own four-fifths of the wealth and pay one-fifth of the cost of protecting it, whilst the rest of the community possess only one-fifth of the wealth and carry four-fifths of the burden of protecting all. I have roughly tested Mr. Mahon's figures by taking out the number of workers in the several callings enumerated in the census returns, and the results support his conclusions. In wealth production per head of population Australia stands very high, but the bona-fide producer gets probably a smaller percentage than those in older lands.

The proportion of the parasite class is enormous. We have had a vigorous young manhood putting forth their energies in the wide field of a young, unpeopled country, with splendid natural resources.

The men and women who came here brought
old-world ideas with them. The wage rate was
on old-world lines, and,. as almost all wage-earners
are content with a very limited standard of comfort,
it took a long time to awaken in the toiler's
mind the demand for his own. He is now coming
to understand how foolish he has been to allow the
swarm of suave but entirely needless middlemen to
fatten big bellies and bank accounts out of his hard
labor.

The uncertain nature of the wage-workers'
occupation deterred him from attempting to secure
a home of his own, hence it gave a splendid field
for landlordism. The rent-taker was able to secure
tenants for any sort of insanitary, old, jerry-built
dog-box. The absence of a Building Act enabled
him to erect four alleged cottages on one allotment
in either Sydney or Melbourne. Cheaply run up
terraces, with a thirteen-feet frontage to each
dwelling, are common. Even under the more settled
conditions of to-day, our electoral rolls show thirty
per cent. of new electors in each city electorate every
three years. All this unsettledness is against the
worker and in favor of the parasite.

Australia has been the happy hunting-ground
for capitalists in search of splendid bona-fide
investments. Last year very few companies paid
under ten per cent., and over fifty paid dividends
ranging from ten up to one hundred and sixty per
cent. The parasite has found the Commonwealth full
of openings, and he has not been slow to take
advantage. Prior to boom time scores of companies

grew up, all tapping the pockets of the easy-going public for cash. Banks started with half-a-crown capital.

We have still a swarm of parasitic institutions which will have to be wiped out of existence. Some of the worst " take-downs " are fire insurance and fidelity guarantee companies. A few friends get together and decide to form an insurance company. They provide themselves and their friends and relatives with billets, and the fool public provides the money. They charge needlessly high premiums and the public pays, as it does not take the trouble to inquire as to whether such sum is required or not. One has only to look at the cost of management to see what a fraud the whole thing is as run under private enterprise.

Statistician Coghlan says it is impossible to get at the real facts as to insurance companies, as they hide them away in the accounts and do not separate the work as they should do. Taking five of the sixteen Australian life insurance companies, it is seen that the expenses of management use up from fifty to seventy-seven per cent. of the gross receipts. In relation to premiums paid, it takes from £3 to £4 out of every £5 received to carry on the society. When we think of all the other companies—such as land, building, investment, trustee, agencies, trading, commercial, tramway, etc.—we can form a dim conception of what becomes of the workers' labor-product and of the swarm of parasites sucking his life-blood without giving an equivalent. So long as the worker allows a class to rule him, not only in

Parliament but in all the other branches of social influence and power, so long will he suffer.

The worker must take possession everywhere, and clear out the gangs of boodlers now using public positions, such as municipal councils, to help themselves and their friends. They are interested in an insurance company—say fire and fidelity guarantee—and naturally the company gets the council's favors. The biggest profits are made out of public bodies, such as municipalities. The City Council of Melbourne, for instance, paid in premiums for fire risks the sum of £8500 in fourteen years, yet all that the company had to pay out was £480. Thus the City Council took over £8000 out of its ratepayers' pockets and handed it over to a few individuals, whose particular business it is to take down ratepayers in that particular way. A neighboring council has done still more for the enterprising company which deals in that line, as it has paid £18,000 in all, and the company which collared that sum was only called upon for £1200 in payment of claims.

Victorian Railway Commissioners between 1884 and 1903 paid £295,058 10s. 3d. to a private company for insurance of their staff. The company which got the money settled the 449 claims made during the period for £64,400, and thereby made a profit of £230,658 10s. 3d. Thus the cute schemers running the insurance company used the commissioners as instruments to bleed to the amount named the public who use the railways. Of course the press, ever friendly to these parasitic companies, will explain in answer that it is unfair to pick out isolated cases.

Interstate Conference Australian Labor Party, 1908.

Very well; let us take the totals, and we find that the fire and fidelity companies doing business in Victoria received last year £612,288 and only paid out £254,059, leaving them a profit of £358,224.

The most impudent of all private enterprisers are the coal companies. The influence of those who held interests in Newcastle, N.S.W., coal-mines and in shipping—exerted in various ways, but most plainly through the Melbourne " Argus "—was sufficient for many years to stop even a search for coal in Victoria, though geologists said it existed. At last it was opened up, and for years the public have been fleeced to provide dividends for shareholders in the coal-mines of Gippsland. The system was to get up deputations and induce the Railway Commissioners and the Minister to agree to carry the coal at low rates—so low, in fact, as to entail a loss. Then special rates were paid on long contracts for supplies for the railways. Not satisfied with dividends averaging 27 per cent., the companies reduced wages, and with the help of Ministers of the Crown filled the men's places with blacklegs at low wages.

The Jumbunna company put in £12,291, and has drawn dividends to the amount of £22,000. The Coal Creek company had from its shareholders £10,177, and paid in dividends £26,250. The Outtrim mine paid 27 per cent. None of the companies put anything into development, but followed the simple plan of dividing every available penny, and then if things were bad owing to lack of proper management they would get up a deputation and secure more concessions. Practically the companies have had

JJ

their dividends from the railways, as detailed elsewhere, and it emphasises the need for such management of the railways as will get the supplies of coal at cost price by doing their own mining.

These few examples from Victoria illustrate what goes on all over the Commonwealth. It is not possible to get at the totals, as the various devices known to cunning and unscrupulous commercialism hide away the facts from outsiders. Watered stock, misleading balance-sheets, and secrecy keep the public in the dark; but if we only look at what is known through municipalities, railways, and other public bodies coming into contact with these parasites we can realise that hundreds of thousands of pounds are wasted in upholding a swarm of boodlers. By the Commonwealth taking up insurance of all necessary kinds the saving to the people would be enormous. Banking and insurance must both be faced so soon as Labor gets a majority. The average man is ignorant of the fact that he is heavily taxed by such parasitic institutions; and, whilst he will object strongly to direct taxation or to additional taxation, he goes on paying vast sums in an indirect way without a word. It is the duty of a Government to relieve the citizen of all burdens it is possible to take off his shoulders, and to provide at once that all public utilities shall be run at the lowest cost by eliminating the profit-stealing boodler and doing the work by the Nation, State, or Municipality, according to its scope or importance. That it can be done better and cheaper has been proved by Australian and New Zealand experience.

Another peculiar scheme which the politicians of the past are responsible for is the way in which the Savings Banks are controlled. The people have placed about £36,000,000 in the Savings Banks of the Commonwealth, nearly all of those institutions being under Government control. In order to assist in robbing their own people, however, the Governments limit the amounts upon which interest is paid in every State, and in some cases limit also the amount taken on deposit. New South Wales allows interest to depositors other than Friendly Societies or Charitable Institutions only on sums up to £300. Victoria allows interest at three per cent. up to £100, two and a-half per cent. up to £250, but nothing over that. Queensland allows interest only up to £200, but can issue bonds for sums over that amount. South Australia has a limit of £250, and Tasmania one of £150; whilst West Australia limits deposits to £600 and interest is only allowed up to £300. This method forces money into the private banks and gives them cheap money to handle and charge high interest on. The Government, instead of having the use of the people's money, are thus forced to borrow from private banks. The people pay for all this and the bank shareholders pocket the profits.

I have not touched on mining at all, as most people are aware that it is a gamble and is full of wild-cat schemes for taking money out of the pockets of the investor as well as the plunger and gambler. The games are known, and hence those who are taken in cannot grumble, as they took the risk. It is the wily schemes which fit in so well with commercial life and its evils which are most

necessary to expose. I have already mentioned
the fact that the knowing ones who worked the
worst swindles in the land boom of 1889 secured
the passage of an Act of Parliament in Victoria
to allow of voluntary liquidation. It only needed
then to put a friend in as liquidator to have all evils
hushed up. They ran against a straight man
sometimes, and did so in the case I quote below.
It is a fair sample of many others if the truth had
all been made known. In this particular case there
were not enough assets realisable to pay the
liquidator and he went without his payment and
handed all there was to those entitled to claim.
I quote from the " Argus " of 27th April, 1907 :—

" In August, 1891, the Anglo-Australian
Bank Limited went into voluntary liquidation,
and in October of that year Colonel J. M.
Templeton was appointed official liquidator
to conduct the winding-up and to settle the
voluntary liquidation. The way he started off,
and what he discovered, is told as follows :—
' Finding that the liquidators had continued to
occupy the bank's premises, which had been
taken on lease at a high rental, which was still
being paid, I took possession of all the bank's
assets, and its books and papers, and removed
them to an office which I secured at a small
weekly rent, and left the landlord to make a
claim for the breach of contract made by my
leaving the premises unoccupied. I immediately
appointed a chief clerk, and, with his assistance,
made an examination of the books and papers,

and a complete investigation of the bank's affairs. I discovered that the bank was a sham and a swindle from its inception, and that it was an offshoot of another sham bank—the British Bank of Australia Limited—which had been put into voluntary liquidation some months before.'

" On Colonel Templeton's advice, a criminal prosecution of the chairman and directors and the manager and auditors of the Anglo-Australian Bank was undertaken by the Crown, which resulted in the conviction of all of them, and they were sentenced to various terms of imprisonment. ' Thus,' he said, ' the swindlers were punished without trenching on the very small funds of the bank for the expenses of the prosecution. The so-called assets of the bank, for the most part, consisted of uncompleted contracts for the purchase of large blocks of vacant land at exorbitant prices, and of contracts of sale, also uncompleted, of small allotments into which the large blocks had been subdivided. The sale money was payable by monthly instalments extending to twelve years, and many of the purchasers were quite unable to pay what they had undertaken under the glamor of the bank's representations as to value, while others refused to pay on the ground that they had been swindled. The position was very difficult, for the bank could not give titles to the small allotments, because it had not yet paid the original vendors of the large blocks which it had subdivided. . . . The next step was to look up shareholders so as to compel them to pay, under the order of the Supreme Court, the full amount of their shares. These shareholders having been victimised by the promoters of the bank, strove, as far as possible, to avoid the payment of calls.' . . . The cause that led to the delay in the completion of the liquidation was Colonel Templeton's objection to admit the preferential claim of the liquidator of the British Bank, which had been allowed by the Court at £286,630. He had opposed the claim, on the ground that the two banks were practically the one institution, but the Court had overruled his objection. Therefore, the winding-up of the Anglo-Australian Bank was delayed by Colonel Templeton until he heard that the British Bank had been finally dissolved. That information now being forthcoming, he was in a position to declare a final dividend, and make a report. . . . The total claims allowed by the Court against the bank were £420,299, of which £119,790 represented the claims (alleged to be preferential) of depositors and debenture-holders. By excluding the British Bank a dividend of 3 1-16d. in the £1 is possible when payments are made for clerical work, etc., the net amount available being £1528. This is the ignominious end of one of the prominent creations of the land-boom period.''

In these brief quotations we see disclosed the methods followed then and still adhered to by the parasites of society. A few persons form a company,

take up a block of land, cut it up, advertise and sell
it at an enhanced price pocketing the difference.
It seemed alright until the bubble burst—then it was
a swindle, and everybody agreed that it was. What
the public do not seem to realise is that it is a
swindle none the less when it succeeds.

Amongst other evils to be remedied are the
methods adopted under State and municipal control
to save the rich from paying their honest taxation.
Recently portion of a big estate was purchased by
the Victorian Government. It had to pay £17 an
acre, whereas the valuation upon which land tax
has been paid for some years past was only £1 per
acre. All over the State it is notorious that the big
landowner dodges his land tax, and no Government
has had the courage to discharge the valuators
responsible. Under the Shire Councils the same
under-valuation for municipal taxes goes on.
Recently under a new Act the Water Commissioners
made a valuation, and it turns out to be from 75 to
90 per cent. above that upon which rates have been
paid. Especially is it the case with regard to the
value put upon the land. Taking four places as
samples, the respective values per acre are:—

	By Municipality.	By Commissioners.
Bacchus Marsh ...	£51 0 0	£72 14 0
Benjeroop	2 18 10	4 11 0
Campaspe	3 5 0	5 16 0·
Gunbower West ..	2 7 0	4 10 0

The total values by the shires amount to £122,810.
That is the sum upon which rates are paid. The

valuation by the independent Commissioners is
£195,799. £1,172,027 was spent on free head works
on which no interest was charged. £142,506 was
given in free grants and £1,106,852 written off by
the Government for various Water Trusts in country
districts. It is not surprising also to find that the
Shire of Rodney, which asked and secured from the
Government a remission of £202,000, which they
alleged they were unable to pay on an irrigation
scheme from which they had all the gain, was
collecting rates on a valuation of £59,565, whilst the
Commissioners find it is a fair value to put £105,908
on the Shire. This place was the headquarters of a
recent conservative political movement which swept
Victoria off its feet and sent in a big party pledged
to economy and reform in administration. It is
characteristic of that class that no sooner had they
closed their big conference in Melbourne after
launching the scheme which was going to save the
country than they fairly rushed the various departments asking concessions for their several districts.
It is only another way of taking down the masses,
who have no personal axes of this kind which they
can grind.

The majority of those who now run municipal
government have been trained and lived their lives
in the atmosphere of profit-making by taking
advantage of every opportunity which presents itself,
and hence they apply it to municipal and political
work. They are ever for class—always against the
masses. The great working masses are but a field
for exploitation, and must be kept in that position

or the classes will no longer enjoy incomes without effort and escape taxation by keeping control of the man who would impose the tax.

It has been the boast of Australians that our political and municipal life has been clear of that bribery and blackmailing " graft " of which we hear so much from America. To a large extent that is true, but we have not quite the same system here in many things, such for instance as railways. By having them State-owned we have blocked the boodlers. Also, we have not yet reached the same high pressure of social life, nor have we many extremely rich men. Our Australian commercial and land-owning class are just as clever in carrying out a " graft " as our American cousins, and if social conditions are not soon changed we shall see just the same development of corruption and bribery as has disgraced the public life of the great American people. Like conditions produce like results. The social system here is the same in principle if not in detail as in the U.S.A. and older lands. Australians have produced many champions in various fields, and it will just as surely produce champion " grafters " and swindlers as other countries unless the class rule up to now dominant is done away with altogether.

The hope of Australia is with the Labor Party in politics, in local government, and in every social force. Labor has a better record for honest, economical, and efficient management than any other class. In Friendly Societies, in Co-operation, and in Trade Unions where the workers dominate, the

ability of practical men who know how to manage
has been displayed. When they take charge of the
public affairs of the nation in all their ramifications
an era of healthy prosperity based upon justice to
all and privileges to none will begin, and will
never end.

CHAPTER XXXVI.

LABOR'S OBJECTIVE.

THE Labor Movement in Australia is a political as well as a propagandist movement. Its leaders realise that before we can have social reform the people must be educated to demand and carry out such reforms. The platforms, Federal and State, indicate the practical proposals for which public opinion is considered ripe. The objective and the general platform give an idea of the propagandist side. The first part of the Federal objective declares for. '' The cultivation of an Australian sentiment based upon the maintenance of racial purity and the development in Australia of an enlightened and self-reliant community.'' The party stands for racial purity and racial efficiency—industrially, mentally, morally, and intellectually. It asks the people to set up a high ideal of national character, and hence it stands strongly against any admixture with the white race. True patriotism should be racial. True self-government means the government of Self—the prevention of Self from trespassing on the rights of others. No class-ruled people can ever be a self-governing people. No people are self-reliant who are under the control of landlords or who depend on a brother man for the right to work for daily bread.

587

Labor stands for giving to Australians the opportunity to become an enlightened people. Every child must be educated at the expense of the community. Education must be made free right through, from the primary school to the University. The child must be protected from the careless or greedy parent, hence we must keep to a compulsory system, with technical training in every case to follow the teaching in the primary schools. Every citizen must also be educated politically, so that we may have an active and enlightened democracy. We want a people self-reliant in moral character and manhood able and willing to defend their hearths and homes in case of invasion. We aim at being self-reliant in regard to defence—in being able to manufacture all our own requirements of guns, ammunition, and food supplies. We should also manufacture all our own requirements for everyday life. Labor takes the home as the unit of the nation and works for all that is calculated to make it happy. It desires that the makers of the useful and the beautiful shall have the pleasure of enjoying all that is best in modern civilisation.

The second part of the Federal objective runs: " The securing of the full results of their industry to all producers by the collective ownership of monopolies and the extension of the industrial and economic functions of the State and Municipality." Some of the States go further and declare for the " nationalisation of all the means of production, distribution, and exchange," and hence have given grounds for the Labor Party being called Socialists. The party does not deny being socialistic in its aims, but as practical men its members put forward such proposals as will improve conditions, while at the same time they are sound on general principles. When doing propaganda work most of the members of the party in any of the Parliaments will advocate Socialism, but as candidates for the suffrages of the people they keep closely to the definite proposals contained in the Fighting Platform which has been adopted by the Political Labor Leagues, and which represents enough work for three years even if Labor had a majority.

Australians generally are Socialistic, most of them as yet unconsciously so. The most Socialistic in their demands are those calling themselves " Anti-Socialists." They are great in asking for State assistance for practically everything they are connected with. The Victorian farmer declares himself against Socialism, yet he escapes much local taxation by securing Government subsidies for roads, bridges, parks, and gardens, and other public utilities which, were he a true individualist, he would scorn to ask aid in supporting. Likewise he gets money for agricultural shows, and experts of all kinds are sent around to teach him how to grow things in the most profitable manner.

The farmer has had so much done for him by the State that he is greedy for more, and at the same conference at which he declared himself politically opposed to Socialism root and branch he formulated the following list of things he wanted from the Government. He wanted water conservation, land on deferred payments, manure protection, reduced grain freights on the railways, reduced rates for starving stock, wire netting on deferred payments, bonus on fox scalps, help in bush fires, cold storage, a subsidy for the Agricultural College, special grants for shows, markets for fruit, instruction in tobacco growing, Credit Foncier for loans, and they also seriously discussed the question of asking for help to pay for reapers and binders. Many of these requests have been granted, but the hypocrisy of those who receive them calling themselves individualists is simply amazing. A very lengthy list could be added, but my object is merely to show the trend of thought.

In Australia a mass of things is done, and well done, by the Government which in other countries is left to private enterprise. The Labor Party say these can be increased with advantage to the community. They draw no line, leaving each step to be followed by the next as experience suggests. If anyone proposed to transfer any of the big things now carried out by the Government to private enterprise the professed Anti-Socialists would themselves oppose it. The conscious dividing line between the Labor Party and all others is the fact that the old political parties, no matter by what name they called themselves, favored using the powers of State to help a minority of the people, whilst Labor wants to use it for the equal good of all the people. The only class which has hitherto not asked for State help has been the workers. The farmer, the commercial man, and the manufacturer have all been strongly Socialistic in seeking help of all sorts for their own personal advantage, but the wage-earner has had no consideration in any way.

There is also this great difference between the new party and the old. Labor understands the problem and has a well-thought-out plan of social evolution, and each step it proposes will be permanent and will not have to be receded from. The old parties were and are still mere opportunists, doing such things as they felt would keep them in office or proposing such things as would appeal to the people, and when put into power either forgetting their promises or keeping them only in name. Labor is in favor of taking over certain monopolies now operating in Australia, such as the manufacture of tobacco, the running of steamships on the Australian coast, the refining of sugar, etc. At present the Commonwealth Constitution is against the Party, and it will take a little time to educate the people up to carrying an amendment, but it will come. A State, which comprises but a section of the people, can take up the refining of sugar or the manufacture of iron, yet the Commonwealth, which includes the entire population, does not at present possess that power.

Then there is but little of Municipal Socialism in Australia, and there is a big field in that department of social life. There is great alarm amongst those who have been making fortunes out of the people in various forms of private enterprise, and they are leading in the fight against Labor, but just as the people awake to the fact that such persons are not friends, but in many ways parasites on society, so will Labor gather strength.

The influence of self-interest was exemplified recently in New South Wales, where a Government

parading itself as a Reform Government, and one
in favor of economy, refused to allow railway
engines to be made in Government workshops, even
though they could be produced better and cheaper
than by private enterprise. In this they stood true
to the traditions of old parties. They granted favors
to the big firms at the expense of the taxpayer, and
openly call it helping private enterprise. The
railways are run by the State under Commissioners,
but, instead of having their own coal mines like
New Zealand, the people who use the railways—the
country producers—have to pay higher freights and
fares than there is occasion for in order that a coal
ring may have big dividends. New South Wales
railways consume 400,000 tons of coal per annum,
and if they owned coal mines they would save at
least £30,000 per annum and the freights could be
reduced by that amount. When Labor gets into
power that is one of the Socialistic things it will do.

There are scores of economies of a similar kind
which a good live Labor Government could at once
effect, and which the people would applaud once
they had the object lesson. Carl Snyder in his
'' New Conceptions in Science '' says: '' The
scientific organization of industry illustrated in
the great trusts is going on under our eyes. It
should give no alarm. When the work is complete
public utility will necessitate governmental control,
and from this to the complete unification of the
whole machinery of production and distribution will
be but a step. With this will come, too, the
disappearance of the leisured and parasitic class

generally. The invidious distinctions of wealth, with their attendant vulgarity and their inevitable debasing influence, will disappear. Under a rational regime men and women will satisfy their instinct for activity and work, while they will have ample time for that recreation and change which alone make life agreeable or supportable. Ostentatious riches and depressing poverty, greed and want, crime and prostitution will cease to exist, and with them the physical and moral maiming and stunting of the children of the poor.'' That represents the economic faith of the Australian Labor Movement, which is already prepared for taking over several monopolies, such as tobacco, shipping, sugar refining, etc.

As to whether Labor will nationalise the land, the means of production, distribution, and exchange, the question is hardly worth discussing at this stage, except as an abstract proposition. Every intelligent student of our social system agrees that universal co-operation must come. The law already declares that there is no such thing as private ownership of land. Monopoly of land is admitted to be an evil. There are only two factors in production—labor and land. The owner of land, if unrestricted, practically owns all the people. Presently the people will see that the ownership of machinery is on the same plane. Machinery must become the property of the community, and production must be for use and not for profit-making.

The present competitive struggle for existence will disappear, and a new condition will arise, but it will not and cannot be brought suddenly into

KK

being. Revolutionary Socialism is an impossibility.
No practical man can conceive it possible. It is not
a healthy form of doing things. There is such an
immense amount of clearing away of rubbish ere we
can begin the foundations that no Parliament could
do the work, even if it was a desirable thing to
spring it suddenly on a people grown up under an
entirely different set of conditions. There is ample
work for a succession of Labor Parliaments staring
us in the face, and until the Tory Second Chambers
are got rid of we cannot even make a start.

There is one brake beside that, and that is the
people. It is slow work getting right ideas knocked
into the masses. They are mostly so mentally lazy
that they take their views ready-made from a
misleading press. The Labor Movement is a people's
movement. Labor trusts the people, and it cannot
travel faster than the people will permit. The
leaders ought to be and are ahead of the people,
and legislation which now lags behind the aggregate
intelligence of the masses will under a Labor
Government take the opposite course and keep just
ahead of the thought of the people. Much of their
first work will be palliative; much of it preparatory
to the introduction of bigger things.

The inglorious muddle made of land and finance
alone by all past Governments will hamper Labor
for a time. The very staff it has to depend on in
administration of departments will have to be
educated and trained to new ideas and to new
methods. There will be so little difference apparent
to the people between a Labor Government and

others that the alarmists will cease to worry, whilst some of the impatient extremists will be disappointed. Those in close touch will realise how inevitable it is that progress must be comparatively slow. The thoughtful student of history will see in the advent a turning point, however, which will mark a revolution for the future historian.

Labor undertakes to change the whole tenor of the world's ideas. It undertakes to change a social system which has been the growth of century upon century. It has thousands of years of heredity to overcome, and some are foolish enough to expect it to be done in a year. The Labor Party is dominated by two moral convictions—the Ethics of Usefulness and the Ethics of Fellowship. It holds that all work must have a social value to entitle to an income. In the state of society Labor aims at setting up there will be no room for the idler. Every individual will have to contribute some service having a social value. The teacher, the artist, the writer, the scientist, the medical man, and those who entertain as well as those who make things are all entitled to income, but there is no place for the profit-grabber—the being who lives on rent or usury. Governed by the Ethics of Fellowship there will only be one class, and that the producing class. All will have to be producers, using the term in the broad sense to apply to all who aid in production and in making men better and happier. Such a condition must come sooner in white Australia than in older lands.

Give Labor a chance—give it reasonable time— and it will start such an era of growing prosperity in Australia as will make it the envy of the world. There must be patience and solidarity. There must be faith in the greatness and soundness of the cause which, while it can be retarded in its progress by individual action and unwise haste, can never be prevented from steady advance—leading whither we cannot now tell, but certainly to better and brighter days as time rolls on.

THE END.

APPENDIX.

NEW SOUTH WALES LABOR PLATFORM, 1891.

(1) Electoral Reform—to provide for the abolition of plural voting; the abolition of money deposits in Parliamentary elections; the extension of the franchise to seamen, shearers, and general laborers by the registration of votes; the extension of the franchise to policemen and soldiers; the abolition of the six months' residence clause as a qualification for the exercise of the franchise; the establishment of single member electorates and equal electoral districts on an adult population basis; the holding of all Parliamentary elections on one day—that a public holiday; and that all public-houses shall be closed during the hours of polling.

(2) Free, compulsory, and technical education—higher as well as elementary—to be extended to all.

(3) Eight hours to be the legal maximum working day in all occupations.

(4) A Workshop and Factories Act, to provide for the prohibition of the sweating system; the supervision of land boilers and machinery; and the appointment of representative working men as inspectors.

(5) An amendment of the Mining Act, to provide for all applications for mineral leases being summarily dealt with by the local wardens; the strict enforcement of labor conditions on such leases; the abolition of the leasing system on all new goldfields; the right to mine on private property; the greater protection of persons engaged in the mining industry; and that all inspectors shall hold certificates of competency.

(6) The extension to seamen of the benefits of the Employers' Liabilities Act.

(7) The repeal of the Masters and Servants Act and the Agreements Validating Act.

(8) The amendment of the Masters and Servants Act and the Trades Union Act.

(9) The establishment of a Department of Labor; a National Bank; and a national system of water conservation and irrigation.

(10) Election of magistrates.

(11) Local Government and decentralization; the the extension of the principle of the Government acting as an employer, through the medium of local self-governing

bodies; and the abolition of our present unjust method of raising municipal revenue by the taxation of improvements effected by Labor.

(12) The Federation of the Australian colonies on a National as opposed to an Imperial basis; the abolition of the present Defence Force, and the establishment of our military system upon a purely voluntary basis.

(13) The recognition in our legislative enactments of the natural and inalienable rights of the whole community to the land—upon which all must live and from which by labor all wealth is produced—by the taxation of that value which accrues to land from the presence and needs of the community, irrespective of improvements effected by human exertion; and the absolute and indefeasible right of property on the part of all Crown tenants in improvements effected on their holdings.

(14) The execution of all Government contracts in the colony.

(15) The stamping of all Chinese-made furniture.

(16) Any measure which will secure for the wage-earner a fair and equitable return for his or her labor.

NEW SOUTH WALES LABOR PLATFORMS, 1909.

OBJECTIVE.—(1) The cultivation of an Australian sentiment based upon the maintenance of racial purity, and the development in Australia of an enlightened and self-reliant community. (2) The securing of the full results of their industry to all producers by the collective ownership of monopolies and the extension of the industrial and economic functions of the State and Municipality.

STATE PLEDGE.

I hereby pledge myself not to oppose the selected candidate of this or any other Branch of the Political Labor League. I also pledge myself, if returned to Parliament, on all occasions to do my utmost to ensure the carrying out of the principles embodied in the Labor Platform, and on all such questions, and especially on questions affecting the fate of a Government, to vote as a majority of the Labor Party may decide at a duly constituted caucus meeting. I further pledge myself not to retire from the contest without the consent of the Executive of the Political Labor League of New South Wales.

STATE PLATFORM.

Fighting Platform.

1. Constitutional Reform.
   (a) Abolition of the Legislative Council and the office of State Governor.
   (b) Electoral reform to provide proper machinery for the true representation of the people in Parliament.
2. Land and Financial Reform.
   (a) Cessation of further sales of Crown Lands.
   (b) A proper system of Closer Settlement.
   (c) Water Conservation and Irrigation.
   (d) Restriction of Public Borrowing.
   (e) State Bank.
   (f) Graduated Land Tax.
3. Free Education.
   (a) Secondary.
   (b) Technical.
   (c) University.
   To be available on the Bursary System to all children passing a qualifying test.
4. Re-enactment of the Industrial Arbitration Act.
5. The Zone System of Railway Fares and Freights.
6. Regulation of Hours of Labor.
7. Workers' Compensation.

Details of Fighting Platform.

1. Constitutional Reform.
   (a) Abolition of the Legislative Council and the substitution therefor of the Initiative and Referendum.
   (b) Abolition of the office of State Governor and other unnecessary offices.
   (c) All citizens, other than criminals or lunatics, to be entitled to the franchise, after six months' residence in the State, irrespective of electoral boundaries.
   (d) Full civil and political rights to all State and Municipal employees.
   (e) Provision to enable electors when travelling to record their votes for their electorates in any part of the State, and facilities for seamen and others to record their votes by post.
   (f) State elections to be held early in the year, from February to April inclusive; polling day to be a Saturday, and be proclaimed a public holiday; hours of polling, 8 a.m. to 8 p.m.

(g) All polling returns for the small centres in country electorates shall be sealed in the ballot-boxes at close of the poll and forwarded to the Returning-officer for the electorate, who, with his Scrutineers and Poll Clerk, shall be the only persons authorised to count them.

2. Land and Financial Reform.

Land Reform.

(1) Immediate cessation of Crown Lands Sales.

(2) Land Acts to be consolidated and simplified, and to provide for—

(a) Compulsory resumption of private lands for Closer Settlement, value to be determined by a competent tribunal; such value not to exceed that fixed by the owner for taxation purposes plus 10 per cent., together with the value of the improvements at the time of the resumption.

(b) Where areas of country lands are subdivided by private owners for sale, purchasers to be subject to such conditions as to residence, area, etc., as may be approved of by the Government for Closer Settlement purposes.

(c) Rents payable by settlers on private lands to be determined by a competent tribunal on application by the tenant or landlord. Security of tenure and tenant right in improvements effected by tenant.

(d) No land suitable for bona-fide settlement to be set apart for improvement or scrub leases. Land proposed to be offered under these tenures to be made available for settlement for a period of not less than twelve months.

(e) Existing improvement and scrub leases to be viewed with a view to the withdrawal of those suitable for settlement, and the forfeiture of any improperly or illegally granted.

(f) Every Australian citizen not already holding land to the value of £500 to have a preferential right to acquire an area of land up to that value. Preference to be given, first, to persons holding no land, and, second, to small holders requiring additional holdings, such areas not necessarily to be deemed living areas.

(g) Any person acquiring ordinary Crown lands for permanent settlement to be entitled to remission of rent for the first five years, conditional upon permanent improvements of not less than the value of the remitted rent being effected.

(h) The reappraisement of homestead selections and settlement leases at the instance of the Crown shall not take place oftener than once during each 20-year period, the first reappraisement to take place 25 years after the date of application.

(i) Rentals of homestead selections in no instance to exceed a sum equal to the difference between the shire or municipal taxation on such holdings and freeholds in the same shire or municipality, together with interest at 2½ per cent. on the capital value placed on lands alienated from the Crown of similar quality in the same locality.

(j) Provision for workingmen's blocks in centres of population.

(k) Provision to be made to prevent speculators from monopolising business and residential allotments in towns and villages.

(l) Election of local members of Land Boards.

(m) Crown land agents to be compelled to fill in forms for applicants for land free of charge.

(n) Lands Agents to be made officers of the Court.

(o) Members of Parliament to be debarred from acting as paid agents in Crown lands matters.

(3) Water Conservation and Irrigation with resumption of all frontages to water so conserved, together with such lands as are benefited thereby which are suitable for Closer Settlement.

(4) Existing legislation providing for the distribution of wire-netting to be amended to provide for the direct supply of wire-netting to landholders by the Government.

(5) The duties of the Pastures and Protection Boards to be taken over by the Shire Councils.

(6) That immigration be not encouraged until sufficient land is made available for eager and desirable settlers at present in this State.

FINANCIAL REFORM.

Public Borrowing.

(1) Cessation of borrowing except for
  (a) Redemption.
  (b) Completing works already authorised by Parliament.

    (c) Undertakings which will pay interest from the
       beginning, and provide 1 per cent. sinking fund
(2) Provision to be made for a sinking fund in connec-
    tion with renewed loans.
(3) Loans to be converted locally as far as practicable

State Bank.

(1) Amalgamation of existing Savings Banks into a
    State Bank; a portion of the funds to be available
    for—
    (a) Repurchase of private estates for Closer
       Settlement.
    (b) Advances to settlers on the land held by them or
       the improvements thereon.
    (c) Conditional advances to be granted for the
       purpose of effecting permanent improvements;
       such advances to be made in instalments as
       required during the progress of the work at the
       rate of £75 for each £100 worth of permanent
       improvements effected.
    (d) Advances to workmen and others to build homes
       themselves.
(2) All charges in connection with loans made by the
    Advance Department of the Savings Bank to be
    added to the amount advanced and be paid off
    with the loan.

Fresh Taxation.

(1) Graduated Land Tax on all estates over £5000 in
    value on an unimproved basis, increasing ½d. for
    each £5000 in value over that exemption.
(2) Graduated Income Tax.
(3) Special taxation of land owned and incomes derived
    by absentees.
(4) Increased Probate Duties on estates of over £20,000
    in value.
(5) Probate duty on the estates of absentees to be
    double the ordinary rates and without exemption.
State Socialistic Services.
(1) Receipts and Expenditure to be kept separate from
    the Consolidated Revenue Account.
(2) Any surplus accruing after paying working
    expenses and charges for upkeep and depresiation
    to be used—
    (a) For the reduction of charges to users;
      (b) For paying off capital cost.

    (3) Estimates of receipts and expenditure in connection with all Socialistic services to be submitted an-annually to Parliament.

3. Free Education.
    (a) Secondary.
    (b) Technical.
    (c) University.
       To be available on the Bursary System to all children passing a qualifying test.

4. Re-enactment of Industrial Arbitration Act.
5. The Zone System of Railway Fares and Freights.
6. An Eight Hour Bill on similar lines to that introduced by the Parliamentary Labor Party.
7. Workers' Compensation Act, to embrace all classes of labor, including Seamen and Waterside Workers.

GENERAL PLATFORM.

8. Industrial Reform.
    (a) Anti-Sweating Legisation, providing for punishment by imprisonment for breaches.
    (b) Arbitration Act Amendemnt.
       (1) The general provisions of the Act to be so enlarged as to make it impossible to apply for a writ of prohibition, except in cases where the Court flagrantly goes beyond its powers.
       (2) An amendment of the Act in its definitions and general provisions so as to make it clearly apparent that the Arbitration Court is a Court with power to determine the general conditions of any industry for given periods at the instigation of either Unions of employers or employees.
       (3) An amendment which will enable the Court in dealing with different industries to appoint Boards of Conciliation to assist it in the making of its awards.
       (4) An amendment permitting the Court to grant a common rule on any industrial agreement where the parties thereto substantially represent an industry.
       (5) An amendment directing the Court to take the profits of an industry into consideration in fixing minimum wages, such minimum not to be less than a living wage.
       (6) An amendment excluding the legal profession and paid advocates, excepting bona-fide representatives of Unions of employees or bona-fide servants of employers from the Courts of Arbitration or Boards of Conciliation unless by consent of both parties to a reference.

(7) An amendment providing expressly that all contract and piece work, where employees supply labor only, shall come under the jurisdiction of the Court.

(8) An amendment providing that all awards and orders of the Court shall be enforced by the Department of Labor, with power to Unions to proceed on mandamus to compel the Minister to act where necessary.

(9) An amendment to provide that if an employer is represented on the taking of evidence in camera, employees shall also have the right of representation, and to empower the Court to appoint accountants to assist in its deliberations.

(10) An amendment providing for effective preference to Unionists.

(11) The Act if satisfactorily amended to be made permanent, and an additional Court to be appointed for two years to deal with mining and such other cases as may be referred to it by the Chief Court.

(12) An amendment to include domestic service as an industry under the Act.

(13) An amendment to give power to Unions to sue members in a local Court of Petty Sessions for the recovery of all arrears of subscriptions, levies, and fines, provided in their Rules.

(c) Regulation of hours of labor.

(1) The general reduction of the hours of labor to 44 per week on account of the increased productivity of Labor.

(2) That six hours be the recognised day for all underground workers.

(3) Amendment of the Early Closing Act on the lines as agreed upon at the Trades Union Congress, 1908.

(4) The abolition of night work in bake-houses.

(d) A minimum living wage in all occupations, sufficient reasonably to provide for the contingencies of a civilised life. A minimum wage for adult labor shall not be less than 8s. per day. Equal pay for women for equal work.

(e) Legislation to provide that payment of wages be a first charge on any assets available in connection with any occupation in which wages are earned.

(f) A Lien Bill.

(g) Amending legislation to secure to Trade Unions the legal position occupied from the legalisation of Trade Unions until the Taff Vale decision altered the application of the law.

(h) Repeal of the Masters and Servants Act and the Agreements Validating Act.

(i) Amendment of the Trade Unions Act and the Apprentices Act to provide for compulsory apprenticeship and the abolition of premiums, and to provide that employers shall be compelled to properly teach their apprentices the trade or trades to which they have been indentured; also that a limitation be placed upon the number of apprentices in accordance with the number of tradesmen employed. The Act to be administered by the Department of Labor and Industry.

(j) A Right to Work Bill.

(k) The Labor Agency business to be conducted entirely by the State.

(l) Amendment of the Shops and Factories Act, 1896, on the lines agreed upon by the Trade Union Congress, 1908.

(m) Abolition of the age limit for employment in all Government Departments.

9. The Encouragement of Agriculture.

(a) By the establishment of State mills for sugar, grain, and other produce.

(b) The establishment of a State Export Department.

(c) The establishment of the bulk system of handling grain.

(d) Any other matter which will be effective in assisting in the development of agriculture.

10. State Pensions or Annuities to Residents of the State over 60 years of age and to Invalids; and abolition of State pensions, except those provided under the Old Age Pensions Act.

11. Amendment of the Mining Laws to provide for—

(a) Mining on private property without payment of royalty other than to the State, or of rent or compensation except for actual value of land taken or damage done to land or improvements.

(b) The abolition of authorities to enter and the substitution therefor of mining on private land licenses.

(c) Qualified persons only to be appointed to administer the mining laws.

(d) Abolition of the leasing system on all new gold-fields.

(e) Greater protection to persons engaged in the mining industries; inspectors to hold certificates of competency.

(f) Strict enforcement of the Labor conditions on leases.

12. (a) All Government work to be executed in the State without the intervention of contractors.

(b) Prohibition of sub-letting.

(c) Standard Union wages to be the minimum paid on all Government and Municipal work.

13. A Land Boiler and Machinery Inspection Bill to provide for the more effective supervision of all land engines, boilers, and machinery, and that all persons in charge of engines and boilers hold certificates of competency.

14. Liquor Traffic Reform.

(a) State Option, with right to vote as to compensation.

(b) Plebiscite of electors, as to nationalising the Liquor Traffic.

15. Amendment of the Navigation Act to provide for the more efficient control of navigation in connection with traffic on harbors and rivers, the suppression of crimping, and the restitution of the six months' survey clause.

16. (a) With a view to the more equitable administration of justice, when a charge is preferred against a person and fails, expenses may be awarded against the Crown.

(b) A Crown Defender to be appointed and paid by the Government in all cases where a Crown Prosecutor is employed.

17. Amendment of the State Children's Relief Act to provide that the mother of a State child should receive for its maintenance an amount equivalent to the maximum allowed a foster mother. Such amount to be payable until the child is 16 years of age.

18. State Subsidy to Maternity.

19. (a) All public hospitals to be supported by shire and municipal rates, together with Government subsidies.

(b) Boards controlling hospitals to be elected by adult suffrage.

(c) Women to have the same rights as men to be on the medical staff.

(d) The working hours of nurses to be forty-four hours per week.

(e) In serious cases where patients are unable to reach hospitals, Government medical officers shall attend them in their homes or wherever located.

(f) All country hospitals should have a lunacy ward.

(g) A maternity ward to be attached to all hospitals, with provision for home treatment where necessary. .

(h) All school children to be examined periodically by competent medical and dental officers and treated free where necessary.

(i) The establishment of Foundling Homes.

20. (a) All Chinese furniture factories be restricted to forty-eight hours per week, and that the forty-eight hours be worked between 7.30 a.m. and 6 p.m. Mondays to Fridays inclusive, and between 7.30 a.m. and 1 p.m. on Saturdays, and that overtime can only be worked after obtaining the sanction of the Department of Labor and Industry.

(b) Stamping of Chinese furniture and other manufactures.

21. (a) Workers' dwellings to be constructed by the Government in suitable localities, and be let to those requiring them at reasonable rentals.

(b) Provision of small cottage homes for indigent aged couples.

(c) Amendment of the Landlord and Tenants Act to provide that in distress for rent cases the landlord shall leave in the possession of the tenant all necessary goods and chattels to the value of £20, together with tools of trade.

22. Absorption of the Unemployed by—

(a) The establishment of State ironworks.

(b) The establishment of State farms and labor colonies.

(c) The establishment of State woollen mills and clothing factories.

23. Nationalisation of any industry which becomes a private monopoly.

24. The Nationalisation of Land.

25. Nationalisation of Coal Mines.

26. All iron required for State use to be produced from State mines.

27. (a) Amendment of the Metropolitan Water and Sewerage Act so that rates shall be assessed on the unimproved value of the land.

(b) Members of all Water and Sewerage Boards to be elected by adult suffrage.

28.   MUNICIPAL COUNCILS.
          Objective, Regulations, and Platform.

OBJECTIVE.

The Objective shall be the acquisition of the right to exercise any or all the powers provided for in Section 109 of the Local Government Act, 1906, and broadening its scope, and extending the powers of Council in the direction of communal activity.

REGULATIONS.

1. Leagues in any municipal area shall have the work of formulating municipal programme suitable to local requirements.

2. Such programme must be in accord with the general principles of the P.L.L. Municipal Platform.

3. The Rules and Regulations of the P.L.L. governing the selection of candidates for Parliament shall, as far as practicable, apply to candidates seeking selection for municipal honors.

PLATFORM.

1. To advocate and support measures to amend the Local Government Act to gain—

  (a) Full adult suffrage on a one month's residential qualification.

  (b) That it shall be the duty of Councils to collect the roll annually of all adult residents.

  (c) That the present power of Council to vote Mayoral allowances be extended to include aldermen.

  (d) Extending the hour of closing the poll till 8 p.m.

2. Day Labor where practicable, with preference to Unionists in all municipal work.

3. Rating on the unimproved values of land only, with no exemption.

4. The adoption of and wielding of all communal powers and activities possible under the Act, especially of the activities hereunder:—

  (a) Infants' milk depots.

  (b) Ferries.

  (c) Gas and electric light.

  (d) Hydraulic or other power when desirable.

  (e) Night shelters.

  (f) Public shelters.

  (g) Public markets, abattoirs, and retail meat depots.

  (h) The arrangement and beautification of the area, and the acquisition of land, streets, buildings, etc., therefor, together with the lease of land or building after such rearrangement.

(i) The subsidising of public bands or orchestras.

(j) The regulation and licensing of public vehicles, and of the drivers and conductors thereof.

(k) The regulation and licensing of hawkers of goods.

(l) Provision for separate lavatories for men and women.

5. The adoption and enforcement of provisions requiring the payment of Union rates of pay for all municipal work.

6. Readjustment of finances and the establishment of a Loans Redemption Fund.

7. Taking over the control and maintenance of parks and reserves.

29.   SHIRE COUNCILS.

Objective, Regulations, and Platform.

Objective.

The Objective shall be the acquisition of the right to exercise any or all of the powers provided for in Section 109 of the Local Government Act, 1906, with amendments as herein suggested.

Regulations.

1. Leagues in any local government area shall have the work of formulating a County Council programme suitable to local requirements.

2. Such programme must be in accord with the general principles of the P.L.L., and shall be forwarded to the Executive for confirmation.

3. The Rules and Regulations of the P.L.L. governing the selection of candidates for Parliament shall as far as practicable apply to candidates seeking selection for County Councils.

Platform.

1. Election to Shire Councils to be on the basis of adult suffrage.

2. That no land shall be sold by the Shire Council, and that the Local Government Act shall be amended in Part 12, Section 104, and wherever else necessary, to prevent the sale of lands by the Council.

3. That no new licenses be granted to Asiatics. This not to apply to renewals of existing licenses.

30.   GREATER SYDNEY MUNICIPALITY.

In the constitution of the Greater Sydney Municipality and Council, the following things to be observed:—

(a) The powers, rights, and liabilities of any one and all of the civic bodies referred to to be the powers, rights, and liabilities of the Greater Sydney Council.

LL

(b) The Council to have control of all services affecting the communal life of the citizens, such as water and sewerage, tramways, gas supply, electric supply, harbor control, parks and open spaces, housing of the working classes, trans-harbor ferries, hydraulic power, roads and bridges.

(c) The municipality to be divided into forty wards, each ward to return two aldermen.

(d) Any person (except such as are disqualified by Section 70 of the Local Government Act, 1906) whose name is on the roll to be eligible for election and to act as alderman.

(e) The aldermen to be elected for three years; the elections to be held on the same day as other municipal elections in the State, and the poll to remain open till 8 p.m.

(f) The election of aldermen to be by adult suffrage.

(g) Each elector to have one vote only, to be exercised in ward where resident.

(h) The Mayor to be elected annually by the electors.

(i) Provision to be made for payment of Mayor and aldermen.

(j) One general rate to be struck for all requirements; such rate to be on the unimproved value of the land.

(k) The Railway Commissioners, the Australian Gaslight Company, the Telephone Department, and all other public or private bodies interfering with or permanently using any of the public ways to pay rates.

(l) The Council not to sell any land acquired by it.

PROGRESSIVE POLITICAL LEAGUE OF VICTORIA, 1891.

The Object of the League is to secure for all classes such legislation as will advance their interests by

(a) The enrolment of all persons desirous of promoting progressive legislation.

(b) The return of candidates to Parliament pledged to support the Platform of the League.

All persons over 18 years of age shall be eligible to become members of the League. The subscription shall be not less than one shilling per annum payable in advance.

PLATFORM.

1st—Electoral Reform.

(a) Abolition of plural Voting. One general roll on the basis of manhood suffrage.

(b) Special proVision for Seamen and others following migratory occupations to record their Votes at Parliamentary elections.

(c) Extension of the hours of polling from 9 a.m. to 9 p.m., to be uniform throughout the colony.

(d) Equal electoral districts on a population basis, and single electorates.

2nd.—Reform of the Labor Laws.

(a) Repeal of the 6 Geo. IV. cap 129, and other Acts relating to conspiracy in Industrial Disputes.

(b) A law enacting a maximum Labor day of eight hours.

(c) The repeal of that portion of the Employers and Employees Act formerly known as the Master and Servants Act.

(d) Amendment of the Factories and Shops Act.

(e) Extension of the proVisions of the Employers' Liability Act to seamen.

(f) A Mining Act proViding for the proper Ventilation and safety in gold, coal, and other mines.

(g) All Inspectors under any Act of Parliament requiring practical knowledge to be appointed from workers in their respective trades and occupations.

(h) Prohibition of the importation of Chinese and Coolie laborers and of laborers under contract.

(i) The establishment of a Department of Labor.

(j) The establishment by law of Courts of Conciliation for the settlement of disputes between Employers and Employees.

3rd—Social Reform.

(a) The application of the principle of the Referendum to the opening of public libraries, museums, and art galleries on Sundays.

(b) The application of the same principle to the closing of public houses on Sundays.

(c) No more Crown lands to be alienated, the land and material therein being the common property of the people.

(d) A tax on land values, exclusive of improvements, sufficient to secure for the community the unearned increment.

(e) A cumulative tax on all incomes over £300 per annum.

4th—Federation.

Federation of the Colonies on a Democratic basis.

VICTORIAN LABOR PLATFORM, 1908.

STATE PLATFORM.

Land Policy.

1. Compulsory resumption of land for closer settlement.

2. (a) No further alienation of Crown land; (b) restriction of the aggregation of large estates; (c) the establishment of a State Forestry Department.

3. The sustaining of village settlements, and the creation of small landholders under a new system of perpetual lease, with periodical Valuations.

Financial Policy.

4. Restriction of public borrowing, except for conversion of existing loans.

5. A graduated tax on the unimproved value of land, subject to an exemption of £500.

6. A cumulative tax on incomes over £200 per year.

(Note.—This resolution was carried unanimously by Annual Conference, March, 1907:—" The Conference regrets that any misconception exists in relation to the respective fields of operation of the land and income taxes, and affirms the principle that the income tax is not intended to apply to land, or the produce of land that is subject to a land tax.")

7. The establishment of a State Bank, and extension of the Credit Foncier system to the whole State.

8. The establishment of a State Life and Fire Insurance Department.

Constitutional Reform.

9. One adult one vote (State or Municipal).

10. Initiative and Referendum.

11. Abolition of the Legislative Council.

12. Abolition of State Governorship.

13. Amendment of the Local Government Act, in order to facilitate the realisation of the Municipal Platform.

14. Civil equality of men and women.

Industrial Regulation.

15. (a) The establishment of a Department of Labor, with a responsible Minister; (b) abolition of private registry offices, and establishment of Central Labor Bureau, with branches throughout the State.

16. The legalisation of the eight hour system and a minimum wage for all workers.

17. Equal pay for equal work.

18. The establishment by law of Courts of Compulsory Arbitration between employers and employees.

Educational.

19. (a) Education—Primary, Secondary, Technical and University—to be free and secular, with all requisites to be provided by the State. Primary education to be compulsory; (b) the maintenance and extension of technical education by the State; (c) free night schools for persons over 16 years of age.

Social.

20. (a) Adequate pensions for all aged or disabled persons; (b) children's pensions.

21. Socialisation of the drink traffic.

22. Family Homes Protection Act, to exempt family homes, registered under the Act, to the value of £2000, from seizure.

Municipal Platform.

1. Adult Suffrage: (a) all electors resident for six months to be qualified representatives; (b) election of mayors and presidents by the people.

2. All municipal taxes to be assessed on the unimproved value of land.

3. (a) All community enterprises, such as tramways, lighting, water supply, and markets, to be conducted and controlled by the municipality; (b) no extension of leases to tramway, electric lighting, or other companies.

4. Direct employment of all labor where possible.

5. An eight hours day. The wage payable to municipal employees shall not be less than the minimum trade union rate.

6. Erection by the municipality of healthy homes for the people.

7. All officers administering the Health Act to be appointed by, and under the control of, the Board of Health.

8. Municipal insurance of ratepayers' property.

9. Representatives to all trusts and boards to be elected by the people.

10. Creation of recreation reserves in populous neighborhoods for the free use of the people, and as playgrounds for children.

11. Provisions for the regular entertainment of the people by concerts, lectures, and theatrical performances, and any other means of elevating the popular tastes.

12. No alienation of land the property of the municipalities.

13. Strict enforcement of the Weights and Measures Act.

14. Initiative: By which 5 per cent. of qualified voters in any municipality may, on petition, demand that a referendum on any and every proposition submitted by such proportion of qualified voters shall take place at the next municipal elections.

15. All meetings of municipal councils to be held at night in cities and boroughs, and at the hour most convenient for the attendance of the public in country municipalities, and to be open to the public.

16. The establishment of municipal Montes de Piete.

17. Municipal ownership and control of milk, bread and meat supply.

AUSTRALIAN LABOR FEDERATION.

PLATFORM ADOPTED IN QUEENSLAND, 1890.

1. The Nationalisation of all sources of wealth and all means of producing and distributing wealth.

2. The conducting by the State Authority of all production and all exchange.

3. The pensioning by the State authority of all children, aged and invalid citizens.

4. The saving by the State authority of such proportion of the joint wealth production as may be requisite for instituting, maintaining, and increasing national capital.

5. The maintenance by the State authority from the joint wealth production of all education and sanitary institutions.

6. The just division among all the citizens of the State of all wealth production, less only that part retained for public and common requirements.

7. The reorganization of society upon the above lines to be commenced at once and pursued uninterruptedly until social justice is fully secured to each and every citizen.

THE PEOPLE'S PARLIAMENTARY PLATFORM.

1. Universal White Adult Suffrage for all Parliamentary and local elections; no plural voting; no nominee or property qualification chamber.

2. State registration of all citizens as electors.

3. Provision for full and complete enfranchisement of the floating population.

4. All Parliamentary elections on one day, and that day to be a close holiday and all public houses closed.

5. Equal electoral districts on adult population basis.

6. Annual Parliaments.

7. Abolition of veto.

CONDITIONS OF LABOR CANDIDATES.

1. All Labor representatives to occupy seats on opposition cross-benches no matter what party is in power.

2. Previous to election a Labor candidate shall give a written pledge to resign on a requisition signed by a two-thirds majority of his constituents.

QUEENSLAND LABOR PLATFORM, 1893.

Electoral Reform.

One man one vote. Special provision to be made for all whose occupations necessitate a constant change of residence. Six months' residence in the Colony to be the qualification for franchise.

All Parliamentary elections on the same day, and that day to be public holiday and all public houses to be closed. Abolition of the Nominee Chamber.

National Work.

State control of water conservation and irrigation.
State aided village settlements.

Education (Secular).

Elementary compulsory, higher optional, both absolutely free in State schools.

Regulation of Industry.

Statutory eight hours day where practicable.
Shops and Factories Act, with elected inspectors.
Mines Act, giving complete protection to miners.
Machinery Act, providing for inspection of land boilers and machinery. Persons in charge to have certificates of competency.

Labor Rights.

State Department of Labor to which men can apply for work at a minimum wage as a right.

Wages Act, giving complete lien for wages over work performed, and full security for wages against all forfeiture whether by agreement or Court order.

A progressive tax upon land values irrespective of improvements. Realisation of adequate returns from the unalienated public estate.

Repeals.

Abolition of State-aided immigration.

Abolition of all conspiracy laws relating to industrial disputes.

Law Reform.

All magistrates to be elected.

Referendum.

The submission of measures for the approval or rejection by the people.

Miscellaneous.

Revision of the Railway tariff.

The legal cancelling of a members' right to represent a constituency on a two-thirds majority adverse vote of his constituents.

Exclusion of colored Asiatics and contract or indented labor.

State construction and ownership of the railways.

And any measure that will secure a fair and equitable return to labor and promote the progress and prosperity of the Colony.

As regards local questions, including that of separation in Central and North Queensland, local organizations are free to determine their own course of action.

On no account shall the fiscal question be regarded as a Labor Party question.

Recommended.

To secure sober men as Labor candidates for Parliament.

The following pledge was signed.—

"I, the undersigned candidate for selection by the ....Branch of the...................
Workers' Political Organization, hereby give my pledge that if not selected as a candidate for Parliament by the Branch I will not in any way oppose the candidature of the duly selected nominee of this or any other branch, and if selected, I agree to advocate and support the principles contained in this platform.
Signed...................

THE QUEENSLAND LABOR PLATFORM.

As adopted at the Rockhampton Convention, March, 1907.

Fighting Platform.

1. Abolition of Legislative Council.
2. Trade Disputes Bill.
3. Old Age Pensions.
4. Conciliation and Compulsory Arbitration.
5. Public Sugar Refineries and Smelting Works.
6. Pure Food (by legislation and administration).
7. Tax on publicly created land values and absentees.
8. Immediate stoppage of all further sales of Crown Lands (fixity of tenure—leasehold only, with periodic re-appraisement of rents).
9. State Bank (extension of the principle) and Loans to Settlers and Miners.
10. Local Government Reform—One adult one vote, no disfranchisement for arrears of rates, election of mayors and chairmen of local government bodies by electors.

General Programme.

1. Constitutional Reforms.
   Amendment of Elections Act.
   Initiative and Referendum.
   Elective Ministries.
   Abolition of the position of State Governor.
2. Industrial Reform.
   Amendment of Shearers and Sugar Workers' Accommodation Act.
   Amendment of Workers' Compensation Act.
   Machinery Act, providing for the inspection of all boilers, only certificated persons to attend to them.
   Statutory Eight-Hour Day where practicable.
   Amended Mines Regulation Act, with provision for better inspection and ventilation of mines, allaying of dust of mines, and election of inspectors by popular vote of miners.
   Amendment of Wages Protection and Lien Act.
   Minimum Wage and Abolition of the Contract System in Government Work.
   State Settlements at which persons out of employment may obtain work as a right.
3. Taxation Reform.
   Progressive Tax on publicly-created Land Values, with £300 exemption.
   Progressive Income Tax, with £200 exemption.

4. Land Reform.

      Mining on Private Property.

      Equalisation of Pastoralists' and Selectors' Rents.

      No Asiatic, Polynesian, or African aboriginal to hold land in freehold or leasehold from the Crown or private owner.

5. National Work.

      Extension of State Department of Labor.

      Public Control of Water Conservation (artesian and otherwise) and Irrigation.

      Public Ownership, Construction, and Maintenance of all Railways.

      Public Fire, Life, Marine, Accident, and General Insurance.

      Public Crushing Batteries, Smelting and Metallurgical Works.

      Purchase of Mineral Ore and Free Assaying.

      Public ownership of coal and iron industries.

      State manufacture, importation, and sale of intoxicants, with the ultimate view of total prohibition.

6. Education (Secular).

      Elementary, compulsory; higher, optional. Both absolutely free in State schools.

      Technical Education Reform.

      University, free, to all qualifying by examination.

7. Miscellaneous.

      Establishment of Sinking Fund to meet maturing Loans.

      Nationalisation of all Hospitals.

      Public Trust Office.

      Repeal of the Contagious Diseases Act.

      Law Reform, including the appointment of Public Defenders.

SOUTH AUSTRALIAN LABOR PLATFORM, 1892.

1. Protection for the purpose of encouraging local industries, and the further development of the resources of the Colony.

2. Progressive tax on land values, or failing this an increase in the present tax, with exemption on small holdings.

3. Liens Bill, for the better protection of workmen's wages.

4. Workshops and Factories Act, for the purpose of securing adequate breathing space, to regulate and limit the hours of labor, limit the age at which young persons may be employed, and provide sanitary arrangements in all buildings used as workrooms and factories.

5. Steam boiler inspection.
6. Free education.
7. Part 719 (amendment of Land Values Act).
8. Tax on goods and passengers carried intercolonially in foreign vessels.
9. Amendment of the Railways Commissioners Act.
10. Establishment of a Department of Labor.
11. Re-distribution of Seats on the basis of population, and the adoption of adult suffrage.
12. Reform of the Legisatilve Council in the direction of shortening the term of election.
13. Establishment of a State Bank.
14. An Act to secure to tenant farmers just compensation for improvements.
15. Working men's blocks, and loans to blockers.
16. Trades Hall site.
17. Eight Hours Bill.
18. Removal of duties on tea, coffee, cocoa, and kerosene.
19. Opposed to free and assisted immigration.

This platform was revised prior to the elections of 1894, and a plank added urging the establishment of an Export Department.

UNITED LABOR PARTY OF SOUTH AUSTRALIA.

PLATFORM, 1908.

FIGHTING PLATFORM.

1. Progressive Land Tax on the lines of New Zealand.
2. Abolition of the Legislative Council; failing that, adult suffrage for both Houses.
3. Compulsory Conciliation and Arbitration Bill.
4. Public ownership and control of all railways, tramways, and wharfs.
5. Cessation of borrowing, except for (1) conversion of loans, (2) completion of public works already authorised, and (3) works which will show interest on capital borrowed and provide for a sinking fund.
6. The right of the Government to resume land for Closer Settlement and public purposes on the valuation accepted by the owner for taxation purposes, plus 10 per cent.
7. Stopping further alienation of Crown lands.

GENERAL PLATFORM.

Constitution.

1. Abolition of the Legislative Council; failing that, adult suffrage for both Houses.
2. The Initiative and the Referendum.

Land.

3. Progressive Land Tax on the lines of 'New Zealand.

4. The right of the Government to resume land for Closer Settlement and public purposes on the valuation accepted by the owner for taxation purposes, plus 10 per cent.

5. A more equitable system of allotment of Crown Lands.

6. Stopping further alienation of Crown Lands.

Industry.

7. Compulsory Conciliation and Arbitration Bill.

8. Extension of Wages Boards, to prevent sweating.

9. Steam Boilers' Inspection Bill, to make the user of steam responsible for the inspection of his boiler.

10. Amendment of Workmen's Liens Act.

11. Amendment of Workmen's Compensation Act.

12. Inspection of Scaffolding.

Public Works.

13. Public ownership and control of all railways, Tramways, and wharfs.

14. Conservation of Murray River Waters for irrigation and navigation.

15. Extension of functions of the State Bank.

16. Extension of the State Export Department.

17. Minimum wage of 7s. per day for all adult males employed by the State or on State contracts.

Local Government.

18. Amendment of Land Values Assessment Act.—Part XIX.

19. Abolition of Plural Voting in Municipal Elections.

General.

20. Cessation of borrowing, except for (1) conversion of loans, (2) completion of public works already authorised, and (3) works which will show interest on capital borrowed and provide for a sinking fund.

21. Maintenance and extension of present system of education.

22. Old Age Pensions.

23. Amendment of Food and Drugs Act with a view to better safeguarding the public health.

24. Mortgagors' Limitation Liability Bill.

25. Encouragement and Fuller Development of the agricultural, pastoral, and mining resources of the State.

26. Amendment of Landlord and Tenants Act, to place all creditors on an equal basis.

WEST AUSTRALIAN STATE PLATFORM.

(Adopted at the Sixth Congress, held at Kalgoorlie,
September 19, 1908.)

FIGHTING PLANKS.

1. Effective reform of the Legislative Council with a view to its ultimate abolition.
2. Taxation of unimproved land values without exemption or rebates.
3. Establishment of State flour mills and State agricultural development and export departments.
4. Initiative and Referendum.
5 Nationalisation of the Liquor Traffic and Local Option as to continuance, increase, or reduction of licenses.
6. Maximum day of eight hours.
7. State bank of issue.
8. Graduated income tax with exemption up to £250 with special impost on absentees.
9. Old age pensions.

GENERAL PLATFORM.

1. Nationalisation of Crown lands with a view to the ultimate nationalisation of all lands.
2. Departmental construction of public works.
3. Limitation of State borrowing except for the purpose of reproductive works.
4. State Fire, Life, and Accident Insurance.
5. Government manufacture of Government clothing and uniforms.
6. Progressive absentee tax. .
7. The abolition of the present system of State Governors and Government House, the office to be filled by the Chief Justice.
8. The establishment of mining boards.
9. Free technical, scientific and general education.
10. The day of Parliamentary elections to be a public holiday.

TASMANIAN LABOR PLATFORM 1896.

1. One adult one vote.
2. Adequate payment of members.
3. Reform of the Legislative Council.
4. A graduated tax on the unimproved capital Value of land.
5. Constitutional and Parliamentary Reform.
6. The Referendum.
7. No further alienation of Crown lands.

8. Mining on Private Property Bill.

9. Graduated Income and Succession Duties.

10. Legislative enactment of the eight hours system.

11. A Shop Assistants Act, providing for early closing.

12. An amended Factory Act, including clauses for the suppression of sweating.

13. An amended Employers' Liability Act.

14. State old age pensions.

15. Reproductive works for the unemployed.

16. A uniform franchise for the Federal Parliament, such franchise to consist of adult suffrage exercisable upon the principle of one adult one Vote.

17. Municipal reform.

18. Fair rents for farmers and other producers.

19. State bank.

TASMANIAN LABOR PLATFORM, 1909.

OBJECTIVE.

1. Cultivation of an Australian sentiment based upon the maintenance of racial purity, and the development in Australia of an enlightened and self-reliant community.

2. The securing of the full results of their industry to all producers by the collective ownership of monopolies, and the extension of the industrial and economic functions of the State and municipality.

PLATFORM.

Electoral and Constitutional.

One adult one vote.

Adequate payment of Members, with proVision for penalties for non-attendance.

Abolition of Upper House; provision for initiative and referendum.

Abolition of State GoVernorship as at present constituted.

Abolition of nominee boards.

Extension of hours of polling; a compulsory two hours leave to all employees during polling hours.

Land.

Progressive Tax on Land Values, town and country, exclusive of improvements.

Self assessment; right of resumption by the State on the basis of such assessment.

Repurchase of estates for Closer Settlement.

Government advances to settlers on easy terms.

No further alienation of Crown lands.

Education.

Free primary, secondary, technical, and University education, with all requisites supplied by the State. Attendance at primary schools to be compulsory.

Finance.

Restriction of State borrowing; loan moneys to be used solely for reproductive works.

Exemption from direct taxation of incomes under £125 per annum in the case of unmarried persons, and £150 in the case of married persons, with £10 further exemption for every child dependent on the taxpayer.

Establishment of a Public Trust Office.

Old age pensions.

ProVisions for all permanently disabled persons and widows and orphans.

Industrial.

Establishment of a Department of Labor.

Legalised eight hour day, and 5½-day week of 44 hours, where practicable.

A Workmen and Contractors' Lien Act.

Minimum wage in all Government and municipal contracts.

Compulsory Arbitration.

Wages Boards.

Equal pay for equal work for both sexes.

Shops and Factories Act; compulsory early closing and weekly half-holiday.

Workman's Compensation.

Abolition of the Truck system.

State pulping works.

Liquor.

State ownership and control of the liquor traffic, with proVision for local option.

Gambling.

Referendum as to whether Tattersalls should continue as at present, be abolished, or conducted by the State.

State Pledge.

Candidates for selection must sign, prior to nomination, the following Pledge:—I hereby pledge myself not to oppose the selected candidate of this or any other Branch of the

Tasmanian Workers' Political League. I also pledge myself, if returned to Parliament, on all occasions to do my utmost to ensure the carrying out of the principles embodied in the Labor Platform, and on all such questions affecting the fate of a Government, to vote as a majority of the Labor Party may decide at a duly constituted caucus meeting.

FEDERAL CONVENTION, 1897.

LABOR PLATFORM OF NEW SOUTH WALES AND TASMANIA.

1. The name of the Federation shall be the Australian Commonwealth.

2. The Federal Parliament shall consist of a House of Representatives elected on a population basis of single seat electorates, by adult suffrage, and a Second Chamber elected on the same franchise, each Colony voting as one constituency.

3. Limitation of the power of veto on the part of the Second Chamber.

4. Introduction of a system of non-party Government by the election of Ministers.

5. Direct initiation of legislation by the people, and the Referendum.

6. Payment of members.

7. The future exclusion from residence and citizenship within Federal territory of undesirable aliens.

8. Governor-General, all State Governors, judges and magistrates to be elected.

FIRST FEDERAL LABOR PLATFORM.

(Adopted at an Interstate Conference held January 24, 1900.)

GENERAL LEGISLATION.

1. Electoral Reform, providing for one adult one vote.
2. Total exclusion of colored and other undesirable races.
3. Old age pensions.

CONSTITUTIONAL REFORM.

4. The Federal Constitution to be amended to provide for—

(a) The Initiative and Referendum for the alteration of the Constitution.

(b) Substitution of the National Referendum for the double dissolution for the settlement of deadlocks between the two Houses.

PLEDGE.

I hereby pledge myself not to oppose any selected candidate. I also pledge myself, if returned to the Commonwealth Parliament, to do my utmost to ensure the carrying out of the principles embodied in the Federal Labor Platform, and on all such questions to vote as a majority of the Federal Labor Party may decide at a duly constituted caucus meeting.

COMMONWEALTH LABOR PLATFORM, 1908.

NAME—AUSTRALIAN LABOR PARTY.

OBJECTIVE.

(a) The cultivation of an Australian sentiment, based upon the maintenance of racial purity, and the development in Australia of an enlightened and self-reliant community.

(b) The securing of the full results of their industry to all producers by the collective ownership of monopolies, and the extension of the industrial and economic functions of the State and Municipality.

FIGHTING PLATFORM.

1. Maintenance of White Australia.
2. The New Protection.
3. Nationalisation of monopolies.
4. Graduated Tax on unimproved land values.
5. Citizens Defence Force.
6. Commonwealth Bank.
7. Restriction of public borrowing.
8 Navigation laws.
9. Arbitration Act Amendment.

MM

GENERAL PLATFORM.

1. Maintenance of a White Australia.

2. New Protection—Amendment of Constitution to ensure effective Federal legislation for New Protection and Arbitration.

3. Nationalisation of monopolies—if necessary, amendment of Constitution to provide for same.

4. Graduated Land Tax—Graduated tax on all estates over £5000 in value on an unimproved basis.

5. Citizen Defence Force, with compulsory military training, and Australian-owned and controlled Navy.

6. Commonwealth Bank of Issue, Deposit, Exchange, and Reserve, with non-political management.

7. Restriction of Public Borrowing.

8. Navigation Laws to provide—(a) for the protection of Australian shipping against unfair competition; (b) registration of all vessels engaged in the coastal trade; (c) the efficient manning of vessels; (d) the proper supply of life-saving and other equipments; (e) the registration of hours and conditions of work; (f) proper accommodation for passengers and seamen; (g) proper loading gear and inspection of same; (h) compulsory insurance by shipowners against accident or death.

9. Arbitration Act Amendment, to provide for Preference to Unionists and exclusion of the legal profession, with provision for the inclusion of all State Government employees.

10. Old age and invalid pensions.

11. General Insurance Department, with non-political management.

12. Civil equality of men and women.

13. Naval and military expenditure to be allotted from proceeds of direct taxation.

14. Initiative and Referendum.

PLEDGE.

I hereby pledge myself not to oppose the candidate selected by the recognised political Labor organization, and, if elected, to do my utmost to carry out the principles embodied in the Australian Labor Party's platform, and on all questions affecting the Platform to vote as a majority of the Parliamentary Party may decide at a duly constituted caucus meeting.

POSTAL BANKING SCHEME.

The general principles of the following scheme for the establishment of a National Postal Bank were adopted at the Interstate Conference of 1908. The scheme was drafted by Labor member King O'Malley and formed part of his proposal for handling the finances of the States and Commonwealth:—

THE NATIONAL POSTAL BANK.

1. In order to facilitate and economise the carrying out of the financial transactions of the Commonwealth and the States, and especially those connected with the conversion, redemption, renewal, and issue of loans, it is proposed to establish a National Bank of Deposit, Issue, Exchange, and Reserve.

2. It is proposed:—

(i.) That this bank shall be conducted purely as a Government Department, absolutely free from political control.

(ii.) That it shall be so constituted as to possess all the powers and immunities requisite to its security, to the recovery of its debts, and to the disposal of its property.

(iii.) That its capital shall be represented by 12,000 shares, of £100 each, of which at least 6000 shall be in the hands of the Commonwealth Government, and that of the balance no State Government shall hold more than 1000 shares.

(iv.) That the shares of the bank shall be transferable only to the Governments of the Commonwealth and the States; that the failure of any or all of the States Governments to subscribe shall not prevent the bank from commencing operations; and that in the event of a State Government desiring to dispose of shares in the bank, the Commonwealth Government shall have the first option of purchasing.

(v.) That the Commonwealth and State Governments holding shares shall be jointly and severally liable in respect of all transactions of the bank.

(vi.) That the bank shall act as the agent for the Mint in the purchase of raw gold and silver and the issue of coin.

(vii.) That the bank shall be empowered to issue notes which shall, throughout the Commonwealth, be legal tender at all places except the head office of the bank in each State; and that at such head offices payment of the value of notes presented may be made in gold or Commonwealth Consols, at the option of the Comptroller-General of the bank.

(viii.) That the bank shall become the repository for the payments from time to time in respect of the Consolidated Revenue, Loan, and Trust Funds of the Commonwealth and State Governments, and the funds of municipal bodies, and shall pay interest on the daily balances thereof

(ix.) That the bank shall provide for temporary advances by way of overdraft to Commonwealth and State Governments and municipal bodies.

(x.) That the bank shall, in other respects, carry on an ordinary banking business, receiving from the public moneys on current account or fixed deposit, and making advances on good security.

(xi.) That the bank shall carry out the inscription of all Commonwealth and State Inscribed Stock, and make all arrangements necessary for the conversion, redemption, renewal or issue of Commonwealth, State, and Municipal loans.

(xii.) That the Board of Management of the bank shall consist of a Comptroller-General, representing the Commonwealth, and one representative from each of the subscribing States.

(xiii.) That the Treasurer of the Commonwealth shall be entitled to attend all meetings, and inspect all proceedings of the Board of Management.

(xiv.) That all payments to be made in London by Commonwealth or State Governments shall be made through the medium of the bank.

(xv.) That the General Post Office in each capital shall be the head office of the bank in that State, and that any post-office within the Commonwealth carrying on the business of a money-order office may be constituted a branch of the bank.

(xvi.) That the bank shall be a bank of reserve for the deposit of reserves of the banking companies operating in the Commonwealth.

(xvii.) That the regulations requisite for controlling shall be drawn up by the Board of Management of the bank and the Council of the Associated Banks of Australia, and approved by the Governor-General in Council.

(xviii.) That a branch of the bank shall be established in London.

(xix.) That at the London office, and at the head office of the bank in each State, Commonwealth Consols shall be obtainable in sums of £10 and upwards.

HONOR LIST OF UNION PRISONERS.

The following Unionists were sent to prison for periods varying from four months to seven years for alleged breaches of unjust law vindictively administered. The list is not complete. It is for New South Wales for 1891-1894.

Ashton, J.
Armstrong, Alex.
Belfitt, A. A.
Bruce, G.
Brown, J.
Berkely, Henry
Blair, Wm.
Bonner, Thomas
Bolger, John
Casey, James
Collins, Alfred
Cama, J. E.
Costello, Michael
Coleman, Wm.
Currie, Thomas
Davidson, W.
Donnelan, James
Douglas, A.
Devlin, B.
Enright, J.
Elliott, T.
Ewan, W.
Ferguson, W. J.
Fitzpatrick, P.
Glindon, P.
Graham, Hugh
Graham, Jack
Gearing, J.
Gerstenkorn, H.
Hewitt, R. H.
Heberle, Herman
Herr, Albert
Hogan, M.
Hurley, F.
Innes, David
Jones, John
Jackson, W.
Kelly, Matt.
Keogh, M.
King, W.

Laracy, J.
Lawless, Henry
Lee, Brian
McDonald, Jack
McOid, Hugh
McLean, Wm.
Murphy, John
Murphy, Charles
Montgomery, Alfred
Moss, H.
McKenzie, G.
Marsden, J.
Noble, J.
Olsen, Peter
Osborne, Hector
O'Neill, Andrew
Oliver, C.
Price, Wm.
Polkinghorne, E. C.
Pahae, Paul
Parker, John
Ross, A.
Reinecke, E.
Richardson, Robert
Ryan, J.
Stiff, Joseph
Sleath, Richard
Skelton, C.
Sullivan, Thomas
Springfield, Frank
Thomas, W.
Townsend, S.
Tyson, Wm.
Thomas, T.
Vergin, John
Williams, Henry
White, J.
Williams, W.
Woodcock, John J.
Wyend, W.

The following list comprises Queensland Unionists who were sent to jail by a corrupt capitalistic Government for periods of from three to fifteen years—1891-4:—

Bennet, W. J.
Bowes, D.
Cowling, E.
Fotheringham, W.
Forrester, A.
Griffin, P. F.
Hamilton, W.
Irwin
Jeffries
Latrielle, C. F.
Loyola, John
MacNamara, J.
Martin, James
Murphy, D.
Murphy
Prince, E. R.
Prior
Stuart, J. A.
Smith-Barry, H. C.
Taylor, George

The Worker Print, 129 Bathurst St., Sydney.

CPSIA information can be obtained
at www.ICGtesting.com
Printed in the USA
BVHW04*0017210818
525056BV00018B/2015/P